THE
NEW STATESMAN

THE
NEW STATESMAN
Portrait of a Political Weekly,
1913–1931

ADRIAN SMITH

FRANK CASS
LONDON

First published in 1996 in Great Britain by
FRANK CASS & CO. LTD
Newbury House, 900 Eastern Avenue, London IG2 7HH, England

and in the United States of America by
FRANK CASS
c/o ISBS, 5804 N.E. Hassalo Street, Portland, Oregon 97213–3644

British Library Cataloguing in Publication Data

Smith, Adrian
"New Statesman": Portrait of a Political
Weekly, 1913–31
I. Title
320.05

ISBN 0-7146-4645-8 (cloth)
ISBN 0-7146-4169-3 (paper)

Library of Congress Cataloging in Publication Data

Smith, Adrian, 1952–
The new statesman : portrait of a political weekly,
1913–1931 / Adrian Smith
   p.   cm.
Includes bibliographical references and index.
ISBN 0-7146-4645-8. -- ISBN 0-7146-4169-3 (pbk.)
1. New statesman.   I. Title.
PN5130.N4S65 1996   95-21578
052--dc20   CIP

Printed in Great Britain by
Bookcraft Ltd, Midsomer Norton, Avon

To Mary and Adam,
Frances and Alf

Contents

List of illustrations

Illustration acknowledgements

Photographs 1, 2, 3 and 15, from the National Portrait Gallery; photographs 4, 5, 6, 7, 8, 9, 10, 11, 12, 13, 14 and 16, by courtesy of *New Statesman & Society*.

Preface and acknowledgements

> Crossman is not a Communist or a fellow-traveller but he is that most pernicious of all characters in our national life, the persistent anti-patriot. And he has the talent of deploying *New Statesman* arguments at *Sunday Pictorial* level. *New Statesman* arguments were pernicious enough when they destroyed a whole generation of dons, schoolmasters, journalists and education officers; given the emotional twist that appeals to millions of typists, office-boys and conscripts, they can wreck what remains of our strength as a nation.[1]

Could this book be the product of a brainwashed threat to all that the nation holds dear? I can claim to have grown up in Dick Crossman's constituency, read the *Sunday Pictorial* as a teenager (frustrated by all those exposés that ended abruptly with 'I made my excuses and left'), and stayed faithful to the *New Statesman* for nigh on two decades. There have been times – most notably in the early 1980s when every feature read like a seminar paper – when my subscription has lapsed. Always, however, guilt has brought me back to the fold: I know they need my money, never more so than now, and I keep telling myself that to read the *New Statesman* is to feel you are upholding a certain set of liberal values; dare I say even maintaining a tradition? I'm well aware that I am leaving myself open to ridicule by suggesting that a weekly sampling of Steve Platt and his team is somehow a declaration of faith (making 'I'm a *Guardian*-reader, and proud of it' pale into insignificance), but at its best the magazine still stands for certain common decencies – everything George Orwell thought was best about the British in *The Lion and the Unicorn*. The irony is of course that Orwell deemed such values – fraternity, tolerance, compassion, humour, idealism – wholly absent from Kingsley Martin's 'generally negative, querulous' paper.[2]

True, there have been plenty of occasions when the *New Statesman* has been out of touch, dogmatic, sanctimonious, insensitive, or just plain wrong, but even when articulating the battiest of viewpoints, it has rarely been mendacious or malicious. This book is no whitewash – Clifford Sharp was a singularly unattractive individual, and Martin on occasion acted in an indefensible manner, not least when censoring Orwell – but it does assume that for over 80 years the *New Statesman* has on balance been a force for good, and that its survival has never been more important than at the present time. For good or ill, in 1913 the paper set out to stamp its influence on a young Labour Party still struggling to maintain credibility as the instrument of democratic socialism. By the time Sidney Webb and Arthur Henderson sat down to draft the 1918 constitution the *New Statesman* was clearly more than a mere passenger on Labour's journey to the New Jerusalem.[3] With today's Labour leadership ready to revise and replace that constitution, the left's great survivor, for too long out on a limb, can again be at the heart of the policy debate.[4] It seems therefore an opportune moment to examine the *New Statesman*'s early years in the light of its subsequent chequered history. Over 30 years ago, when Edward Hyams was writing his authorised history, 'glorious' would have been substituted for 'chequered'. A Whiggish version of events was still possible with weekly sales nearly five times as great as today. Not only that, Martin, G.D.H. Cole and Leonard Woolf were all still alive and well – and no doubt eager to vet the manuscript.

Hyams's book appeared in 1963, celebrating 50 years of the *New Statesman*. The seventy-fifth anniversary was marked by Stephen Howe's splendid anthology.[5] This volume does not tie in with any anniversary, which is perhaps just as well given the disaster in 1993: the *New Statesman*'s eightieth birthday was nearly its last, libel suits by John Major and Clare Latimer almost bringing the paper to its knees.[6] I never envisaged my book as a successor to Hyams's official history, although when tackling a PhD many years ago I felt that I could do a lot more than simply rewrite the early chapters. Hyams had very little material to draw on, which was something of a relief given the timetable he was working to. I on the other hand have had an abundance of material, and, although working to a deadline when a graduate student, have had a further 15 years to reflect upon the early *New Statesman* when teaching, or researching and writing on other facets of life in twentieth-century Britain.

Yes, this does override anything Hyams wrote in the first half of his book, but I have never had any inclination to produce a full history of the paper from Sharp to Platt. Apart from the fact that much has already been written about Kingsley Martin (and Richard Crossman), any account of events in recent years would no doubt have suffered from my background in education, not journalism. As it is, I am acutely aware that this 'portrait of a political weekly' invites criticism from practising journalists all too well aware that I have no comparable experience. My only defence is that I am writing *as a historian* about a world separated from our own by almost the whole of the twentieth century – none of us can claim any inside knowledge of life at Great Queen Street in an era when desk-top publishing meant an Imperial typewriter, a pair of scissors, and a tub of glue.

My principal thanks must go to those who were able to draw on their direct experience of working for or in competition with the *New Statesman* between 1913 and the early 1930s, all of whom are, sadly, deceased: Lord Fenner Brockway, Dame Margaret Cole, and Raymond Mortimer CBE. I shall never forget aiding the nonagenarian Fenner Brockway to the chamber of the House of Lords where he was still a front-bench spokesman, nor listening to Raymond Mortimer reminisce in a bed-sit surrounded by a dazzling selection of Post-Impressionist paintings picked up for a song in Paris half a century earlier, nor watching G.D.H. Cole's widow under a huge Lowry in her tiny Highgate flat cast the most recent biography of her husband into the waste-paper bin. Regrettably, the late Sir Victor Pritchett and the late Dame Rebecca West both refused to see me, the latter's letter explaining why in no uncertain terms. Kingsley Martin's foil and eventual biographer, C.H. Rolph (C.R. Hewitt), died in March 1994. He was a marvellous man, full of good advice for a young, naive postgraduate. Similarly, Martin's assistant editor in the 1940s and 1950s, and the University of Sussex's first professor of education, Norman MacKenzie, was enormously helpful. Without his assistance, particularly over access to the Webbs' correspondence and Leonard Woolf's papers, I should never have been able to complete the thesis which provides much of the material for this book.

In London, my thanks must go to Peter Hennessy, at Queen Mary and Westfield College, whose enthusiasm and commonsense never fails to amaze me; the editorial and technical staff at Frank

Cass; the staff of the House of Lords Reference Office, the British Library of Political and Economic Science, and the PRO; and Anthony Howard and Bruce Page for giving me the run of the *New Statesman* archives in the late 1970s. In Cambridge, the late Sir Austen Robinson and his assistants advised me on the papers of John Maynard Keynes, whose official biographer, Lord Robert Skidelsky, showed the patience of a saint when a quiet Sunday afternoon was ruined by my daft telephone query. In Canterbury, at the University of Kent and at Christ Church College I must thank the administrative staff of the university library and of Keynes College; Graham Thomas for being a lousy supervisor but a great inspiration; Colin Seymour-Ure for his dry sense of humour, his abundance of good suggestions, and his pioneering work in studying the British press; Sean Greenwood for 20 years of reminding me what history and rock'n'roll are all about; and above all, Derek Crabtree, walking companion and ceaseless source of intellectual stimulation. In Southampton, at LSU College I must thank Liz Upson and her fellow librarians; Amanda Astill, secretary *extraordinaire*, who has given me back my sanity; and all my colleagues in the Department of Historical and Political Studies. Of the latter, I am especially grateful to David Dunn and to Frank Cogliano for relieving me of all administration in the autumn semester 1994 in order that I could finish the book, and to Jane MacDermid whose wisdom knows no bounds. Frank read each draft chapter, and his suggestions and criticism were invaluable, but any failings in this book are mine alone.

Last but by no means least, a special thanks to my mother and to my late father for their patience and understanding when I went back to being a student; and in more recent times to Mary and Adam for putting up with me through a succession of projects, but especially this one. I promise, I will *never* mention the *New Statesman* again.

Adrian Smith
Lymington, Hampshire
November 1994

Abbreviations

BEF	British Expeditionary Force
CID	Committee of Imperial Defence
CPGB	Communist Party of Great Britain
CUFC	Cambridge University Fabian Society
DORA	Defence of the Realm Act
EAC	Economic Advisory Council
ELF	East London Federation
ILP	Independent Labour Party
IAOS	Irish Agricultural Organisation Society
IGS	Imperial General Staff
ITGWU	Irish Transport and General Workers' Union
FRD	Fabian Research Department
LCC	London County Council
LII	Liberal Industrial Inquiry
LRC	Labour Representation Committee
LRD	Labour Research Department
LSE	London School of Economics and Political Science
MOI	Ministry of Information
NAC	National Administrative Council – Independent Labour Party
NCF	No Conscription Fellowship
NCPD	National Committee for the Prevention of Destitution
NEC	National Executive Committee – Labour Party
NEP	New Economic Policy
NFRB	New Fabian Research Bureau
NGL	National Guilds League
NJC	National Joint Council – Labour Party/TUC
NUJ	National Union of Journalists
NUR	National Union of Railwaymen
NUWSS	National Union of Women's Suffrage Societies

PID	Political Intelligence Department (previously Division)
POUM	Partido Obrero de Unifacación Marxista
RIC	Royal Irish Constabulary
SSIP	Society for Socialist Inquiry and Propaganda
TGWU	Transport and General Workers' Union
TUC	Trades Union Congress
UDC	Union of Democratic Control
UVF	Ulster Volunteer Force
WEA	Workers' Educational Association
WSPU	Women's Social and Political Union

1

Introduction

On 16 October 1994 the *Sunday Times* published the first extract from Jonathan Dimbleby's biography of Prince Charles. The newspaper cost 50p, albeit for one week only, and weighed a staggering 2lb 16oz. Multi-sectioned, groaning with AB advertisements, and padded out by glitzy trivia, the *Sunday Times* is understandably accused of having drifted down-market to satisfy Rupert Murdoch's profit margins. Yet, to be fair, the column inches devoted to reportage, analysis and commentary maintain their inexorable growth, as does coverage of the arts (and belatedly, science and technology). The same would be true of the *Sunday Times*'s rivals, most notably the *Observer*. That same week's *New Statesman & Society* boasted a neat, eye-catching format, a list of contributors that ranged from Nick Hornby to Anthony Giddens (taking in two members of the shadow Cabinet on the way), an illuminating supplement on poverty – and a cover price of £1.65. Excluding photo-caption references to new books, the magazine contained five review articles. The *Sunday Times*, on the other hand, ranged across the contemporary publishing scene in a self-contained, tabloid-size literary supplement. In both quality and length there was little to distinguish between the two publications' individual reviews, and one suspects that if the Sunday paper had been the *Observer* the writers might even have been the same. The plain fact is that, if narrowly judged in terms of value for money, the *Spectator* or *New Statesman & Society* cannot compete with the weekend press. Clearly the weeklies have to offer something distinctive in order to survive into the twenty-first century.

To blame the growth and popularity of the Sundays (and now also the Saturday broadsheets) for the demise of the weeklies is nothing new. Departing from the *New Statesman* in 1978, Anthony Howard bewailed the way in which since the early 1960s the *Sunday Times* had led the way in fulfilling a role traditionally filled by magazines such as his own.[1] Howard was not the first journalist to point out that, in terms of price, let alone breadth of coverage, these papers could no longer compete. Kingsley Martin's retirement in January 1961 had symbolised the end of an era in which the weeklies genuinely complemented the national press. Martin's paper was expensive to run, but not to buy: sales of well over 80,000 copies a week ensured a plentiful stream of advertising revenue.[2] Certainly, it withstood fresh competition better than many less resourceful rivals, the magazine's regular contributors maintaining a high profile courtesy of Lord Reith's BBC. The changing face of public service broadcasting after 1956, the proliferation and diversification of newspapers, changing reading habits, and an ageing list of subscribers, all signalled the decline of the weeklies. Among the editorial staff, raw talent now found its way into television, or was attracted by exciting new opportunities in Fleet Street, *vide* the *Sunday Times*. Despite all this, the *Spectator*, and even more the *New Statesman*, appeared to reverse the trend: with Labour in the ascendant, circulation peaked in the mid-1960s at an astonishing 93,000.

Nevertheless, within a decade all but the *Economist* (and more specialist titles such as *New Society* and *New Scientist*) looked outmoded, tired and, worst of all, irrelevant. In an increasingly harsh environment, the weeklies sought desperately to carve out new roles for themselves, not always successfully – the *Listener* repeatedly relaunched itself, but finally went to the wall when a cost-conscious BBC withdrew its subsidy. Having become a nursery for Conrad Black's *Telegraph* group, the *Spectator* rode on the back of 'Young Fogeyism' and Thatcherism to emerge in the mid-1990s with a healthy profit and a circulation of around 50,000. The *Spectator* saved itself by fostering a reputation for style and vivacity, mixed with more than a dash of controversy.[3] Under Bruce Page, Howard's successor, the *New Statesman* enjoyed plenty of controversy, but became more and more indigestible. The sacking of the humorist Arthur Marshall symbolised for many the magazine's conscious abnegation of wit and good writing. Page had been a pioneer of investigative journalism at the *Sunday Times*. As the *New Statesman* moved sharply towards what might loosely be labelled the Bennite left, he encouraged journalists like Duncan Campbell to file a succession of *exposés* related to issues of national security. Page's legacy was a reputation for turgid prose and leftist puritanism, made worse by the *Spectator*'s growing esteem.

Three editors in rapid succession laboured hard to bring the *New Statesman* more into the Kinnockite mainstream of Labour politics, rid the paper of its reputation for being dull and uninteresting, and stem a haemorrhage in sales. In the 1990s the current editor, Steve Platt, while not securing a spectacular turn-around in the merged *New Statesman & Society*'s fortunes, has made it once again readable. The magazine scores in terms of content and of appearance, and as a result is both gaining and regaining readers. Like his immediate predecessor, Stuart Weir, co-author of Charter 88's call for constitutional reform, Platt is a propagandist, using *New Statesman & Society* as a platform for various campaigns against executive abuse of state power. In 1993 he survived a libel suit from John Major and a subsequent transfer of ownership.[4]

Simply by staying, Platt has brought stability. In September 1994 he master-minded a second relaunching in 18 months, tongue only partly in cheek when comparing a now much glossier magazine with the self-proclaimed 'new politics' of Tony Blair and Gordon Brown. That week's editorial made a plea for fresh thinking in the Labour Party over how to mobilise sceptical young voters. Echoing G.D.H. Cole 80 years earlier, Platt lauded a 'democratic, libertarian socialist strain' always present within the party but all too often marginalised.[5] He bewailed the British left's 'cul de sac liaison, the love affair with the state', for which the *New Statesman*'s Fabian founders bore much of the responsibility. Beatrice and Sidney Webb were no doubt turning in their grave.

As Chapters 2 and 3 explain, of all the reasons advanced to justify the Webbs' costly and time-consuming new enterprise, one argument was judged incontrovertible: that progressive opinion in Britain needed to be as one in acknowledging a powerful yet benevolent state apparatus as the generator of prosperity, efficiency, opportunity and social justice. Renegade Fabians like Cole and his fellow guild socialists on the *New Age* were urging shopfloor and constituency activists to follow an alternative, decentralised path to the New Jerusalem.[6] After the First World War a rehabilitated yet unrepentant Cole became arguably the most important member of the *New Statesman*'s editorial staff. Yet in 1913 his ideas were seen by the Webbs as a pernicious influence upon organised labour, encouraging rather than countering the impact of syndicalism up and down the country. The fact that precious few shop stewards knew anything about guild socialism was irrelevant. As we shall see, for years very few of them knew anything about the *New Statesman* either, but this did not stop the paper playing an important role in the wartime evolution of the modern Labour Party, nor in the debate over future relations with the Liberals following the return of peace.

As early as 1896 Beatrice Webb was clear in her own mind that any future venture had one over-riding purpose, namely 'to make the *thinking persons* socialistic' (author's italics).[7] At that point she had in mind a homogeneous middle-class intelligentsia of recognised progressive sympathies: the 'intellectual proletariat' whose technical, managerial and professional expertise would one day be so crucial to the Webbs' well-ordered collectivist oligarchy. With over a tenth of its male members full-time writers, the Fabian Society should have been ideally placed to emulate the commercial success of the *Spectator*.[8] Chapter 2 explains why it took until 1913 for the Webbs, aided by a reluctant George Bernard Shaw, to take up the challenge. By that time of course, not only had the *New Age* become the left's most glamorous review, but the *Nation* had emerged as a flagship of 'New Liberalism'.[9] Belatedly abandoning permeation and mass propaganda, Beatrice and Sidney swallowed their pride, nailing their collectivist colours to Labour's mast. Henceforth they hoped to influence the movement from within; and here the *New Statesman*, like the Webbs' other great creation, the London School of Economics (LSE), clearly had a role to play.[10]

The longest and most wide-ranging chapter – on the *New Statesman* during the First World War – is also the most important. It considers the quality of reporting and commentary, the question of censorship, and the paper's standing among the political elite by 1918. Chapter 5 also highlights the magazine's value to Sidney Webb during his meteoric rise to membership of Labour's National Executive Committee (NEC); not only was he appointed to key policy-making bodies, but he was the joint author, with Arthur Henderson, of the new constitution. The war was as crucial to the

New Statesman's fortunes as it was to Labour's. The 1918 general election saw the paper an unequivocal supporter of the Labour Party, but that clear-cut commitment was lost for a decade following the return of Clifford Sharp, editor from 1913 until destroyed by drink in the late 1920s.

This book is a history of the first *New Statesman*, but it is also the story of Clifford Sharp. The Webbs and GBS founded the paper, but Sharp masterminded its creation. For good or ill, he stamped his persona on the paper, gave it an identity, and ensured that within a surprisingly short space of time politicians and policy-makers, ministers and mandarins, became familiar with his no-nonsense approach to problem-solving. A singularly unattractive individual, whose post-war affair with the hip-flask brought out all his worst attributes, Sharp was in awe of no-one, least of all his wartime masters in the Foreign Office. Chapter 6 considers the *New Statesman*'s coverage of the Russian Revolution and its aftermath, focusing on Sharp's espionage and propagandist activities – all with the approval of Sidney Webb. Pausing to consider the magazine's coverage of the arts, and in particular the very different personalities of its first two literary editors, Jack Squire and Desmond MacCarthy, later chapters explain the disruptive effect of Sharp's post-war infatuation with the Liberals. Chapters 7 and 9 trace his rapid decline in the 1920s, leaving the paper bereft of vision and direction: tension between the editor and his socialist colleagues and directors is seen in the context of the wider struggle between Labour and the Liberals, and the battle for survival between the *New Statesman* and a rejuvenated *Nation*. Attention is focused on the impact on their respective papers of Douglas Cole and Mostyn Lloyd, and Maynard Keynes and Leonard Woolf. Chapter 10 looks at the individual contributions of all four men, and of the new editor Kingsley Martin, to the very different magazine born out of the *New Statesman*'s 1931 merger with the *Nation*. The origins of the *New Statesman and the Nation*, and the working relationships between Martin and Keynes and between Cole and Keynes are explored against the backdrop of Labour's disastrous second term in office. This final section explains why, despite being the superior weekly in the late 1920s, the Liberal *Nation* was in effect taken over by a *New Statesman* loyal to Labour (albeit critical of Ramsay

MacDonald's premiership), and free from the inconsistency and equivocation that marked the final phase of Sharp's editorship. Thus the book concludes by looking backwards, and forwards, to the heyday of the 'Staggers and Naggers' from the mid-1930s to the early 1960s.

The monetary and political crisis of August 1931 was Martin's baptism of fire. It confirmed his worst fears, reinforced his prejudices, and redefined his understanding of democratic socialism's future direction. Ironically, Labour's demise was the best thing that could have happened to the new magazine, fuelling the fires of radicalism, and deepening Martin's healthy disrespect for all aspiring ministers. With respect to the latter, the magazine had come full circle.[11] For all its Fabian associations the *New Statesman* was founded as a genuinely independent political review, and Sharp was the ideal person to demonstrate that here was a paper owing allegiance to no-one. Arguably he carried his cynicism too far, as for instance in a decade-long feud with Lloyd George and a lifelong contempt for MacDonald. With the exception of the *New Age*, in many respects the very reason for its existence, the *New Statesman* was unique. Unlike the *Nation* it was not at the heart of what sometimes has been labelled the 'press of opinion': the small-circulation reviews and clubland evening papers that until 1916 kept the Liberal flame burning brightly, and in the case of the *Westminster Gazette* boasted a direct line to the corridors of power.[12]

Nor was Sharp's paper part of an often ignored publishing phenomenon in late Victorian and Edwardian Britain: the appearance of well over 200 newspapers, newsletters and periodicals, all affiliated directly or indirectly to the Independent Labour Party (ILP) and the Labour Representation Committee (LRC), and all addressing a predominantly working-class audience. The ILP published around 70 regional weeklies, each complementing the nationally distributed *ILP News*. The keenest cardholders also read the *Labour Leader*, edited by Keir Hardie from 1894 to 1903, and by Fenner Brockway from 1912 until his imprisonment four years later as a conscientious objector. However, sales of the *Labour Leader* never matched those of the *Clarion*. Robert Blatchford's unconventional, unpredictable and increasingly idiosyncratic weekly first appeared in 1891, and staggered on until as late as 1934.[13] In 1913 neither of these journals – one the mouthpiece of a party, and the other a jolly ego trip for its founder – was seen by the Webbs as serious rivals, in the same way that the *Nation* and the *New Age* clearly were.

Unlike, say, the *Clarion*, Sharp's *New Statesman* had no visible roots in nineteenth-century dissent. The *Political Register* and the *Black Dwarf*, and later the Chartist newspapers, had struggled to keep alive the voice of the freeborn Englishman as a new commercial press emerged in the wake of industrialisation. Kingsley Martin would certainly have seen William Cobbett as a man after his own heart. Sharp and Squire, however, had more in common with those mid-Victorian journalists who found goliaths like the *Edinburgh Review* and *Blackwood's Magazine* far too staid and reactionary, and looked to launch a new generation of small, cheaply subsidised political and literary reviews. Many such enterprises were Radical in leaning, like the *Speaker*, but they expressed scant interest in extra-parliamentary politics, and addressed a narrow – and overwhelmingly metropolitan – middle-class audience. With a growing reservoir of well-educated and intelligent potential readers, it is not surprising that the weekly press blossomed in the second half of the nineteenth century. At the same time, technological innovation and the emergence of a vibrant urban artisan culture spawned a new popular press, with Northcliffe's *Daily Mail* in the vanguard. Neither development can be seen in isolation. Nor can any individual newspaper over the succeeding 150 years be subject to scrutiny without noting all processes of 'change, owners, editors, committee and policy meetings and agendas, sources of capital, labour skills, technology, marketing and distribution'[14] – an exhaustive check list, courtesy of *The Times*'s former archivist, but a useful reminder of focusing too much on personalities at the expense of processes.

This book purports to be a 'portrait of a political weekly', and as such tries to capture the flavour of the *New Statesman* at a crucial yet often forgotten period in its history. Although clearly there is continuity with the years after 1931, the magazine produced by Sharp and his colleagues had its own very unique identity, hence an occasional reference to 'the first *New Statesman*'. August 1931 was a watershed for the Labour Party, leaving a new generation to assume the political mantle and rebuild. Similarly, Kingsley

Martin's arrival accelerated changes initiated by Cole and Lloyd following Sharp's final departure. Yet Martin's paper was built on firm foundations, for all the travails experienced in the years immediately preceding the merger with the *Nation*. In any history of the *New Statesman* Sharp will always be overshadowed by Martin, and rightly so, but it is time to rescue him from semi-obscurity.

To a lesser degree the same applies to Jack Squire, reborn in the 1920s as Sir John Squire, the notoriously conservative editor of the *London Mercury*. Squire has been all but forgotten, but G.D.H. Cole has been rediscovered in recent years as a Labour guru with ideas still relevant to the next millennium. Cole's 40-year commitment to the *New Statesman* is well known. Less appreciated is how much he influenced the paper's treatment of domestic issues throughout much of the 1920s, particularly after the fall of the first Labour government. While lacking Keynes's intellectual rigour, Cole's imaginative approach to monetary and economic policy fuelled a debate within the Labour Party on reflation, even if ultimately his advice was repeatedly ignored.

Cole is only one of several prominent figures seen from a different perspective by virtue of their involvement with the *New Statesman* and/or the *Nation*. For example, most leading lights in Bloomsbury, except for Vanessa Bell and Duncan Grant, became involved with either or both magazines during and after the First World War. When working for the *New Statesman*, Leonard Woolf was a major presence in the leader columns and on the review pages, highlighting the importance of viewing the magazine as a whole: editorial policy *and* engagement in cultural debate.

Ideally, the story moves seamlessly backwards and forwards between the two halves of the paper. At the same time, while concentrating on a clearly defined time-span, it ranges across the eight decades that separate Sharp's sombre, sober journal from today's experiment in harnessing hip design and polemic to Tony Blair's image-conscious 'social-ism'. In 1913, for all Beatrice Webb's apprehension, the long-term prospects for an independent left-of-centre weekly, strong on principle if sadly lacking in passion, were good. In the mid-1990s, a permanent revolution in communications technology, with immense implications for print journalism, and a gradual breakdown of all the familiar assumptions on which British politics has been based for most of this century, means that today's magazine is entering uncharted waters.[15] The problems encountered by Clifford Sharp and Kingsley Martin were of a very different magnitude to those facing Steve Platt today, but their respective success in launching and relaunching the *New Statesman* has lessons for historians and practising journalists alike. When the centenary issue enters the Internet, Martin will doubtless be praised for ensuring the paper survived an early mid-life crisis. Although largely responsible for generating that crisis, Sharp will not be forgotten. His contribution was belatedly recognised when the *New Statesman* celebrated 75 years as an icon of the left. Well before 2013 the full extent of that contribution will at last be on the record.

2

Perplexed Fabians: Sidney and Beatrice Webb by 1912

THE WEBBS AND EDWARDIAN PARTY POLITICS: INNOCENTS ABROAD

The most surprising aspect of the *New Statesman*'s early history is that the idea was not conceived at least ten years earlier. The first Fabians produced a flood of tracts, pamphlets, collected essays, histories, research findings and committee reports. If there was a problem to investigate or a posture to adopt, then the Society usually had a position – or would soon adopt one. The most obvious omission among all this frenetic publishing activity was an organ of publicity regularly available to non-members. Members received the *Fabian News* every month, but a proposal in October 1906 that it appear weekly and seek a wider circulation had received a mixed reception. Despite Shaw's enthusiasm for the new venture, it never materialised.[1] A year later, the arrival of the *New Age*, of which more later, appeared at first to obviate any need for the Society to launch its own political weekly. Long-serving secretary Edward Pease assured members that the new paper would be run 'on Fabian lines'.[2] It soon became clear to Shaw, and to Sidney and Beatrice Webb, that the *New Age* was not at all the kind of magazine they envisaged. Indeed, its very existence was seen to confirm the need for a rival weekly independent of the Society, but rarely dissenting from the views of the executive, which at this time was still dominated by what H.G. Wells labelled the 'Old Gang'.[3] The success of the *New Age* suggested that there might be enough readers, writers and advertisers around to make such a project viable, *provided* that the new magazine was attractive, provocative, and well-written. Needless to say, that same success offered no evidence that bulky supplements containing early results of pathfinding social investigations, or multi-part reflections upon the meaning and purpose of socialism, would attract anyone other than the most selfless subscriber. Of course, for Beatrice and Sidney – their lives devoted to investigation, report and propaganda – inclusion of such worthy material could only enhance rather than detract from any publication with which they might wish to be associated. But in 1907 talk of yet another political review was largely academic. For the Webbs, if not for GBS, there were too many other preoccupations. Nor had their political fortunes sunk so low as to require such a costly and time-consuming initiative. In fact another five years were to pass before all three felt ready to plunge into the unfamiliar and decidedly uninviting waters of weekly journalism.

The Webbs' lengthy world tour of 1911–12 was as much an escape as a vacation. Despite Beatrice's determination to embrace the 'democratic movement', needless to say leading from the front, never had their reputation slumped so low, nor their policies appeared so suspect. As early as March 1910 Beatrice had tacitly acknowledged the final failure of permeation, a strategy she and Sidney had pursued with mixed fortunes for nearly two decades.[4] Permeation consisted of educating and lobbying whichever members of the two main political parties appeared at any given moment most sympathetic to adopting and implementing particular social reforms. Often it entailed a bipartisan approach, wining and dining opponents who shared a common interest, for example, the many discussions on educational reform attended by Arthur Balfour and R.B. Haldane. The additional presence of Robert Morant, from 1903 permanent secretary to the Board of Education, would reflect Sidney's success in courting senior civil servants or London County Council (LCC) officials. Yet confirmation of permeation's ultimate failure could be found in Webb's ineffective role during his latter years as a Progressive councillor (representing Deptford from 1892 to 1910), and in Lloyd George's refusal to accept en bloc the package of proposals Beatrice proposed in the Minority Report of the 1909 Royal Commission on the Poor Laws.

The 1902 and 1903 Education Acts (the latter for London only) appeared at first a vindication of the Webbs' endeavours to influence key figures from both sides of the political divide as well as inside Whitehall: Sidney even helped Morant draft the bills. Yet his indifference towards Nonconformist complaints over public funding of Anglican and Roman Catholic voluntary aided schools confirmed a clear lack of political intuition. The episode lost 'Wily Webb' many Radical friends and natural supporters, did little to mend bridges with MacDonald, cost him his chairmanship of the Technical Education Committee, and exacerbated tensions already evident within the Fabians.[5]

The very essence of permeation was that you dealt with those individuals you felt were sympathetic and could deliver. The Webbs made the most of their contacts, enjoying access to Opposition spokesmen and to senior ministers, notably Joseph Chamberlain and Balfour before the latter entered Downing Street in 1902, and Lloyd George and Haldane after 1905. Yet in the early 1900s Sidney repeatedly paid the price for failing to appreciate how much the prospect of gaining or retaining power can concentrate minds wonderfully and bind even the most factious of parties. His support for government legislation on education, his underestimation of Sir Henry Campbell-Bannerman, and his announcement that Lloyd George was 'absolutely apathetic' towards social reform, not only antagonised the Liberals' powerful Nonconformist element, but led to a complete misreading of the revival in the party's fortunes after 1902.

Scarred by his LCC experience, and badly advised by Beatrice and GBS, Webb eschewed a rising generation of Radicals who looked to Lloyd George for leadership, particularly during the Boer War. Instead he looked to the Liberal Imperialists who had supported the war – Haldane, H.H. Asquith, Sir Edward Grey, and even the erstwhile premier Lord Rosebery – to forge a realignment of 'progressive forces' at the very highest level. However small in number, the 'Limps' constituted the coming generation in the Liberal Party, and would have included the leader himself if Asquith's expenses had not necessitated his continuing to practise at the Bar. According to Beatrice, they expressed, 'no prejudice against our views of social reform: whilst their general attitude towards the Empire as a powerful and self-conscious force is one with which we are in agreement'. Accordingly, in November 1902 the Webbs established the 'Co-efficients' dining group in order to 'discuss the aims and methods of Imperial policy' and draw up a programme of reform in advance of the Liberal Imperialists joining forces with the 'more progressive wing of the Unionist Party'. Drawn from Oxford and the LSE, the fringes of Fleet Street, Cape Town, and Westminster itself, Liberal Unionist tariff reformers and Liberal Imperialists gathered around the same table. A jaundiced observer of this imperial think tank's early meetings was H.G. Wells, soon to became a formidable foe of the Webbs.[6]

The obvious weakness of the 'Co-efficient' dinner parties was that, no matter how glittering the guests, they failed to represent the bulk of their respective parties. Not a single Tory freetrader or Radical was present. The much anticipated realignment never took place of course: while tariff reform was destroying the Unionist hold on power, the Gladstonian Campbell-Bannerman successfully rebuilt a Liberal Party that had been in disarray for over a generation. Confirmation of that success came in December 1905 when the 'Limps' tore up the Relugas Compact in order to enjoy high office, and in January 1906 when the Liberals secured an historic election victory.[7] In fact, collectively if by no means individually, the Liberal Imperialists were already a spent force. Rosebery's abortive attempt in 1901 to launch a Liberal League – designed to revive his own political ambitions and dislodge Campbell-Bannerman as leader – had crashed spectacularly, a victim of inertia, lack of interest, and a lamentable misreading of the mood of party activists at constituency level. Sidney Webb's fatal mistake was in publicly expressing enthusiastic support for the Liberal League, especially when Asquith and others close to Rosebery were quick to recognise that enthusiastic support was tantamount to political suicide. Unduly influenced by Shaw, who 'inserted some of the brilliance' in what was to prove a fatal article for the *Nineteenth Century*, Webb urged the Liberal Imperialists to follow through their rejection of 'Gladstonian Liberalism' by endorsing the collectivist alternative of 'national efficiency' as a first step to arresting incipient decline. Domestic regeneration, let alone imperial survival and prosperity, depended upon addressing every problem presently undermining the efficiency of the nation, from inadequate welfare and educational provision through to cumbersome parliamentary procedure.[8] To be fair, Webb's pessimism reflected a prevailing mood, fuelled by evidence of American and German industrial and commercial success, and the manifest failure to inflict a swift, inexpensive defeat upon the Boers. Support for Rosebery and his supporters was a gamble based on a forlorn hope: that having jettisoned 'old Liberalism' before embracing a viable alternative, the Liberal Imperialists would look to the Webbs for a collectivist solution to the nation's ills. As a gamble, it was doomed from the outset. When Campbell-Bannerman crushed Rosebery's pathetic challenge at a Chesterfield rally of the party faithful in late 1901, Sidney had the uncomfortable experience of being singled out as a malign influence totally out of touch with a resurgent Liberal Party whose leader's power base lay in Celtic regional federations, not in English country houses. To judge from Beatrice's diary entries for December 1901, neither she nor Sidney realised how much their close association with the 'Limps' was damaging their reputations (whenever she attempted to foresee future developments in Liberal politics, she was usually spectacularly wrong).[9]

With Campbell-Bannerman in Downing Street the Webbs had scant opportunity to advise on policy, and the situation scarcely changed after Asquith became Prime Minister in April 1908. They paid the price not just for antagonizing the Liberal leader, but for ignoring the bulk of his party. Furthermore, although Haldane had always been happy to work with Balfour when in opposition, the overwhelming majority of his parliamentary colleagues viewed with suspicion the Webbs' cosy relationship with key Unionists. Ironically, it was Balfour who gave Beatrice her one clear opportunity to influence future Liberal social policy: one of his last acts as Prime Minister was to appoint her to the Poor Law Commission. The Unionist government had been forced to respond to an alarming report from the Interdepartmental Committee on Physical Deterioration. Beatrice was the *de facto* voice of 'national efficiency', as well as an effective intellectual counterweight to the most articulate advocate of a less mechanical approach to alleviating poverty, Helen Bosanquet.[10]

Rarely has a royal commission generated so much public discussion, the publication of majority and minority reports in 1909 serving only to fuel further controversy. Attention focused on the familiar question of whether bad moral character was a consequence or a cause of pauperism. The Majority Report assumed the latter, identifying an underclass whose 'instincts of independence and self-maintenance' warranted as much attention as their material needs. In the Minority Report, Beatrice and Sidney blamed the inadequacy of welfare provision rather than individual culpability for the poor's propensity to engage in anti-social behaviour. Recognising the interdependence of education, health, care of the young and the elderly, and regular employment, they called for an ambitious programme of public services to be available to all. Rich and poor alike would share in a common citizenship. Identifying with a protective yet resourceful state, all but the most degenerate would acknowledge their individual and collective responsibilities. Their reward would be the by now familiar 'National Minimum of civilised life'. However, the Majority Report took the notion of individual responsibility much further, arguing that in an increasingly pluralist society the price of political equality was controlling one's own destiny, for good or ill. The Webbs insisted that, in the face of harsh reality, such an argument was academic: victims of social deprivation had to accept that – for their own good and that of society as a whole – central and local government had their best interests at heart. They therefore put forward a 'logical alternative to pauperisation, the package of compulsory labour exchanges, enforced remedial training and penal repression set out in the Minority Report'. Tory and Liberal critics labelled them profligate and reckless. Renegade Fabians at the *New Age* accused them of merely substituting 'a governmental despotism for a capitalist one'. [11]

Lloyd George's polite indifference to the Minority Report, no matter how intense the lobbying, was the price paid for ignoring the Radicals in the dogdays of the Balfour administration.[12] If any event highlighted the bankruptcy of permeation as a political strategy it was the determination of the Chancellor and the President of the Board of Trade to push ahead with their own agenda, effectively sidelining four years of single-minded research and intellectual endeavour. Rebuffed, the Webbs went on to the offensive. For the first time Sidney found himself sharing a platform with his wife, who by all accounts was a much better speaker than he was. They launched an all-party campaign of mass propaganda, intended to extol the virtues of the Minority Report

15

the length and breadth of the nation. Its contents were repackaged, and published in two bulky volumes of impenetrable prose as *The Break Up of the Poor Law*. With attention firmly focused on the constitutional crisis – let alone the excesses of the WSPU, the naval race with Germany, and the deterioration in industrial relations – Poor Law reform was never going to fire the imagination of the general public.[13] The Webbs were trying to get across to the general public an exceptionally complex set of arguments, and an equally demanding package of proposals. Even in a pre-soundbite era they were expecting a lot of the layperson, but they tried their best. The National Committee for the Prevention of Destitution (NCPD) had a staff of seven – including the young Clement Attlee – and at the peak of its campaign boasted around 16,000 members. The bulk of the membership did little more than read the NCPD monthly journal, the *Crusade*, and many of the most active were Fabians and/or ILP members. First published in February 1910 as a rather amateurish 12-page campaign paper, by the time it appeared for the last time in February 1913 the *Crusade* had become a very distinctive, albeit very dry, 35-page magazine.

Clifford Sharp, the *New Statesman*'s first editor, and the central figure in this book, served his apprenticeship on the *Crusade*. Over 36 issues Sharp learnt his trade as an editor, taking over full responsibility for the campaign following the Webbs' departure for Quebec in 1911. It was Sharp who the following year received a cable instructing him to wind up the National Committee. The war had been lost, and it was time to call a cease-fire: that July the 1911 National Insurance Act came into operation, Lloyd George having overcome guerrilla tactics by a resurgent Unionist Party in the Commons and dogged resistance by a deeply suspicious labour movement in the country. The Act was consistent with the spirit of the Majority Report, in other words, assuming that the function of the state was to supplement individual initiative, not to replace it. Thus Poor Law institutions remained as a safety net for those too poor or 'unworthy' to benefit from the piecemeal reforms already enacted or in the pipeline. If the National Committee, and in particular the *Crusade*, had a villain, it was clearly the Chancellor, architect of the legislation. The deep enmity between Lloyd George and Clifford Sharp, such a marked characteristic of the

New Statesman's first decade, dates from the years of the NCPD campaign.[14]

A coda to the Poor Law campaign was the 'War against Poverty' rally on 11 October 1911, organised by the Standing Committee of the ILP and the Fabian Society as part of their joint lobbying for a national minimum wage. It attracted little attention, but it did show the Webbs had not lost their appetite for politics while away. More importantly, it was the first sign that they were ready to work closely with Labour. Nevertheless, Beatrice recorded in her diary at the end of 1912, 'the plain fact is that Lloyd George and the Radicals have out-trumped the Labour Party'.[15] In reality the parliamentary Labour Party, as opposed to the trade union movement on the shop-floor and in the friendly societies, had never really been in a position to be 'out-trumped'. If this applied to anyone then it was the Webbs themselves. For too long the older Fabians failed to acknowledge that most leading Liberals, if not the party as a whole, would only initiate improvements in working conditions and welfare provision on the scale envisaged by the Webbs if threatened by a credible electoral challenge. Even the most cost-conscious member of Campbell-Bannerman's Cabinet acknowledged that socialism and a widening franchise concentrated Liberal minds wonderfully.[16]

The years 1906–8 marked an Indian summer for the traditional Gladstonian causes of free trade, sound finance, disestablishment and temperance. The attraction of 'New Liberal' ideas to hard-headed ministers desperate to retain power in an era of unprecedented party political conflict was obvious. 'New Liberalism', a coherent but never a cohesive package of ideas, drew on the idealism of T.H. Green to redefine Liberalism in terms of reconciling greater individual freedom and the collective good. But it was always more than an intellectual exercise, offering Liberal politicians the means of matching Labour's appeal to a growing working-class electorate. In the 1890s 'New Liberal' writers such as Herbert Samuel, L.T. Hobhouse, and J.A. Hobson had forlornly sought a progressive alliance of organized labour and their own party: the Rainbow Circle discussion group and the short-lived *Progressive Review* were intended to promote cross-party co-operation in reforming an inefficient and immoral capitalist system. The Rainbow Circle's failure to generate much interest beyond Hampstead Garden Suburb illustrates how Liberal intellectuals were invariably following a separate agenda from the parliamentary leadership. For men who had spent most of their political careers in opposition, alliance with the Labour Party – whether to win general elections or retain a working majority – was based on expediency not Radical idealism, as witness Herbert Gladstone's electoral pact with Ramsay MacDonald. For very different reasons, within the ILP and the LRC MacDonald also saw a working relationship with the Liberals as purely tactical, and finite: through playing the long game, and by 'assimilating and not being assimilated', Labour could become the dominant left of centre party. After the heady euphoria of 1909, the government's readiness to trim, and in particular Lloyd George's refusal to carry the Radical flag in Cabinet, fomented disillusion, even despair, among the less patient of its natural supporters. Increasingly harsh moral judgements were passed on ministerial performance, not least regarding *entente* with tsarist Russia, and the delay in granting full female suffrage. Even before entry into the war and the issue of conscription brought matters to a head, some fully paid-up members of the progressive intelligentsia were looking to Labour as a party better qualified to secure a peculiarly British synthesis of 'experimental collectivism' and Liberalism that pertained to be social democracy.[17]

From the outset the Fabian Society had an uneasy relationship with the ILP, and in London members might join but would rarely become branch activists. Although not party to the formation of the Progressive coalition in 1889, Sidney Webb's LCC work drew him towards like-minded, reassuringly middle-class Radicals. He had only modest contact with ILP organisers among the trade unions and the handful of self-educated 'full-time propagandists' who within a very short time in the mid-1890s became fiercely antagonistic towards the Liberals, notably Philip Snowden and Ramsay MacDonald.[18] Thus, as the labour movement consolidated its presence in turn-of-the-century London, local Fabians remained largely aloof, even obstructive. This inevitably reduced any influence they might have exercised nationally when the idea of the LRC was first floated.[19] Always uneasy about an independent party of the working class, and yet conscious of the need to be involved, the Webbs and Shaw for too long failed fully to

appreciate the significance of Labour's 1906 electoral breakthrough.[20] Robert Ensor, an early ILP enthusiast, later recalled how
'absurdly' the 'Old Gang' underrated Labour by failing to
appreciate the scale of Keir Hardie's appeal. Beatrice's diary,
though shrewd in her assessments of say MacDonald and Arthur
Henderson, is full of snobbish and disparaging references to the
bulk of the parliamentary party.[21]

By the autumn of 1906 Ensor was ready to support Wells and
Haden Guest in their abortive attempt to convert the Fabian
Society into an independent socialist party either affiliated to, or
working closely with, the ILP. Their reform committee, chaired by
Sydney Olivier, himself technically one of the 'Old Gang', met at
the central London offices of the ILP. In the event, Ensor and
Wells proved incapable of overcoming a mutual loathing in order
to organise an effective reform group. In December 1906, when
complaints were silenced only by Shaw's eloquence, Wells had
come remarkably close to overthrowing the 'Old Gang'.[22] A
reflection of his success and popularity among younger members
was a very respectable fourth in the following March's executive
elections. Three months later Sidney Webb tried convincing Wells
how their 'political society' could justify its existence. He insisted
that electoral considerations were secondary, and that the Fabians'
success in exercising 'a good deal of political influence' confirmed
how 'More is done in England in politics whilst ignoring elections
& parties than by or with them'.[23] Although technically no longer
a member after September 1908, Wells continued to stir the pot.
Eventually, in 1911, he wreaked revenge on the Webbs in *The
New Machiavelli*, lampooning all they stood for, with permeation
and sexual propriety particularly fond targets.

Beatrice and Sidney were an easy mark. The eventual collapse of
the Poor Law campaign confirmed what was already evident: that
by 1911 the Webbs' political clout inside Whitehall was minimal.
The government was working to its own agenda, albeit increasingly
in the form of crisis management; the Unionists by virtue of their
behaviour in the wake of vetoing a finance bill were clearly beyond
the pale; and the Labour Party had established a parliamentary
presence at Westminster with minimal help from the very people
who should have been at the heart of policy formulation. By
distancing themselves from Labour the Webbs had opted not to

play the party political game. They had paid the price, even if in her diary Beatrice continued to exude optimism long after the Poor Law campaign had lost its early momentum.[24] Not only did they have minimal influence among the great and the good, but they had no political home (power base sounds too grand) other than an increasingly fractious and dispirited Fabian Society.

THE *NEW AGE*, YOUNG FABIANS, AND GUILD SOCIALISM

There probably never would have been a *New Statesman* if its chief rival on the left in the final years of peace had been the joyless organ of collectivist orthodoxy most likely to find favour with the 'Old Gang'. The *New Age* was relaunched in 1907 and survived until 1926, although its heady days as a barnstorming iconoclastic forum for new ideas were all but over by the middle of the First World War. For Margaret Cole, it was '*the* left-wing paper which everybody who was anybody read'.[25] Like so many Edwardian reviews, the *New Age* survived thanks to a small but loyal readership, and friendly publishers with generous advertising budgets.[26] The magazine's reputation and popularity far exceeded actual sales, not least because its best-known columnist Arnold Bennett ('Jacob Tonson' 1908–11) never missed an opportunity to praise its editor as a man receptive to fresh thinking and with a fine eye for spotting new talent at an early stage.[27] That editor was A.R. Orage, theosopher, Platonist, Nietzschean, co-founder of the legendary Leeds Arts Club, and one-time schoolmaster and ILP lecturer. Moving to London in 1906, Orage was reunited with fellow northerners A.J. Penty and Holbrook Jackson. Penty, an architect active in the 'arts and crafts' movement, was about to publish *The Restoration of the Guild System*, quickly to become the bible of guild socialism. Holbrook Jackson, once a lace merchant in Leeds, shared Orage's dream of a new and exciting career as a writer.[28] Having previously met all three men at the Leeds Arts Club, in January 1907 Shaw encouraged them to set up a similar discussion group in London. As it grew, the Fabian Arts Group never found itself in open conflict with the executive, but the presence of an increasingly disaffected Wells soon made it attractive to those younger members who found the society stuffy and staid. In the summer of 1907, when an ailing 13-year-old weekly came up for sale, GBS offered Orage and his friends £500 plus a promise of regular contributions. Further support came from an unexpected source, a merchant banker called Dr A.R. Wallace. An early sign that the New Age had become a thorn in the flesh of the older Fabians was when Jackson stood down as co-editor to improve his chances of joining the executive. From the outset poets were judged as important as polemicists, reflecting the new weekly's preoccupation with the cultural basis of socialism (a legacy of the Leeds Art Club was a keen interest in William Morris and John Ruskin). The Arts Group had little in common with the Webbs, with their narrow interpretation of the New Jerusalem. Although early issues refrained from endorsing any contributor's criticism of the 'Old Gang', Orage and Penty were more and more convinced that the Fabian leadership was out of touch with new thinking and unwilling to explore alternatives to their own brand of bureaucratic collectivism.[29]

Left to edit the New Age on his own, Orage adopted the principle of publishing any radical-minded contributor with strong views and the capacity to express them with style and panache. Needless to say the quality of writing was not always consistent, but the depth of conviction certainly was. If at times this scattergun approach suggested the editor was doing little other than hold the ring, Orage insisted that at least one reader would feel inspired by even the most eccentric commentary. Bennett applauded the New Age's capacity to think the unthinkable: the very fact that it had no consistent editorial line was actually its strength. One would expect Shaw to have been a natural admirer of such eclecticism, and yet he grew increasingly exasperated with the paper. By 1918, admittedly long after the New Age had gone into decline, he complained that 'Its freedom is the freedom of the explosive which is not confined in a cannon, spending itself incalculably in all directions'. Shaw drew, with hindsight, an interesting contrast between a weekly such as Orage's, with its instant but short-lived impact on the reader, and a genuine opinion-former such as the New Statesman. Clearly the New Age never lived up to Shaw's original conception of a review as keenly read in the Reform Club as in an Oxbridge junior common room.

This was a lesson learnt, and in GBS's mind any future venture into publishing had to bear close scrutiny in the corridors of power.[30]

The Fabian Arts Group had been founded at a time when the Society was growing as rapidly as in the years following publication of the *Fabian Essays*. Here the Poor Law campaign was visibly successful – it revived interest in the Society, revitalised flagging spirits among longstanding members, and encouraged a new generation of educated humanists to embrace the 'Basis', the statement of basic principles all Fabians technically subscribed to. By 1908 total membership was around 2,000, and for the first time was genuinely nationwide. The executive accepted that in the past it had only really been interested in what was happening in London. Provincial branches were formed or revived, including the Oxford and later the Cambridge University Fabian Societies. The latter were for all intents and purposes outposts of the Fabian 'Nursery' in London, with regular visits from executive members and those ILP leaders not intimidated by precocious undergraduates and enquiring young dons. As befitted the co-founders of the LSE, Sidney and Beatrice placed great store by their regular contact with students attracted to Fabianism, utilising the brighter ones as research assistants: today's undergraduate was tomorrow's stalwart of the 'intellectual proletariat'. Yet until the mid-1900s the Society had been singularly unsuccessful in trawling the universities. In the 1890s, when Wallas and the Webbs were especially keen to recruit more students, their reliance on Leonard Hobhouse (Oxford) and Charles Trevelyan (Cambridge) was a mistake: most undergraduates who fell under their spell became active in the Liberal Party.[31]

Victorian Oxbridge had established a tradition of student philanthropy, if only to ease consciences among the more guilt-ridden progeny of a privileged middle-class. Attlee was by no means the first graduate to embrace socialism while a voluntary worker in the East End. In Cambridge from 1906 philanthropy, progressive politics, and above all, female and sexual emancipation, came together in one form or another within the University Fabian Society (CUFC). Frederic Hillersden Keeling, known to all his friends as Ben, had become a Fabian while still at Winchester. Only a term after arriving at Trinity he set about reviving the Society. Keeling's success in securing support from Keynes, and in attracting star speakers like Shaw and Wells ensured over 100 members within a year. Few who came into contact with Keeling proved indifferent to his idealism, enthusiasm and socialist evangelism, and an early convert was Hugh Dalton, who cut his political teeth proselytising the Minority Report among Cambridgeshire rustics.[32] An added incentive to sign up was the presence of women undergraduates, notably Newnham's Amber Pember Reeves and Ka Cox. Among the Apostles, Keynes's active involvement with the group diminished following his return to King's in July 1908. Nevertheless, he did give a paper on foreign investment to the Society in 1910, and at the Union in February 1911 he went so far as to second Sidney Webb's proposal 'That the progressive reorganisation of Society along the lines of Collectivist Socialism is both inevitable and desirable'. Other Apostles active in the CUFC were Gerald Shove, the future psychoanalyst James Strachey, and Rupert Brooke, Dalton's successor as president. A fellow economist, Shove soon came to share Keynes's deeply sceptical view of Fabian Socialism. Strachey on the other hand was hugely enthusiastic, encouraging brother Lytton to adopt a less complacent, more combative view of politics. Brooke, who unlike many of his fellow Apostles was unreservedly heterosexual, embodied a rather macho, glamorous brand of socialism. He was a far more glamorous figure than Dalton, while in no way matching him intellectually. At Fabian Summer Schools, Brooke, Ka Cox and their circle (nicknamed the 'neo-pagans' by Virginia Woolf) shocked Beatrice Webb with 'their anarchic ways in sexual questions'. An older, more inhibited friend of Brooke was Jack Squire, an early acolyte of Keeling's and the CUFC's first secretary.[33]

J.C. Squire was to be the *New Statesman*'s first literary editor, the acting editor 1917–19, and a key figure in the early part of this story. After graduating he very quickly got married, and through his new wife was introduced to Alfred Orage. Meeting Orage led to freelance work for the *New Age*, either translating verse or contributing his own. Regular review work followed, and then in December 1909 came 'Imaginary Speeches', a popular feature in the magazine which revealed Squire as a master of parody. The future Sir John Squire spent the rest of his life coming to terms with the fact that he wrote his best poetry when pretending to be someone else. By 1910 he was effectively the *New Age's* literary editor, learning all the time but proving himself extremely able in dealing with the technical side of weekly journalism. Bennett held Squire in the highest regard, as did the Irish critic and essayist, Robert Lynd. Both men sponsored his membership of the National Liberal Club, where he quickly befriended the more amenable pillars of the Edwardian literary establishment. Similarly, although he worked with Orage, Squire never shared his politics, maintaining links with the Fabian leadership established at Cambridge. The passion for cricket, the Georgian penchant for rustic nostalgia, and the carefully cultivated image of the urban Bohemian, all disguised Squire's growing determination to make his mark as a man-of-letters. Bennett noted this quiet ambition, even if Beatrice and Sidney did not. However, by 1913 they were won over, raising no objection when Sharp chose Squire as the *New Statesman's* first literary editor. Sharp had no time for cricket and ale on the village green, but he had seen his new assistant in action alongside Orage. Whoever was charged with setting up the back half of the paper had to be highly professional, and capable of being left to work on his own for long periods. Squire clearly filled the bill, but he had two further advantages. First, despite feigning an amateurish interest in politics, he was able to take over full editorial responsibility at a moment's notice, as he proved in the final two years of the war. Second, within the small incestuous world that was London literary life Jack Squire knew everybody – he was one of the great networkers, and the *New Statesman* benefited accordingly.[34]

Squire remained in close touch with Ben Keeling after the latter left Cambridge with a double first in 1908. Although Keeling wrote prolifically over the next eight years, for example publishing two books based on his experience running labour exchanges in London and Leeds, his importance as an investigative journalist and student of urban social work was only properly acknowledged after he died on the Somme in 1916. Having written regularly for the *Crusade*, he was a regular contributor to the *New Statesman* before joining up in August 1914. Highly regarded by his peers, not least Clifford Sharp who was a hard man to please at the best of times, Keeling owed much of his early career to the patronage of the Webbs. However, by the final year of peace he seemed to be drifting, increasingly cut off from his family and friends. Seeking a fresh start in politics, Keeling flirted with the idea of becoming a Liberal. Had he survived the First World War it is likely he would have been back in the Labour fold, the chances of his adoption as a parliamentary candidate being that much greater than in 1914. He would certainly have provided the *New Statesman* board with an alternative to the increasingly unreliable Sharp. With Keeling as editor the history of the paper in the 1920s would have been very different.[35]

Someone else denied his chance to edit the *New Statesman* was G.D.H. Cole.[36] Douglas Cole discovered socialism in 1906 while still a schoolboy, by reading William Morris's utopian *News From Nowhere*. On his arrival at Balliol two years later he co-founded a newsheet, the *Oxford Socialist*, and in late 1909 the *Oxford Reformer*. The Webbs took a close interest in both papers, with Sidney writing an article on the Poor Law campaign for the *Oxford Reformer*. Cole had been drawn to their attention because of his efforts along with William Mellor to resurrect the university's Fabian Society. This generation of Oxford Fabians had no time for the Liberal Party, or for permeation. Nor did they have much in common with their Cambridge contemporaries, remaining firmly committed to their cause long after going down. Their chief spokesman was an extremely bright young man with firm views, few inhibitions, and an almost complete lack of discretion. By 1912, the year Cole gained a fellowship at Magdalen, he remained a Fabian only in so far as he renewed his annual subscription, railed against the executive at the AGM, and always made a point of attending the Summer Schools – if only to shock Beatrice Webb by his manifest intention to enjoy himself while on holiday, preferably in female company.[37] Cole's intellectual wrestling with syndicalism, his growing interest in Penty's conception of guild socialism, and his support of workers' mass action, equally alarmed the Webbs, even if they felt no great personal hostility towards him. Indeed, throughout his early career, even when he did things guaranteed to infuriate them, Cole was always a welcome weekend guest. Beatrice clearly regarded him as a bit of a rogue, wrong regarding every matter on which he held an opinion; but in her diary she usually let him off lightly, compared with, say,

25

MacDonald or Mosley. Furthermore, although she disagreed violently with much of what Cole stood for, she was determined to keep him somehow within the fold. He was too bright, and too hard-working, to abandon to revolutionary socialism.[38]

In her history of the Fabians, Margaret Cole argued that her husband's generation joined only after making a conscious decision that the Society was the most effective way of bringing about socialism.[39] For a few this may have been true, but in Oxford and Cambridge there was a whole variety of reasons why people joined, many of them quite trivial. Thus, for some, joining the Fabian Society brought the prospect of sexual liberation, even if the reality was invariably disappointment: listening to H.G. Wells lecture on the libido proved a lot easier than satisfying it.[40] Despite Wells's failure to change the face of Fabianism in late 1906, the next ten years were marked by a succession of constitutional wrangles. Wells himself happily encouraged any evidence of dissent among the more restless and ambitious of the Society's burgeoning membership. Rising stars like Cole and Mellor not only disagreed profoundly with the 'Old Gang' over the nature of socialism and how to achieve it, but they insisted on their own views being accommodated within the 'Basis', and thus the prevailing ethos of the Society. Despite ferocious personality clashes, the executive usually survived by soaking up criticism and then responding with contrite gestures and token reforms.[41] Serious disruption took place in 1911 when Shaw, the ageing roué Hubert Bland, and the genuinely reverend Stewart Headlam, all resigned from the executive, albeit with an absent Beatrice Webb providing some continuity by being elected for the first time. The upheaval caused by the departure of GBS and his fellow founding fathers was evidence enough that a clash of generations had, following the failure of permeation, further neutralised Fabianism as a potent force in British politics.

This then was the Fabian Society that Beatrice and Sidney returned home to – a body at one time bonded by their common 'moral earnestness', but now split asunder by deepening ideological differences. The ideas adopted and articulated by Cole, Mellor, and their supporters owed a great deal to Orage, Penty and the *New Age*, and before them to John Ruskin. Indeed the *New Age* rapidly became a convenient means of attacking the Fabian

26

executive, at first in coded language but later in quite brutal terms. By 1909 Orage was espousing an ostensibly libertarian brand of socialism that rendered class loyalties redundant and eschewed the centralist state. Years later he recalled how, as 'Avowed opponents of political labour in any shape or form, antagonists of the Fabian Society from the moment of its surrender to class politics, our situation was, indeed, that of Ishmael'.[42]

The libertarian Orage could happily go along with Hilaire Belloc's claim that Liberal welfare reforms were in reality undermining fundamental civil liberties.[43] In the *New Age* both men decried the compulsory element in the 1911 National Insurance Act as fiercely as once they had denounced the Fabian executive's support for compulsory arbitration. The *New Age* kept hitting the 'Old Gang', but they chose never to fight back. GBS and the Webbs' reluctance to answer the magazine's criticisms when invited to do so particularly irritated Orage.[44] Penty, from the outset a trenchant critic of Sidney and Beatrice's penchant for central direction and control, was until the latter part of the First World War a major influence on Orage. In *The Restoration of the Guild System*, Penty argued that Fabianism constituted little more than a bourgeois revolution, with only a token acknowledgement of workers' rights to determine their wages and conditions. The high level of industrial unrest of 1909–13, and the syndicalist ideas imported by agitators such as Tom Mann, encouraged Penty and Orage in their call for genuine workers' control. Unlike Sorel, Penty looked to medieval England for inspiration: deskilled and alienated as a consequence of industrialisation, workers had to follow the example of craftsmen in the guilds and agree among themselves – and with their managers – on mutually satisfying processes of manufacture. Today's trade unions would transmogrify into yesterday's guilds. Instead of expensive, poorly made goods, articles manufactured by guildsmen who took a pride in their work would be of high quality and priced fairly. Unlike syndicalism, with its call for revolutionary strike action and class warfare, guild socialism envisaged a peaceful fusion of organised labour and management. Penty rejected capitalism's intense competitiveness, and its indifference to labour as anything other than a faceless factor of production. Yet he was equally dismissive of socialism's materialistic, functionalist view of workers' needs.

27

One reason why he came to loathe the Fabian leadership was that they were largely indifferent to working men and women's spiritual and cultural needs. In Penty's far less complex and spiritually far more rewarding post-capitalist society, the state's only role would be to lease industrial assets back to the guilds, each of which would be run on an open and democratic basis. These ideas were refined by another renegade Fabian, S.G. Hobson, in a series of articles published by the *New Age* in the winter of 1912–13. Hobson stressed the importance of a 'functional democracy'; in other words, the presence of representative institutions to complement the guilds as forums for discussion and decision-making: guild socialism had to find a middle way between syndicalism's anarchical view of the state, and Fabianism's centripetal tendencies. Hobson's essays made a deep impression on Cole, who was himself by now a *New Age* contributor.[45]

Over the next two years Cole elaborated upon Penty and Hobson's ideas in the *Daily Herald* and the *Labour Leader*, as well as in the *New Age* itself. In 1913 he published his first book, *The World of Labour*, a combative and idealistic defence of workers' rights demonstrating a contempt for parliamentary socialism worthy of Ben Tillett or James Connolly. In his 'Notes of the Week' Orage echoed its sentiments, but when Cole and Mellor founded the National Guilds League (NGL) in 1915 he refused to join. Insisting that formality stifled the free exchange of ideas, Orage predicted the NGL would quickly become as moribund as the Fabian Society. By the time he did become a member, in late 1917, Orage had come to suspect that guild socialism was based on a naive and romantic view of medieval artisans. Disillusioned by the realisation that guilds were wholly unsuited to advanced industrial societies, and desperate for an alternative all-embracing solution to the nation's ills, Orage's flagging spirits were revived by Major C.H. Douglas. Douglas, an engineer turned economist, was the first to advocate a scheme for 'social credit'. At its simplest, social credit was intended to engineer a demand-led revival of the economy: to enhance individual purchasing power the state would pay a regular dividend to every adult citizen. By 1919, to Penty's great annoyance, the *New Age* was enthusiastically promoting Douglas's ideas. In April 1920 Orage failed to convince the NGL executive that the theory of social credit should be incorporated into guild socialism. Without a mouthpiece in the weekly press, and after 1917 under increasing attack from a new Marxian revolutionary left, guild socialism was a dying cause. The *New Age*'s prospects were equally bleak, its circulation tiny and its editor discredited by his association with social credit and theosophy. In 1922 Orage left for Fontainebleau to study with the mystic G.I. Gurdjieff, becoming a close friend and confidant of fellow theosophist Katherine Mansfield. Within four years his paper had closed down. By that time Orage was himself a guru of theosophy, in New York. He returned home in 1930 to resume his career as a journalist. He launched the *New English Weekly* 12 months later, editing the magazine until his death in the autumn of 1934.[46]

The sad fate of the *New Age* could scarcely have been predicted in 1912–13, when the paper's popularity was at its peak. In public Shaw and the Webbs ignored their renegade review. In private they feared its visible influence on a younger generation of Fabians singularly unimpressed by the caution and conservatism of their elders and betters. In any future struggle for the soul of the Fabian Society, the latter's voice had to be heard. In any wider debate on the future of organised labour – whether on the shopfloor, across the council chamber, or in the conference hall – the case for state socialism had to be made. If the *New Age* was to be challenged, perhaps even silenced, then there was only one obvious course of action: to establish a rival magazine. However, Beatrice Webb was not alone in appreciating that any such initiative had to run parallel with giving the Fabian Society a new lease of life *and* redefining its relationship with the ILP.

While abroad the Webbs were quietly mapping out a new role for the Fabian Society – as Labour's think-tank. The ILP had organisation, members, and trade union links, but as far as Beatrice was concerned it was singularly lacking in ideas (one reason why she had not previously been a member). Even worse, the parliamentary party was stuffed full of sinecured trade unionists happy to act as lobby fodder for the Liberals. And yet, 'there seems to be a clear call to leadership in the Labour and Socialist Movement to which we feel we must respond'. Plans were laid for launching a magazine, but the first thing the Fabians had to do was to liaise more closely with the Labour leadership. The result might be a far more vital role for the Society, particularly if it could fill an obvious policy vacuum by putting forward legislative proposals based on recent research.[47] Back home, in October 1912 Beatrice secured executive approval for two new policy-making committees. As a major benefactor of the whole enterprise, Henry Harben was rewarded with chairing a modest inquiry into rural problems, the results of which appeared in an early *New Statesman* supplement and then sank without trace.[48] The other committee, on the control of industry, grew and grew, until nearly 200 members were in one form or another associated with it. It took over the offices of the NCPD, spawned sub-committees and a secretariat, and eventually acquired formal recognition as a semi-independent organisation operating under the Fabian umbrella. The fact that Cole, Mellor, and other 'natural insurrectionists' were leading lights in the new Fabian Research Department (FRD) signalled that the inquiry would not run smoothly. With most *New Age* articles unsigned it was always possible to maintain niceties, albeit in an increasingly cool atmosphere. The drafting of the control of industry report meant fundamental differences between orthodox collectivists and guild socialists could no longer be ignored: the latter saw the FRD as a springboard for securing control of the Fabian Society as a whole.[49]

Both Beatrice and Sidney made clear, publicly and privately, that the final report of the control of industry committee should contain an unequivocal denunciation of syndicalism and any other form of workers' control. Impressionistic young Fabians and uneducated labourers might easily be swayed by a seductive and simplistic syndicalist message, hence the urgent need for 'constructive proposals' with which to counter 'fervent apostles of anarchic impulse and catastrophic revolution'.[50] The answer was obvious, so the only requirement was empirical evidence to support it. Cole, Mellor, and the most militant of their researchers, Robin Page Arnot, felt the same – except that the answer they wanted to come up with was diametrically opposite to that of the Webbs. As early as April 1913, the month Cole led the FRD's first major revolt against the executive, Beatrice was wishing she had never had the idea of an inquiry in the first place. At the same time, Arthur Henderson's view of the Society as a fountain of cash not a foundation of knowledge had left her wondering 'if we should have been stronger if we had kept clear of the Labour Party'. At the end of 1913, despite the successful launch of the *New Statesman*, she looked back on a torrid year of endless confrontation. She and Sidney had never felt so isolated or so unpopular, not least in the eyes of 'the revolutionary socialist or fanatical sentimentalist [who] see in us, and our philosophy, the main obstacle to what they call enthusiasm and we call hysteria'.[51]

Cole, Mellor and the FRD secretary H.J. Gillespie relished demolishing the Webbs' draft submissions for the final report, and most of this material was to see the light of day only in a post-war edition of *The History of Trade Unionism*. Needless to say, a commonly agreed report never appeared, and one reason for establishing the NGL was that, having failed to secure control of the Fabian Society, the guild socialists needed an alternative publishing outlet. The NGL might never have materialised if Cole and his allies had succeeded in severing the Fabians' connections with Labour and formally established research as the Society's overriding concern. Sidney fought such a course of action furiously, arguing that research was important but not the sole function of the Society. Beatrice still had great hopes for the FRD, envisaging that it could prove 'extraordinarily useful' to the *New Statesman*, as well as the focal point for collaboration with the 'finer intellects of our German, Belgian and Dutch comrades'. However, she had no illusions about what the guild socialists really meant when they talked about 'research': in reality it was 'a new form of propaganda and a new doctrine', which placed the control of manufacturing industry directly in the hands of the workers. At the 1914 annual general meeting, with the unsolicited support of Shaw, the rebels came within one vote of securing their objectives.[52] Six months later, during which time 'the Oxford men' continued to battle with Beatrice in her capacity as FRD conference director, war split the Society, albeit not as deeply as in 1899. Ironically, for the first ten months of the conflict relations between the Webbs and the anti-war guild socialists improved, leaving Beatrice optimistic over the FRD's long-term future. However, in May 1915 Cole stormed out of the AGM following the guild socialists' poor showing in the executive election and in the vote on their manifesto demanding the expulsion of all Liberals, 'The Right Moment'.[53]

Cole and Mellor clearly behaved appallingly throughout

1913–15, and beyond. Yet Beatrice Webb always admired their enthusiasm, industry and determination to get what they wanted. Whether Sidney shared her generosity of spirit is open to question, but with hindsight we can see that the Webbs' battered faith in Cole as the Fabian crown prince played a large part in bringing him out of the cold in the latter part of the First World War.[54] By that time, not only was the National Guilds League on its last legs, but the FRD had carved out a new role for itself as an investigative agency for the whole labour movement. Free from Fabian supervision, the renamed Labour Research Department (LRD) received £150 in 1918 from the Labour Party for providing research support. Post-war industrial upheaval revived latent syndicalist sympathies among the researchers, much to the annoyance of Henderson, who had helped most of them escape conscription in 1916. In July 1921 Labour ceased to provide accommodation and financial support. Lack of cash meant that the LRD faced closure unless it accepted the offer of Communist funding – and control. Dissuaded by the Webbs from accepting Moscow gold, Cole broke with Page Arnot and sought rehabilitation within the Labour mainstream.[55]

As we shall see, by the early 1920s Douglas Cole was already emerging as a key figure in the post-war survival of the *New Statesman* – and yet, without actually doing anything, in 1912–13 he had made an enormous contribution to the paper's very existence. His espousal of guild socialism, in the columns of the *New Age* and in the normally dull proceedings of the Fabian Society had convinced Beatrice and Sidney Webb of the need for effective counter-propaganda. Along with Shaw, they decided to take action on an idea that had been floating around for at least five years. A 'loyal' political weekly would not simply act as the voice of a Fabian silent majority outraged by the antics and opinions of Cole and his comrades, but – far more important – would give the progressive intelligentsia (including, most especially, the Webbs and other like-minded Fabians) a platform from which to launch a 'hearts and minds' offensive upon the ILP and the Labour Party in Parliament. It took Beatrice and Sidney half their political lives to realise the importance of working from within the labour movement.[56] Once that realisation had sunk in, and with spirits recharged by their world cruise, they acted with purpose and speed. The *New Statesman* was conceived during weekend parties and long walks across Beachy Head in the summer of 1912. Within a year the necessary capital had been raised, an editorial staff recruited, and the first heavyweight challenger to the *New Age* was on sale at all quality newsagents from Hampstead to Bloomsbury.

3

Pre-war paper-making: Founding a new radical weekly

CLIFFORD SHARP (AND ROSAMUND BLAND)

Clifford Dyce Sharp is an unlikely hero in the history of the *New Statesman*. All the evidence suggests he was an obnoxious character, indifferent to the affections and feelings of his wife and, for all but the very closest of his colleagues, a fair-weather friend. Early ambitions drowned in a post-war sea of alcohol, and long before his final dismissal in 1930 he cut a pitiable figure. The more he drank, the more morose he became. As a result he tested to the limit the patience and loyalty of those few friends he retained. Never a man of sound political judgement, in the 1920s he shared Asquith's affection for the bottle *and* his politics. The *New Statesman* suffered accordingly. Yet until around 1927 he could somehow still put a paper to bed on time, and here lies the secret of Sharp's success: as a technician he was extremely able, pioneering new standards in newspaper composition with his innovatory ideas in layout and typography. A master editor, he was the Fabian mechanic *par excellence*. He even had an engineering degree. Described by Leonard Woolf as 'a curiously chilly and saturnine man . . . who had the sentimentality of those who make a fuss about being anti-sentimental', Sharp proved ideally qualified for editing papers founded by Beatrice and Sidney Webb, tapping loyal readers' sense of duty rather than their desire for pure entertainment.[1]

Sharp was no romantic, but if he had a passion for anything it was journalism. He never stopped producing copy, even on his deathbed. Born into a strictly Nonconformist family in Surrey,

34

Sharp progressed through school and university college to a position in his father's firm of solicitors. He practised law, but all too often his mind was elsewhere. Even when studying engineering he had shown far more interest in the intellectual ferment that was progressive politics in late Victorian London. Deeply conservative, and yet desperate to live in a nation both efficient and humane, he had joined the Fabian Society in 1900. Not only did Sharp intend to write, but he wanted one day to be an editor. He knew he had to serve his apprenticeship, and that a burgeoning weekly press offered the best openings. All his spare time was spent in London or on the South Coast cultivating the 'Old Gang', particularly Shaw and Hubert Bland.[2] As a would-be journalist of the left, Sharp was in the right place at the right time.

In 1906, when Sharp was 23, some of the Society's younger members formed the 'Fabian Nursery'. Sharp was elected treasurer, and Rosamund Bland the secretary. Rosamund was the daughter of Hubert Bland and the successful children's writer, E. Nesbit. Their two houses, at Dymchurch on the edge of Romney Marsh and at Well Hall in Eltham, provided twin focal points for many of the Society's less arduous activities. It was probably while enjoying Edith Nesbit's legendary hospitality that Sharp met his future editorial partner, Jack Squire. The latter would have relished the Bland household's rather Bohemian lifestyle, while the former was no doubt mildly disapproving. Sharp nevertheless was a great admirer of Hubert Bland, although it is hard to think why. Never was a writer more aptly named. Before trying his hand at journalism, Bland had demonstrated that he was equally ill-equipped for business. He never abandoned the *persona* of the prosperous Victorian gentlemen, his top hat, tailcoat and black-ribboned monocle contrasting sharply with the familiar Fabian uniform of Norfolk jacket and knicker-bockers. Demonstrating a deep scepticism that verged on outright hostility towards most forms of female emancipation, Bland's stern moral pronouncements contrasted sharply with his sexual proclivities. Of his children, Rosamund was the favourite, inspiring Bland's 1906 moralising volume, *Letters to a Daughter*. Drawing on Wells's admittedly hostile memoirs, Edith Nesbit's biographer has speculated on whether Bland strayed beyond acceptable paternal affection.[3] He certainly was not averse to seeking to seduce

Rosamund's schoolfriends, and he tried his wife's patience with a succession of mistresses. Not long before helping to found the 'Nursery', Rosamund discovered that Edith, with whom she never really got on that well, was not her real mother. It transpired that when Alice Hoatson, the Blands' first housekeeper, gave birth to an illegitimate daughter, Edith had acceded to her husband's request that they adopt the baby as their own. Three years later Bland confessed that he had seduced Alice, and that Rosamund was in fact their offspring.[4]

While never as uninhibited as Brooke's Cambridge circle a few years later, the second generation of Fabians were far livelier than their temperate, indeed rather severe elders (including the public Bland, and even the abstemious GBS). Creation of the 'Nursery' coincided with H.G. Wells's intellectual and constitutional assaults upon the 'Old Gang'. In print and in conversation Wells was a seductive figure, his novels and essays exciting a young audience with their vision of a new world order, and above all a new morality. Sharp was unimpressed, remaining loyal to the executive as most of the other young Fabians enthused over Wells's mission to turn the Society into a crusading parliamentary party. Always happy to massage a rising star's ego, he nevertheless voted against Wells's motion in December 1906, advising him to take defeat gracefully.[5]

Wells was keenly aware that nearly a quarter of all Fabians were now women, most of whom were eager for their enhanced representation to be reflected in the organisation and in the prevailing ethos of the Society. Arguing that women were victims of economic and sexual exploitation, Wells had little difficulty in splitting the Bland household. Rosamund, emotionally stifled by her father, and desperate to step out of her mother's shadow and establish herself as an author in her own right, found herself in the spring of 1907 the focus of Wells's attention: Bland could keep his outmoded, self-satisfied, *petit bourgeois* gaggle of do-gooders, but it was about time his daughter was set free. Wells was determined Rosamund should have a clear idea of what her father was really like, and what a hypocrite he was when it came to sex. It was a bold if rash ploy, and it worked. Rosamund's affair with Wells appears to have lasted about a year. It was discreetly conducted, and yet throughout 1907–8 she was assiduously courted by Sharp, who Bland felt would make an admirable match. The affair ended when father and cuckolded suitor confronted the couple at Paddington Station. Bland knocked Wells to the ground, warning him that he would create a public scandal unless the relationship ended at once.[6] It did, and not long afterwards one of Wells's more celebrated affairs – with Amber Pember Reeves – began. Rosamund's glamorous successors in Wells's tempestuous love-life (Rebecca West succeeded Amber Reeves, both women bearing him children) have left her looking a rather sad and pathetic figure. Although she did live an unhappy life, idolising Wells long after he had forgotten about her, she was also by all accounts an intelligent, strong-willed and resourceful woman. She needed to be, as in September 1909 she married Sharp, spending the next 24 years mostly alone and mostly penniless.[7]

Wells stuck the knife into the Blands in *The New Machiavelli* (the Booles are a far nastier couple than the Baileys/Webbs). In *Experiment in Autobiography* he twisted the blade, while also slipping in a snide reference to Sharp.[8] The latter's reward for loyalty in 1906 was election to the Fabian executive two years later. Despite Wells's feeling that Sharp had somehow betrayed him they appeared to remain on good terms. In March 1908, when still unaware of what was going on behind his back, Sharp congratulated Wells on the series of essays on socialism that made up *New Worlds For Old*. The letter confirmed that Sharp had at last 'burnt his law boats' by accepting an offer to assist Orage on the *New Age*. At this time the *New Age* had yet to break away from its Fabian roots and raise the standard of guild socialism. Even so, Sharp was an unusual choice. By 1910 he must have been horrified by Orage and Penty's rejection of the state, while at the same time revelling in the distinctive 'Englishness' of their thinking: the reason he admired *New Worlds For Old* so much was that it marked 'an epoch – the end of orthodoxy & the beginning of a *national* (i.e. English) movement'.[9] It is clear from Sharp's three-year tenure editing the *Crusade*, and then the successful launch of the *New Statesman*, that he learnt a great deal from Orage. The *New Age* taught Sharp all he knew about editing a political weekly and literary review. He left the magazine in 1910, and three years later he set about destroying it.

RAISING CAPITAL AND RECRUITING SUBSCRIBERS

> The world's great age begins anew;
>   The Fabians return;
> The Webb doth like a snake renew
>   His social creed outworn.[10]

Wells gave the *New Statesman's* first issue a jaundiced reception, gently reminding Shaw and the Webbs that the notion of the Fabians spawning an independent political weekly was originally his.[11] Convincing a target audience among the reformist middle class that this was a genuinely independent platform for progressive thinking was seen by Sharp to be of paramount importance. In March 1912 he objected strongly to Beatrice's suggestion that a revamp and relaunch of the *Crusade* would suffice.[12] Even so, it was several months before the Webbs accepted that their provisional title, 'The Fabian', would also send out all the wrong signals. If they were going to get their ideas across in a fresh and innovatory fashion then they had to indicate that the new weekly was precisely that: new. The risk was not merely that of operating on insufficient capital and an almost total lack of experience in newspaper management and production: survival depended upon convincing potential readers that advancing unashamedly collectivist arguments and ideas could be squared with the principle of full editorial freedom.[13] After all, if the 'Old Gang' could not get their message across, why waste time launching a new magazine? Conversely, if every leader parroted Beatrice and Sidney, then the the project was doomed from the outset.

For this reason alone, Shaw's name – as well as his money – was vital. The attraction of reading GBS was that you never knew what you were going to get next. For the Webbs he was a lifelong ally and friend, unpredictable but trustworthy. For the general public he was the voice of the age, *the* man of letters in an era of great men of letters. Shaw had an opinion on *everything*, and an appeal that transcended class and gender. As far as Beatrice was concerned, the venture was doomed without his active involvement. Yet Shaw's initial response was scarcely encouraging. The memory of his unhappy experience with the *New Age* was still fresh in his memory.

In a long letter to Beatrice he warned that launching a new title was a hazardous undertaking. She would have to exercise tight control over whoever was appointed editor, and rely heavily on a 'team of young lions (coaching them to some extent at a weekly lunch or dinner)'. All of this would be extremely time-consuming. With glorious irony, given the emotional upheaval caused by his recent affair with Mrs Patrick Campbell, Shaw expressed concern that handling difficult writers might place an unexpected pressure on the Webbs' marriage. Shaw went on to recall his ten years with the *Star*, and the relief he felt when no longer expected to produce scintillating copy every week. Sidney's many and remarkable talents sadly did not stretch to 'fascinating' the 'sixpenny public', and yet it was unfair to expect classic GBS week in, week out. He could not therefore make any commitment on contributing until he knew who the editor would be. Utilising a favourite Shavian ruse, he blamed his inertia on the onset of old age. Nor, he insisted, could Sidney escape the passing of the years (among myriad future activities, Webb was yet to be a co-author of the Labour Party constitution and serve in two Cabinets). It is worth recalling that, at 57, Shaw was by his own standards a mere youth. For a man whose 'bolt is shot' he remained remarkably prolific, and, although starting to question the theatre's value as an appropriate medium for his ideas, he was still to write *Pygmalion*, perhaps his most popular play. If Shaw was not yet ready to offer his pen, he was prepared to dip into his purse. Ignoring his own advice, he ended the letter to Beatrice by generously offering to match the largest individual investment.[14]

Five months later Shaw handed over a cheque for £1,000, the sum invested by each of the three other major contributors: Henry Harben, Edward Whitley and E.D. Simon. Whitley had made a lot of money as an applied chemist. Like Harben, he was an active Fabian and had helped sponsor the Poor Law campaign. Ernest (much later, as Chairman of the BBC, Lord) Simon was a Manchester businessman who, having built up a fortune, practised politics to the extent of becoming a Liberal backbencher. As major shareholders all three men were to play a major role in determining the fortunes of the *New Statesman* until well into the 1920s. The Webbs themselves were only two of several small investors who together held the remaining £1,000 of stock. In

October 1912 'The Statesman' Publishing Company Ltd. was established, the board holding its first meeting in the NCPD's old Norfolk Street premises two months later. These offices were to be the new paper's home, until the move to 10 Great Queen Street. Having agreed on Sidney Webb as chairman, the directors decided that the paper would be launched in the spring and be called 'The Statesman'. The name had come from, of all people, A.J. Balfour, perhaps the only Tory leader ever to read the magazine purely for pleasure. 'New' was added to the future masthead in February 1913 after S.K. Ratcliffe pointed out that India's largest-selling daily was *The Statesman*.[15]

Given that Sidney and Beatrice had been in Calcutta as recently as January 1912 it is odd that they failed to recall a mass circulation newspaper Ratcliffe himself had edited only a few years earlier. The fact that Ratcliffe was sounded out about the editorship not long after the Webbs' return home shows that Sharp's appointment was by no means a foregone conclusion. He had an ideal *c.v.*, three years at *The Statesman* having followed editorship of the *Echo*, a London evening paper that had supported the Progressives. After returning from India Ratcliffe had worked alongside H.W. Massingham on the then new Liberal weekly, the *Nation*, as well as editing the *Sociological Review*. For the Webbs, Ratcliffe would have been an ideal choice, but he turned them down, preferring to act in an advisory capacity.[16] For much of the time after 1914 he was based in New York, his network of contacts and nose for a good story providing the *New Statesman* with exceptional coverage of American politics. Throughout the autumn and winter of 1912 Ratcliffe put the Webbs in contact with those journalists who could offer practical advice on how a new weekly could survive, and even achieve profitability.

Another adviser was C.M. Lloyd who, on the basis of his research for the NCPD and his expertise as a barrister, was a regular lecturer on social administration at the LSE. Mostyn Lloyd had enjoyed a glittering early career at Oxford and as a private secretary, before a spell at Toynbee Hall led to his joining the ILP and taking seriously his Fabian membership. An executive member, he enjoyed the unusual distinction of his views being respected by both the Webbs and the Coles. Highly regarded as a writer on social deprivation and industrial relations, Lloyd would have made an ideal editor for the *New Statesman*. The trouble was that he had no relevant experience. His input to the paper before the First World War was therefore modest, but, as we shall see, after 1918 his influence was immense.[17]

In December 1912 Sharp was at last made editor, at a salary of £500 per annum. There was no great enthusiasm about the appointment, Sidney judging Sharp 'weak, timid and slow', a view with which Beatrice concurred. She did, however, highlight his 'method, sense and good journalist manners', and Sidney qualified his very negative assessment of Sharp by maintaining that he would probably work best if left to get on with it. Thus, from the outset the chairman followed Shaw's advice of having a weekly lunch, and his own advice of not getting involved in purely editorial matters.[18] In the New Year Sharp was given £50 and sent to France where he was to meet the Anglophile historian Elie Halévy. The idea was that Halévy would introduce him to useful contacts in Paris as part of a grand tour intended to familiarise a previously parochial Sharp with politics across the Channel. Although he was later rather good at persuading foreign correspondents to write for the *New Statesman* in their spare time, Sharp appears to have achieved little during his brief sojourn on the continent.[19] The only significant appointment was made at home: Jack Squire agreed to become literary editor for the princely sum of £300 per year, a modest but timely income for a struggling poet.

Squire must have been pleased to learn that 'The Statesman' would henceforth be Shaw's 'habitual medium of communication with the public through the press'. Unfortunately, in the interest of editorial uniformity GBS would be as anonymous as everybody else. Sharp was particularly keen on this, and Shaw was similarly insistent. He had no intention 'of being the funny man and the privileged lunatic of a weekly paper'.[20] If the seductive initials 'GBS' were not to feature on the cover, then there had to be other equally enticing delights: only Beatrice and Sidney Webb could have come up with the idea of selling a new political weekly on the strength of a *twenty*-part series, 'What Is Socialism?'. The greater the number of subscribers, the greater the appeal to advertisers. They needed 2,000, but if subscriptions scarcely exceeded 500 then Beatrice anticipated closure within two years. At the *Nation* Massingham reassured himself that survival was impossible with weekly sales under 3,000, and that the best this new 'one-idea-ed' paper could secure was 1,500, mainly thanks to Shaw. Beatrice pooh-poohed the *Nation*'s confidence that it would speedily see off a fresh rival. However, the initial signs were not good The mailing lists of the Fabian Society and the NCPD had provided 20,000 names, of which the most promising received personal letters. Yet the first fortnight's herculean efforts brought in a mere 150 subscriptions. In early February Shaw and Sidney took over from an exhausted Beatrice. With help from Harley Granville-Barker, the Fabian founder of the Stage Society, Frederick Whelen, and the companies' register at Somerset House, they drew up a list of 5,000 people with an interest in drama. All these potential admirers of GBS duly received a special letter and a subscription form.[21]

The Shavian card was played again and again. The letter to 'Fellow-Fabians' was a 'Private and Confidential' letter from Shaw reassuring them that the new weekly had its roots firmly in the Society. Fellow members had to appreciate that only the 'most urgent necessity' was obliging him to join the Webbs in sacrificing their valuable time so late in life. Moral blackmail was probably more persuasive than the prolix efforts of the four-page *Preliminary Memorandum* to discount any hint of a Fabian conspiracy. The gist of the latter's message was that sectarianism hindered progress, and that the community would benefit best from the 'steady development of Collectivist theory and policy'. This necessitated a new and wide-ranging weekly in which feedback from readers would have an especially important role to play. Perhaps the correspondence column was the only guarantee of decent prose: one can only presume Shaw had no role in drafting an appeal that sought subscribers 'neither disinclined for controversy, nor unable to express themselves'.[22] The few surviving subscribers to the *Crusade* now received their final issue, the last page announcing that a new weekly review of politics and literature would appear for the first time on 12 April 1913. *Crusade* readers would be either reassured or horrified to learn that Mr Clifford Sharp would assume the editorship of the magisterially named *New Statesman*. On 11 March a somewhat larger audience read of the announcement in *The Times*.

Beatrice's calculations were just about right. The mailshot produced 2,450 subscribers, with around another 150 signing up after seeing the first issue. Casual sales were between 500 and 600, growing to nearly 2,000 by the time of the First World War. The crunch came of course when subscriptions had to be renewed in the spring of 1914: allowing for fresh subscribers, around 650 decided not to continue. Thus, the circulation at the end of the first year was over 3,000. However, income was failing to keep up with costs, and the price of paper was rising with alarming speed. The supplements were always intended to be a crucial feature of the paper, but they were extremely expensive to produce, and only became economical with a large print run.[23] By the end of the first financial year over half of the initial capital had been used up, despite Harben, Whitley, and Shaw each contributing a further £500. All three made clear their reluctance to subsidise the paper *ad infinitum*. The Webbs promised to tighten up arrangements for subscription renewal, and held a fund-raising event in the Kingsway Hall. The attraction was GBS speaking on 'The Press', and according to Lytton Strachey the event was a disaster: every time Sharp tried to answer a question, 'The three Gorgons surrounding him kept leaping to their feet with the most crushing replies'.[24]

INITIAL REACTION

The first issue of the *New Statesman* appeared, as announced, on 12 April 1913. It is unlikely that many of those involved, whether directors or contributors, would have imagined the paper celebrating its eightieth anniversary and still going strong. After six issues Beatrice summarised a mixed response:

> There are all sorts of conflicting criticism – the paper is dull: it is mere brilliant writing and there is not enough solid information; the political articles are good but the literature 'rot'; the literary side is excellent but the political articles not sufficiently constructive.[25]

Clearly confusion ranged. The only obvious conclusion was that, however uninspiring he was as a writer, Sharp had a clear aptitude for business – he was a born editor and administrator.[26]

One person who had a very clear idea what he thought of the new paper was Orage. Sharp and Squire had learnt all they could about editing from him. Now they had set up in direct competition to him. Feelings ran high. Although he thought the *New Statesman* was appalling, Orage soon began to feel the pressure. The *New Age*'s circulation dropped to 4,500, and when the price doubled, from 3d to 6d, in November 1913 another 1,000 readers drifted away. By the end of 1914 the two weeklies shared similar sales, but Orage was finding it harder to control costs and maintain standards. To compensate for having to pay so much for newsprint Orage reduced the number of contributors, and wrote far too much himself. No wonder that when he bumped into Sharp in Chancery Lane during the first year of the war there was an icy exchange.[27]

Wells recognised straightaway who the *New Statesman*'s target was. In the first issue he found 'not so much as the tenth of an *Orage* in the whole enterprise'. With the honourable exception of Desmond MacCarthy's theatre column, this was 'not journalism but printed mumbling . . . as dull as a privet hedge in Leeds'. Wells's review was a triumph of vitriol, guaranteed to shatter any hope of reconciliation between him and Sharp.[28]

The *Nation* was of course the *New Statesman*'s other principal target. Its editor, the veteran Liberal journalist H.W. Massingham, provided a thoughtful response to the first issue. He argued that liberalism constituted a genuinely libertarian alternative to Fabian collectivism. In office the Liberal Party had on the whole stuck to its principles, witness the pursuit of Home Rule and defence of free trade. The party was worthy of support so long as it continued reconciling individual liberty with the adequate provision of 'all that is good in Socialism'. If GBS and Sidney Webb largely concurred with Massingham's sentiments then why did they intend to replace the present administration, let alone how?[29] Massingham was never going to succeed in convincing the Webbs that their paper was unnecessary, so his priority was to fight back. He had the advantage of having already built up a glittering array of contributors, but he went on the offensive by trying to tap Shaw's early disillusion. Needless to say, he failed.[30]

Like the *New Age*, the *Nation* relied on regular copy from Arnold Bennett. However, neither magazine had exclusive rights to Bennett, who was invariably available to the highest bidder. Bennett was no great admirer of the Webbs, even though he appears to have got on reasonably well with Sidney after joining the *New Statesman* board in 1915. However, as the literary editor's friend and mentor he was happy to write for far less than he normally charged, as well as putting Squire in contact with Paris-based writers such as Rémy de Gourmont and Romain Rolland. Bennett had a generally poor opinion of Sharp's half of the paper, albeit acknowledging that after six months it had improved dramatically.[31]

In contrast to Bennett, Ernest Simon felt happy with Sharp, but questioned whether Squire was up to the job. Webb's reply was suitably diplomatic, mixing flattery, self-deprecation and firmness: yes, Sharp was 'quite to be trusted for politics', but doubtless he would welcome Simon's advice; Squire had come highly recommended, and was clearly a 'very clever and charming fellow'; no he didn't have a clue what Squire was up to, if only because modern literature was incomprehensible; if he judged the paper exactly right then 'the sum total would not commend itself to anyone not named Webb'; frankly, the best course of action was to let these young men have their head and not intervene in editorial affairs.[32] The chairman's view of his staff was tolerant, enlightened and rooted in common sense. Perhaps because he had a lot more money invested in the paper, Simon found it difficult to adopt a similar air of equanimity. He regularly sought reassurance from Sidney about the project's viability, until an encounter with the editor of the *Manchester Courier* at last eased his fears:

> He [Acland, *Manchester Courier* editor] spoke rather highly of the 'Statesman' and said it was obvious it must succeed because Bernard Shaw had invested money in it, and whatever else Shaw might be he was essentially a first class business man and would not have put in a penny unless he was quite sure he would get a good return on it![33]

Within three years Shaw had resigned from the board of the *New Statesman*, and the *Manchester Courier* had ceased publication.

'I [GBS] AM MR JORKINS ON THE NEW STATESMAN; CLIFFORD SHARP IS MR SPENLOW'[34]

With around 2,400 shares and a £1,500 loan, Shaw had the biggest financial interest in the *New Statesman*. His generosity and good-will were legendary, but by no means inexhaustible. Most editors would have been wary of antagonising GBS, particularly as he was the main reason anyone bought the paper. Not so Clifford Sharp.

Unsigned paragraphs of 'Comments' took up the first two or three pages of the new paper, with Sharp explaining that anonymity was crucial for establishing a common style and tone.[35] He had already earned the board's approval by making it clear that the *New Statesman* would most definitely not be a ragbag of conflicting styles and opinions *à la* the *New Age*. Readers were assured at the outset, however, that Mr Bernard Shaw would be a regular contributor.[36] In theory, therefore, identifying Shaw's contributions was to be a matter of guesswork. In reality of course it was very easy, with his witty, fantastic and sometimes wholly bizarre musings upon the modern world contrasting sharply with the brisk, no-nonsense approach Sharp considered *de rigueur* throughout the front half of the paper.

Shaw had no intention of being a lightweight eccentric, but at the same time he wanted some fun. This was a concept Sharp found difficulty with, complaining that Shaw's flippancy undermined his efforts to create the sort of paper Treasury mandarins packed in their weekend bag. Shaw and Sharp disagreed on everything, except 'Ireland, Municipal Trading, and the death duties'. Tension between the two men became evident even as the first issue was going to press. Shaw adopted what was to become a familiar habit of keeping his editor totally in the dark about the content of his copy. Then, as if to compound his sins, successive drafts of an article on the *New Witness*'s muck-raking role in the Marconi scandal were so inaccurate and potentially libellous that Sharp and Squire found themselves tearing the proofs up and starting again.[37]

It was Squire who soon succeeded Sidney Webb in the role of arbitrator. Both Sidney and Beatrice were clearly sympathetic to Sharp's position, quarrelling with Shaw as early as the third issue over a funny but outrageous article about the Belgian general strike.[38] For GBS, the 'capable editor' had to have 'ability enough and to spare for literature and yet deliberately prefer journalism to literature as an occupation'.[39] If he really believed this, then it's not surprising that he preferred Squire to Sharp. Michael Holroyd has suggested another reason why the two men did not get on. Sharp was too much like Shaw's father. Here was another 'moral teetotaller who drank: a man also of late hours and cloudy scandals over money and women'.[40]

At first Sharp was in no position to dispense with the services of the principal shareholder, who just also happened to be the foremost writer of the day. His solution was to suggest that Shaw would be the exception that proved the rule, and would sign his articles. This of course was what Beatrice had wanted at the outset. Shaw, however, was adamant that the original arrangement would remain. In the words of his biographer, 'Collectivism did not mean to him a regimentation of tone, but the release of differing individual talents for a generally harmonious purpose'.[41] Shaw's mission was to capture his readers through the old familiar sparkle, and then get them thinking about issues deeper than the mechanics of local government or the failings of national insurance.

Shaw had better things to do than squabble with the likes of Clifford Sharp, and his input to the *New Statesman* declined rapidly in the course of the first year. When Israel Zangwill complained that a letter criticising MacCarthy had not been published, Shaw answered, 'That's nothing, you're not a proprietor; I am; and he won't print my articles'.[42] Sharp's willingness to quote this against himself suggests a lingering affection for his old adversary. Even at the time he made light of, 'the good-humoured contempt which he [GBS] never concealed. I think he is much the most generous and sweetest-tempered person I ever came across.'[43] This is clearly nonsense given the abuse heaped on Shaw's head over the next 18 months. Sharp encouraged the notion that he was the injured party simply to protect his job. As we shall see, the First World War led to Shaw reviving his interest in the paper, with ultimately unhappy results. His reluctance to write for Sharp in the final months of peace forced the *New Statesman* to rely on its own efforts and look elsewhere for dazzling prose. In this respect Shaw did his investment a favour.

The most striking feature of Shaw's involvement in the *New Statesman*, both before and during the war, is his generosity and good humour. Sharp's claim to like and respect GBS should be taken with a pinch of salt – as Chapter 5 confirms, all the evidence suggests that he loathed him. Shaw on the other hand displayed no trace of ill-will towards either the editorial staff or his fellow directors.[44] Sharp had no sense of humour, seeing Shaw's behaviour as cavalier and irresponsible. Shaw saw Sharp as a well-intentioned social engineer but an emotional cripple. In the spring of 1918, two years after his final break with the *New Statesman*, Shaw reassured a worried left-leaning correspondent thus:

> I [GBS] am delighted to hear that there is an Anti-Socialist magazine in existence. If it does half as much to hinder its own course as most of the Socialist magazines and societies, the triumph of Socialism is assured.
> Go ahead, hard.[45]

Of course, had the correspondent been Clifford Sharp, he simply would not have got the joke. He and Shaw could easily have come from different planets.

4

The *New Statesman* in Liberal England

Bernard Shaw never intimidated Sharp, but then nobody ever did. His attitude towards readers reinforces one's impression of an Evelyn Waugh of the left, in temperament if not in talent. Letters to the editor might take up as many as four pages, many of which were articles in all but name (no need to pay contributors of course if the great and the good were writing *gratis*). Sharp would happily lay into a hapless correspondent, or encourage a colleague to do so. Debates and quarrels could go on for weeks until the editor called a halt. This established an instant *New Statesman* tradition of the correspondence columns as a battleground for entrenched opinions. Just occasionally a serious debate of national importance has taken place, most notably the storm created by Keynes's public avowal of protection in early 1931.[1]

Like any other young journal, the *New Statesman* had to establish an identity as speedily as possible. However impenetrable the prose, Beatrice's research reports clearly had a role to play. But the supplements in which they appeared were precisely that – supplements. Only a tiny percentage of the *New Statesman*'s potential readership would buy it solely for the great wads of indigestible information that accompanied the actual magazine. How many of the worthier supplements entered the Aga not the filing cabinet? Sharp and his colleagues were not in the frontline of reportage, so the *New Statesman*'s capacity to survive depended on the quality of their commentary. In other words, they had to proffer a view of the world which educated left-leaning members of the Edwardian middle class could not easily acquire elsewhere.

The cinema was in its infancy and the wireless still a decade away. Television was the stuff of science fiction, and Sunday supplements half a century in the future. Thus the only serious competition was the daily press. The morning papers had the edge in terms of up-to-the-minute hard news, but had only so much scope for careful reflection and breadth of opinion. The evening titles, particularly in the heart of the capital, came the closest to the weeklies. But when all was said and done they were still *news*papers, and functioned as such. Whatever the Webbs' fears, this was a highly propitious time to launch a new weekly. Aggressive marketing and high-quality journalism, if properly combined, could ensure the viability of a new title in a crowded market. Furthermore, the level of domestic upheaval in the final years of peace ensured no shortage of subject-matter. Working-class militancy, the travails of the young Labour Party, the unprecedented level of party political conflict, the struggle for female emancipation, and above all the issue of Irish Home Rule, provided the *New Statesman* with a rich agenda in its first 16 months of publication.[2]

COVERING THE HOME RULE CRISIS, 1913–14

Needless to say, Ireland was seen as crying out for a supplement: it would educate the English, but, more importantly, it might help put 'new spirit' into Irish domestic politics.[3] Sidney Webb's assumption that the likes of Sir Edward Carson and John Redmond would eagerly digest an obscure weekly's views on Home Rule has a charming naivety. He had a relentless optimism, albeit underpinned by more than a hint of intellectual arrogance. The supplement duly appeared, on 24 July 1913, with an introduction by Shaw, who had provided unusually sober coverage of the continuing crisis in Ireland since the first issue. This is one supplement worthy of closer examination as it introduced to the paper a number of writers who would become familiar to the readers over the next ten years.

One name missing, although an unsigned article could easily have been written by him, was Ireland's foremost agrarian reformer, Sir Horace Plunkett.[4] A former Unionist MP and founder of the Department of Agriculture and Technical Instruction, Plunkett had been closely if unfairly associated with Balfour's policy of killing nationalism through kindness. Plunkett argued that economic not political activity was a priority, his greatest achievement being the establishment of a hugely successful co-operative, the Irish Agricultural Organisation Society (IAOS). Having only partially convinced tenant farmers and Anglo-Irish estate owners to pioneer practical solutions to rural distress, Plunkett became a deeply sceptical supporter of Home Rule once its appearance on the statute book appeared inevitable. He firmly resisted the Webbs' repeated requests that he write on Home Rule, and that he edit the supplement, although he did recruit for them the IAOS's secretary, George Russell, better known as the poet 'AE'. The Webbs had stressed to their friend that the new weekly would have no firm line on Home Rule, as indeed it did not before the winter of 1913–14.[5] Yet, despite Beatrice's assurances that his semi-neutral position would not be compromised, Plunkett clearly did not relish seeing his name in print alongside radical writers such as Francis Sheehy-Skeffington, of whom more later. This refusal to help old friends clearly caused no lasting enmity. Plunkett's pronouncements, particularly his case for an eventual plebiscite, were always reported in hushed tones.[6] Having said this, events moved so rapidly in the spring and summer of 1914, and Sharp in particular became so infuriated by Unionist intransigence, that Plunkett's last-minute appeal for loyalist moderation attracted only polite interest.

In contrast to Plunkett's indifference, another scion of the Ascendancy, *The Times*'s Joseph Hone, happily provided the supplement with a study of the Gaelic League. Hone, a quiet, sensitive man, equally at home in Liberty Hall or the Gresham Hotel, within weeks became 'our Dublin correspondent'. Hone was a close friend of the Yeats family and active in the cultural regeneration at the heart of an 'Irish Ireland'. At the same time, his Anglo-Irish background, and the high regard in which he was held at Printing House Square, ensured easy access to the highest echelons of the Unionist movement, not least Carson himself. Like so many southern Protestants, Hone, the product of an English public-school education and devoutly High Church, could scarcely empathise with the atavistic loyalties and traditions of marching Presbyterian Ulstermen. What was more, as a convinced Home Ruler he thought they were misguided and wrong. Nevertheless, he was remarkably good at articulating the fears of Belfast's working and lower middle classes. Their leaders accorded similar respect, Hone's principal target being those Unionists at Westminster happy to foster civil strife in Ulster as a means of bringing down the government.[7] The *New Statesman*'s policy of anonymity meant that as Hone began to appear more frequently via 'Comments' or in specially commissioned articles so the paper's position on Home Rule began to firm up. This was despite Shaw becoming more and more of a loose cannon in his writings on Ireland, to the obvious annoyance of an editor still struggling to establish consistency of opinion.[8]

The third native authority on Home Rule was Robert Lynd, literary editor of the *Daily News* and a freelance writer. Lynd was unusual in that he was a keen supporter of the Gaelic League and a nationalist pamphleteer, but the son of a Presbyterian minister. Returning to Belfast in the summer of 1913 he provided the *New Statesman* with an insider's view of 12 July, warning that latent violence and religious bigotry could explode at any moment.[9] Eyewitness accounts were still rare in the *New Statesman*, and on the strength of this very powerful piece Sharp invited Lynd to write the weekly 'middle'. Although Lynd was familiar with the magazine, having been persuaded by Jack Squire to review, it was some months before he made a regular commitment. All the weeklies at this time had at least one columnist whose reflections on a topical issue acted as a bridge between the political commentary and coverage of the arts. The *Nation* published no fewer than three middle articles, featuring the formidable trio of H.N. Brailsford, J.A. Hobson and H.W. Nevinson.[10] With competition like this Sharp had to be sure that he had the right man.

Ideally, a regular columnist should be like a cartoonist, enjoying the privilege of expressing views that are not always in accord with editorial policy. Sharp was reluctant to give Lynd this freedom so long as he wrote under his own name. The topic for the week was discussed in advance, and the editorial 'we' used throughout. Surprisingly, Lynd adhered to these conditions throughout the war, real freedom of expression only coming in 1918 when he became 'X' (later 'XX', and then, until 1945, the much better-known and extremely popular 'YY'). The reason appears to be that Lynd found great difficulty in deciding on a topic and then sitting down to write – Sharp provided the inspiration and the discipline.[11] Lynd's essays were whimsical and witty, but always had a serious point, not least when he was writing about Ireland. His writing gives the impression of a very gentle man, and yet he could be abrasive and damning if he chose. Early targets were St Loe Strachey for the *Spectator*'s Cassandra-like warnings of nationalist carnage, and the *Daily Telegraph* for fomenting sectarian violence within the Orange lodges. Even when writing about unrelated subjects Lynd could rarely resist an irreverent, if irrelevant, reference to Carson. Eventually a memo from an exasperated Sharp simply asked: 'Can't you forget your bloody country for *one* week?' [12]

Growing dependence on Hone, plus pressure from Lynd, meant Sharp was abandoning the Webbs' sympathetic yet non-partisan view of Home Rule as early as the summer of 1913. The uncompromising position evident by the end of the year was brought about by the Dublin transport strike. In late August, amid rioting and arson, the tramwaymen in James Larkin's Irish Transport and General Workers' Union (ITGWU) went on strike. The Employers' Federation ordered its members' employees to tear up their ITGWU membership cards. A mass refusal to do so meant that by the end of September 28,000 had been locked out. Wholly out of character, Sharp threw caution to the wind, joining Lynd, Hone and Keeling in condemning RIC connivance with the employers, urging support from the rest of the UK, and even lauding Larkin's role in radicalising the Irish TUC.[13] Lynd still had reservations about Larkin, but not so a new Dublin correspondent, with a style and passion very different from the more contemplative Hone. The presence of Francis (sometimes Frank) Sheehy-Skiffington confirmed a radicalisation of the *New Statesman* regarding Irish matters that contrasted sharply with the sober and sombre posture older Fabian readers normally found so reassuring. It was almost as if, when it came to Ireland, Sharp had lost control of his paper. While sympathetic to the strikers, the directors must have been astonished by what sometimes appeared as tacit approval of workers' control. After all, the *New Statesman* had been deliberately set up to ridicule such a concept, not endorse it. The fact that these events were taking place on the other side of the Irish Sea was irrelevant. Sheehy-Skeffington was a dangerous man, not that the authorities in Dublin Castle needed reminding of this. He had been a pain in their side (along with everybody else) for many years before his despatches from the front line left Sidney Webb bemused and irate.

Francis Sheehy-Skeffington was a fearless and inveterate campaigner, ever eager to enlighten a Phoenix Park audience. A pacifist, feminist and vegetarian, he derived his nationalism from the veteran land campaigner Michael Davitt, his socialism from Shaw, and his commitment to women's emancipation from his wife, Hannah. For nearly a decade Sheehy-Skeffington had argued in small-circulation papers such as the *Nationist* for female emancipation, better working conditions and a free Ireland. With Hannah he had helped establish the militant Irish Women's Franchise League, and in 1908 was a co-founder of the Irish ILP. Closely associated with Larkin, and with James Connolly's Citizen Army, Sheehy-Skeffington threw himself into supporting victims of the lockout. The losses of the *Irish Citizen*, his small pro-suffrage weekly, and an appeal from his old friend Robert Lynd, persuaded him to write for the paper of his hero, Shaw. Sheehy-Skeffington's dramatic accounts of what was taking place out on the streets complemented the more urbane Hone's appraisal of regular party politics. In addition to reporting for the *New Statesman*, he continued as leader-writer for the *Freeman's Journal*, and as Dublin correspondent for an assortment of newspapers, including the *Manchester Guardian*, *Daily Herald* and *L'Humanité*.

Throughout the autumn of 1913 it was invariably Sheehy-Skeffington who exhorted English trade unionists to provide material as well as moral support. Sharp complained of police brutality and made uncharacteristic pleas for action in the face of Larkin's arrest. By this time the railwaymen were on strike at home, and the NUR had joined the transport workers and miners in a Triple Alliance. Undiluted class war both sides of the Irish Sea was taking place against a backdrop of growing loyalist resistance in Ulster and a republican backlash in the south. Sidney Webb confined his demands to the familiar plea for a minimum wage and working conditions, albeit bemoaning government reluctance to force a compromise on the employers. However, by December early reports of Connolly's efforts to recruit a Citizen Army left

Webb fearful that an escalation in the dispute might bring in its wake social chaos and revolution.[14] The alarming prospect of republicanism and workers' control advancing simultaneously prompted a subtle shift in editorial policy after Christmas. The paper began to distance itself from the dispute. Events in Dublin attracted far less coverage, particularly the amount of space given to Sheehy-Skeffington's graphic accounts of squalor, anger and increasing recrimination. Sharp's willingness to fall into line with his chairman was quickly noticed. The *New Age* had despatched an early warning of the need for continued solidarity. The gist of Cole and Mellor's message was that Dublin was witnessing a historic struggle between labour and capital, and the *New Statesman* had better make sure it stayed on the right side of the barricades.[15]

Before further accusations of sell out appeared in the correspondence columns, the dispute was over. Hone and Sheehy-Skeffington were left with the task of explaining why the employers had won. By the end of February attention was again sharply focused on Home Rule, but with the passing of the strike the tone was now very different. The nightmare scenario of syndicalism and republicanism fusing in a new proletarian mass movement was seen by both Webb and Sharp to make the need for Home Rule that much more urgent. Calls for the smack of firm government rang out loudly even before the Unionists rejected Asquith's March proposal that each of Ulster's six counties could vote on exclusion from Home Rule for an initial six years. Sharp, who much preferred Plunkett's alternative of inclusion for six years, foresaw anti-Catholic discrimination and plebiscites being quietly dropped if partition was agreed. While the editor was at least prepared to study the options, for his Irish staff it was all or nothing. With the *Observer*'s J.L. Garvin clearly in his sights, Hone called on the Cabinet to ignore 'scarifying Sunday prophets' who predicted civil war.[16] Lynd, despite his Orange roots, took a long time to acknowledge that Home Rule for all 32 counties now appeared untenable. It was left to an unusually restrained Shaw to persuade Carson that genuine leadership meant never flinching from the more difficult path, in this case eschewing bigotry for compromise. His argument against partition was well-reasoned, persuasive and prescient, but of course it was ignored.[17]

Coverage of the Curragh 'mutiny' a few weeks later illustrated how ill-informed Sharp and his colleagues could be, despite having a full seven days before going to press (every weekly editor's nightmare – the big story breaks on a Thursday). To be fair, nobody else – including the Cabinet – had a clear idea of what was going on after Brigadier General Gough and his staff effectively vetoed the possibility of being ordered north. Events at the Curragh, and the repercussions at home that culminated in Asquith himself taking over the War Office, must have brought home to the more intelligent *New Statesman* reader how difficult it was to maintain a consistent and credible line over Ireland. On the one hand the paper was telling ministers to come down hard on the UVF if necessary, and on the other it was stating clearly that the Army should not be placed in an invidious position. Similarly, when arms were landed at Larne, the government was told to deal with the gun-runners or resign, a ridiculous ultimatum given the alternative of a Bonar Law-led administration.[18]

With growing polarisation and an ever deepening crisis, editorial policy lost its coherence and became simply reactive. Sharp's predictions and prognostications invariably proved wrong, although he, Lynd and Hone were as one in damning the Tory peers' amending bill of permanent exclusion. They were also united in giving the Irish Volunteers the benefit of the doubt, seeing them as a useful bargaining lever if all parties accepted a constitutional convention.[19] A Speaker's Conference finally took place at Buckingham Palace in late July, and it ended in deadlock. Sharp was already distracted by disturbing developments in the Balkans. From Dublin, Hone warned readers that if Asquith now embraced permanent exclusion on grounds of expediency, the consequences would be fatal.[20] Within days Austria had declared war on Serbia, and the second reading of the amending bill was postponed indefinitely. In the Commons Redmond and Carson pledged their respective forces to fight a common enemy. Squire's delight at 'the spectacle of an Ireland solid in its loyalty to the flag' was predictable, and if Sharp had not been absent on holiday he would probably have written the same. Hone might have been been expected to temper such enthusiasm, but he too was quite happy to engage in misplaced optimism, parroting Irish Party MPs' insistence that sacrifice on Flanders field would heal division and bring consensus.[21]

The one correspondent who knew all this was nonsense had been silent for weeks. Sheehy-Skeffington viewed war as an abomination, largely attributable to the untamed male ego. In the *Irish Citizen* he insisted his country had no interest in a struggle between rival imperialist powers. The first anti-recruitment meetings were held in Beresford Place as Francis joined Hannah in mobilising pacifist opinion against early efforts to place Ireland on a war footing. As we shall see, within a year he was in Kilmainham gaol, and by the time his work next appeared in the *New Statesman* he was dead.[22]

Once Britain was at war Sheehy-Skeffington was clearly *persona non grata* with Sharp. Hone on the other hand was seen as the respectable face of Irish nationalism, sharing as he did the *New Statesman*'s support for the war effort. For nearly two years, until Easter 1916, his copy was relegated to the final paragraph of 'Comments'. Ireland was no longer newsworthy, but Sharp wisely held on to Hone. Both men still stood to gain from collaboration. The *New Statesman* could draw on the doyen of the broadsheet correspondents in Dublin, with all that implied for access to the highest political circles. The anonymous Hone could write what he wanted, as opposed to what *The Times* wanted him to write. During the transport strike he was an effective counterweight to Sheehy-Skeffington, and in the ensuing months he acted as a conduit for nationalist opinion inside and outside the Irish Party. Hone helped ensure that by the winter of 1913–14 the *New Statesman* was firmly in favour of Home Rule because it was in Ireland's best interest (and not just because it was Liberal policy, as in the case of the *Nation*).

But of course Hone was not the only influence upon Sharp, who seems to have been genuinely shocked by events surrounding the transport strike. The sufferings of the strikers and their families, the failure of the Dublin housing commission to expose municipal corruption, and the impotence of an official inquiry into police handling of picket lines and rallies were all highlighted in the magazine, even after Webb suggested the dispute was getting out of control. Although direct communication was almost non-existent, Shaw and Sharp for once had no trouble in agreeing on the folly of Unionist behaviour at Westminster and on the streets of Belfast. Lynd did enjoy the ear of the editor, with the latter consequently failing to appreciate how unrepresentative his columnist was of middle-class, let alone working-class, feeling across Protestant Ulster. Only after the Curragh incident and the landing of guns at Larne did Sharp realise the strength of resistance within the Ulster Unionist Council, let alone the UVF. From then on, rather like the Prime Minister himself, he was floundering – his heart told him that Home Rule for all was an incontrovertible principle, but his head told him that 'No Surrender' meant precisely that. Subsequent events subverted all attempts at adhering to a clear and purposeful editorial policy, even if it turned out to be a reluctant embrace of partition.

If the Webbs intended their paper to lead from the front, then in the case of Ireland it failed. Yet what else could it do? It provided some first-class reporting from Dublin and Belfast, reminded readers of the general principles underlying Irish self-determination, and reacted to an astonishing sequence of events as best it could. Not glamorous, not glorious, but not any worse than the record of its main rivals in covering an issue where clear thinking and breadth of vision were always going to be of rare value.

COVERING THE 'WOMAN QUESTION'

With the exception of Rebecca West, all too briefly reviewing new fiction, women at Great Queen Street were thin on the ground. To be more accurate, they were non-existent. Contemporary photographs suggest pipe-smoking men in tweeds whose working day divided between jockeying for bar space with off-duty barristers and sitting purposelessly in dank, draughty rooms with grim decor and antique office equipment. Of course it could not always have been like this, otherwise the paper would never have gone to press. Nevertheless, much depended on the reliability of the support staff, particularly Sharp's secretary, Mrs Vincent. These were the women on the front line in terms of production, but editorial influence was at a distance and at a premium. The Coles may have been heirs to the Webbs as intellectual partners on the road to the New Jerusalem, but as far as the post-war *New Statesman* was concerned Margaret remained a non-person. In the early years acknowledgement was made of the contributions of

Maud Reeves and Margaret Bondfield to the paper, either directly via the supplements or indirectly via the very occasional leader on women and social deprivation. Other women, such as the eminently sensible and sadly underused Dr Ethel Bentham, were given a platform, but their influence over editorial content and policy was non-existent. The only woman with any sort of control over what the *New Statesman* said and did was of course Beatrice Webb.[23]

It was Beatrice who ensured that two special supplements on women appeared within the first 12 months. Seventy-five years later the *New Statesman* could justifiably claim that 'The Awakening of Women' and 'Women in Industry' were together the 'most thorough statement of socialist feminism of its times'.[24] Introducing the first supplement, Beatrice declared that, along with the rise of labour and nascent anti-imperialism, female emancipation was 'one of three simultaneous world-movements towards a more equal partnership among human beings in human affairs'. Needless to say, the triumph of all three were but a matter of time. Sharp was expected to publish a woman he found infuriating. On behalf of the Women's Social and Political Union (WSPU), Christabel Pankhurst set out to convince *New Statesman* readers of the case for direct action. More congenial to the editor was a supplement piece by Millicent Garrett Fawcett, founder of the National Union of Women's Suffrage Societies (NUWSS).[25]

Christabel Pankhurst and her mother had broken with the ILP as early as 1907. Sharp and Shaw, sickened by forcible feeding and police harassment, lauded the suffragettes' aims and sacrifices, but attacked their methods and their leadership's reluctance to ally with Labour. The NUWSS on the other hand was subject to regular approval. The suffragists had recently allied themselves to Labour, refusing to consort with the Liberal Party until it dumped Asquith and any other waverers over votes for women. In February 1914 Beatrice personally reported on an NUWSS rally at which delegates from several Labour organisations were present, rightly predicting a future coalescence of feminist awareness and class consciousness.[26] From the outset the Webbs and Shaw had publicised Sylvia Pankhurst's and George Lansbury's struggles in the East London Federation (ELF). When the WSPU's *The*

Suffragette returned Sylvia's article on East End slums, Webb ensured its publication.[27] Frustrated by the Labour leadership's apparent passivity in promoting female suffrage, Lansbury had resigned the whip and then his seat. Having deliberately created a by-election to publicise the franchise issue, he unfortunately lost. To make matters worse he was then arrested in April 1913 on a trumped-up charge, serving four months before being released under the 'Cat and Mouse' Act. Lansbury's incarceration was an early example of the *New Statesman* in an unfamiliar role as a campaigning paper fighting against injustice.

Sharp always insisted that his paper should be concerned with 'principles not persons', and yet he matched Orage in exposing the horrors of forcible feeding, even though he himself judged hunger strikes stupid and pointless. Shaw was the obvious candidate to lambast the government and the prison authorities, his acerbic wit matching the combined efforts of Nevinson and Brailsford in the *Nation*. In early 1914 GBS championed Sylvia Pankhurst, then on hunger strike in Holloway. The Shavian argument was logical if unorthodox, pragmatic and yet principled. The gist of his message was, why fuel East End resentment by making repeated arrests, and why defend prison as a deterrent when in this case it quite clearly was not?[28]

Although more respectful of the rule of law, Sharp was largely in agreement with Shaw when it came to treatment of suffragettes. Their tactics annoyed him because they gave waverers an excuse to stay on the fence and opponents an excuse for moral indignation. All the furore surrounding suffragette militancy obscured the fact that the Liberal Party when in office had reneged on its basic principles of free speech and political equality.[29] An end to direct action would call the government's bluff. Ministers would then have to act swiftly, resisting any temptation to humiliate the WSPU by insisting on a period of inactivity:

> It is not so much upon the possession as upon the gaining of the vote that this section of the movement have set their hearts. The vote is to them but a symbol of women's new-found respect. To ask them to abandon that self-respect in return for being granted the vote is to ask them to sacrifice the substance.[30]

The temptation is to emulate Shaw and portray Sharp as a gut Tory with a taste for Fabian blueprints. Yet his writing on women suggests that, in the early days at least, native chauvinism was tempered by an unexpected sensitivity and perception. Much of the *New Statesman*'s editorial treatment of the 'woman question' is incredibly patronising, and yet Sharp's brisk approach and abrupt manner (like his style – he often wrote staccato-fashion) belied an unexpected sensitivity and perception. Unlikely as it may seem, perhaps Rosamund Sharp influenced her husband's public attitude towards women. If she did not, Beatrice Webb almost certainly did.

Given Sharp's cavalier treatment of indignant readers, it is unlikely that he was swayed by those correspondents who saw throwing a brick or torching the outhouses as somehow symbolic of a wider struggle to assert the rights and status of a 'new woman' in a new age. From the second issue it is doubtful if any other topic featured so regularly in the editor's postbag. Given his experience with the *New Age*, Sharp should have expected this. By 1913 Orage was a veteran campaigner in support of equal rights and equality of opportunity. Six years earlier the *New Age* had enthusiastically supported the campaign to have the Fabian Basis incorporate support for full female suffrage. In 1908 Orage had welcomed the establishment of the Fabian Women's Group, even if in his eyes it failed to act as an acceptable channel of dissent. Under the patronage of Charlotte Wilson, Maud Reeves and Beatrice Webb, the Group was a pillar of Fabian orthodoxy. In February 1914 it produced the supplement on 'Women in Industry'. Partially supplanting the notorious, much delayed 'Control of Industry' report, the supplement called on the trade unions to encourage greater female involvement, and exposed inadequacies in working conditions.[31]

'The Awakening of Women' had included an article on motherhood by Lady Balfour, and this formed the theme for a third supplement, edited by the science correspondent 'Lens', who for once was allowed to write under his own name of Caleb Saleeby, MD. 'Lens' was an evangelising eugenicist and acolyte of Francis Galton, whose belief in training for motherhood accorded with the Webbs' own views on the family.[32] He was, however, a well-known eccentric, and Sharp insisted on a pseudonym in order to protect the paper. Nevertheless, Saleeby was very good at explaining basic scientific concepts to the layperson, as were

Ritchie Calder in the late 1930s, C.P. Snow in the 1950s, and Sarah Hutchings in the 1990s. The *New Statesman* periodically rediscovers science, although Kingsley Martin was always a close associate of key figures in the scientific establishment such as Julian Huxley, Solly Zuckerman and, of course, Snow. Sharp, soaked in Positivism and writing at a time of tremendous optimism regarding scientific discovery, had committed his new paper to 'the cultivation of the scientific spirit and its application to society's problems'. The supplements and Blue Book summaries had to be seen in this context: all social reform had an empirical basis, and all empiricists analysed society with the objectivity and emotional detachment of the natural scientist.[33] Assumptions such as this spurred Bertrand Russell to produce within the first month of publication a two-part defence of the scientist as a creative artist and not as an industrial operative. Intellectually outgunned he may have been, but Sharp was unlikely to alter his mechanistic view of the world. Fortunately, he was surrounded by writers willing to adopt more flexible and subtle standpoints – the world could not be seen in simple black and white terms, and there were no easy solutions rooted in the inductive process.

Thus, although Saleeby was a eugenicist, he poured scorn on those 'counterfeit' Darwinists who saw natural selection and even selective breeding as the keys to national survival. Like many Fabians of his generation he believed healthy, well-trained mothers could stem the racial degeneration of an urban under-class. Unlike many Fabians, Saleeby placed his faith in breast-feeding, good housekeeping, and little else.[34] A Dr Forsyth shared this blind faith in 'preventive eugenics', albeit at the same time acknowledging the need to monitor inner-city children's health. It took a woman, Ethel Bentham, to point out that training in parenthood was a worthy but completely one-dimensional form of social amelioration.[35]

Concrete proposals were contained in the supplement's main feature, written by Margaret Bondfield. Ten years before becoming Britain's first woman minister, she was busy on behalf of the Shop Assistants' Union and the Women's Labour League. An executive member of both the ILP and the National Federation of Women Workers, Bondfield was also a vocal member of the Fabian Society. As if all this was not enough, in early 1914 she was working with Margaret Llewelyn Davies of the Women's Co-operative Guild. It was the latter's introduction to the 1915 collection, *Maternity Letters From Women*, based on her collaboration with Bondfield, which helped kill off the cult of motherhood.[36] In the supplement Bondfield previewed Davies's proposal for a Public Health Authority to co-ordinate and implement all maternity and infant care at municipal level.[37] Beatrice enthusiastically supported an idea at least 30 years ahead of its time, placing it in the context of the wider campaign:

> Every occasion on which a fresh link is forged in the relationship between Maternity and the State renders the exclusion of women from citizenship a more obvious anomaly. The recognition by the State of motherhood as a social service leads direct to the conception of the mother as a citizen.[38]

In this essay, and in a five-part series on 'Personal Rights and the Women's Movement' just before the war, Beatrice ridiculed the notion of the vote as a universal panacea. Complaining that the WSPU was too narrowly-focused, she echoed Margaret Bondfield's call for free maternity and child care. Assimilating a vast array of research, Beatrice argued forcefully, if not always especially eloquently, for women's unrestricted entry to all occupations, and their equal remuneration under a national minimum wage. With the onset of war this series was a timely reminder of how far women still had to go to in the battle for equality. Wartime mobilisation necessitated a whole new agenda, but the basic demands remained the same. A common theme running throughout the *New Statesman*'s pre-war treatment of women's issues was the need for them to become more actively involved in all facets of the labour movement. The fight for female emancipation was portrayed as part of a much wider struggle, in which the forces of progressivism would finally break down (male-dominated) bastions of privilege and reaction. Women, young or old, 'new' or not so new, all had a role to play. It would be ridiculous to portray the *New Statesman* as rallying women round a purple and green banner or indeed a red flag, but thanks to Beatrice Webb the paper did far more than the odd token gesture. Its principal writers exposed the folly and iniquity of the government's position, Sharp revealing a sympathy and sensitivity at odds with everything else we know about him. The supplements for once justified their existence, each one postulating a series of demands which when taken together constituted a coherent and credible package of proposals. No historian of the women's movement before the First World War is going to start with the back numbers of the *New Statesman*, and yet in its own quiet way the paper went well beyond merely preaching to the converted. By putting forward proposals for equal opportunity, maternal support and so on, it forced a largely male readership to see that socialism involved much more than just taking over the gas works and regulating the price of a pint. This point needed hammering home, however sophisticated and well-educated the reader. The war brought special circumstances, but sadly the momentum was not maintained after 1918. With Beatrice Webb gone, the paper reverted to type – written by men, for men. To quote Sarah Benton, 'When women stopped making united political demands, the *New Statesman* stopped making them'.[39]

LOOKING AT LABOUR

When readers were not busy defending the suffragettes, they were usually putting pen to paper over the future of the Labour Party. Scarcely a week went by without leaders or letters engaging in increasingly arcane arguments as to whither Labour. Yet at the same time the paper's position *vis-à-vis* the parliamentary party was consistent and straightforward: it was largely made up of sinecured trade unionists who were inept, unimaginative and looking for leadership from the ILP.[40] The early issues set the tone for the next 15 months. Sharp and Webb criticised MacDonald for tacitly accepting the National Insurance scheme, questioning his reluctance to bow to pressure from within the party and distance Labour from the Liberals. It was no wonder activists in the constituencies and on the shop floor were becoming angry and disillusioned when Labour MPs were little more than lobby fodder for a well-intentioned but discredited government. While not directly critical of MacDonald for refusing to support a socialist candidate in the Leicester by-election, Sharp gave plenty of coverage to the subsequent debate within the ILP and beyond, not least within the Fabian Society.[41]

Two months later, in August 1913, controversy surrounding the

Chesterfield by-election prompted yet another call for Labour to assert its independence inside the House of Commons. This time MPs were told where they should be putting pressure on ministers to keep up the momentum of reform. Sharp's shopping-list was for all intents and purposes the *New Statesman*'s action programme for 1913–14: abolition of the Poor Law; extension of the Trade Boards Act; revision of the National Insurance Act; shorter working hours, especially on the railways; slum clearance; tightening up of the Factory Acts; better child welfare; public ownership of rail and coal; and finally, preparation for recurring unemployment.[42] With the exception of the last, gloriously vague request, this was a set of demands consistent with the Webbs' thinking ever since publication of the Minority Report. It offered the parliamentary party an opportunity to regain the reformist high ground. Needless to say, it was totally ignored. Sharp's message was falling on deaf ears; at this time perhaps only a handful of MPs read the magazine. This did not stop people like Mostyn Lloyd from establishing the great *New Statesman* tradition of writing interminable pieces on constitutional wranglings, invariably focused on conference and/or the power of the trade unions.[43] *Plus ça change...*

As secretary of the Bethnal Green ILP, Lloyd had some claim to speak on behalf of the rank-and-file. Beatrice Webb had scarcely had time to renew her membership. Yet there she was at the 1914 Labour Party conference having her worst prejudices about the leadership confirmed. To be fair, unlike Sharp she did at least make some effort to understand why MacDonald's reluctance 'to cut loose' from the Liberals was scarcely challenged.[44] As we shall see, Sharp's insistence that Labour make a clean break is particularly ironic in the light of a post-war love affair with Asquith and his circle.[45] Returning to the *New Statesman* in 1919 he found himself a lonely voice arguing for Labour and the Independent Liberals to recast the progressive alliance. Five years earlier the situation was reversed, with Ben Keeling in the role of Liberal plaintiff.

Keeling had moved so far into the centre ground since leaving Leeds (let alone Cambridge) that he was just about ready to jump ship and join the Liberals: 'the only line of practical political activity open'. Chapter 2 speculated on Keeling as a possible editor had he lived. Admittedly circumstances had changed dramatically and who knows what might have happened, but in June 1914 Keeling painted a bleak picture for his Great Queen Street colleagues:

> The Fabian or *Statesman* point of view does not stand for any large movement or section of English society as it is. It represents very able criticism and a very constructive policy which is too logical for English politics. Now I [Keeling] do care about seeing the concrete circumstances of the life of the English ameliorated – as Liberal legislation has in fact appreciably ameliorated them.[46]

A defence of pragmatism, but with more than a hint of truth (especially if applied to the whole of the United Kingdom, as Keeling no doubt intended). Sharp and the Webbs had a clear idea of what the *New Statesman* stood for in 1914. But *whom* did it stand for, other than a Fabian clique? If the magazine had collapsed with the onset of war it would scarcely warrant a footnote in any history of the British labour movement. Indeed the brevity of this chapter compared with its successors reflects the paper's relative insignificance. The story of the *New Statesman* before 1914 is important only because of what it was to become. Like so much else, the Great War changed everything, not least the fortunes of the Liberal Party. Keeling of course did not enjoy the benefit of hindsight. For him the important thing about the Liberals was that they were in office, and therefore able to get things done. Ministers might procrastinate and make mistakes, but at least they could exercise power. The crisis in Ireland notwithstanding, it was a compelling argument. It was also an argument that Sharp, let alone the Webbs, wholly refuted: now they were paid-up members they would stick with Labour, but unless the parliamentary party aggressively pursued its own political agenda then it had no right to expect a shift in voters' allegiance.[47]

The same message was reiterated time and again right up until the outbreak of war. Similarly, sniping at Ramsay MacDonald continued until his resignation as chairman in August 1914. Sharp, Lloyd, and the Webbs all shared a deep suspicion of MacDonald's ministerial ambitions. Overtures from Lloyd George were common knowledge, witness delegates' unambivalent message to their MPs at the ILP annual conference in April.[48] Beatrice attended that conference as the Fabians' fraternal delegate.

Buoyed up by Herbert Samuel's news that the *New Statesman* was already a 'considerable force' in the corridors of power, she found time to sample Labour's twin-pronged attack on Fleet Street: the *Daily Citizen* was 'smug, common and ultra-official', while the *Daily Herald* remained 'iconoclastic and inconsistent in the policies it takes up and drops with fiery levity'.[49] Lansbury's paper flirted with syndicalism. It depicted the Triple Alliance as step one on the road to workers' control of industry, anathema to Fabian orthodoxy. Again and again Sharp's editorials warned Labour leaders that the price of inertia was popular support for the preachers of class war.[50] Not only had the parliamentary party failed to entice wavering middle-class voters away from the Liberals, but it had given the advocates of direct action every encouragement.

This then was the *New Statesman*'s message to Labour on the eve of the First World War – the morale of the movement as a whole, and the case for parliamentary socialism, depended upon a more visible presence in the Commons, a clear demonstration that the party was not at the beck and call of the Liberals, and an equally clear demonstration that MPs had an agenda of their own and were not merely trade union lobbyists. In short, the parliamentary party had to be proactive not reactive. It also had to improve the intellectual calibre of its members, a message increasingly explicit as time passed. Implicit in such a message was that Labour MPs would benefit greatly from reading the *New Statesman* every week. One can fairly safely assume that they all read the *Labour Leader* and the local ILP papers, as well as the *Daily Herald* and *Daily Citizen*; but there is little evidence to suggest that anyone other than MacDonald, Henderson and Snowden found time to familiarise themselves with the latest in Fabian thinking. When it came to Labour at Westminster, the *New Statesman* was certainly never short of advice. The fact that it was invariably ignored was because it was invariably unread. Like the Labour Party itself, its time was yet to come.

Unlike Labour, the coming of war brought no division. Grey's address to the Commons on 3 August insisting that Germany's entry into Belgium constituted a *casus belli* may not have convinced a sizeable minority within the ILP, but it was good enough for everyone connected with the *New Statesman*. In a complete *volte-face* from the view expressed only seven days earlier – that Britain was under no obligation to aid republican France, let alone tsarist Russia – Squire, Keeling and Robert Ensor devoted several pages to explaining why the nation had 'never gone to war with cleaner hands'.[51] Given Keeling's recent change of heart towards the government, his hostility towards MacDonald and Hardie must have come as no great surprise to Squire, deputising that week for Sharp. However, Ensor's change of heart was wholly unexpected. Always deeply sceptical towards the continental commitment, within the ILP he must have seemed a natural opponent of the war. Yet on 3 August he experienced a conversion of Damascene proportions.[52]

Crisis or no crisis, Sharp had insisted on taking his annual fortnight's holiday. Seizing a rare opportunity to escape the blue pencil, Shaw provided the first issue of the war with two predictions, one right and the other horribly wrong: Russian autocracy was doomed whatever the outcome, and the fighting would be over in no time at all.[53]

5

Common sense about the war: The *New Statesman*, 1914–18

REPORTING THE GREAT WAR – AND DEALING WITH THE CENSOR

Today's *New Statesman & Society* rightly proclaims a long and honourable tradition of cocking a snook at state censorship, formal or informal, voluntary or imposed. That tradition has its roots in the years 1914–18, when even Sidney Webb was not averse to challenging the power of the state over fundamental issues of press freedom, *if* he felt his paper was in the right. Although acquiescent and co-operative for most of the First World War, at the height of the conflict both Webb and Sharp took issue with a government enjoying unprecedented statutory powers of control over information and opinion. This willingness to take on the principal agency of censorship – the Press Bureau – in defence of pacifist papers, with which the *New Statesman* was in almost total disagreement, clearly enhanced the magazine's standing and influence within a previously sceptical labour movement. As has been seen, chairman and editor never intended their paper to be a campaigning voice of protest; its principal purpose was to educate, instruct and above all persuade. However, when confronted by a powerful executive increasingly indifferent to civil liberties, a still fledgeling weekly enthusiastically took up the challenge.[1]

The *New Statesman* had of course never been envisaged as a self-appointed champion of free speech. The Webbs were not interested in a campaigning magazine that challenged the establishment of the day head-on; this was simply not their style.

Such a posture would, by definition, have been confrontational, and thus wholly at odds with a strategy of influencing rather than alienating the exercisers of power. Whitehall mandarins and their political masters in the final years of peace were no less hostile to charges of conspiracies of silence than their contemporary counterparts. On no known occasion did the *New Statesman's* directors and editorial staff address the very topical issues of censorship; and the growing statutory power of government, whatever its political persuasion, to control information and/or suppress dissent. It was, after all, one of their closest friends, Richard Burdon Haldane, who had steered the Official Secrets Act through Parliament in the summer of 1911.[2] The freedom of information, with the benefit of hindsight, was clearly a major area of concern in Edwardian England; and yet, perhaps not surprisingly, it was always near the bottom of the Fabians' ideological baggage. In a golden age of empiricism, guaranteed dissemination of information was not a tangible, easily resolvable problem, on a par with pension provision or improved public utilities; and as such it did not attract the remorseless attention of social investigators and reformers. To be fair, it took the onset of 'total war' to make news management and the systematic suppression of information and dissent a visible political issue, and to jolt all but the most radical and sensitive journalists out of their complacency. Thus, the fact that the *New Statesman* was not in the vanguard of uninhibited freedom of expression from its inception should not, it may be argued, constitute a cause for serious censure. In any case, one particularly prominent director could always be relied upon to deride the nation's moral guardians. The shadow of the Lord Chamberlain made Shaw as a playwright particularly sensitive to official complaint; yet his journalism during the first two years of the war confirmed an earlier impression of characteristic indifference to the views of authority, censorious or otherwise.

On the literary pages Jack Squire displayed a similar insouciance regarding freedom of speech. As editor of the *London Mercury*, he was later to become a notorious scourge of D.H. Lawrence. The winter of 1915 offered an early indication of what was to come, when the *New Statesman* failed to condemn the government's obscenity charge against *The Rainbow*. Clive Bell and Lytton

Strachey, neither of whom actually liked the novel, urged Squire to take a stand, but he declined: the book was not only poor, it was 'perverse', and its prosecution was clearly not a veiled response to Ursula Brangwen's denunciation of war. To be fair, Squire did eventually come around to the view that, for a writer 'of an earnestness ... almost awe-inspiring', censorship was absurd.[3] Yet Bell could scarcely have expected the paper to demonstrate support for Lawrence given his own experience a few months earlier. In September 1915 Bell's pamphlet, *Peace At Once*, had been destroyed by order of Salford magistrates. Its author wrote asking whether the *New Statesman* could justify an infringement of civil liberties that not even the Germans would tolerate. A terse reply, while acknowledging that such suppression was wrong, pointed to the folly of Bell's pacifism; similarly, to believe that England ranked second to any nation in respecting the freedom of its press was a delusion.[4] On this evidence the *New Statesman* could scarcely be considered a fearless wartime champion of free speech, and yet, as we shall see, within a few months of spurning Bell and Lawrence the paper was directly challenging the authorities over this very question.

In August 1914 Robert Ensor, in his capacity as chief leader-writer on foreign affairs, had assumed responsibility for military matters. Nobody sought to challenge him, and Sharp was probably relieved that someone was prepared to take on such a thankless task: war correspondent may not always prove the easiest of roles for self-proclaimed socialists, especially those formerly of a pacifist disposition. However, Ensor reported the progress of the war, or rather the lack of it, with all the fervour of the true convert. While many of his former ILP colleagues soon joined the anti-war Union of Democratic Control (UDC), Ensor now spoke for the pro-war faction within the Fabian Society. For the next four years, in the *New Statesman* and the *Daily Chronicle*, he urged the uncompromising defeat of the 'Prussian militarists' and the dismemberment of their empire. Although the editor invariably added his own equally ill-informed views on the fighting, after Sharp's call-up in 1917 Ensor was left to get on with it.

While Sidney Webb and Leonard Woolf drew up blueprints for national and international reconstruction, Ensor indulged in military punditry. Rarely able or willing to challenge orthodox strategic thinking, he became especially adept at manipulating news to ensure an almost permanent optimism. Sharp shared Ensor's enthusiasm for the Imperial General Staff (IGS) and for a 'Western' strategy based on attrition, if only because it was consistent with an editorial policy of opposing Lloyd George. Even after Gallipoli the Welshman remained at heart an 'Easterner', seeking final victory away from the Western Front.[5] Not surprisingly therefore, the leader-writers swallowed whole the generals' strategic orthodoxies. Criticism of attrition was *ipso facto* criticism of the High Command itself. Yet disaffection with Lloyd George, particularly after his accession to the premiership in December 1916, necessitated Sharp's and then Squire's approval of Haig and Robertson.[6] The *New Statesman* found itself in the novel position of supporting soldiers whom before the war it would have berated as unreconstructed Unionists abusing every long-established tenet of civil–military relations. Instead, they were portrayed as convenient scapegoats for politicians, and one very important politician in particular.[7]

Until May 1915 the *New Statesman* shared the same problem as the dailies, upon whose sources it so often relied: irregular and unreliable information in the absence of recognised war correspondents. The government had tacitly encouraged a pre-war assumption that the Army would welcome reporters, but Kitchener imposed a blanket-ban upon his appointment as Secretary for War. In terms of Asquith's administration maintaining goodwill with the national press this was a public-relations disaster. However, as controls were relaxed following the establishment of the first Coalition, so contributors began visiting the front. Touring the trenches in July 1915, Arnold Bennett was unhappy with what he saw, but a reluctance to risk controversy ensured a bland report in the *Illustrated London News*. At the same time, however, he passed his true feelings on to Sharp for unattributed use.[8] Sharp's own tours seldom involved the front-line.[9] All they generated were jingoistic accounts of high morale and dogged determinism among the troops; no doubt to the disgust of subscribers such as Graves and Sassoon. A favourite of the IGS and an 'authority' in Fleet Street was that singularly unqualified pundit on military matters, Hilaire Belloc. Quoted almost in awe by the *New Statesman*, Belloc would pass on his information and opinions to Squire, a fellow contributor to the wartime propaganda magazine *Land and Water*. Needless to say, the soldiers in the line held him in total contempt, and the *Wipers Times* lampooned him as the ludicrously optimistic 'Belary Helloc'.

The irony is that Sidney Webb had predicted at the outset an enormous credibility-gap between the general public's preconceived, romantic notions of warfare, and the harsh reality of history's 'least actually observed, least contemporaneously reported, and most imaginatively lied, war'. Thus, the *New Statesman* would provide a weekly summary of the best-authenticated news, 'The Progress of the War'.[10] The demise of Webb's initiative after only a month symbolised the ease with which the magazine unconsciously adapted to the style and content of those newspapers whose coverage of the war it so frequently criticised. By fulfilling its propagandist function just as smoothly as so many other non-pacifist publications, the *New Statesman* failed to justify its claim to independence and the high moral ground. Sharp and Ensor rarely displayed any real understanding of what conditions were like in the trenches, and in this of course they were by no means unique – neither did the overwhelming majority of the civilian population. Nevertheless, there still remained this prevailing attitude that somehow *New Statesman* reportage was different from – and, by implication, superior to – the majority of newspaper coverage and commentary. Such an attitude rendered Ensor's propaganda even more insidious and unattractive. It is scarcely surprising that so few people at home were interested in the depressing and distressing news that soldiers brought home on leave. Ignorance was bliss, and civilian sources of information – professional writers such as Ensor, Sharp, and Squire – conveniently lacked the imagination, the language and, above all, the motivation to convince the public of the Western Front's real horrors. By the final year of the war the combination of Squire's sentimental jingoism and Ensor's clinical audit of the slaughter was alienating a growing number of progressives from their allegedly independent weekly. Why was it that bad news always had to be counter-balanced by good news, with casualty figures glossed over? Why, in every advance or retreat, victory or defeat, must optimism always prevail?[11]

To be fair, the paper was quick to appreciate the importance of technological innovation in shifting the tactical advantage away from defence in favour of offence. Regrettably, Ensor's speedy perception of what modern warfare entailed made little difference when it came to defending the generals. For example, he noted the potential of the tank even before Cambrai, but only as an auxiliary to – never a substitute for – the familiar combination of barrage and 'over the top'. The novelty of Plumer's 1917 successful attacks on Messines and the Ypres–Menin road was rightly acknowledged, but like Haig – and unlike Hindenburg – Ensor failed to see the new tactics as a model for future campaigns. As early as May 1915 he had come out strongly in favour of attrition, and for the next two years he never failed to remind readers that when it came to the crunch the total male population of the *Entente* would always outnumber that of the Central Powers.[12] The loss of Russia made little difference to Ensor: Pershing's doughboys would bring about the final triumph of demographic warfare. Like so many other papers, the *New Statesman*'s coverage of the Somme had been a triumph of passivity and gullibility. When Bapaume fell on 17 March 1917, an exuberant Ensor omitted to mention the village's importance as a first-day objective nine months earlier.[13]

Although never as bad as Ensor or Squire, Sharp was not above embracing this illusory, unreal world of cheerful Tommies impatient for another crack at their quivering foe. Following a final visit to France before joining the Army himself, Sharp was quite happy to assure readers that the Germans' confidence had been critically undermined by daily trench raids where, 'as individual fighters they cannot meet our rank and file on equal terms'. Leaderless and lacking initiative, the hapless Hun was surrendering in the face of superior British morale.[14] During Passchaendale (third battle of Ypres), the rain was dismissed as merely 'bad luck', at a time when hundreds were drowning in the mud: minimal advance was in actual fact a 'conscious plan' to prevent troops advancing beyond artillery range. When the offensive came to a halt, so too did Ensor's coverage. Events at home and in Russia meant that news of the Western Front disappeared from the front pages of the magazine in late 1917. Only GHQ's formal confirmation of deadlock forced Ensor to acknowledge that the attack's success was 'altogether harder, costlier and riskier than its three predecessors', but did guarantee a superior 'winter position locally'. With the likes of Robert Ensor controlling coverage of events in France and Flanders, one may wonder how the *New Statesman* ever fell foul of Britain's wartime agency of censorship, the Press Bureau.

The final years of peace had seen a system of voluntary censorship and self-regulation work remarkably smoothly; for example, the formation of the BEF only became public knowledge in August 1914, two years after the event.[15] The Boer War and the subsequent creation of the Committee of Imperial Defence (CID) had generated an extensive and, at times, cantankerous debate between newspaper proprietors and the guardians of the nation's secrets.[16] The heat was only taken out of these negotiations when the Official Secrets Act was rushed through Parliament at the height of the Agadir crisis. Predictably, attention focused on the clauses concerned with espionage in Section 1. The indiscriminatory nature of Section 2 – with all that it implied regarding coverage of defence matters – was scarcely acknowledged. Such a vague and draconian measure necessitated urgent agreement between the military and the press on ground rules regarding what could or could not be published; in other words, a buffer needed to be established. In October 1912 a new liaison body, the Joint Standing Committee of Admiralty, War Office and press representatives, was empowered to issue 'D' (for Defence) Notices formally advising non-publication of material specifically related to national security. Then, as now, editors would receive directives advising them on the treatment of a news item, and the parameters within which coverage of a particular story should operate.

The success of the voluntary system exacerbated Fleet Street's annoyance over the arbitrary imposition of direct controls following the outbreak of hostilities. Regulations 18, 27, and 51 of the 1914 Defence of the Realm Act (DORA), together with the 1911 Act and Lord Kitchener's ban on war correspondents, gave the government all the power it needed to underpin editorial self-censorship. Nevertheless, on 7 August 1914 the Press Bureau was set up, responsible both for the dissemination of official information and the censorship of all material voluntarily submitted by the press (cables were compulsory). Technically speaking, on a day-to-day basis non-statutory censorship still prevailed, and the majority of editors and proprietors were remarkably acquiescent when advised via 'D' Notices as to tone and content. Such acquiescence was often deemed irritating and inconvenient, but nevertheless in the national interest. Whatever restraint Fleet Street exercised with regard to overtly military matters, it more than made up for in its coverage of domestic issues, especially the politicians' record in conducting the war. The pacifist press suffered the most hardship, but in an ostensibly liberal democracy the government was unwilling to use DORA to impose permanent and comprehensive suppression. Such an act would have offered invaluable ammunition for enemy propaganda, particularly when targeted at the United States.

Resentment towards the Press Bureau was based on the feeling that the pre-war system of self-censorship was both more efficient and more effective. Newspapers now submitted relevant copy, excepting editorials, to censors drawn from the Services. The latter – rarely former journalists – were responsible for the control of front-line and naval news, and the suppression of any information potentially useful to the enemy. However, the Press Bureau rapidly acquired a reputation for incompetence under its first Director, F.E. Smith (the future Lord Birkenhead). As a prominent barrister and uncompromising Unionist before the war, Smith had acquired many enemies at the height of the Home Rule crisis – particularly in the Liberal press. Fleet Street pressed Asquith's government for a replacement familiar with the mechanics of producing newspapers to a deadline. But, neither the sympathy expressed by Smith's equally inappropriate successor, the Solicitor-General, Sir Stanley Buckmaster, nor the wholesale reforms pioneered from June 1915 by Sir Edward Cook offered adequate recompense for the inevitable delay in processing all-too-scarce news stories. The War Office and the Admiralty failed to encourage the same co-operation with Fleet Street which the earlier Joint Standing Committee had secured from 1912 until the BEF completed its disembarkation on 18 August 1914.

Cook, a former editor and an unrepentant Liberal Imperialist, was the first Director of the Press Bureau who genuinely appreciated the problems involved in going to press on time. Until his appointment, delays were a regular occurrence, with censors' decisions often arbitrary and confused. In November 1914 Lord Northcliffe had complained to Asquith that 'our people have nothing but the casualty lists and the mutilated scraps with which it is quite impossible to arouse interest or follow the war intelligently'.[17] In response, Downing Street eased cablegram censorship and sent Buckmaster to placate the Commons. Soothing words, and a promise to do better, clearly failed. Northcliffe's *Daily Mail* still insisted that the failings of the Press Bureau reflected the performance of the Liberal government as a whole.[18]

With the exception of Lloyd George, who throughout his career assiduously cultivated editors and owners, Asquith and his colleagues were notoriously indifferent towards the press. They failed to utilise the Press Bureau, or indeed any other Whitehall machinery, as a means whereby ministerial briefings could facilitate informed and intelligent comment. Both the Prime Minister and the Foreign Secretary would confide only in J.A. Spender, whose *Westminster Gazette*, for all its eminence, rarely sold a copy beyond the confines of St James's and Pall Mall. Before the war *The Times* correspondent at the Foreign Office received a daily briefing, and C.P. Scott would exercise the *Manchester Guardian*'s historic right to quiz Liberal grandees, but that was about as far as the party's news management stretched. Antagonising Fleet Street by tolerating incompetence at the Press Bureau further provoked Unionist – and some Liberal – newspapers. The press destroyed Haldane in the spring of 1915, and within 18 months had hounded Asquith and Grey from office. There are many reasons why Asquith's wartime administrations collapsed, not least the Prime Minister's ineffectual handling of the war, but the press's relentless undermining of his authority clearly had a corrosive effect.

Naturally the weeklies were far less dependent upon the Press Bureau than was the daily press, although early in the war St Loe Strachey was convinced that a Liberal bias caused the *Spectator* to be especially victimised.[19] Heavily dependent on secondary news sources, the *New Statesman* submitted very little for censorship. But this did not stop Ensor and Sharp bitterly criticising the Press Bureau from the outset. After the first month's fighting they joined other journalists in petitioning the War Office to remove F.E. Smith. The magazine's position was simple and consistent: all creditable information not of benefit to the enemy should be available for publication; the Press Bureau's work should be limited to preventing the leak of vital military information; maximum discussion should be encouraged; and there should be absolute frankness in the interests of public morale.[20] Until the summer of 1916 Sharp was a great believer in the 'stimulating effect' that reverses would have on the British temperament: announcement of a defeat could act as a great morale-booster. Even after the failure of the Somme offensive, Ensor continued to suffer from similar delusions. Even so, the paper adhered to 'D' Notice requests for silence on the 1915 Zeppelin raids and the surrender of Kut-el-Amara to the Turks in April 1916. In September 1915, 35 socialist and pacifist papers were removed from the 'D' Notice list, either for ignoring the Press Bureau's directives or for not submitting contentious material. Pro-war and respectable, the *New Statesman* retained establishment approval.[21]

Sharp explained to Wells in January 1917 that he respected the Press Bureau's wishes, 'unless I am pretty sure of my ground'. Thus, Cook's only contact had been a letter to 'warn' Sharp about publishing the Glasgow ILP's account of the stormy reception they gave Lloyd George. Sharp claimed that 'being quite sure of my ground I replied suitably and published a fuller account the following week'. Military matters were 'a much more tricky question'. He would risk attacking the generals, but would never take issue with the censor over criticising soldiers in the field, 'because I don't think any such general right can reasonably be held in wartime'.[22] We must return to Sharp's and Sidney Webb's unexpected assertion of anti-war ILP members' right to publish. This marked a rare occasion when discretion was abandoned. It was different when dealing with Wells, a man who of course had never hidden his disdain for the paper. He offered the *New Statesman* copy which had already been heavily censored by the Press Bureau when submitted by the *Daily News*. Always wary of Lloyd George, Sharp rejected the offer, despite boasting that the *New Statesman* was, 'the only paper in England that has made any serious attempt to criticise the military people'.[23] This was of course absolute nonsense. The *Nation* was a far more trenchant critic of the High Command, to the extent that in April 1917 overseas sales were banned: the government claimed enemy propaganda had quoted Massingham lambasting Haig. This was less than three months after Sharp's warning to Wells that he would never risk the same penalty, 'just for the fun of having a row with the authorities'.[24]

By the time news of the *Nation*'s ban had caused uproar in the Commons, Sharp was in the Army. At Massingham's request, Bennett and Squire campaigned for the order to be revoked: such a course of action would see Lloyd George 'vindicating his Liberalism and his common-sense'.[25] In October 1917 the restriction was lifted, by which time the War Office was busy filtering and sanitising news from the killing fields of Passchaendale.[26] In his weekly column Bennett castigated the Press Bureau as 'the most unsatisfactory, exasperating and inefficient war-organisation on the island'. The general public needed the positive, direct instruction and guidance which an official review of operations might periodically provide, but which the Services were clearly loath to initiate.[27] Bennett and Squire's patriotism was obvious to all. Above suspicion, and indifferent to prime ministerial threats, they felt little need to follow the same pragmatic path as Sharp. Nevertheless, in the following year the *New Statesman* did come under Foreign Office scrutiny when an article on deserters was taken up by German propaganda. As this was a solitary example, and any action against the magazine would surely have focused on Bennett – director and author, but also by now a prominent Ministry of Information propagandist – the incident was quickly forgotten. Prosecuting a small-circulation weekly was one thing; silencing the nation's most popular novelist was quite another.[28]

Administratively, it proved extremely difficult for the authorities to impose a rigorous censorship policy across a sophisticated pluralist society for over four years of war. Politically, it proved a major undertaking, albeit not impossible, to over-rule a combination of sectional interests within the British press. The government correctly perceived that among newspapers of all political persuasions there existed a certain bond. The *New Statesman* was no exception; for example, in attacking the April 1916 restriction on references to Cabinet proceedings. In

November 1917 it was to join the rest of the Liberal and Labour press in endorsing backbench opposition to the compulsory censorship of pamphlets. Both incidents offer an interesting insight into the contrasting views of Clifford Sharp and Jack Squire on free speech in time of war. In 1916 the former genuinely feared that the new DORA regulations would affect only the weakest papers, those with 'no special Cabinet friends'. By November 1917 the acting editor's only concern was a deepening conviction among the pacifist 'dissentient majority' that the right to free speech was their's alone.[29] What Squire meant by such a remark is open to interpretation, but it does not place him in a very flattering light. In contrast, Sharp, the unashamed pragmatist, could stake a modest claim to defending the freedom of the press. In this respect, his finest hour was undoubtedly in the early months of 1916 when he found himself an unlikely hero of the ILP.

As an editor, Sharp demanded of his writers no more than sound intellect, technical expertise and journalistic competence. It was these criteria (note the absence of individual talent), as opposed to straightforward loyalties of party and class, that had at first led to the *New Statesman* naively ignoring the Labour press, and most obviously the *Daily Herald*. Demoralised by the split in the Labour movement at the outbreak of war, and starved of trade union backing, the *Herald* staggered on as a weekly newspaper. More resilient, retaining a circulation of between 1,500 and 2,000 readers, was the *Labour Leader*. Edited by Fenner Brockway, the ILP's main organ was a vociferous opponent of the war. Sharp regularly challenged Brockway's views, but after January 1917 was prevented by DORA from mentioning any pacifist newspaper. This ban followed a German wireless broadcast quoting a *Labour Leader* call for civil disobedience in the face of conscription. Brockway felt honour-bound to resign as editor and, no longer enjoying exemption, was ultimately imprisoned as a conscientious objector.

Before 1917 Brockway's paper had already been prosecuted twice. Sharp's protests were characteristically ambivalent: why prosecute, given the government's forbearance of several equally damaging Unionist newspapers, and why enhance the prestige of the ILP's anti-war faction among trade unionists?[30] So begrudging a protest was hardly heroic, with scant risk of martyrdom.

However, in January 1916 Sharp surprisingly sprang to the defence of the Glasgow ILP's broadsheet, *Forward*. The voice of 'Red Clydeside' had been silenced for mocking Lloyd George's unsuccessful efforts to appease striking shipbuilders. Sidney Webb paid tribute to the ILP newspapers and the *Herald* for publishing the truth about the Minister of Munitions' visit, as opposed to the 'official' version carried by the established press.[31] The following week Sharp revealed that the *New Statesman* had been contacted by the Press Bureau, no doubt on Lloyd George's orders. At issue, apparently, was not Webb's leader, but correspondence from 'A Glasgow Labour man', a pseudonym for P.J. Dollan. Dollan, a conscientious objector and later a well-known figure in the ILP, had given his version of Clydeside's welcome for the Minister.[32] So too had another comrade's letter, in a subsequent defiance of the Bureau's warning. With the skill of a trained lawyer, Sharp dissected and demolished Lloyd George's parliamentary defence of *Forward*'s suppression. However much it differed from the *New Statesman* in its thinking, the paper had always scrupulously adhered to the principle of free speech and had provided its readers with a balanced and truthful account of the visit. This was certainly more than could be said for the government.[33]

Shared antipathy towards Lloyd George demanded that this unholy alliance with the Glasgow ILP be maintained. Tom Johnston, *Forward*'s editor and a future Labour minister, wrote in appreciation of the *New Statesman*'s stand, thus prompting yet another thundering leader: had Parliament ever been subjected to such 'a tissue of misrepresentation and calculated misquotation'?[34] By the following week the order suppressing the Glasgow ILP's Civic Press had been lifted following a visit by Johnston to the Ministry of Munitions. Sharp naively looked to Asquith for reassurance that any future action along similar lines would receive Cabinet, not simply departmental, clearance.[35] This was a distinctly peacetime understanding of wartime decision-making, at precisely the moment when the War Cabinet was consolidating its control of both military and domestic affairs. A more obvious irony was Lloyd George's subsequent protection of the *Herald* and the ILP newspapers once the retention of Labour support for the second Coalition became of paramount importance.[36]

The *New Statesman* was never again as uncompromising in its support of the pacifist and socialist press. Fabian readers must have been puzzled to find their paper insisting on more than one occasion that, in agreeing to disagree over the war, the ILP had abdicated the intellectual leadership of the Labour movement. Even in 1918, with Henderson, MacDonald *and* Webb eager to paper over the cracks within the embryonic Labour Party, the latter refrained from demonstrating overt sympathy when the *Labour Leader* and its sister papers were harassed. As we shall see, after Sharp's departure Webb was happy to hand over supervision of editorial matters to Bennett and Squire, with both men sharing a good working relationship and similar views on the conduct of the war. As a result the *New Statesman*'s views regarding the well-being or otherwise of the pacifist press noticeably hardened.

Nevertheless, when faced with a clear threat to the freedom of the press, the paper had been prepared to stand up and be counted. Whatever Sharp's motives, the editor, secure in the support of his chairman, had stood his ground. Such a gesture, so clearly identifiable with a man who in the last year of the war was playing a crucial role in remoulding the Labour Party, gives us a partial insight into why the ILP and indeed the whole of the labour movement were able to reunite when faced with a general election in the winter of 1918. Socialists supporting or opposing the war held fundamentally different views right until the bitter end; but where they clearly did agree was on the need to resist a residual erosion of basic civil liberties, and here censorship was a key issue. The *New Statesman*'s record of resistance was, to say the least, patchy, but at the same time it was by no means dishonourable.

BOARDROOM CHANGES: SHAW'S DEPARTURE AND BENNETT'S ARRIVAL

When peace finally did come Sharp no doubt argued that, as far his paper was concerned, the position adopted in August 1914 had been scrupulously maintained: the government was entitled to assume a nation united in a common cause, but equally, the press was entitled to express positive criticism when confronted with ministerial complacency. From the outset the Unionist press, and Northcliffe's papers in particular, had been berated for not playing by the rules of the game – as so stoutly maintained in Great Queen

Street. Why, came the plaintive cry, were *The Times* and the *Daily Mail* allowed to get away with smear campaigns against Haldane, and even the Premier himself? In retrospect, Sharp's fascination with Asquith, so potentially fatal in the post-war years, dates from the Liberals' final months alone in office. The Prime Minister was now seen as a healing, unifying figure, he and his Cabinet uniquely qualified to lead a once divided nation into the cauldron of war. By the spring of 1915 Sharp's previously sound judgement and healthy scepticism had abandoned him. He dismissed reports of intrigue against the 'most popular Ministry for a century' less than a month before the government fell, unconvincingly portraying Asquith as an ideal wartime premier, and gleefully mocking Lloyd George's pretensions to such a role. An unconvincingly Whiggish editor, moulded in late nineteenth-century certainties of party politics, derided coalition government as a phenomenon alien to British political culture and a dangerous infringement of parliamentary sovereignty. Sharp's judgement, even if flawed, was certainly pervasive: throughout the following seven years of coalition government the *New Statesman* rarely veered from this initial suspicion.[37]

Shaw found such support for Asquith irritating, but an equally stout defence of Sir Edward Grey – the walking embodiment of 'smug and selfish squirearchy' – was well-nigh intolerable. Accepting that Britain had to fight, but adamant that all nations were culpable, Shaw explained to Sidney and Beatrice that the *Daily News* was better value than their own 'mere waste paper basket'. A prescient GBS demanded to know why Sharp refused to 'strike at the vital parts', and instead risked ultimate retribution by apotheosising Grey as an 'angel of peace'. Shaw poured scorn on the notion of England's peace-loving aristocracy reluctantly taking up arms against the belligerent Hun. The war would be fought in vain if it failed to discredit 'Junkerism', a phenomenon embracing the Wilhelmstrasse *and* Carlton Gardens. Shaw promised an early manifesto setting out his ideas on why the old order had finally broken down.[38]

The *New Statesman*'s staunch support for Grey, who according to Beatrice was 'terribly concerned that he had not been able to prevent the war . . . suffering, I think, from an over-sensitive consciousness of personal responsibility', did little to improve relations with the anti-war faction of the ILP and their nominal leader. Unwilling to encourage Fleet Street's savage assault on MacDonald, Sharp had registered only mild protest at the executive's manifesto denouncing British intervention. But, when MacDonald questioned Grey's integrity in both the *Labour Leader* and the *Nation*, and then implied in the Commons acquiescence should France have violated Belgian neutrality, it was too much for Jack Squire. A vituperative denunciation of MacDonald, followed by repeated attacks on the ILP executive in succeeding months, fuelled a mutual suspicion which for the next 16 years over-shadowed relations with Labour's parliamentary party, and on at least one occasion provoked a major clash between Sharp and his directors. Although not differing from his staff's view that the ILP had 'separated itself from enlightened and patriotic working-class opinion', Webb was more sensitive to the breadth of opinion within the party. Unequivocal pacifists such as George Lansbury, and idealistic international socialists like Brockway and the Fabian Clifford Allen, defended MacDonald and guaranteed him column inches in the *Labour Leader*, but nevertheless remained deeply suspicious of his capacity for compromise. In contrast, Sidney Webb noted approvingly MacDonald's tacit approval of recruitment as an acceptable alternative to conscription, his analysis of the war as a consequence of inept diplomacy rather than the inevitable collapse of advanced capitalism, and his efforts to cultivate a tiny forum of opinion receptive to any eventual opportunity for negotiated peace. If their views on the war appeared at first sight incompatible, Webb and MacDonald did in fact have much in common, notwithstanding Beatrice's dismissal of the UDC as a bunch of 'sentimental whigs'.[39]

Meanwhile, in Torquay Shaw penned his manifesto, and in London Sharp pondered possible litigation. A protracted correspondence focused on the editor's right to avoid the possibility of Grey taking libel action by proof-reading a final draft. An impatient Shaw, confident of the triumphant logic of his argument, was eager to satisfy an impatient popular press. Ignoring assurances that he would bathe in 'eternal glory' by association with such a 'superb performance', the lawyer-turned-editor insisted on a byline. Dismissing charges of being pro-German, Shaw replied that his essay on Belgium in the *Daily Telegraph*'s fund-raising *King Albert's Book* would reassure sensitive *New Statesman* readers that here was no 'Back Down and Stop the War Man'. The 35,000-word 'Common Sense About the War', finally appeared as a supplement to the issue of 14 November. Its author was still basking in the limelight of the previous week's 'Open Letter to the President of the United States of America' in the *New York Times*, in which Shaw had called on Wilson to intervene over the collective destruction of Belgium. At home the *Nation* had published the article, prefaced by Massingham's own views, after Sharp had refused to publish it as a letter.[40]

'Common Sense About the War' provoked a flood of letters, almost all of them long and angry. Shaw twice provided lengthy, detailed and courteous replies: in essence, he ridiculed any suggestion that his views gave the Germans encouragement, insisting instead that they enhanced rather than hindered Allied efforts to generate goodwill in America. A popular misconception that the *New Statesman* disclaimed its own supplement derived partly from Squire's alleged comment that the chief shareholder should be tarred and feathered, and partly from the latter's eventual resignation. Agreed, an accompanying leader refuted both Shaw's indictment of Grey, and his suggestion that the war was partly Britain's fault, but that same leader found much to endorse, praising Shaw's 'constructive criticism' as a welcome challenge to the prevailing 'conspiracy of silence'.[41]

The essay can be read as a prelude to the *New Statesman*'s discussion of post-war reconstruction, and to a hardening attitude over more immediate problems on the home front. 'Junkers' was an over-emotive term, but Shaw's insistence on landed wealth's reactionary bias across Europe towards militarism, discipline and autocracy foreshadowed Sidney Webb's call for a 'conscription of wealth', Ensor's more muted criticism of regular officers monopolising staff posts, and Sharp's concern over growing executive abuse. Webb shared Shaw's concern over the exploitation of diluted labour in the munitions factories, and his continued faith in the 'band of international socialism'. From the first week of the war he was arguing that regular employment in a war economy could prove highly advantageous to British workers and their dependants. Exemplifying Arthur Marwick's argument half a century later that participation on the home front benefited underprivileged sections of society, Webb drew up a list of proposed ameliorative measures, all funded by a genuinely progressive fiscal policy and universal national insurance. Many of his ideas preceded the terms of the 'Treasury Agreement' signed by Lloyd George and the trade unions in March 1915, although repeated calls for sanctions such as the punitive treatment of corporate war profiteers invariably fell on deaf ears.[42]

Clearly the government needed the support of the whole labour movement, if only to render credible at shop-floor level TUC endorsement of the 'Treasury Agreement'. The leading Fabians and their magazine naturally encouraged such support, and yet Sidney Webb never fell victim to that 'patriotic blackmail' which Ralph Miliband saw as reinforcing 'the trade union leaders' propensity to pitch their claims very low'. Indeed, it was precisely the sort of moral blackmail which Lloyd George was so expert at exercising that Webb's journalistic endeavours sought to expose.[43] Neither was Sidney prepared to compromise over conscription (tolerable only after a genuinely universal 'conscription of wealth'), even if by 1918 Squire and Bennett clearly were. Increasingly, the *New Statesman* – with or without GBS – was to form a microcosm of what A.J.P. Taylor once described as wartime British politics'

> great underlying conflict ... between freedom and organisation.... could the war be conducted by 'Liberal' methods – that is, by voluntary recruiting and laissez-faire economics? Or must there be compulsory military service, control of profits, and direction of labour and industry?[44]

Few contemporary historians would wish to portray the debate over organisation of the home front in such stark terms, with even Asquith's harshest critics accepting that the message of 'business as usual' reflected unfairly and unfortunately on the efforts of his two administrations to come to terms with the strategic and logistical consequences of waging war on the grand scale. Yet clearly a debate did take place at the time, and predictably the pro-war Fabians accepted that, 'for the war to be waged with all practical vigour and efficiency', a major extension of state intervention and control was unavoidable; perhaps even welcome if ultimately it benefited labour at the expense of capital. However, should such intervention extend to individual freedom, culminating in that ultimate infringement upon civil liberty, conscription, then equally predictably the Fabians' house magazine railed against an abuse of executive power that was fundamentally at odds with the moral argument for Britain entering the conflict in the first place: the volunteer was 'the universally accepted symbol of the things we are fighting for'. Progressivism (for which, in the case of Sharp, increasingly read plain Liberalism) had fought the good fight in peacetime, and it would win the war – on its own terms. Sharp repeatedly challenged the Unionist press to refute his claim that conscription would entail sacrificing the moral basis on which Britain fought, would generate disunity and apathy, and in consequence would transform a common struggle into a 'war of the governing classes'. For Shaw of course such sentiments were, on a bad day mendacious nonsense, and on a good day evidence of an amusing if dangerous naivety.[45]

From the outset Ensor and his editor had confidently anticipated an eventual realignment of power blocs, with Russia still seen as a future threat; these men could not easily abandon lifelong prejudices. In this respect Shaw's views were consistent with the rest of the paper: 'Common Sense' had similarly concluded that today's Allies were tomorrow's enemies, and vice versa. Thus GBS, Sharp, and later Leonard Woolf, were all in agreement that after the war the now discredited dependence on a European balance of power must be replaced by a credible 'League of Peace' which would be prepared to use force if necessary. With hindsight we can see that the magazine's perspective on international relations throughout the war years was clearly influenced by Shaw's case against imposing reparations on central Europe, and his call for a sensitive redrawing of national boundaries rooted in consensus and constitutional reform. To sum up, the staff of the *New Statesman*'s attitude towards 'Common Sense' was actually very simple: like Arnold Bennett at the time, they agreed with much of the content; what they found themselves unable to stomach was the outrageous and quixotic way in which a fundamentally sound message was being put across.[46]

Before Christmas GBS had again written of the government's partial responsibility for the war, correctly anticipating that victory would bring, not stability, but an even more dangerous world.[47] Sharing Shaw's fears, Beatrice Webb paid tribute to her old friend's clarity of thought and intellectual honesty in keeping

> the crucial purpose of Socialism before us as distinguished from
> the machinery for getting it. And his protest against the
> righteousness of British public opinion about the causes of the war
> is, in my humble opinion, justified.[48]

At the same time stories had reached Shaw of the abuse being
poured on his head by Sharp and Squire. He avoided Great Queen
Street, and tolerated the Young Turks' hostility with characteristic
good humour:

> I [GBS] am a shareholder in the company, and Mr. Clifford Sharp
> is a young and rising man and I am an elderly and declining one. I
> am much more scrupulous in respecting his independence than I
> am with editor-contemporaries of mine who are equally accessible
> to me.[49]

In the spring of 1915 Sharp was still publishing some of Shaw's
less contentious views on the conduct of the war, and had even
been persuaded to accept another attack on Sir Edward Grey. But
by the summer, a furious exchange with Wells notwithstanding,
Shaw's contributions had shrunk to the occasional letter previously
rejected as an article.

On 3 July Beatrice Webb received a draft of the sequel to
'Common Sense' and a request for her impressions. Finding the
essay 'ill-tempered and illogical', she passed it on to Sharp, who
wholeheartedly concurred. Much of this second manifesto was
taken up with defending and updating earlier contentious
statements, but Wells and Rebecca West were not alone in
condemning its excessive praise of the Anglo-German Social
Darwinist, Houston Stewart Chamberlain. The essay was never
published in its entirety, but amended extracts did appear, even in
the *New Statesman*.[50]

GBS still attended the monthly board meetings, but Sharp's
hostility was bound to provoke an eventual withdrawal of financial
support. The paper would then cease publication, unless a new
director purchased Shaw's shares. Closure appeared a very real
option given that the chairman was, if forced to make a choice,
happy to back his editor. Of course Shaw's generosity of spirit was
such that Webb knew their friendship would weather such an
unfortunate conflict of loyalties. But Webb also knew that a

potential white knight had already joined the board: at the conclusion of his first visit to Great Queen Street, on 2 March 1915, Arnold Bennett had been invited by Sidney to become a director.[51] Nevertheless, as Hyams observed, Shaw's refusal to use his financial firepower against Sharp demonstrated an unusual degree of tolerance and good humour. He explained his reluctance to sell by claiming that the shares' value might one day be such that he would be relieved to have retained them. The reality was that Shaw appreciated only too well the importance to the paper of Bennett injecting extra capital.[52]

Within a month of his appointment an enthusiastic Bennett was offering Squire extracts from his journals; a magnanimous gesture never in fact taken up, perhaps because of American copyright problems.[53] The two men also began a regular correspondence. By April 1917 this had become a weekly commentary on Squire's endeavours as temporary editor. Sharp still met his chairman every Tuesday for a frank and 'invaluable' exchange of ideas, but now he began to dine regularly with the new director.[54] Towards the end of 1916 Bennett offered to pay for a monthly lunch of editors, contributors and directors which would complement formal board meetings and the Webbs' weekly lunches. His journals suggest that the offer was never taken up. They do, however, record an increasingly frequent attendance at the Tuesday discussion on editorial policy.[55]

Although Bennett was to be a key influence on the magazine in the final years of the war, there is little evidence of direct intervention during the period of the first Coalition. This was, with hindsight, regrettable, as Sharp's disappointment with Asquith for not riding out successive controversies over ammunition, admirals and alcohol swiftly degenerated into righteous indignation over the role of Unionist politicians and their Fleet Street allies in ending nearly a decade of Liberal rule. That indignation equally swiftly became fury, and a convenient target of abuse was the man who as long ago as the summer of 1910 had argued the case for a suspension of party conflict in the interest of national unity – David Lloyd George. Throughout the second half of 1915 the *New Statesman* attacked Lloyd George at every opportunity. Anonymity meant that Webb's measured reflections upon the delay in fulfilling the government side of the 'Treasury

Agreement', and the prospect of social unrest if Unionist ministers secured a Cabinet majority in favour of conscription, were to become increasingly indistinguishable from Sharp's ever wilder attacks on a blatantly 'insincere and dangerous' Munitions Minister. One would have thought Lloyd George far too busy to deal with a small-circulation weekly's portrait of a professional politician intent on usurping his leader and erstwhile ally. Yet in late 1915 the minister answered Sharp's 'utterly discreditable' allegation that he had insulted that autumn's TUC Congress: 'Dulness [sic] has but one excuse, that it is popularly supposed to be conducive to accuracy of statement. When it ceases to justify this popular exception, it becomes truly intolerable.'[56]

The neat put-down indicated that here was no carefully drafted reply for which a loyal permanent secretary had required his master's signature. The lesson was clear: Sharp was by now a marked man. He complained that the Ministry of Munitions, having despatched the letter too late to meet the previous week's deadline, had prematurely released its contents to the national press: such hasty and irresponsible action against one of the few papers prepared to expose the 'blundering injustice and futility of the Munitions Act' suggested an overworked and overwrought minister in need of a very long rest.[57] Sharp may have been foolhardy, but he never lacked courage.

What he clearly did lack was sound judgement. Again and again, editorials lauded Asquith as irreplaceable, foolishly ignoring or sometimes even deriding Lloyd George's suitability as Prime Minister. By now Shaw was finding Sharp's refusal to countenance Asquith's and Grey's resignations increasingly intolerable; he was quite happy for any number of Cabinets to be experimented with before a suitable group and/or strong man emerged.[58]

The notion that this strong man might be Haldane, so ruthlessly hounded out of office by the Unionist press six months earlier, was, to say the least, bizarre. Yet at the board's November meeting Shaw chose the former Lord Chancellor when challenged by Sharp to name an alternative Prime Minister. By comparison, Sharp's own suggestion that Haldane return to the War Office following Kitchener's death in July 1916 begins to assume a degree of reality. Having learnt that, despite a general slump in advertising revenue, the paper had lost £800 on the first six months of the financial year, Shaw urged a less predictable editorial line as the most obvious means of attracting fresh readers. In the street afterwards, GBS explained that he had 'talked like that as a "hygiene operation", and that it was necessary to exaggerate in such hygiene . . . to stir Sharp up'. Like the Webbs, Bennett had disagreed with Shaw, and yet could not fail to be moved by his 'fundamental decency and kindliness' throughout an unusually tense meeting.[59]

Bennett's contacts within the Liberal Party ranged from Radicals active within the UDC such as Arthur Ponsonby and Charles Trevelyan right through to ministers as senior as Reginald McKenna. The Chancellor's distrust of Lloyd George, compounded by the humiliating terms of his temporary tenure at the Treasury, was no doubt common knowledge in Great Queen Street. Before the war the *New Statesman* had been swift to lambast McKenna for the Home Office's treatment of imprisoned suffragettes. However, as the months passed and the new administration consolidated its position, Bennett encouraged a far more mellow view of at least one old adversary. Shaw's final *New Statesman* attack, 'Wanted: a Coalition of the Intelligentsia', prompted a reply from Bennett in the *Daily News*. Discussing the relative merits of both articles with the novelist, the Webbs again adopted an ambivalent view of GBS, finding him '"common" (which he is) and "slack" (which he apparently is), but they admitted his incomparable skill'.[60] Apart from yet another tussle with G.K. Chesterton in the spring of 1916, Shaw's contributions now all but ceased. One last major contribution to the magazine appeared after the 1916 Easter Rising in Dublin. After all, it would have been unthinkable for Sharp not to seek the major shareholder's view of revolution in his native city.

Not surprisingly, coverage of Irish affairs had dropped off following the outbreak of war, and the apparent suspension of inter-party hostilities over enforcing Home Rule in Ulster. Joseph Hone continued as Dublin correspondent throughout the war years, but Francis Sheehy-Skeffington was now busily engaged with his wife Hannah in organising Ireland's pacifists.[61] Imprisoned for campaigning against recruitment, Sheehy-Skeffington got out of Kilmainham by going on hunger strike. He wrote to Shaw in the spring of 1915 thanking him for his efforts to secure an early release. A year later he wrote again, enclosing a widely distributed pacifist appeal to the Army urging the avoidance of any confrontation with the Irish Volunteers and Citizen Army (this request counter-balanced Sheehy-Skeffington's earlier *Open Letter to Thomas MacDonagh*, calling on republicans not to take up arms). He complained to GBS that further copies had been forwarded to the *New Statesman* and to all leading newspapers, but that there was little hope of publication.[62]

The *New Statesman* did eventually publish Francis Sheehy-Skeffington's appeal: a fortnight after he was murdered on Easter Tuesday 1916 by an allegedly insane English officer. Why did the document not appear earlier? Did Shaw's support no longer count for anything? According to Sharp the appeal was not printed as 'we did not think that to do so would serve any useful purpose'. He went on to explain to readers that the rapid execution of the Dublin rebels had forced the paper to reconsider the appeal's importance as evidence supporting the republicans' claim that they were simply pre-empting a violent clash with the military authorities. This was nonsense given that Sheehy-Skeffington did not enjoy the confidence of the uprising's leaders, and thus – even if like many informed Dubliners he anticipated violence – was largely ignorant of any imminent revolution. A man who abhorred any resort to political violence, he died as he lived, intervening after he saw an unarmed youth shot dead. His murder influenced many Dubliners previously indifferent to the reprisals taking place in the aftermath of the initial bloodshed.[63] Sharp, ever the pragmatist, regretted the government's 'abstract retributive justice', but primarily on the grounds that ministers had transformed 'foolish fire-brands' into national heroes and martyrs. In a similar vein Hone wrote from Dublin condemning James Connolly and James Larkin outright; but with careful calculation went to great pains to exempt his Sinn Fein friends from direct responsibility, as if somehow there was a respectable republicanism untarnished by the spilling of blood. Back in London, Robert Lynd plaintively pleaded for Redmond to receive the government's full support in reasserting his own and his party's national authority. To be fair, the immediate aftermath of the uprising was too early to appreciate that as a credible political force the Irish Party was for all intents and purposes dead.[64]

Only Shaw made a real effort to understand the 'dense

ignorance and romantic folly which made these unfortunate Sinn Feiners mistake a piece of hopeless mischief for a pathetic stroke for freedom'. Thus, the rebels' infatuation with the 'romantic separatism of Ireland' was exasperating, but their patriotism, bravery, honesty, and adherence to the 'republican political ideal' was indisputable. This moving tribute to misplaced idealism, easily the best of GBS's wartime work for the *New Statesman*, regrettably degenerated into an infuriatingly absurd, but all too typical conclusion: rebel prisoners were unlikely to admire the Protestant monarchy of Prussia, so why not send them to the French who needed good republicans and knew of old the value of an Irish brigade? If this was the famous Shavian wit, then it was in the poorest of taste. Sharp must have felt that Shaw's final flourish did little to help the paper's laudable plea for clemency. Beatrice Webb concluded that Shaw was alarmingly ignorant of the pain caused by his 'jeering words and laughing gestures'.[65]

Throughout 1916 the *New Statesman* monitored the effects of the Military Service Acts passed in January and May. The legislation facilitated the call-up of single men, and amended previously favourable terms of service for survivors of the pre-war Territorial Army. Although Sharp judged conscription an 'impoverishment of moral resources' and an unwarranted erosion of civil liberties, he refused to condemn it outright. Thus, unlike Woolf, who was active within the No Conscription Fellowship (NCF), Sharp urged compliance, particularly if resistance might be seen to undermine the war effort. Although, to the horror of many readers, adamant that 'political' conscientious objectors should expect civil imprisonment, Sharp was genuinely appalled by the Army's control of exemption tribunals, and illegal use of field punishment in France. He, and later Bennett, constantly drew attention to the ill-treatment of COs.[66]

Despite Asquith's reassurances to the labour movement, Webb was soon questioning Arthur Henderson's presence in the same Cabinet as the Minister of Munitions. Never happier than when attacking the latter, Sharp yet again lauded the unique trust inspired by the Prime Minister. He poured scorn on *The Times*'s War Cabinet proposals. As we have seen, protests over Lloyd George's suppression of *Forward* reflected a mellowing towards the ILP in the face of a common enemy.[67] Yet by Easter 1916 much of the temporary goodwill towards the anti-war socialists had been exhausted. The *New Statesman* had no problems concerning the ILP's opposition to conscription; and indeed it was Sidney Webb who had stood alone as Labour's NEC capitulated to a Cabinet demand for extending the upper age limit. The main issue was the ILP's (and by implication, given the heavy presence of the ILP in its ranks, the NCF's) continued objection to voluntary recruitment. When the party's annual conference restated this position, the *New Statesman* deemed it to have 'abdicated its intellectual leadership of the working-class movement'. Fenner Brockway was still arguing over 60 years later that Sharp's claim was prejudicial nonsense given the growing rank-and-file discontent and war-weariness, especially in the ILP strongholds of South Wales and southern Scotland. This was a fair point, particularly when one takes note of the impressive array of former Radicals becoming associated with the party by the middle of the war.[67]

Almost every leading member of the Union of Democratic Control (UDC) – that small, essentially metropolitan, but nevertheless highly vociferous voice of pacifist dissent – was in the ILP or by 1918 joining the nascent Labour Party. The ranks of the Liberal intelligentsia lost such people as Charles Trevelyan, Norman Angell and the driving force behind the UDC, E.D. Morel, all of whom joined Arthur Ponsonby in supporting MacDonald. Most of them of course were veterans of the Rainbow Circle, the irony being that 20 years earlier MacDonald had been almost unique in his loyalty to the ILP.[68] For advocates of a negotiated peace Asquith was as guilty as Lloyd George in perpetuating the war, both before and after December 1916, and in consequence, 'MacDonald and the anti-war minority of the Labour Party were able to run off with the liberal conscience'.[69]

David Marquand is by no means the first to recognise that, without recruitment among those self-same intellectuals, Labour could never have justified 'its claim to be the heir of all that was best in Liberalism', let alone appear a potential party of government. More contentious is his claim that the 'progressive intelligentsia' were attracted by Labour's 'wartime record as much as by its economic doctrines', to the extent that they would have remained loyal to a Liberal Party whose leader was willing to suffer short-term unpopularity by urging peace, in order to retain the moral high ground in the longer term: 'As things were, the tradition of mandarin progressivism which Asquith's Government had embodied more fully than any other before or since flowed, in the main, into Labour's channels.'[70]

The fact of the matter is that Asquith *did* support the war effort, even after being forced out of office, and the consequences of projecting himself as an alternative 'man of the people' to MacDonald would have been catastrophic in terms of losing his natural support: a support that ranged from the tea rooms of the House of Commons to the constituency clubs of the National Liberal Federation. Where Marquand finds himself on firmer ground is in quoting with approval Peter Clarke's distinction between New Liberal 'moral reformists' and Fabian 'mechanical reformists'.[71] The former's often painful and soul-searching transfer of loyalties constituted an implicit challenge to the latter's pretensions as the intellectual vanguard of the Labour movement – pretensions to which, having so recently jettisoned the wreckage of permeation, the Fabians themselves could lay only a tenuous claim.

Not surprisingly, Sharp, the very model of a 'mechanical reformist' was openly suspicious of the UDC, and in particular the efforts by sympathetic Radical backbenchers to stimulate a broader discussion of war policy and the basis upon which peace might be made. Webb was less antagonistic, yet made no attempt to mute even the most intemperate of the *New Statesman*'s attacks upon Morel and his fellow dissenters. The chief shareholder, on the other hand, could tolerate Sharp no longer. Shaw and Sidney were again working in close harmony, collaborating on a joint address to the Fabian Summer School's distinguished gathering of *New Statesman* 'readers and admirers'. Beatrice noted that 'GBS was at his best – witty, wise and outstandingly good-natured'. Yet by mid-September Shaw was back in London accusing Sharp of being a 'suburban-Tory' disciple of Cecil Chesterton. Pledging that he would never haunt Great Queen Street again, Shaw announced that the American press would always welcome his views. In consequence, Sharp was 'free for ever of your GBS'.[72]

On 5 October 1916 the company secretary received a short note from Shaw announcing his intention to resign from the board but remain a 'simple shareholder'.[73] Webb immediately posted a letter of regret, which crossed with the recipient's letter of explanation. Shaw argued that Sidney, Beatrice and himself, despite a continuing editorial input, could no longer control their editor's suburban *petit-bourgeois* admiration for the 'social prestige' of the Prime Minister and the 'plutocrat-professionals'. Given Sharp's fascination with Asquith's faded fortunes in the 1920s this was very astute. In Shaw's eyes the *New Statesman*'s information was first-class but, as this failed to form an adequate foundation for the campaigning paper he had originally envisaged, he saw no purpose in continuing to sponsor Asquith's 'gratuitous and hysterically fervid testimonials'. The now ex-director expressed no personal bitterness, especially towards the harassed Sharp, whom Shaw claimed to find amusing ('and I help with his salary to let him amuse himself').

The Webbs were gently criticised for a lack of concern over foreign affairs, but Shaw felt certain that they too would ultimately clash with Sharp over German disarmament, which the latter 'calmly tells me . . . is the policy of the Fabian Society as formulated by me'. This was harsh on Sharp who had never advocated a 'Cecil–Chestertonic Last Judgement On the Huns', and always restrained Ensor if ever his commentaries threatened to do so.[74] *Common Sense*'s prediction of a future realignment confirmed the brilliant intuition of an unrivalled polemicist; the subsequent infatuation with such a realignment being Anglo-German and Francophobe confirmed a tiresome Shavian infatuation, fuelled by dabbling in some of the Reich's worst Social Darwinist preoccupations.

Sharp, singularly unperturbed by the present course of events, was mildly amused that Shaw found his published views on peace terms severe given that Berlin's *Deutsche Tageszeitung* had already denounced them as an officially sanctioned attempt to convince ordinary Germans that they could escape harsh retribution.[75] Beatrice wrote separately to the two antagonists urging reconciliation. Sharp reacted fiercely to what he saw as her implicit support for Shaw. Had she *any* conception of the frustration experienced in negotiating endlessly with this 'most grossly egotistical and unreasonable of beings'?[76] For herself, Beatrice saw only an unsentimental, unimaginative, and to be honest rather unattractive, younger man's loathing for an ageing 'professional rebel': yet if Sharp refused to publish Shaw – if he even dispensed with Sidney – then these were his decisions. Protest was pointless, for 'if the paper succeeds, we do not grudge Sharp his independence. . . . We shall watch the *New Statesman* cutting itself loose from us . . . . with placid content'.[77] Sharp himself rejected this, urging a policy that commanded common agreement:

> I [Sharp] do not regard the paper as representing my personal views, but rather the views of an indefinable Fabian entity which it is my business to interpret . . . . if you [Webbs] are silent about differences of opinion because the paper is more my affair than yours – well, it *will* become more my affair than I think it ought to be. I've no desire at all to have a personal organ . . . .[78]

Sharp's respect for the Webbs was no doubt sincere. There was no hidden agenda, no private ambition to establish a 'personal organ'. Over the years Sharp has come in for a lot of criticism, much of it justified. But at the time of Shaw's departure he was still ungrudgingly sharing leader-space with Webb and Ensor, respectful of Squire's autonomy, and rarely averse to seeking advice from his paper's two most involved directors. This was hardly the style of a proto-Garvin or St Loe Strachey, or even an Orage. Sharp's talent lay in assimilating disparate and often very dry material; but also in creating a magazine with a clear identity, and in consequence an unequivocal – if on many occasions wholly mistaken – editorial line. Sharp rejected any 'romantic' notion of the *New Statesman* as a paper campaigning relentlessly against every injustice that arose. He told Beatrice Webb that their concern should be for principles *not* persons, protesting only when there was '*a reasonable chance of producing results*'. Sharp despised idealism as much as he loathed sentimentality; no wonder Beatrice judged him to possess 'neither imagination nor emotion'. Sharp's distinctiveness as an editor lay in a neutral, highly functional view of his paper as an instrument for promoting 'social machinery to improve the condition of life'. Such an unglamorous, albeit worthy vision scarcely suggested an ambitious and calculating exploiter of the elder Fabians' goodwill. What it did suggest, of course, was a world-view the complete antithesis to that of GBS, and indeed that of his eventual successor, Kingsley

Martin. Sharp practised journalism as, in Beatrice Webb's words, a 'hard-minded conservative collectivist', while every week Martin embarked on a fresh – if often disastrous – socialist crusade.[79]

Shaw, in his reply to Beatrice, insisted that their editor was in 'fundamental opposition' to her and Sidney, and that without strenuous efforts to regain GBS's support the situation would deteriorate. A second letter portrayed Sharp as a 'man of late hours and plenty of strong coffee' under immense stress. Given his unimaginative and unconvincing coverage of the conflagration it was hard to answer Shaw's charge that Sharp as a writer was psychologically incapable of offering a humane – and human – response to the challenge of war. Shaw bewailed the absence of humour and generosity, adding that he had resigned solely to ease the nerves of a 'shaken man' fearful of conscription. The Military Service Acts enabled editors to seek exemption, but Beatrice anticipated Sharp's call-up if he carried on criticising Lloyd George. In such circumstances, could the paper survive? With characteristic lack of tact Shaw insisted that the *New Statesman* was now so decrepit and unadventurous that neither he, nor most definitely the Cabinet, would notice its demise. He had sought to 'rally old England in the interests of New England . . . and achieve the political destruction of the worthless people who have been blocking us for the last ten years', but the 'amazing journalistic feat of sacking Bernard Shaw does not indicate much taste for that sort of thing in Great Queen Street'.[80] Such sentiments were hardly likely to accord with those of a man ever more convinced that only the Prime Minister could unite the nation in both war and reconstruction. At the time Sharp may have judged Beatrice to be more in sympathy with Shaw than himself, but within a few years she was dismissing him as a 'failure' who had contributed little to the *New Statesman*'s survival.[81]

In formally acknowledging Shaw's departure, Bennett acknowledged his 'in some ways . . . excellent influence upon the enlightened', but also insisted upon paying tribute to Sharp's editorial achievements. Shaw's early biographers on the whole found few redeeming features regarding Sharp's handling of the affair, most notably St John Ervine in whom GBS confided at the time. When researching his book 40 years later, all St John Ervine's prejudices were reinforced by reading Desmond MacCarthy's shaky recollection of events. No doubt MacCarthy was right to claim 'no other literary man of anything like his eminence . . . would have taken such treatment so good-naturedly', but did this mean Sharp was wholly to blame, especially when portrayed as an unreasonable youth eager to 'slash and cut' the great man's copy 'unmercifully'?[82] A more judicious reflection upon Shaw's behaviour came from Sidney Webb, who concluded that: 'From his [Shaw's] own point of view he has been long-suffering & generous. Even to magnanimity; But [*sic*] he is utterly unable to "co-operate" – he must do as he likes, when he likes, & how he likes, without regard to others!'[83]

Bennett and Webb were the only directors present at the reconstituted board's initial meeting, on 15 October 1916. The tone of the meeting was gloomy, with those present discussing for several hours how to keep the paper afloat. Circulation was reported to be stuck at around 6,000 copies per week, with an anticipated loss for the current financial year of £1,900 (it turned out to be £2,071). The serious decline in advertising revenue and the rising cost of paper effectively negated any ambitious plans to increase the size and thus the appeal of the magazine. Sidney reluctantly declined to provide further funding, but offered to write to E.D. Simon and Edward Whitley, asking them to increase their stake in the company. Both men, while expressing regret and concern over Shaw's departure, demonstrated via their wallets a mutual approval of the prevailing editorial line. Bennett could easily afford an extra £400, but in December A.K. Bulley made way for Glynne Williams when asked for a further £500. By August 1917 escalating costs suggested an annual deficit of at least £2,000, improved sales and advertising income notwithstanding. Again, Bennett responded unhesitatingly to Webb's renewed appeal, becoming the third largest shareholder behind Whitley and Simon when loans were converted into ordinary shares in 1920.[84]

Writing as 'Sardonyx', Bennett received no payment for his weekly set of 'Observations'. This column, starting on 28 October 1916 and clearly intended to fill the vacuum caused by the loss of GBS, was rather naively labelled by Sidney as 'personal impressions about political events', and later by Beatrice as 'an article of the hard-pro-liberal-minister line'.[85] Bennett found this new commitment satisfying for at least three reasons: it fulfilled a propagandist role (how can we improve war effort?); following his break with the *Daily News*, it offered a fresh opportunity, at least in theory, to address a national audience; and finally, it helped boost the *New Statesman*'s circulation, even if the impact was not as dramatic as when Beaverbrook recruited him to the *Evening Standard* in 1923. Even when unwell Bennett gave priority to this forerunner of 'London Diary', and Hyams was mistaken in suggesting that Squire and Ensor finally took it over. 'Onyx' (Squire) wrote only when 'Sardonyx' was seriously ill, on holiday, or, as in the final months of the war, over-burdened by work at the Ministry of Information. Indeed, Bennett complained in March 1918 that his paragraphs had been cut, 'because sometimes the editor shies at them'. Hyams was equally wrong to claim that 'Sardonyx's' gossip was incompatible with the rest of the paper when in fact it drew drew heavily on an intimate acquaintance with Whitehall's corridors of power, and as such effectively complemented the leader columns.[86]

FIGHTING LLOYD GEORGE, AND EMBRACING THE LABOUR PARTY

Although by late 1916 Sharp was urging drastic changes in the machinery of government, he could never have envisaged that they might entail Asquith's departure. Webb was assured by his editor that the Prime Minister's closest colleagues were indifferent to 'newspaper screaming' (when had they not been?), but Sharp himself was concerned at the degree of disaffection within the Liberal press. Even as the crisis broke in the first week of December, 'Comments' could still discount reports of ministerial conflict inside a Cabinet supported by the overwhelming majority of the population. Yet again Sharp seemed to have abandoned sound judgement at precisely the wrong moment. One week and a resignation later, he was insisting that government support had shrunk to that minority of the population who could somehow sympathise with an administration conceived through conspiracy and born out of utter contempt for the expressed wishes of the House of Commons. Needless to say, none of these assertions could be quantified and justified; they were rooted solely in Sharp's own perspective and interpretation of events.[87]

For the issue of 9 December Sharp drafted a leader spread over nearly five columns and entitled 'Had Zimri Peace?'. This was intended as a caustic and highly critical account of how the unscrupulous Lloyd George had finally supplanted an unsuspecting Asquith. In describing the political realignment that spawned the Great War's second coalition, the *New Statesman* claimed 'no exclusive or private knowledge', referring merely to 'facts which are known throughout the inner circles of politics and in the offices of every newspaper in London'. On the basis of this ostensibly common knowledge the paper decided that without doubt an alliance of Lloyd George and Lord Northcliffe had landed the dastardly final blow: in contemptuously ignoring *The Times* and the *Daily Mail* for so long the hapless Asquith had shirked a national duty to 'find means of counteracting the disruptive and demoralising effect of a wearying stream of Press misrepresentation'. As so often in the history of modern British politics, when in doubt blame the press. Needless to say, according to Sharp the Minister of War had devoted much time and energy over recent months to cultivating 'all his Press connections with extreme assiduity and really remarkable adroitness'. Of course Lloyd George spent the whole of his political career cultivating the press, usually on the links at Walton Heath. Teeing off with Lord Riddell and Sir Henry Dalziel, or being lectured to by C.P. Scott, was seen as a natural part of the job. By contrast Grey and Asquith regarded currying favour with Fleet Street, or even Manchester Piccadilly, as a vulgar activity unworthy of them. Thus, their only confidant was the *Westminster Gazette*'s J.A. Spender, and, useful though this was in briefing London clubland, it served little purpose beyond the confines of St James's. Having ignored the signs in May 1915, they paid the price 18 months later.[88]

Sharp was right therefore to emphasis the role of the press barons (although ironically ignoring the key figure of the *Daily Express*'s Sir Max Aitken), but mistaken in blaming Asquith's fall entirely on them.[89] At the heart of Sharp's insistence on collusion between Lloyd George and Northcliffe was the claim that after the Prime Minister had resigned, on the evening of Tuesday, 5 December, Lloyd George fed lobby correspondents a wholly distorted account of the preceding seven days' tumultuous events: 'The story was accepted by some newspapers and rejected by others, but those who rejected it did so rather on the ground of its inherent absurdity than because any authoritative denial of it could be obtained.'[90]

There was no 'authoritative denial' because the next morning's edition of The Times had been perfectly correct in reporting that Asquith had informed Lloyd George and Bonar Law how, contrary to the agreed terms of their weekend compromise, the Prime Minister and not the Minister for War must after all be chairman of any new War Committee. Having that Monday morning read The Times's deliberately provocative editorial disparaging his qualities as a war leader, Asquith had belatedly chosen to make a stand. He now saw that his prestige and authority would be irreparably damaged should he agree to Lloyd George publicly assuming full responsibility for the war effort. But it was too late: he was already fatally compromised. Furthermore, over the next 24 hours it became clear that Bonar Law, spurred on by Aitken, would no longer distance himself from Sir Edward Carson's public insistence on a change of leader. Isolated, and with a successor acceptable to the Unionists waiting in the wings, Asquith asked to see the King. After eight years in office, he left Downing Street for the last time. By the time the *New Statesman* went to press that Wednesday, Sharp knew the truth. He left blank the final two columns of 'Had Zimri Peace?', save for the following explanation:

> After we had gone to press the official announcement was made that the Rt. Hon. David Lloyd George had kissed hands upon his appointment as Prime Minister and head of His Majesty's Government. In face of that accomplished fact we consider it undesirable in the national interest that the matters dealt with in the latter part of this article be publicly discussed.[91]

In 1949 S.K. Ratcliffe – in New York and not Great Queen Street throughout the First World War, and therefore scarcely the most reliable of witnesses – suggested that this self-censorship was to let readers infer that, having provoked the Press Bureau, the editor preferred cancellation to recasting. This *might* have been in Sharp's mind, despite the reality being that an overworked Press Bureau had little time to monitor editorial opinion: official disapproval was inevitably retrospective, and usually by channels that circumvented Sir Edward Cook and his scrutineers. As

Beatrice Webb quickly acquired the proofs there seems no reason to dispute her explanation that 'The printer refused to set it up unless the unfavourable criticism of Lloyd George was omitted'. But as Kingsley Martin noted in his memoirs, Sharp could scarcely have felt inclined to protest publicly at his printer's decision.[92] Arguably, he had every reason to be grateful for the suppression of the final four paragraphs. In this particular case discretion was definitely the better part of valour.

Sharp's original conclusion had been that, whatever his qualities as a leader, and those were highly questionable, Lloyd George had now conclusively demonstrated that he was a moral bankrupt incapable of inspiring the nation's confidence:

> Moral confidence may be plainly seen to be half the battle . . . .
> Can a man who has intrigued against his Prime Minister as he has done be described as loyal? Has he taught working men to expect a square deal from him? Is it conceivable that a man of high principle should have been mixed up as he was in the affairs of the Marconi shares? . . . . Will the Allies trust a man with such a genius for intrigue?[93]

Predictably, the answer was an unequivocal 'no'. England's real force was her 'high moral purpose', and yet here was a potential war leader – the nation's 'spokesman and representative' – whose appointment 'at one of the greatest moments of her history would be not only a profound humiliation but a disaster'. A recent alleged libel by Marconi's managing director, Godfrey Isaacs, against the former Postmaster-General, Sir Charles Hobhouse, had revived interest in the original scandal. Thus, any mention of the new Prime Minister's involvement in such a notorious *cause célèbre* constituted more than a mere passing reference (particularly as Lloyd George's survival in 1912–13 owed much to Asquith's loyalty). Despite rattling one very large skeleton in the Premier's cupboard, Sharp made clear that the case against Lloyd George really only rested on the 'inherent absurdity' of his 'false' account of the previous weekend's haggling.[94]

By insisting on the final paragraphs' withdrawal, R.B. Byles, the magazine's publisher, saved himself, Sharp, and the shareholders from becoming ensnared in very expensive litigation. By Thursday the situation was a lot clearer, with Sharp and the Webbs enjoying access to two intimate observers of the crisis: the only journalist welcome inside Downing Street, J.A. Spender, and the author at the King's request of a constitutional memorandum, Lord Haldane. Acknowledging Asquith's vacillation and miscalculation, Sharp must have realised how close he had come to being sued for libel. Arguably, the printed paragraph denouncing Lloyd George's handling of the press left him still exposed, albeit on slightly thicker ice. To have published the whole leader would also have courted closure under DORA, let alone its author's early entry into the Army. Even so Beatrice considered the published article 'sufficiently defiant' as to risk the *New Statesman*'s suppression. Furthermore, the 'new dictator' would ensure Sharp lost his exemption from conscription.[95]

Did Sharp consult the Webbs before *and after* putting pen to paper? Sidney and Beatrice were responsible for the accompanying article on how 'the Lloyd George–Curzon group want to mobilize labour whilst retaining for the ruling class property intact and the control of trade and industry'. In her diary Beatrice railed against a clique 'indifferent to democracy', imperialist, militaristic, and happy to 'enslave' the working class in order to win the war: 'It means the supremacy of all I think evil and the suppression of all I think good. Lloyd George would represent Mammon, though Heaven knows that Asquith and Co. do not represent God. God is unrepresented in the effective world of today.'[96]

Here was the crucial difference between the Webbs and their editor, and the basis for so many future quarrels: in the course of the war Sharp had come to the conclusion that Asquith *could* 'represent God'. For Sidney, writing in that week's *New Statesman*, only the labour movement could 'defeat the "Junker" section' that had now captured the Cabinet. Only Labour, still patriotic but fearful of losing for ever hard-won rights, expounded a viable policy of equal sacrifice for winning the war:

> a real organization of the whole resources of the nation – land, investments and business as well as labour – and the compulsory service of all classes, irrespective of the property or social status they have hitherto enjoyed; the elimination of all 'profiteering' and the provision, directly from public funds, for all alike, of a subsistence and conditions no more unequal than those of the several ranks and grades of the Army.[97]

For the next two years this unambiguously socialist strategy was the alternative Webb offered to the second Coalition's crisis management of the war economy.

In the absence of support from those substantial Liberal MPs loyal to Asquith, Lloyd George swiftly secured the backing of the pro-war Labour Party MPs and executive members. Characteristically scathing of those mediocre and myopic trade unionists destined to be the new administration's 'mere office-mongers', Beatrice noted that 'Sidney came back glad that he had done his best to prevent a decision disastrous to the Labour Party, but inclined to be philosophical'. Only in January 1917, when a surprisingly united conference passed Arthur Henderson's motion that Labour maintain its presence within the government, did the Webbs' pessimism at least partially recede. A majority of six to one was rightly seen as an inaccurate reflection of divisions within the movement, but writing in the *New Statesman* Sidney portrayed conference's policy on reconstruction as a step in the right direction.[98]

Shaw saw from the outset that Asquith would never succeed in organising his supporters into an effective opposition. (Sharp by contrast contrived to interpret their benevolent neutrality as the only way of keeping parliamentary democracy alive.) Angered by what he saw as an unwarranted prejudice against the new administration, Shaw complained to Sidney and Beatrice that Sharp had made 'a ghastly mess of this job . . . . I wish you would drop the paper as I did; it will end by disgracing you'.[99] With the Labour Party beginning to formulate fundamental changes in constitution and policy, and with the Webbs for the first time able to exercise a degree of control over such changes, this was no time to leave Great Queen Street. Limited though its circulation remained, the *New Statesman* offered the Webbs a platform from which to address like-minded brethren within what had become in the course of the war an increasingly heterogeneous movement.

Ironically, less than a month after leaving office, two of Asquith's presumed acolytes, Herbert Samuel and Edwin Montagu, had despatched the veteran Fabian Graham Wallas to Sharp with a message: 'would the *New Statesman* become the organ of H.M. Opposition? The younger liberal leaders were anxious to formulate a constructive policy and they liked the tone of the *New Statesman.*'[100]

Instead of dismissing this approach for the mere kite-flying it really was (had the *Nation* been approached with a similar offer?), the Webbs encouraged their editor to meet Samuel and Montagu. Over dinner Sharp insisted that the *New Statesman* must remain independent, and be seen to be so. Yet, clearly wanting the best of both worlds, he raised no objections to 'consultations' or receiving confidential information.[101] Any overt alignment would have been folly. 'Independent collectivism' could scarcely be reconciled with the economic thinking of Asquith and his circle, whatever Sharp's personal feelings. In encouraging Liberal criticism of Lloyd George, Massingham was both better qualified and less threatened: he was not constrained by concern for the sensitivity of organised labour at a time when Henderson was still in the War Cabinet, and he did not face the prospect of conscription. As it happened, both Samuel and Montagu were fair-weather friends of the former Premier. Montagu chaired the Reconstruction Committee from February to August 1917, by which time he was back in office as Secretary of State for India. In 1920 Samuel was knighted and sent to Palestine by Lloyd George as High Commissioner. With hindsight, Sharp was sensible not to be compromised by contacts such as these.

In April 1917 the *New Statesman*'s editor entered the Army, and Jack Squire assumed responsibility for both halves of the paper.[102] By this time Bennett was spending more of his week in London, and in the process keeping a close eye on his investment: Tuesday's lunch with the Webbs and the principal writers preceded the first draft of 'Observations'; Wednesday afternoon usually meant a Turkish bath with the acting editor and, interestingly, the government propagandist C.F.G. Masterman; Thursday entailed discreetly overseeing the paper go to press; and the long weekend provided time for a memorandum to Squire on where the current issue had scored, and where it had gone wrong. Bennett spent the rest of his time engaged either in fulfilling his enormous daily quota of words or in heated debate at the Reform.[103] In reality, Squire rarely enjoyed as much freedom as a letter to James Elroy Flecker's widow implied: 'My political colleague has been called up and I am running the whole *New Statesman* alone. It is a tax; and some of the subjects I have to write about are, to say the least, not thrilling to a person of my taste.'[104] Bennett's always very positive criticism was invariably detailed and professional. Thus, if he judged an issue poor then he dissected it page by page in order to explain why. His most persistent complaint was of wasted space and poor layout, a reflection of Squire's technical inexperience.

Two months into the new arrangement Bennett passed on Sharp's appreciation, while himself acclaiming Squire as 'a decided success as a writer . . . the best critic going'. Although expressing reluctance to criticise individual writers in the front half of a paper being edited so 'excellently', Bennett felt compelled to comment on what he judged Sidney's lack of sound journalism.[105] He deemed Webb unduly biased in his coverage of industrial affairs, and in December 1917 likened the latter's poor juxtaposition of material to 'the makers of an encyclopaedia who give one volume to A.B & another to C, but cram P to Z all into one volume. The last paragraph is crammed with meat, much too crammed.'[106] Bennett explained to Hugh Walpole that, although he got on well with the Webbs, 'they do not understand (what I call) life'. His pupil at Great Queen Street presented a similar problem: 'Squire is an A1 chap. But he is a vegetarian & he doesn't understand life either. And either he or his wife doesn't understand shirts.'[107]

Not surprisingly, a man heavy on creases and short on starch rarely entered the portals of the Reform Club. Over the next 15 years Squire maintained an ambivalent relationship with the metropolis's political and cultural elites: an eccentric *arriviste* in the eyes of London Society, yet for the young and radical a notorious scourge of modernism and 'progress'. In her largely sympathetic portrait of Squire, Beatrice Webb highlighted a mass of contradictions in his character: the Bohemian who was 'a bourgeois born in his devotion to wife and children', the pipe-smoking drinker who abhorred the butcher's shop, and the enemy of capitalism who hated 'the destruction of anything which has charm or tradition; he is in fact a conservative of all that is distinguished because it is old: old faiths, old customs, old universities, old houses and, last but not least, old books'. Throughout the 1920s the *London Mercury* was, for many former admirers of Squire in his Great Queen Street days, a philistine and unashamedly anti-intellectual rag. Yet many others, their ideals and illusions shattered by the war, saw in Squire and his rag-bag of

Corinthians and redundant Georgian versifiers worthy reminders of a world lost for ever. It somehow seems appropriate that Squire, immortalized as William Hodge, editor of the *London Weekly* and the hilariously inept cricket captain in A.G. Macdonell's *England, Their England*, should have ended his days as quite literally a knight of the road.[108]

Squire was largely unacquainted with the stalwarts of the Liberal Party, having previously been happy for Sharp to seek out the political gossip. Thus, only now was he introduced to the likes of Haldane and Asquith himself.[109] In this respect Edmund Gosse proved a valuable new patron; although it was Edward Marsh who facilitated tea at the Savoy with Churchill in September 1918. One can only speculate as to what Churchill made of the bespectacled, curly-haired and rather raffishly dressed refugee from a good razor, but Squire found his host 'fascinating . . . alive . . . Lloyd George is alive. I wish he weren't.' Like Sidney Webb, impressed initially by the new Munitions Minister's efforts to secure industrial harmony, Squire found his old suspicions soon returned. Privately, however, he expressed approval of Churchill's subsequent move to the War Office, where he could 'get a move on' with reforming the Army.[110]

Squire faced a formidable task in following an editor who, according to Beatrice, had 'made a notable success and shown a fine steadfastness and good judgement'. Succinctly and shrewdly, she summed up Sharp's strengths and weaknesses four years into 'this journalistic adventure':

> He has remained a bureaucratic collectivist: he is a conventional patriot, holding the National Guildsmen and C.O.s in contempt, conservative in his heart and instincts, cold and reasonable in his methods of approach and disinterested and public-spirited in the main objects of his life. He has not a sympathetic or attractive personality, he has little emotional imagination, he is quite oddly ungracious in his manner . . . But he gives you confidence, you feel him to be absolutely trustworthy as a colleague.[111]

The quintessential Fabian technician, and not a man one could easily warm to. Yet over the years E.D. Simon had come to share the Webbs' respect for Sharp's obvious qualities as a professional journalist, to the point where he needed reassurance from Sidney that Squire was up to the job.[112] After a further two months of

Simon's ceaseless 'incitements and monitions', Webb pleaded for patience:

> We are running the paper with a crippled office staff and overworked relief or 'understudy'; incessantly dependent on my writing; not paying either me or Bennett; unable to pay for special information; unable to launch out into schemes for increasing circulation or advertisements – all in a perpetual struggle to keep down the deficit.[113]

Despite Sidney's obvious exasperation, Simon remained unhappy; until in May 1918, according to Beatrice, he 'even threatened to withdraw his financial support if this dilution of an essentially political economic paper with the inferior element of pure literature is not effectively checked!'. Won over by Squire's verse, despite a predictable suspicion of poetry, Beatrice acknowledged that, despite his endeavours 'to keep true to the Sharp tradition', the acting editor had made the magazine 'more literary in content': 'The plain truth is that J.C.S., though a good collectivist because he loathes the motive of profit-making and is emotionally on the side of all "underdogs", is not interested in political democracy or in administrative science.'[114] No wonder then that Sidney and Bennett had to invest so much time in keeping the show on the road, let alone convincing the principal shareholder that his investment was safe in the hands of a man full of good intentions but largely indifferent to the detail and the politicking on which the 'Old Gang' had always thrived.

Despite Simon's serious reservations, Bennett and Webb supervised a remarkably smooth transition, assisted by Ensor assuming even greater responsibility for coverage of the war. The Prime Minister derived little relief from putting Sharp into uniform. In exposing 'the contempt of this Government for Parliament and public opinion', Squire's attacks on Lloyd George were never tempered by fear of call-up or suppression. He was officially unfit for active service, and his home defence duties and general enthusiasm for the war easily answered allegations of disloyalty. Indeed, most criticism of Squire pointed to an excess of patriotism tantamount to jingoism, if not outright xenophobia.[115]

For Squire, ever the gentleman of letters, the nation was in the hands of a 'distasteful' – and, worst of all from the point of view of winning the war – wholly uninspiring alliance of opportunists, conspirators, businessmen, and horror of horrors, newspaper proprietors. Sidney Webb, similarly horrified by the motley collection of imperial or industrial buccaneers and 'experts' now gathered in Downing Street, berated a government insensitive to workers' demands, inadequately prepared for peacetime reconstruction, and incapable of implementing immediate reforms in health and education. Yet in February 1918 both men acknowledged that here was an administration which 'failing some disastrous error in "the conduct of the war" or some open perversion of war aims – it will be kept in office so long as the supreme importance of the war and victory are kept constantly in mind'.[116] This was the price Britain was paying in order to win the war, but was there any realistic alternative? In the absence of a credible Labour presence at Westminster, the *New Statesman* acknowledged there was not. Yet events in France over the next two months almost saw the paper's doomsday scenario become reality. At the height of the German offensive, with a BEF evacuation via Dunkirk still a very real prospect, Henderson, J.H. Thomas and George Lansbury met twice at the Webbs' house to discuss Labour's by now substantial demands should defeat provoke a political crisis, resolved only by the King inviting Asquith to form a government of national unity. Sidney insisted to Henderson that the price of Labour's co-operation must be an electoral pact and the full implementation of the party's reconstruction programme, a view he echoed in print albeit anonymously. In the event the Allies' late spring counter-offensive ensured the capture of Amiens and the government's survival.[117]

Only the absent Sharp speculated in print on Asquith's early return to power. Webb was happy for the *New Statesman* to encourage criticism of the Coalition by fellow Liberals, so long as Labour's long-term aims attracted full coverage and endorsement. Pre-war Radicalism, fatally compromised by Lloyd George in August 1914, and outflanked and deserted over the ensuing four years, was a spent force – to the advantage of a labour movement that on the one hand was similarly split, but on the other was proving remarkably cohesive in seeking to consolidate formidable wartime gains. Labour's 1918 constitution and programme, drafted by Sidney, endorsed by Henderson, and applauded by MacDonald, envisaged in theory – if never in practice – an unequivocably socialist party creating a new social order by courtesy of the liberal democratic state. This faith in parliamentary democracy as the motor of the New Jerusalem was reaffirmed when Labour wholeheartedly rejected direct action at the 1919 conference. The final year of the war witnessed a distinct shift in editorial policy, with which Sharp could not have been entirely happy. Coverage of Labour Party affairs increased markedly, including thanks to Sidney a unique diary of the drafting and ratification of both the constitution and the 1918 manifesto (*Labour and the New Social Order*, a document with its roots in the six-part series on 'The Rebuilding of the State' which appeared between 14 April and 19 May 1917). Following Henderson's departure from office in August 1917 the *New Statesman* identified itself more and more with mainstream, pro-war opinion within the party – at the expense of the Asquithian Liberals. Ensor played an important role in the magazine adopting a more clear-cut position, but the most important factor was of course the sheer volume of copy supplied by Webb. Privately Bennett expressed his disquiet to Squire over this, but with Sharp away neither of them felt strong enough to question the paper's new line. In any case, Squire was beginning to demonstrate an appetite for politics, and Labour was the obvious vehicle for his modest ambitions.

As attacks intensified on the UDC, and on the 'defeatist' Lord Lansdowne (by far the most distinguished Unionist advocate of a negotiated peace), so ironically the *New Statesman*'s hostility towards the ILP abated. With an election on the distant horizon, and a new party organisation, Labour's fragile unity had to override all other considerations. MacDonald's view on the war was increasingly compatible with that espoused so vigorously in Great Queen Street: he had helped Webb to draft Labour's *War Aims Memorandum*, published in December 1917. This document differed from the ILP's public posture only over reparations, yet earned Squire's disingenuous approval because the Central Powers' presumed abhorrence at the principle of national self-determination would sink any hope of a negotiated peace.[118] Beatrice now felt the ILP had confidence in Sidney, even if they still disliked him intensely. His substantial weekly input to the paper, exuding pleasure in his 'new role of adviser in chief to the Labour Party', was intended to fill the 'cleavage between the somewhat neurotic intellectuals of the I.L.P. and the Trade Union leaders'; it was a role Webb undertook with relish through to and beyond the next general election.[119]

Meanwhile Bennett was active in the Writers' Group, fellow members of the Reform drawn from the Rainbow Circle and the Liberal press. Unlike the National Executive Committee (NEC), which discussed contingency plans for Labour's position should military calamity or events in Ireland bring about Lloyd George's fall, the Writers' Group were adamant that the government 'must be overthrown' at once. A mixture of older Fabians, veteran Radicals and loyal Asquithians, they propounded a fiscal policy that was a bizarre mixture of Gladstonian retrenchment and 'New Liberal' egalitarianism: they argued for a more steeply-graded super-tax with 'as much of the national debt paid off by conscription of wealth as would enable income tax to stay at 5s in the £'. The group relied on J.A. Spender and the *Daily News*'s A.G. Gardiner for information, and Bennett for initiative. They conspired feverishly from the comfort of their armchairs, but were treated sufficiently seriously by the professional politicians that regular guests at dinner included Asquith, Henderson and Haldane; and of course Sidney Webb, joint architect of the new Labour Party and for the first time being taken seriously as a player at the highest level.[120] This impressive, if in reality powerless, gathering of leader-writers, academics and men-of-letters was articulating ideas on the conduct of the war and on reconstruction similar to those being voiced in the *New Statesman*. Of course the presence of the paper's two most active and influential directors indicates that this was more than mere coincidence. A consensus on how the country should be run during and after the present conflagration was emerging among the capital's progressive intelligentsia, but whether such opinion was influential beyond St James's and Hampstead was a different matter.

Bennett was happy to encourage a broad-based opposition to current government policy, with the *New Statesman* adopting a similar stance; but by mid-1918 Webb was encouraging an even more partisan line, and increasingly Squire did not demur. In the absence of Sharp, and in the aftermath of May's 'Maurice debate', the paper's attitude towards the supporters of Lloyd George and Asquith was generally one of a plague on both your houses: Labour had nothing to gain from remaining part of the Coalition, or from aligning with the rump of the Liberal Party. It was Webb who in the autumn of 1918 encouraged a gloomy Henderson to defeat J.R. Clynes and the other Labour ministers at the end of the NEC debate and of the subsequent emergency conference on Labour's election strategy. According to Beatrice, Sidney was a realist, accepting that the party would win only around 60 seats. Nevertheless, it was in Labour's long-term interest to campaign with the stated intention that in the next Parliament it would stand alone as HM Opposition.[121] Back in June Webb's conference report had seen the *New Statesman* welcoming Labour's withdrawal from an 'out-dated' party truce. In 'Comments' he dismissed the manifesto of the Asquith (Independent) Liberals as the uninspiring, visionless programme of a party which 'even in the earthquake of a five years' war has learned and forgotten nothing'. The following week Squire launched a parallel attack on Lloyd George's proposals for a nation at peace. The announcement of a general election brought the acting editor's confident prediction that a victorious coalition would prove wholly inappropriate to peacetime politics and thus quickly fall apart in the face of insuperable problems. It was an editorial *tour de force* Sharp would have been proud of, and, given that Lloyd George could look forward to a further four years of power before an exasperated Conservative Party decided enough was enough, totally wrong.[122]

By the time an exhausted but triumphant nation went to the polls, the *New Statesman* could legitimately claim to represent a broad consensus of progressive opinion at Westminster and in Whitehall. Modest sales notwithstanding, the paper's readership was no longer confined to Fabian fellow-travellers and disgruntled Radicals, but embraced policy advisers and policy-makers, columnists and commentators, professional politicians and party *apparatchiks*. Its audience was still overwhelmingly metropolitan, but what it lacked in quantity it gained in quality. As far as the Webbs were concerned their last great venture (excluding the Labour Party itself) was reaching the right people and addressing the right issues – and addressing them with an appropriate degree of authority and gravitas. As early as August 1918 Beatrice boasted that 'Fleet Street and Whitehall count it a great success'. She paid tribute to Sidney's 'tact and ability' as a chairman, and there is no doubt his direction of editorial policy was more adroitly exercised in the final year of the war than at any other time, before or after.[123] Bennett's influence over Squire was clearly considerable, but in the absence of Sharp he never openly challenged Webb over the *New Statesman's* overtly pro-Labour stance. Sidney always exercised discretion in respecting his editor's independence, as witness his suggestion that Sharp discuss with Herbert Samuel and Edwin Montagu whether the paper should henceforth fly Asquith's colours. No doubt the Webbs saw this as an appalling proposition, but they refused to forestall the possibility. From April 1917 it was a very different scenario, in which Bennett was a key player, but Webb took centre stage.

Thus, if Sharp's departure left a vacuum then it was Webb, not Bennett, who filled it. Similarly, 18 months earlier Bennett had provided fresh expertise and enthusiasm, as opposed to simply stepping into GBS's shoes. Shaw after all had never been that closely involved in the *New Statesman's* day-to-day activities. When Squire succeeded Sharp he sought Bennett's advice and support, but this was the very moment when the emergence of a confident, reconstituted Labour Party demanded Webb's renewed efforts in the battleground of political journalism. Again and again Beatrice's diary entries in 1917–18 record the enormous amount of time Sidney was spending proselytising on behalf of his adopted party. Much of that time was taken up producing voluminous copy for immediate despatch to Great Queen Street. In advising Squire, Bennett could draw on a wealth of experience and technical expertise – he knew what made newspapers sell, and when not at his desk he was invariably in the company of editors and press barons. Ultimately he was not a political animal, however, and Sidney now clearly was. Bennett supplied plenty of gossip, but Webb produced the polemics. Thus, in the run-up to the 'Coupon Election' it was the drive and political nous of the chairman that ensured unequivocal support for an ambitious and unsullied Labour Party. In the absence of Sharp to argue the case for a vaguer and more sweeping support for the opposition, embracing the Independent Liberals as well as Labour, Bennett's influence was negligible. In December 1918 Webb, Ensor and even Squire all stood as Labour Party candidates: with the *New Age* distracted by

Social Credit and theosophy, and the ILP's *Labour Leader* addressing a much narrower audience, the *New Statesman* became almost by default a semi-official organ of the Labour Party. In the 1920s the paper was to lose its way, and under Kingsley Martin it was to achieve fame and notoriety as a flagship of the left, but for 18 months or so 'Uncle Arthur' and his colleagues on the NEC had a weekly they could rely on. Not a Westminster house magazine *à la* Dick Crossman's brief, unhappy experiment of the early 1970s, nor the safe, some would say rehabilitated (certainly rejuvenated), mirror of the 'modern' Labour Party that is today's *New Statesman & Society*, but rather, small circulation notwithstanding, a paper that could voice party policy *and* embody the idealism and optimism that made Labour such a dynamic force between 1918 and the cooling of ardour that came with office in 1924.[124]

With Sharp's return in the spring of 1919 Bennett lost interest in the paper, other than as an ordinary director. He was soon too busy writing for Beaverbrook to maintain any regular involvement as a contributor. The editorial staff, soon strengthened by contributors such as Douglas Cole and Mostyn Lloyd who were eager to keep one foot in academia and one foot in Grub Street, gradually re-established its autonomy. Webb reverted to his earlier role, as an active but far less interventionist chairman; but the change in Sharp's character, and a continuing obsession with Asquith and his acolytes, led to inevitable clashes with the board. Yet, however much Bennett and Webb did or did not influence editorial decisions in the course of the Great War, it would have been hard in 1918 to challenge Beatrice's conclusion that 'the success is principally due to Clifford Sharp and Jack Collins Squire and the group of young thinkers that they (and not we) attracted as contributors'.[125]

By 1919 the *New Statesman* was still losing money, its circulation stagnant, but its capacity to exert influence at national – and even international – level gave all involved in the enterprise every cause for optimism. Arguably, the only cloud on the horizon was the return of the man many would say had made it all possible, Sharp himself.[126]

6

Editor or spy? Clifford Sharp and Bolshevik Russia

Having successfully kept Douglas Cole out of uniform, Sidney Webb duly attended his editor's military tribunal in late January 1917.[1] With Lloyd George doubtless well aware of Sharp's attraction to Asquith's circle, the result was predictable. Refused further exemption, the Royal Artillery's latest recruit was ordered to start basic training within two months. Bennett bemoaned his investment's uncertain prospects: 'Awful rot. The War Office is adamant. We can exert influence, but not enough to get him [Sharp] off! . . . His departure means extra work for me, and also a constant effort on my part to keep the policy of the paper straight. He & I think alike.'[2] As already seen, Sharp's departure encouraged Bennett to become more directly involved in the *New Statesman*'s day-to-day affairs. The two men regularly exchanged letters, expressing mutual approval of Jack Squire's endeavours as acting editor, and swapping stories of high jinks at the Reform and in the mess. Sharp spent a leisurely and enjoyable four months training as a 'Gunner', spending much of his free time in the saddle; this was not at all the fate Downing Street had envisaged for a journalist on the surface wholly unsuited to life as a junior subaltern.[3]

Having acquired a taste for army life, in the summer of 1917 to his great annoyance Sharp found himself again a civilian: the War Office released him at the request of the Foreign Office. Ostensibly a freelance journalist, he and Rosamund reached Stockholm in time for the autumn conference of European socialists which, until Unionists in the War Cabinet protested, Lloyd George had been prepared to ignore French objections and let Labour delegates attend. On the basis of his recent visit to Russia, plus reports from Arthur Ransome, the *Daily News's* correspondent, Arthur Henderson had joined Ramsay MacDonald in arguing that British opposition to the Stockholm conference would seriously damage the Kerensky government.[4] In defying fellow ministers' wishes by formally recommending Labour's presence in Stockholm, Henderson was of course obliged to leave office; as we have seen, a key development in terms of Labour's immediate post-war fortunes. Although the conference ultimately failed to come up with a universally acceptable compromise, the government now had to counter any popular sympathy abroad and at home for a 'democratic peace' incompatible with Allied war aims. Meanwhile in Sweden Sharp was kept busy canvassing opinion among social democrats from both neutral and combatant nations, as well as monitoring public perception of the war throughout the Baltic. Beatrice Webb learnt that, by exploiting his reputation as editor of Britain's 'most intellectual socialist weekly', Sharp had quickly proved adept at gathering intelligence: 'one of the very best in the service . . . a supplementary diplomatic agent.'[5]

For nearly two years Sharp operated as head of the British Embassy's information service under Sir Esmé Howard. The two men got on well, and when the Ambassador eventually ended his tour of duty Sharp provided a letter of introduction to the Webbs; the result was a briefing on events in Russia as seen from across the Baltic. Given his background, and high tolerance of hard liquor, Sharp encountered few problems in cultivating the Swedish press, from whom he gained much of his intelligence material. During this time he was working closely with the director of the Secret Service Bureau operations in northern Europe, a Major 'S'.[6]

Inside Russia itself, MI1c's station chief in Petrograd was a Lieutenant Ernest Boyce, nominal controller of the notorious 'ace of spies' Sidney Reilly, and rival of the maverick diplomat and conspirator, Robert Bruce Lockhart. Ignoring Foreign Office advice to the contrary, Lloyd George had been persuaded by Lockhart to let him return to Russia and offer Allied assistance to the Bolsheviks if they would keep Russia in the war effort. Lockhart's endeavours in early 1918 to promote the unlikely prospect of Anglo-Bolshevik co-operation were consistently undermined by policy drift within the Foreign Office, and Arthur Balfour's willingness to support any opposition groups within Russia if they were demonstrably hostile to the Germans. By July 1918, no less than four months after the Brest–Litovsk peace treaty, Lockhart finally accepted that the Bolsheviks would never resume fighting. Although he opposed military intervention, Lockhart did little to stop British covert support for a variety of counter-revolutionary conspiracies, and in some cases he is now known to have been the prime instigator. A month of violence in Moscow and Petrograd followed the Allies' landing at Archangel, culminating in the Left Social Revolutionaries' attempt upon Lenin's life on 30 August 1918 and the Cheka's subsequent storming of the British Embassy. Denounced in *Pravda* as having plotted Lenin's death, Lockhart spent a month in and out of the Lubyanka before finally being expelled to Sweden in exchange for Maxim Litvinov.[7]

In Stockholm Lockhart renewed contact with Arthur Ransome, an old friend and a valuable contact when his mission had first arrived in Petrograd. Ransome enjoyed the confidence of leading Bolsheviks, including even Lenin himself. His fiancée and future sailing companion, Evgenia Shelepina, had been Trotsky's secretary; and his closest friend at the time was the mercurial Karl Radek, head of the Commissariat of Foreign Affairs' Press Bureau. As the military situation deteriorated in the spring of 1918 Ransome spent much of his time in Vologda, a bolthole for foreign missions, and Moscow, the new centre of government. Unable because of war and censorship – Bolshevik *and* British – to report back to London, and increasingly convinced that the new regime would collapse, Ransome sought Lockhart's help in getting out. He returned to Petrograd, and in early August recurring ill-health, and concern for the fate of Evgenia in the event of a White victory, forced him to run the gauntlet of German naval patrols and seek sanctuary in Sweden. Ransome was regularly accused by enemies such as Sidney Reilly of being a 'Bolshevik agent', or at the very least an apologist; and, naivety notwithstanding, many of his reports at this time do encourage the latter charge. Yet in his autobiography he recalled his views as being surprisingly apolitical. This somewhat unconvincing claim is qualified by the rider that he always insisted to readers and policy-makers alike that Russia had neither the capacity nor the will to fight on, and that any Allied intervention was counter-productive.[8] Clearly, after the October

Revolution he had at first wanted Russia to fight on, seeing the Bolsheviks as the only credible force capable of defeating 'Prussianism' in the east. However, British policy had given Lenin little choice but to over-ride comrades' objections and accept Germany's terms. Ransome claimed that, abortive efforts to foment counter-revolution notwithstanding, Lockhart always opposed Allied military intervention. Confident that at the Foreign Office Balfour would welcome his advice, on 13 October Lockhart left Stockholm for London, and disillusion.[9]

As 1918 drew to an end Ransome faced a dilemma: go home and sacrifice a relationship with the Bolshevik leadership enjoyed by no other British journalist, or return to Russia and risk the personal consequences of the Allies formally declaring war. In the end the decision was made for him. Under pressure from the Allies, the Swedish government instructed all members of the Russian legation, including Evgenia, to leave. Ransome too was expelled, although he made no mention of this in his autobiography. Should he and Evgenia return to Petrograd? He left the final decision to the Foreign Office, with Sharp as messenger boy. Sharp knew Ransome as a result of odd pieces submitted to the *New Statesman* before the war. In the latter part of 1918 the two men met regularly to exchange information. In January 1919 Sharp passed on London's approval, and Ransome and Evgenia travelled to Moscow at the end of the month. Six weeks later they were again parted, when Ransome went home to answer questions at Scotland Yard, and then confront his critics in Fleet Street and Whitehall. On 7 April he lunched with Sharp, by then back behind his desk in Great Queen Street. As a result the *New Statesman* published two extracts 'From a Moscow Diary', before their inclusion in the hastily written *Six Weeks in Russia in 1919.*[10]

The fact that in Stockholm Ransome approached a fellow journalist rather than a career diplomat suggests, on the one hand, a safe assumption that Sharp would be sympathetic to the problems of a foreign correspondent; but on the other, a recognition that here was someone sufficiently high up in the embassy pecking order as to have influence in London. Arthur Ransome was not the sort of man to tolerate taking orders from a *de facto* controller, but in the winter of 1918–19 Sharp appears to have played out such a role. Both men were appalled by official

British policy towards Russia; and yet in their own idiosyncratic ways both felt that intelligence-gathering for HMG remained a necessity and a patriotic duty. Foreign Office records, albeit incomplete, suggest that Sharp reported to both MI1c and the Political Intelligence Department (PID). In the 12 months since the establishment of the PID in March 1918, the two organisations had co-operated closely.[11]

The PID (originally known as the Political Intelligence Division) was set up within the Department of Information, under the direction of John Buchan, in order to monitor overseas public opinion. A semi-official history of the Foreign Office between the wars suggested that the new organisation merely recorded 'the rapidly changing conditions of foreign countries both from the Press and from official reports'.[12] By the summer of 1918, however, the PID was engaged in a large and sophisticated programme of intelligence-gathering and interpretation, policy briefing, and covert propaganda: activities more appropriate to the collective intellect and imagination of its specially recruited staff than merely digesting the continental press.

From Balliol came Arnold Toynbee, Hamish Paton and – via the ranks of the Royal Fusiliers – Lewis Namier. Their mentor at Oxford, Alfred Zimmern, was also recruited to the PID – by fellow classicist and former Board of Education inspector, James Headlam (later Sir James Headlam-Morley). Headlam was a highly regarded civil servant transferred to propaganda work in August 1914 on the strength of his expert knowledge of the Wilhelmine Empire. He had published widely on the subject, and his wife was German. Between 1915 and 1917 Headlam wrote several controversial books and pamphlets on the origins of the war, before being appointed Lord Gleichen's assistant director at the Department of Information. When the PID settled in Whitehall Headlam retained his administrative responsibilities, while also heading the most important section: Germany. Before the war Alfred Zimmern's closest friend, and travelling companion in eastern Europe, had been that area's keenest observer and commentator, Robert Seton-Watson.[13] His imaginative wartime weekly, *New Europe*, had been effectively silenced in 1917 when Seton-Watson was conscripted as a medical orderly. Demobilised by order of the War Cabinet to write *The Rise of Nationalism in the Balkans* for the Austrian section of Crewe House, Seton-Watson was despatched to Italy in April 1918 to foment anti-Habsburg propaganda: not an especially arduous task at that time, one might surmise. Like Namier, Seton-Watson occasionally wrote for the *New Statesman*, reviewing books on eastern Europe. Alfred Zimmern, like Namier a Fabian, provided Squire with his translation of a defeatist article by the editor of the German journal *Zukunft*. Similarly, Namier provided Jack Squire with occasional unsigned analyses of conditions in eastern Europe. He was probably first attracted to the *New Statesman* by its strong Zionist sympathies. Following the Balfour Declaration in November 1917, Namier began contributing pleas for Britain, as a mandate power, to encourage the creation of a Jewish homeland in Palestine.

These five noted experts were aided and directed by, among others, the highly regarded Leeper brothers, Allen and Rex. The latter became better known as Sir Reginald Leeper, whose distinguished career in the Diplomatic Service included an unenviable stint as Head of the FO News Department throughout the years of appeasement; a post for which, given his wartime involvement with the PID, he was uniquely qualified.[14] Overnight in February 1918 Headlam's high-powered team became the responsibility of Lord Beaverbrook, newly appointed Chancellor of the Duchy of Lancaster and the first Minister of Information. There had been considerable opposition to Max Aitkin's appointment, with the King sharing the concern of those Unionists already angry over Lord Northcliffe's directorship of enemy propaganda. Supporting his deeply suspicious Under-Secretary (and cousin) Lord Robert Cecil, Balfour promised Beaverbrook minimal co-operation.[15] The service ministries rallied round the Foreign Office in jointly rejecting a formal request that the Ministry of Information (MOI) have access to all sections engaged in intelligence activities. Beaverbrook's intention was to channel potentially damaging information back into the overseas press; but Balfour and Cecil argued that this would disrupt their own department's intelligence operations, and thus endanger security. Jan Smuts was the War Cabinet member detailed to arbitrate, but despite his efforts Whitehall in-fighting persisted right up to Beaverbrook's resignation in the final weeks of the war.[16]

Having already co-opted Arnold Bennett to direct propaganda in France, Beaverbrook's last act in office was to nominate the novelist as Deputy Minister.[17] In October 1918 Bennett was instructed not to resign in sympathy, but his departure from government service was not long in coming. The Armistice brought 'a Roneo'd copy of the War Cabinet minute' dispensing with his services. Bennett had made clear to Downing Street that in his opinion the MOI should survive until a peace treaty was signed, or the Allies mutually agreed to abandon overt propaganda.[18] Resentful of Lloyd George's ingratitude, 'Sardonyx' returned to Great Queen Street eager to vent his spleen.[19]

Earlier in the year it had been the Webbs who first informed Bennett that Headlam's team refused to serve under 'that ignorant man', the Minister of Information. A close confidant of Beaverbrook – a fellow self-made man – Bennett deplored the unprecedented desertion of an entire intelligence bureau to the Foreign Office as 'one more instance of the hand-to-mouthism of Ll. George'.[20] Beaverbook complained to yet another implacable enemy, the permanent secretary Lord Hardinge, only to be told that 'independent experts voluntarily serving the country in war time' were not tied by civil service regulations.[21] Supervised by a high-flier, Sir William Tyrell, the renamed Political Intelligence Department was swiftly and smoothly assimilated into the administrative structure of the Foreign Office. In eight years as Sir Edward Grey's principal private secretary, Tyrell had established a reputation as a highly ambitious diplomat. Grey's departure, and a breakdown brought on by the loss in France of his two sons, had brought his career temporarily to a halt. By 1918, however, he was back on the fast track, and his appointment that October as assistant under-secretary confirmed his continued influence at the highest levels of policy formulation. Always well-briefed by Headlam's team, Tyrell was to prove a fierce critic of Lloyd George at the Versailles conference. Perhaps as a result of this, in 1925 Baldwin appointed Tyrell to head the Foreign Office.[22]

The PID was made up of academics, not career diplomats hidebound by tradition and convention. They were unorthodox and, in seeking to lay the foundations of a permanent peace, idealistic. They cherished their independence, and Tyrell respected this; he placed too much value upon their information and their advice not to. A semi-official history that appeared in 1923 took note of the PID's unique status within the Foreign Office, while implying that the bureau's *raison d'être* ended with the return of peace.[23] This impression was later reinforced by Stephen Gaselee, the Foreign Office's chief librarian and former wartime liaison with John Buchan and then Beaverbrook. In 1933 he claimed that the PID was swiftly disbanded after the Armistice, and its personnel either released from duty or recruited into a reconstituted News Department that eschewed propaganda and provided journalists with genuinely 'objective' briefings and press releases: 'Neither the British Government nor the British people had ever regarded propaganda as other than a regrettable and wasteful experiment'.[24] Quite. Needless to say, later research has called into question Gaselee's comforting words for his readers. Yet clearly there was tacit agreement among official historians to ignore any post-war operations carried out by the PID or similar agencies.[25]

By 1955, however, Gaselee's successor in the same series, the former permanent secretary Lord Strang, was arguing that in an age of mass media governments were obliged to exercise 'popular guidance', at home and abroad. With the coming of the Great War, Strang argued, foreign affairs could no longer be ignored (was this in fact so before 1914?), especially with public opinion confronted by a diversity of political creeds: 'Some of these creeds were revolutionary and extremist. All of them tended in some degree to project internal political principles and doctrines into the external sphere of international relationships.'[26] Thus, liberal democracies were, in the interest of survival, reluctantly obliged to maintain, and if necessary extend, those distasteful methods of disseminating counter-propaganda born out of war. However unconvincing his other arguments, Strang was right to highlight government concern over the wider repercussions of the October Revolution: the subsequent collapse of the Central Powers suggested a Bolshevik threat to the established order throughout continental Europe, and perhaps even across the Channel. Long before the Armistice, the PID, MI1c and the service intelligence agencies were active abroad, complementing Home Office measures to counter domestic subversion.[27]

On 3 December 1918 the head of the PID circulated a

memorandum proposing a visit to Finland by Clifford Sharp. The refusal of the German provisional government's dominant party, the Social Democrats, to suppress the Spartacists had given rise to fears of a second revolution in Berlin, *à la* Petrograd 12 months earlier. Tyrell saw an urgent need to counteract a false impression of Bolshevik efficiency increasingly prevalent in sympathetic newspaper reports (including presumably Ransome's copy for the *Manchester Guardian*): 'The best antidote is simply an accurate and remorseless exposure of the failure of Bolshevism as practical business and its depressing effect on the life of the working-man living under it.'[28] To judge from these remarks, Tyrell was more concerned with countering the presumed pernicious influence of the *Daily Herald* and its ilk than with undermining C.P. Scott's editorial judgement. Sources supposedly holding the confidence of the British working class were to supply detailed information confirming that Bolshevism as practised in Russia ran counter to those liberties traditionally upheld by British trade unionism. From Helsingfors (modern Helsinki), Sharp was to forward the *New Statesman* a series of articles hostile towards the current regime in Russia. Tyrell listed 14 particular areas which SIS in Stockholm were to point out to Sharp. These instructions ranged from coverage of the Soviet Army's size and popularity, through arrangements for the distribution of food, to married women's rights. Had Petrograd's population shrunk to 80,000, and were the Workshop Committees handing their factories over to the government (under War Communism, they were)? Presuming the news would be bad – and therefore justifying hostile treatment of the Bolsheviks – Tyrell demanded accurate accounts, ideally with documentary evidence, of the daily rigours of Russian workers, whether at home or in the factory.[29]

On 18 December 1918 Sidney Webb gave his approval for the use of the *New Statesman*. It is highly unlikely that he informed his fellow directors, other than Bennett; although an appeal to their patriotic instincts would no doubt have ensured endorsement. The project was deemed far too important to justify objecting to the delay in Sharp's return home.[30] A month earlier Webb had assured Lockhart over lunch that Lenin knew nothing about economics, and that the Bolshevik experiment was bound to fail.[31]

Webb's perception of events in Russia since February 1917 on the whole matched that of his creation, although it is probably true to say that he adhered for longer than most of his staff to the view that Bolshevism would self-destruct. Sharp's and then Squire's leaders, drafted in consultation with Ensor, voiced a familiar Fabian concern over the failure of the Provisional government to establish a stable liberal democracy and maintain the war effort. When it finally took place, that great desideratum of Victorian and Edwardian radicalism, the downfall of Tsarist autocracy, had been justified on distinctly pragmatic grounds: rather than make peace as planned by Nicholas II, Russia would now enhance its fighting potential. To be fair to both journalists and directors, the paper never underestimated the problems facing Kerensky, and in particular the threat to his survival – and that of the Russian war effort – from the Soviets. Indeed, only a week after reporting Lenin's return, the new regime's central dilemma was correctly perceived as

> the problem of a mainly bourgeois Government in a country where the bourgeoisie is less important and influential than anywhere else in Europe, which has at once to carry on the war and to convince a revolutionary and pacifist working-class population, enormously excited by a recent democratic revolution, that it is carrying on the war from altruistic motives.[32]

Squire and Ensor frankly admitted that, like most British commentators in the spring of 1917, they had little idea of what was really taking place in Petrograd. Yet by the end of June the *New Statesman* could boast its own correspondent, reporting direct from the Duma and the Hermitage.

The son of a Russian *émigré* and a well-known figure in Fabian circles, Julius West was a poet and historian who before the war had supplemented a meagre income by helping out with the paperwork at Great Queen Street and contributing an occasional review. Fluent in Russian, by 1917 he was a prolific writer and translator who, well in advance of the famous Leeds Convention, wrote a pamphlet on the lessons for the labour movement of the Provisional government's early efforts at democratic and social reform.[33] After brief spells in the Ambulance Corps and as a war correspondent on the Eastern Front, West had edited the magazine

Everyman until the death of an ailing wife freed him to return to Russia. When the ILP leadership agreed in early May to accept an invitation to meet the Petrograd Soviet, West decided to accompany the delegation. Unlike Ramsay MacDonald, who was forced by hostile sailors to stay behind, he duly sailed from Aberdeen in mid-June. Over the next seven months, although able to report at first-hand on the October Revolution and its immediate aftermath, West found himself plagued by both ill-health and an increasingly hostile secret police. Sharp looked after him in Stockholm after his escape across the Baltic in February 1918, and was shocked by his physical condition. Back in London Squire was equally dismayed. Within a year West was dead. Over 70 years later, his eye-witness dispatches can be seen as reportage of the highest calibre; like Ransome, he seems to have had easy access to the new regime's corridors of power, and he could readily convey to his readers a keen sense of history in the making. With his work starting to attract the attention of Fleet Street, West clearly had an exciting future as a foreign correspondent. Alternatively, he could have chosen to stay with the *New Statesman*; in which case, like Keeling, he might have filled the vacuum created by Sharp's increasingly erratic behaviour and editorial inconsistency.[34]

Easy access to the Smolny Institute notwithstanding, West was no admirer of the Bolsheviks, thus failing at first to recognise Lenin's authority and singlemindedness. Similarly, Namier clung too long to Kerensky's falling star, portraying the Bolsheviks as amoral and alienated intellectuals doomed to failure in imposing unreal notions of class war upon the ignorant masses; encouraged and exploited by the German government, the new regime's power derived solely from the inertia of an absent opposition. Namier's first article after the second revolution illustrated perfectly how even an ostensibly well-briefed policy adviser in the Foreign Office could be completely out of touch with what was really happening on the other side of Europe. He was of course correct in insisting that Trotsky's programme for peace and self-determination for small nationalities would prove unacceptable to the Central Powers. Yet interestingly Namier's – and the *New Statesman's* – perception of the Commissar for Foreign Affairs shifted in the course of time. While the margin of Lenin's authority and control over events was consistently underestimated, Trotsky was more and more depicted as a man of principle. Thus, Namier applauded Trotsky's success at Brest–Litovsk in exposing the insatiable nature of Germany's annexationist ambitions; and, safe in his anonymity, ultimately he accepted Lenin's argument that Russia must secure peace at any cost.[35]

Such a conclusion was inconsistent with Squire's increasingly naive hope that the views of a wildly overestimated anti-German faction within the Bolsheviks might still prevail; while at the same time recognising that the key to the party's success was its promise to break up the estates *and* end the war. At the same time, any revolutionary movements across central and eastern Europe capable of hastening the Central Powers' downfall were deemed worthy of the *New Statesman*'s support. Needless to say, such sympathy did not extend to those social democrats in western Europe or Scandinavia seeking revolutionary solidarity with their Russian comrades. In the spring of 1918 Sidney Webb was arguing that, no matter how ruthless and effective the present campaign of terror, Bolshevism was destined to self-destruct without the need for any help from outside. In consequence, the *New Statesman* was opposed to Allied intervention, other than in direct response to a specific threat from German forces. Thus, a fine line was drawn between outright condemnation of Japanese and British landings in Siberia and at Archangel respectively, and implicit approval of necessary naval operations off Murmansk.[36]

Six months later, in another rare leader on events overseas, Webb drew attention to the Bolsheviks' continuing reign of terror, pouring predictable scorn on their presumed ideal of full workers' control. This was a fanatical and fundamentally undemocratic political creed upheld by a minority – but capable of spreading west like an epidemic. The best way to thwart Bolshevism in a Britain about to go to the polls was to underpin public faith in parliamentary democracy by establishing the Labour Party as HM Opposition.[37] Seen in these terms, Webb's indirect contribution to countering communism at home had been in co-drafting Labour's new constitution. His direct contribution of course was to turn a blind eye to the *New Statesman*'s government-inspired role as an organ of anti-Bolshevism, but with ostensibly impeccable progressive credentials.

Sidney's co-operation with the Foreign Office is particularly ironic given the Webbs' enthusiastic embrace of Stalin's new order after 1931. But in late 1918 it was probably quite easy for Webb to reconcile Tyrell's ends – however questionable his means – with the aims and ideals of *Labour and the New Social Order*, a document implicitly if not consciously anti-Bolshevik. Delighted with Squire's success as editor, and boasting his own credentials as a professional propagandist, Bennett was scarcely likely to disapprove. Remember that it had been the Webbs who first informed the novelist of the PID's defection to the Foreign Office, while Beatrice was proving surprisingly knowledgeable concerning Sharp's activities in Stockholm. Twenty years after first cultivating Arthur Balfour's friendship, the Webbs were clearly still in contact with the Foreign Office hierarchy: ministers and mandarins. They knew Tyrell through Haldane, and in September 1918 had introduced him to Kerensky.[38]

Tyrrell dismissed the fact that Sharp spoke no Finnish, and would personally prefer Berlin where 'he *would* be of considerable use'.[39] Given their boss's enthusiasm, no one in the PID was keen to point out that scarcely any member of the British working class, other than the most dedicated socialist autodidact, actually read the *New Statesman*. Most workers on the shop floor, or in the yards and mines, had never heard of Sharp's paper, let alone felt the need to seek out its views on the Russian Revolution. From its inception this was a totally pointless exercise, but any suggestion of a supposedly independent political weekly co-operating with the authorities in the transmission of covert propaganda naturally warrants a close scrutiny of what actually appeared in print. With splendid irony, at the same time as the great scam became operational Squire passed on to Labour's Advisory Committee on Foreign Affairs 'a remarkable indictment of our armed intervention' despatched by Sharp before leaving Stockholm. Beatrice noted that as the latter's 'temperamental sympathies are dead against the Bolshevik spirit and his intellect condemns the Bolshevik conception of social order, he is a notable witness against the policy of intervention'. Meanwhile, the *New Statesman* offered readers evidence that the Coalition might maintain long-term military support for a 'small monarchist class' in their struggle with an increasingly popular regime. The message was unambiguous: even if the Bolshevik experiment ended in 'catastrophic socialism', the Allies had no justification for remaining in Russia now the war was over. Furthermore, Fleet Street should put its house in order and cease publishing provocative articles; and the Labour Party should openly campaign for policies based on talks and trade, not isolation and blockade. Hostile correspondence and vehement condemnation of revolution in Berlin and Bucharest notwithstanding, Squire continued to urge conciliation with the Bolsheviks until his editor's return in late March 1919.[40]

Throughout early 1919 Sharp submitted no copy. Squire relied on Lockhart who, early in the new year, had been introduced to this 'Nice young man with a rather milk-and-water Socialism of the bourgeois type – very tolerant in his view and altogether a distinctly attractive type'.[41] After the British expeditionary force had established itself at Archangel Lockhart had made an 'unconvincing *volte-face*'. Back in London he had sent the Foreign Office a memorandum arguing that if the Allies were serious about intervening then there had to be a concerted and carefully co-ordinated campaign. Balfour and his advisers found it a 'very able' document, and promptly buried it. In his memoirs Lockhart recalled a 'feeble' attempt to reconcile his thinking to that prevailing in Carlton Gardens. By the time he met Squire – and also Arnold Bennett – he had come to the conclusion that no intervention was preferable to the present half-hearted engagement. Conversation with Cole, another newly acquired acquaintance, further convinced him of the folly of fighting alongside the Whites. Lockhart did not at first envisage contributing to his new friends' paper, but in no time at all he had been recruited to write on eastern Europe.[42]

Sharp's long-awaited articles only began to appear after he returned home in March 1919. Immersed in peace negotiations, Tyrell had almost certainly forgotten all about the project, let alone found time to read reports 'From a Correspondent' in the Baltic. If he had done so, he would have been horrified at the support expressed for the prevailing editorial line of appeasement. To take but one example: in April Sharp's belated exposé of White atrocities in Finland was justified as a necessary counterbalance to recent allegations of Bolshevik injustice.[43] This was scarcely what the PID had intended, and for the next 12 months their maverick propagandist repeatedly denounced the press, especially *The Times* and the *Morning Post*, for their 'hysterical nonsense' concerning the Bolsheviks. In early 1920 both sides' excessive faith in the power of propaganda was declared wholly counter-productive and regrettable:

> If there is anything stranger that [*sic*] the illusion that the Soviet Government could be overthrown by the plausible misrepresentation in the English press, it is the illusion that the British Empire in Asia may be destroyed by the dissemination therein of Bolshevik propaganda.[44]

Here was someone clearly not prepared to play the ideological Great Game; a veteran hack quite happy to cock a snook at his old Foreign Office minders. As far as Sharp was concerned the only success Lenin could chalk up was the panic provoked across Europe. In such a fevered atmosphere the last bastion of common sense was clearly Great Queen Street.

So what happened to Clifford Sharp in Finland in the early months of 1919? With so few of his papers surviving, and official records conveniently vague, only the account of White reprisals demonstrates that he actually went to Helsingfors (Helsinki). He could of course have been persuaded by local revolutionaries to submit copy sympathetic to their cause, but this seems highly unlikely. Sharp was very much his own man, but ultimately he was always a patriot, taking an odd pride in his loyalty to the Foreign Office. A less sinister and more plausible answer is that he resented being ordered east instead of to Berlin, or better still home to London. Hostilities had ceased, and Sharp shared his paper's opinion that intelligence operations in non-combatant nations could no longer be justified. Years later, in June 1927, he was to call for drastic reform of MI6, including its *de facto* suspension in peacetime. Similarly, during the 1924 election campaign an unusually trenchant editorial damned the intelligence agencies as obsolete and 'indiscriminately credulous' in releasing the Zinoviev letter to the press.

Whatever the best-laid plans of Tyrell and Sidney Webb, Sharp had reluctantly departed for Helsingfors with a healthy scepticism and a reasonably open mind. It was meagre consolation for the Foreign Office to learn that the *New Statesman* attributed

Bolshevism's survival solely to its being the lesser of two evils: to mix metaphors, War Communism could be the last straw if the West simply left the Russians to put their own house in order. Food was the most effective antidote to extremism, and if Bolshevism prospered only in the face of starvation and despair, then relief workers and emergency supplies together constituted a far more potent force than soldiers and martial law.[45]

By 1920, after nearly twelve months of demanding a government U-turn on Russia, Sharp began demonstrating a degree of editorial misjudgement that was to occur again and again in the *New Statesman*'s coverage of Soviet affairs over the next three decades. Lenin was by now an idealist worthy of respect, Dzerzhinsky the subject of a naively flattering obituary, and Kamenev the unexpected beneficiary of Sharp's sycophancy. Although cruel and inefficient, their regime enjoyed popular consent and was a vanguard of democracy Russian-style; a 'proletarian oligarchy', untrammelled by 'hereditary or plutocratic domination', Bolshevism remained a prelude to freedom.[46] Letters of complaint poured in, with accusations of 'Bolshevist sympathies' attracting brusque, even brutal, replies.

Sharp was never a man to worry about a few libertarian leftists or apoplectic Tories. The appeal of firm no-nonsense government reflected a distinctly authoritarian trait too often evident in leading Fabians, witness the Webbs themselves. Sharp's monopolising of his paper's commentary on European affairs throughout 1919–20 was to some extent an extension of this. After Jack Squire left to establish the *London Mercury*, and Bennett returned to fiction, there was nobody strong enough to question Sharp's judgement, query hasty conclusions, and insist on a consistent editorial line. Webb's growing involvement in Labour matters prevented him from re-establishing his previous role in monitoring policy, but by 1921 Lloyd and Cole were clearly beginning to fill that gap.

However arrogant and opinionated Sharp had now become, it is to his credit that when expected to produce cheap and facile propaganda he responded by demonstrating for perhaps the last time that here was a free spirit indebted to none. Abdicating responsibility for Russia in early 1921 gave him more time to ruminate over events at Westminster, where he was far more at home, even if equally at sea when it came to sound political judgement. Lloyd, and later Lockhart, now had the opportunity to draw upon their newly acquired expertise in Kremlinology and Marxist-Leninism; not that this guaranteed any greater insight into Soviet affairs, and indeed some might argue even less.

One man notable by his absence from *New Statesman* commentaries on foreign affairs in the turbulent years between the Versailles and Locarno conferences was Leonard Woolf. Reflecting upon the health of the paper during Sharp's tenure in Stockholm, Beatrice had noted that, 'oddly enough it is in foreign affairs that the unexpected success has principally been made'.[47] Much of the credit for this went to Woolf, who by 1918 was secretary of Labour's Advisory Committee on International Questions. His chairman was Sidney Webb. Their joint four-page article on the remit and structure of a post-war League of Nations, published less than a week after the Armistice, was tantamount to a Labour Party policy statement. This was not just another example of the *New Statesman* providing a forum for Labour's growing army of back-room thinkers. The document marked the culmination of three years' work, during which time Woolf forged a working relationship with the *New Statesman* that, apart from a break in the 1920s, was to last half a century.

At the end of 1914 Joseph Rowntree had given the Webbs £100 to sponsor an 'enquiry into possible developments of supernational law'. Woolf was commissioned to submit a report to a committee of the Fabian Research Department (FRD) chaired by Sidney. Ignoring Keynes's scepticism, he worked on the familiar Fabian premise that any practical scheme could only emerge from a major empirical study, in this case of international relations. The end result was his highly influential book, *International Government*, which appeared in July 1916. Woolf's original report, entitled 'Suggestions for the Prevention of War', appeared as a two-part supplement to the *New Statesman* in July 1915, two months after Woolf had joined Hobson, Brailsford and Goldsworthy Lowes Dickinson as executive members of the newly launched League of Nations Society. Unaware that the conflict would endure for a further three years the paper had already published a wealth of material on organising and policing the post-war world. Most of these articles had been written by Sharp, including a tendentious five-part series on 'An Allied Peace'. Identifying the need for a commission to supervise Germany's forfeited colonies, Sharp had already floated the idea of supranational co-operation. Not surprisingly, therefore, he greeted the first half of Woolf's report, 'An International Authority and the Prevention of War', with enthusiasm. Ensor, more cautious, called for a post-war Supernational Council to judge all global disputes. This call was answered in detail by Woolf and Webb in the second supplement, 'A Draft Treaty on the Establishment of a Supernational Authority'.[48]

Woolf's recruitment in late 1915 to both the UDC and the Non-Conscription Fellowship helps explain the cooling of relations with Sharp. Massingham, a great admirer of Woolf's work, persuaded him to write more for the *Nation*. With jaundiced memories of his seven years as a colonial administrator in Ceylon, Woolf was quite open in his disapproval of Sharp's enthusiasm for the Empire.[49] Yet the differences between the Webbs and the *Nation* writers should not be exaggerated. A conference of leading Fabians (including GBS) and members of the 'Bryce Committee', a number of whom wrote for the *Nation*, gathered in May 1915 to hear Sidney explain the thinking behind Woolf's report. As a result Graham Wallas, Bryce, Lowes Dickinson and Hobson joined the relevant FRD committee.[50]

The events of 1917, from the publication of Wilson's 14 Points to the Bolshevik revelations of secret diplomacy, prompted Webb and Woolf to resume collaboration. Sharp's absence encouraged the latter's return to Great Queen Street, and in the summer of 1917 the *New Statesman* published Woolf's seven-part series on the organisation and role of a future League of Nations. These articles provided a vital input to Labour's policy formulation in the aftermath of the February Revolution and the United States' entry into the war. Open diplomacy and a supranational mechanism for global co-operation were aims and ideals that could unite both factions within the ILP, and the labour movement as a whole. On 27 October 1917 Squire reiterated the *New Statesman*'s view that 'the only conceivable machinery on which permanent peace and national disarmament can rest is that of a League of Nations', while in the same issue Lloyd's review of *The Framework of a Lasting Peace* paid tribute to its editor's dedicated work. Alluding to Woolf's success a year later in brokering a merger of the League of Nations Society and the more conservative, anti-German League of Nations Association, his biographer noted the *New Statesman*'s grand scheme for post-war international collaboration. Woolf and Webb, and by implication, the Labour Party, secure in the knowledge that it was not about to assume office, envisaged a League of Nations that went far beyond a 'mere adoption of existing inter-Allied machinery to serve a "first-stage" limited League'. They envisaged a genuinely supranational body, empowered to impose on member-states cross-border directives governing economic management and employment law.[51] Many of these proposals were of course about 80 years ahead of their time. Nevertheless, Woolf's ideas, as worked out in *International Government*, the columns of the *New Statesman*, and a myriad of memoranda, policy documents and specialist journals, proved highly influential. Lord Robert Cecil's brief for the British delegation at the Versailles Conference, and Alfred Zimmern's Foreign Office memorandum at the conclusion of the war, a standard work of reference for the drafters of the League of Nations Covenant, both drew heavily upon Woolf's portfolio of work.[52]

Leonard Woolf should have been a key figure in the post-war *New Statesman*. Instead, as we shall see, his Bloomsbury connections led to a close association with the *Nation*, and yet politically Great Queen Street was his natural home. Woolf was in many respects a dour, no-nonsense man, but of immense intelligence. He could have proved the ideal counterweight to Sharp in the early 1920s, and thus prevented the paper drifting away from the clear-cut, unequivocal pro-Labour editorial line so apparent at the time of the 1918 general election. Sadly, Woolf's hasty departure was the price – and not the only price – of having Sharp home from the Baltic and hostile to any notion of *his* paper as Labour's flagship in the forthcoming struggle for power.

Labour or Liberal? The *New Statesman* and the struggle for power, 1918–24

SHARP AND THE ASQUITH INFATUATION

In Helsinki – or perhaps even fleetingly in Berlin – Sharp could rarely if ever have seen back-copies of the *New Statesman*. If he had, it would have been a galling experience. Squire and Webb were insistent that, despite Labour's defeats and disappointments, the real victims of the 'coupon election' results was the Liberal Party. Their view that the Liberals were doomed was supported by Ratcliffe, presently back from New York. Also home was Mostyn Lloyd who, much to the annoyance of his pacifist comrades in the ILP, had taken a commission in February 1915. After being seriously wounded on the first day of the Somme, Lloyd had spent the last two years of the war training officer cadets in England and Egypt. In early 1919 he was home, ready to resume writing, and hopeful of a permanent post at the LSE. Although by nature a cautious man, Lloyd joined Douglas and Margaret Cole in encouraging industrial action and the campaign for early demobilization.[1] Squire was now relying heavily on a team of writers who were far brighter, and also much further to the left than he was. In the absence of Sharp, and with Webb's tacit approval, this younger generation of Fabians and unreconstructed guild socialists had for all intents and purposes turned the *New Statesman* into a left-wing paper. Needless to say, it was not to last.

Sharp's rehabilitation of Asquith, and reassertion of faith in 'a broad progressive Liberalism which – in the absence of an effective

Labour Party – has been so marked a feature of English politics for the past fifteen years', began almost as soon as he was home. Sustained criticism of Lloyd George's performance at the Versailles peace conference was invariably accompanied by gushing praise for his predecessor, recalling the 'extraordinary intellectual gifts . . . [of] a man who honours the best traditions of British politics, and so exemplifies them in his own person'.[2] Throughout the first two years of the post-war coalition Sharp, no doubt to the embarrassment of his colleagues, extolled the virtues of a fading statesman whom even his closest confidants now recognised as a 'dignified wreck'. Unlike Ratcliffe, Sharp never doubted Liberalism's survival as a valid and intellectually defensible doctrine. Echoing 'New Liberals' from what now seemed like another age, he could not see the Liberal Party surviving in a traditionally two-party system without adopting a constructive progressive programme akin to that of Labour. Sharp clung to the old progressive alliance as if blind to the harsh new political landscape created by the war, and in particular the events of December 1916: *if* the Labour Party was to form a government at some point in the future then its survival would be dependent upon effective Liberal leadership. Increasingly flattering references in the early 1920s to the 1905–15 administrations confirm Maurice Cowling's claim that 'the Asquitheans thought they had, in the names and traditions of historic Liberalism, an asset of the greatest power'. In reality, many Labour MPs would have found even Lloyd George a more attractive proposition than the poor figure Asquith cut in the Commons once the heady euphoria of his Paisley by-election victory had receded.[3]

All associated with the *New Statesman*, whether directors or contributors, no doubt felt a lot more comfortable when the editor was doing what he did best – lambasting Lloyd George. Here was a corrupt and morally bankrupt executive which defied the 'moral authority' of Parliament, ignored the public will, appeased the rapacious demands of its most 'Die-Hard' supporters, and thrived on the evident weakness and ineptitude of HM Opposition. Cabinet disunity became in Sharp's eyes a crisis of democracy resolved only by the electorate belatedly appreciating 'the vital and *practical* importance of character as well as brain'. Sharp was terrific on indictment, but short on analysis. Until the summer of

1922 the *New Statesman* more than once explained the survival of a prime minister without a proper party as a consequence of Austen Chamberlain *and* Andrew Bonar Law tacitly acknowledging that the old Unionist monolith was a spent force, and therefore forcing rebellious backbenchers into accepting Lloyd George as a necessary 'chartered demagogue'. The next general election would see the end of this unhappy charade, with the 'last of the Romans' reclaiming his rightful place inside No. 10. All nonsense, of course, but many Independent Liberals did share this unreal notion of the Conservative Party being in a terminal condition, and that somehow the country would come to its senses. Close acquaintance with Asquith's circle clearly distorted Sharp's political judgement.[4]

Sharp and his new political cronies were by no means alone in assuming that English Conservatism could not survive without Unionism as its *raison d'être*, and that the 1921 Anglo-Irish Treaty therefore heralded a Tory nemesis. Despite having access to a first-class reporter in Dublin – the *Manchester Guardian*'s James Good – as well as sound advice from Joseph Hone and Robert Lynd, Mostyn Lloyd confidently anticipated a Free State of 32 counties within a year. Lloyd's miscalculations, both about the resilience of Ulster Loyalism and the health of the Conservative Party, belied his paper's generally good record on reporting 'The Troubles'.[5] After 1921 Sharp's admiration for Michael Collins and Arthur Griffith, and his long-standing distrust of Eamon de Valera and Erskine Childers ('a Spanish theologian and a crack-brained English fanatic'), resulted in the *New Statesman*'s adopting an increasingly propagandist role for the Free State – if only to prove that the government should have granted dominion status three years earlier.[6] Needless to say, in his coverage of Irish affairs Sharp rarely ignored an opportunity to attack Lloyd George and to wax lyrical on 'the greatest democrat of all . . . [who] *is* English opinion'. Thus Asquith's letter to *The Times* in October 1920 arguing the Irish case for full dominion status, including a future option to amend the constitution, was hailed as a great essay in that Liberalism which 'is the distinctive political heritage of our race'.[7]

Sharp's infatuation with Asquith is an enduring theme throughout this chapter. I use the term 'infatuation' quite deliberately. Why did such a tough operator, with a healthy scepticism towards politicians that too often degenerated into destructive cynicism, allow himself to become so involved with an extended network of schemers and free-loaders, the fulfilment of whose ambitions still depended on a bibulous septuagenarian and his increasingly embarrassing spouse? As we shall see, the *New Statesman*'s editor emulated and ultimately exceeded his new idol's dependence on the decanter or, in his case, the hip-flask. More and more, drink became the most visible explanation of a talent squandered, and of an editorial staff leaderless. With Sidney Webb preoccupied playing party politics, Jack Squire off in search of respectability, and Mostyn Lloyd eager for tenure at the LSE, it was the work of Douglas Cole which most effectively checked Sharp's efforts to shift the paper from its 1918 position of largely unqualified support for Labour.

G.D.H. COLE, LABOUR AND THE ECONOMY

As Webb's relations with Sharp deteriorated during 1919–20, Cole gradually assumed responsibility for industrial affairs, and for the labour movement in general. A wartime contributor to the *Nation* and the *Manchester Guardian* following his earlier apprenticeship with the *New Age*, Douglas Cole had moved to the *New Statesman* because, he told Edward Hyams, it was 'more appropriate to his pacifism and socialism'. The reference to pacifism is puzzling when one compares the wartime leaders of Squire and Ensor with those of a true Radical like Massingham.[8] In common with Sidney Webb, Cole had belatedly appreciated the need to undertake an active role in formulating Labour Party policy, in his case by joining the Advisory Committee on Trade Policy and Finance. Unlike C.P. Scott who had procrastinated for 18 months before finally dispensing with Cole's services, Sharp surprised colleagues by quickly warming to the young, highly intelligent economist and political thinker whose ideas were so radically different from his own. The feeling was not reciprocated, but Cole respected Sharp as an editor, and both men felt drawn together by their mutual scorn for the first generation of Labour leaders. Unlike Kingsley Martin in later decades, Sharp saw no cause to consult Cole, who anyway was a rare visitor to Great

Queen Street. In any case Cole exercised a far more direct form of influence – through his copy. Topical and unashamedly polemical, Cole's contributions were a sub-editor's dream, being always clearly written and exact in length; *and* they always arrived well before the paper went to press. Rarely a week went by without a contribution: Cole averaged 40 articles annually throughout the interwar period, in addition to his many editorial notes. Given such a prolific output it is not surprising that the quality of all this freelance work was patchy. Much of it strikes the modern reader as worthy but dull (sadly a charge familiar to too many *New Statesman* writers over the years), but there were many exceptions to the rule, especially whenever Cole highlighted Labour's failure in and out of office to come up with credible policies for tackling unemployment.[9]

From January 1921 Cole was writing regularly for the *Labour Leader* which, despite an annual loss, was then selling three times as many copies as the *New Statesman*. Although sales had slipped below 20,000 by the time H.N. Brailsford took over in September 1922, as a relaunched *New Leader* it reached a circulation of 38,000 by November 1923, with a special 1924 conference issue selling 60,000.[10] Contrast such an astonishing performance with Sharp's weekly, which in the same years had a circulation of just over 10,000. Clearly the *New Statesman* was by no means Cole's only means of getting his point of view across, and via the ILP his name was familiar to a far wider audience than the largely metropolitan readership still cultivated by Great Queen Street. This was an audience, in Bernard Crick's words, more receptive to a socialism 'based on the primacy of fellowship, fraternity, community, and cooperation' than the sterile technocratic vision so often associated with the early Fabians. Given Cole's resilient faith in guild socialism, this more organic, more devolved conception of collectivism offered fertile ground for his ideas. It is no coincidence that he was an enthusiastic contributor to the ILP's regional papers, most notably *Forward* in Glasgow.[11] In his *New Statesman* persona Cole consciously avoided any charge of unduly vague speculation as to the nature of the New Jerusalem. Although writing about the economy at a macro-level, he focused sharply on specific problems, returning again and again to the needs of the jobless. By writing anonymously Cole ensured he was read by

139

middle-class Labour supporters normally hostile to anything published under his name.[12] No doubt conscious of his own Oxford/Hampstead background, when writing for the ILP he never encouraged shop-floor suspicion of remote London-based middle-class socialists.[13]

Provincial prejudice was fuelled by the view of those intellectuals relatively new to the party that Labour's adoption of Clause 4 called into question the ILP's continued existence as an autonomous affiliated body – unless it became a powerful pressure group capable of persuading the rest of the labour movement to adopt an even more advanced programme for the ultimate transformation of capitalist society. At branch level, scarred by the experience of wartime mobilisation, the ILP's emerging industrial section shared their armchair comrades' concern over the centralised state's enormous potential for the abuse of power. While at no time suggesting the ILP surrender its strong electoral tradition, within four years Cole and his old ally Clifford Allen had successfully persuaded conference to adopt a guild socialist programme as the basis of a new constitution (a far greater triumph than their spectacularly disastrous attempt to do the same within the Fabian Society in spring 1915).[14] This success was despite a manifest lack of trade union interest in or sympathy for guild socialism, and the continued belief of the political wing – albeit much weakened after the 1918 general election – that state socialism remained the best form of defence against monolithic government. The debate over the future role of the ILP took place almost entirely within the party's own press, and Cole naturally made little reference to it in the *New Statesman*.[15]

Sharp largely ignored the ILP leaders throughout their four years of parliamentary exile. One of the reasons he felt no qualms about publishing Cole was that he similarly held the likes of Henderson, Snowden and MacDonald in such low regard. Both editor and columnist quoted J.H. Thomas's refusal to force a division over the 1921 reparations bill as a classic example of the surviving senior Members' inherent 'political cowardice'. They bemoaned not simply the intellectual calibre of the parliamentary party, but a wider failure to forge a 'great and effective . . . real People's Party round which all the vital democratic forces in this country can gather'.[16] Beatrice Webb lamented that 'men should be bound together, not by common loyalties, but by common dislikes', while Sidney resolved what was for him an increasingly difficult situation by simply contributing less and less.[17]

Throughout the four years of coalition government it was remarkable how often Cole and Sharp were in agreement, the latter's antipathy towards Lloyd George being so great that he found himself adopting previously unthinkable positions. His view that Parliament was unrepresentative and bereft of 'moral authority' and that most Labour MPs were wholly ineffectual led him in the summer of 1919 into justifying a general strike if popular demand for a dissolution was ignored. At the same time Sharp went to great lengths to paint trade union leaders as moderate patriots resisting a government conspiracy of provocation designed to curb Labour's growing middle-class support. Sharp 'exposed' the government's hidden agenda in a special three-page leader on 4 October 1919. He gritted his teeth and praised Jimmy Thomas's 'wise and moderating influence' over those NUR members prepared to display 'reasonableness and responsibility' by going back to work. Cole's absence through illness conveniently removed any dissenting voice, while Webb merely noted that here was an increasingly rare occasion upon which he and Beatrice agreed with Sharp.[18]

By March 1920 Cole and Lloyd had convinced their editor that the miners were only the first to confront Lloyd George's premeditated assault upon organized labour. As a result, throughout 1920 the *New Statesman* unequivocally supported pithead action for public ownership and against wage cuts. In April 1921 the paper even went so far as to justify the whole of the Triple Alliance going on strike in order for it to retain credibility as an instrument of working-class solidarity.[19] But note the context in which Sharp defended mass strike action: most trade unionists were eager for compromise and were consciously avoiding any violent response to the Prime Minister's renewed 'class war' – an open struggle between capital and labour into which most Conservatives had reluctantly been drawn by a renegade politician posturing as their leader.[20] When the railwaymen and transport workers' leaders chose not to strike, Sharp was quick to blame the Miners' Federation executive for its inept handling of negotiations. This time Cole was on hand to disagree, depicting 'Black Friday' as a 'failure of courage'. Boasting access to inside information, he insisted that the other unions in the Triple Alliance had always intended to desert the miners at the earliest opportunity. Beatrice Webb noted similar reports, and quoted Cole as saying that the Cabinet were reconciled to defeat when notified that the strike was off (a statement Cole himself was unable to recall 30 years later).[21]

Cole could do little about Sharp's regular jibes at the ILP for its 'narrow "particularism" and sectarian righteousness'. Indeed for the whole of the 1920s the *New Statesman* was engaged in a running battle with the ILP, which Lloyd and Webb saw as deliberately subverting the Labour leadership's efforts to project an image of moderation and respectability in order to widen the party's electoral base and social composition. 'Red Clydesiders' and other veterans of the class war were further irritated in the early part of the decade by former Radicals and ex-UDC members who, with scant mention of socialism, argued that Labour should focus on campaigning for a fair peace settlement throughout Europe as the basis for domestic economic recovery. MacDonald was by no means alone within the NEC and the parliamentary party in sharing a similar faith in a 'Cobdenite restoration of world markets'. This was an economic policy, as naive as it was fatalistic, which, when lined up alongside the now familiar projection of moderation and aptitude to govern, proved attractive to a wide cross-section of wavering middle-class Liberal voters.[22] The *New Statesman* epitomised this none-too-subtle camouflaging of the 'politics of material advancement' in its coverage of and commentary upon the interaction between foreign affairs and domestic concerns. Whatever his personal feelings towards Asquith and Grey, Sharp unreservedly endorsed MacDonald's insistence that the Labour Party had emerged from the war and Versailles as the sole 'residuary legatee of the dissenting tradition in foreign policy . . . [which] believed in right as against might as the arbiter of international relations, in discussion and compromise as against force and threats of force'.[23] The fact was, of course, that a great many of those Radicals who before August 1914 had upheld that very same dissenting tradition from within the Liberal Party had by the end of the Great War turned to Labour, and in the cases of Arthur Ponsonby and Charles Trevelyan done so with an eye on eventual office. By 1920 there appeared to be precious few dissenters left in the Liberal ranks to challenge MacDonald's claim, and those who had stayed loyal were on the whole keeping their heads down and coming to terms with their party's remarkable capacity for tearing itself apart.[24]

In common with most progressive thinking in the 1920s, the *New Statesman* endorsed Keynes's indictment of the Versailles treaty, and was consistently unsympathetic to France's continuing concern over its own security and that of its east European partners in the 'Little Entente'.[25] Punitive measures against Britain's premier market in Europe, Germany, were seen as delaying an early economic revival across the continent as a whole. Thus, German ambitions could best be checked by a strong League of Nations genuinely committed to collective security, and not the French alternative of insistence on full reparations. This would serve only to reopen old wounds, and undermine recovery in the Ruhr and beyond. Lloyd George's failure to convince Clemenceau and his successors that reparations were actually a disincentive to the revival of international trade was judged a crucial factor in Britain's inability to sustain the post-war boom beyond 1920. Of course, no serious consideration was given to the depth of suspicion still held by France towards a neighbouring state that had invaded it twice within 50 years. Recession at home was further linked to the Coalition's conduct of foreign affairs via the delay in restoring trade or diplomatic relations with Russia and Turkey, the reluctance to appease influential Americans incensed by events in Ireland, and the commitment to a costly and unwarranted occupation of Mesopotamia. Lloyd's vision of the 'New Europe' was one based upon universal co-operation and mutual aid, with international credit facilities restoring German manufacturing industry to full productive capacity. Thus, rather than demand indemnities, Britain had to 'finance our customers or lose them and share in their ruin, sinking deeper every month into the morass of doles and relief works'.[26]

This excessive emphasis upon events overseas as the cause of Britain's economic ills conveniently camouflaged Labour's poverty of thought regarding the resolution of structural unemployment. Nevertheless, Webb and Lloyd at least fostered the impression that HM Opposition had a set of well-formulated proposals: an independent and uncompromised Labour Party had to resist appeals for assistance, if not advice, once the Coalition begrudgingly agreed to provide 'productive relief and relief works'.[27] This was all pretty unreal stuff. The government was looking to Sir Eric Geddes for advice on slashing public expenditure, not across the floor of the House for suggested job creation schemes. Anyway, among the government's opponents Philip Snowden was not the only slavish adherent to financial orthodoxy. Keynes might have already perceived the state's obligation to control credit, check the outward flow of capital, and then sponsor major capital investment; but Sharp feared the consequences of a budgetary deficit as deeply as any Treasury mandarin. His criticism of current fiscal policy focused, not on a predictable absence of any attempt at redistributing wealth, but on concerns shared by most left of centre critics. Sharp complained as much as Lord Rothermere's editors about 'Waste', the crucial difference being that he pointed to the unnecessary cost of military engagement in Russia, Mesopotamia and Ireland. Despite advising Asquith to avoid 'specious economic orthodoxies', he himself demanded tighter control of public borrowing; and bemoaned the negative impact of excessive taxation on consumer demand, and on the incentive to work and invest.[28]

To be fair, Cole and Lloyd acted as effective counterweights to Sharp's enthusiastic embrace of Gladstonian Liberalism. Nevertheless, an underlying assumption remained the necessity of the balanced budget: readers were assured that once a future Labour government had improved industrial relations, and above all, secured greater harmony and stability in Europe, then its domestic measures would not constitute a major drain upon the public purse. Cole faithfully stuck to this line, whatever his private reservations, while at the same time advocating an action programme which would have dramatically transformed an infrastructure starved of public funding. On the eve of the 1923 election he defended expenditure on: energy, transport and communications; rural and industrial improvement; a comprehensive system of town and country planning; and a complementary welfare, education, and industrial retraining programme. Cole was 22 years and a world war ahead of his time, but he argued convincingly that state investment across such a broad front must generate growth. He contrasted his (ironic) endeavours to make capitalism work with Baldwin's recent embrace of protectionism – an alternative intended solely to disguise manufacturing industry's inefficiency and chronic lack of capital investment.[29]

CLIFFORD SHARP AND THE LIBERALS

More and more Sharp was at odds with his chairman and his immediate colleagues as to Labour's electoral strategy. He clearly did not accept the premise that coalition should be publicly discounted, if only because he had no intention whatsoever of helping hasten the demise of the Liberals as a potential party of government – a task effectively achieved by Labour (with Tory tacit approval) in the general election of October 1924. Yet no major realignment in editorial policy took place before the 1922 general election, and arguably beyond. Sharp still had the sense to ridicule Asquith's claim to be a 'Labour member in quite as full and ... true sense as any man who, representing a great Trade Union ... comes to the House of Commons with a Labour mandate'.[30] In March 1922 it was the editor – clearly unfamiliar with the mind of Philip Snowden – who contrasted the Liberals' rigid adherence to the twin 'shibboleths' of retrenchment and free trade with the 'empiricist' Labour Party's public expenditure programme designed to boost growth. Yet five months earlier an indignant, if despondent, Beatrice Webb was bewailing Sharp's insistence that, although still a Fabian, he had never joined the Labour Party.[31] In December 1922 she provided a gloriously censorious and snooty account of his seduction by the 'Squiffites':

> Clifford Sharp had a natural affinity for the Asquiths and their set, and when the door was opened wide to this delectable social abode and Margot [Asquith] with her wit, flattery, and caressing familiarities, beckoned to him he was doomed to enter in and to have the door sharply closed behind him. The liking was spontaneous on his side. Sharp had the same political temperament as Asquith; the same coarse grained character and strong commonplace intelligence; the same conventionality of culture and outlook; the same contempt for enthusiasm and idealism; the same liking for heavy drinking, smoking and card

playing, the same taste for ornamental and parasitic women. And brought up in ugly undistinguished suburban society, the glamour of the past power and the present social prestige and luxurious living of the Asquith set were irresistible. Of course this new attraction meant repulsion to his old associates.[32]

Asquith had every reason to befriend an editor whose paper had given him solid support from the earliest days of the war. Here was a useful contact, and a reassuringly sycophantic drinking companion, but no more. Sharp, a man with a permanent thirst, no doubt relished his invitations to the Reform and Bedford Square, and scarcely gave a thought to the fact that he was abandoning old comrades and genuine friends. Out of loyalty Beatrice flatly denied St John Ervine's charge that Sharp was a drunkard, yet she could scarcely help noticing how sustained heavy drinking was wreaking havoc upon his mental condition and physique.[33] Evidence would suggest that as early as 1922 the *New Statesman*'s editor was an alcoholic. Such a development scarcely augured well for the future well-being of the magazine, let alone of Sharp himself.

The final break with the Webbs came in October 1922, following Lloyd George's resignation. Looking ahead to the next Parliament Sharp rightly anticipated a marked improvement in the quality as well as the number of Labour MPs. Ignoring MacDonald's excellent prospects at Aberavon and the ILP's continued respect for his bearing throughout the war, Sharp assumed Henderson would be back at Westminster as party leader. Anticipating that neither Labour nor the Liberals would secure a clear majority, he made an early plea for co-operation. Sharp now argued that any policy differences were 'purely personal' and no threat to an effective coalition. With all the signs pointing to victory for Bonar Law, this speculation was as pointless as it was damaging. One week, and a bulging mailbag later, Sharp admitted to being baffled by so many objections to a view 'too commonplace and too obvious to need defence' – it was in the nation's interest for both opposition parties to offer 'the best of all imaginable combinations'.[34]

In the remaining two issues before polling day it was left to Lloyd to revive the *New Statesman*'s fading pretensions to being a genuine paper of the left. Sending a very different message from that of earlier editorials, Lloyd polarised the election into a naked struggle between Labour and the Conservatives over 'whether the work of turning Great Britain into a civilized country is to stand still or go on'; whether a responsible party offering working people a minimum standard of living could successfully challenge the powerful and repressive protagonists of class conflict. Reviving the fiery rhetoric of 1918 had come too late: despite Cole's warm welcome for new ILP MPs, and Sharp's acknowledgement of MacDonald's impressive start as Leader of the Opposition, the newly elected Member for Seaham used the excuse of 'pressure of parliamentary duties' to resign as chairman of the *New Statesman*: 'For some time Sidney [Webb] has felt his position . . . untenable: in the notes and editorials there were too frequent deprecations of the Labour Party and all its works. . . . The parting was quite amicable . . . [but] inevitable and was foretold by GBS before the war.'[35] The Webbs' relations with Sharp were 'practically though not ostensibly severed'. For her part, Beatrice took the view that Sharp had grown increasingly resentful of his debt to the founders of his paper: 'it was as Editor of the NS that he had got his start in life.'

In exposing Sharp's 'mediocre spirit' and unchivalrous behaviour ('he merely lacks all the finer loyalties of life'), and 'the measure of his partisanship for the Liberal as against the Labour Party', Beatrice was clearly appalled by his eagerness less than two months after the fall of the Coalition to welcome Lloyd George and Churchill 'back into the Liberal fold . . . statesmen that he has virulently criticized and condemned'.[36] Like so many, Sharp was always fascinated by Churchill, but there was little evidence of any genuine *rapprochement* with Lloyd George for at least another year.

Ironically, it was in a letter to Lloyd George in 1930 that Sharp claimed to have known 'the Old Man fairly long & very intimately'. He even made the spurious claim that, so long as Asquith retained his mental faculties, he would 'talk quite openly' only to Sharp and Venetia Montagu, and 'certainly never' to Spender, Maurice Bonham Carter, or Vivian Phillips.[37] For one who claimed to be such a close political confidant, Sharp scarcely features at all in Asquith's papers. In fact the letter to Lloyd George is highly unreliable as its main purpose was to purport intimate knowledge that the late leader would have supported his usurper in his quarrels with Phillips and another Asquithean stalwart and one-time Chief Whip, Geoffrey Howard.[38] If Frances Stevenson had had any sense she would have filed Sharp's letter away under 'Ramblings of a drunken fantasist' and not wasted Lloyd George's time. Unfortunately for the *New Statesman*, for much of the 1920s its readers had to put up with the same sort of sentimental nonsense.[39] The paper was the victim of an ego massaged, not by sycophants, but by the bottle. Thus, four years earlier, in January 1926, a suitably obsequious Sharp had felt sufficiently confident to advise Lloyd George on how to cast off the 'last traces of the Coalition tarbrush', consolidate his parliamentary leadership, and 'make the Labour people understand that you are "left-wing" and mean business'.[40]

When Sidney resigned in late 1922 Beatrice had suspected that Sharp's reputation as a heavy drinker would thwart his progress into a 'more lucrative journalistic enterprise'.[41] Yet his post-war embrace of Liberalism, and respect in Fleet Street for his technical skills, had resulted in offers to edit both dailies owned by the 'Cocoa Press'. As early as August 1919 the Cadbury family had invited Sharp to succeed A.G. Gardiner at the *Daily News*, admittedly an appointment already turned down by J.L. Hammond, the *Observer*'s Arthur Greenwood, and the *Manchester Guardian*'s W.P. Crozier. Like Hammond and Greenwood, Sharp refused out of respect for Gardiner, whose enforced departure after attacking the Peace Treaty was deplored by both the *New Statesman* and the *Nation*. Given Edward Cadbury's desire to placate Lloyd George, one wonders why on earth he approached Sharp. His choice may well have been influenced by Ratcliffe and Lynd, senior correspondent and literary editor respectively at the *Daily News*. The terms of Gardiner's departure allowed him to resume his famous Saturday column 12 months later. Unlike his employers, he refused to acknowledge in public the parlous state of the Independent Liberals, anticipating a great recovery in the aftermath of the Paisley by-election. In many respects therefore Gardiner's views paralleled those of Sharp, and his support for the 'Wee Frees' so infuriated Edward and Henry Cadbury that they got rid of him for good in March 1921. Sharp wrote occasionally for the *Daily News* in the early 1920s, but Gardiner's fate suggests that any tenure in the editor's chair would have been both short and stormy.[42]

In October 1921 Sharp informed the Webbs that he would be writing leaders for a replacement morning edition of the capital's surviving Independent Liberal newspaper, the early evening *Westminster Gazette*. J.A. Spender would remain nominal editor, but it had been suggested to Sharp that he might assume direct control if the venture was a success. For the moment, however, the rising star would continue to concentrate on editing the *New Statesman*. With an alarming number of previously sympathetic national and provincial papers now either controlled by Lloyd George or sympathetic to him, Asquith's supporters had seen an urgent need for the voice of unsullied Liberalism to be heard across the nation's breakfast tables. The *Westminster Gazette*'s circulation was well under 30,000, and its owner Lord Cowdray faced a choice of cutting his losses by closure or launching a new company and an exciting new venture.[43]

Spender had refused to bow to popular tastes and advertisers' demands, and in consequence his paper was a commercial disaster; but his lucid, well-informed and on occasion highly influential leaders were read by about a third of the St James clubland elite of politicians, permanent under-secretaries, financiers and establishment men-of-letters. The one editor who had enjoyed the confidence of Asquith and Grey throughout their years in office, Spender had successfully resisted an attempt by Lloyd George in 1917 to have him replaced, and for the next four loss-making years Lord Cowdray had rarely interfered. Although nominally responsible for the new daily, throughout the first three months of its existence Spender was absent reporting the Washington Conference and relied on Sharp among others for news of the new daily's progress. The finances of Westminster Press, for whom Sharp now worked, were so enmeshed with those of the Independent Liberals that his independence as a reporter and leader-writer was, to say the least, questionable. As events transpired, however, this proved no problem. Sharp was horrified by the first issue, warning Spender that it was 'an outrage – the *Westminster* transformed into a third-rate provincial sheet and offered at 2d'.[44] Such indignation would suggest only a marginal input to the pilot editions, and in fact Sharp's connection 'with the vulgarisation of something that we have tried to keep clear of that kind of taint for these thirty years' was to prove both tenuous and short-lived. His early departure was no doubt hastened by Spender's insistence on resigning as soon as he arrived home in late January 1922.[45]

Neither of these offers should be lightly dismissed as minor appointments. Both the *Daily News* and the *Westminster Gazette* were still in their Indian summers immediately after the First World War. Whatever Asquith's personal nostalgia for the power and security of Liberal England, their news-gathering and commentary were 'as relevant to the real problems of the post-war world as anything offered by either of the other parties'.[46] To sum up, Sharp's peers in Fleet Street had judged him sufficiently talented and experienced that he might succeed two of their most highly regarded colleagues – Gardiner and Spender – and edit two national dailies still clinging tenaciously to their pre-war prestige, if not necessarily their pre-war sales.

THE *NEW STATESMAN* AND THE *NATION* – THE ABORTIVE MERGER, 1923

In the early 1920s Sharp was still quite adept at concealing his drink problem, particularly when in the company of his directors, and relations with the *New Statesman* board remained generally cordial. With the exception of Edward Whitley and the Webbs, all the major shareholders were Liberals and unlikely to question their editor's call for a progressive coalition. The former chairman and his wife felt that they had 'lost control' of the magazine only because it relied so heavily upon the financial support of E.D. Simon, Arnold Bennett and Glynne Williams: 'A melancholy ending to our one journalistic adventure. Poor poverty-stricken Labour!' In her diary Beatrice indicated that if she and Sidney had exercised greater financial muscle they could have retained control over Sharp, but there is little evidence to support such a claim.[47] A relatively new director was Sir Hedley Le Bas, originally called in as a consultant and in January 1921 the author of a largely positive report. A specialist in regenerating unprofitable magazines, Le Bas recommended various economies and innovations which he forecast would reverse the 1920 deficit of £6,500. In the medium term his optimism was vindicated: by April 1923 Sharp was predicting an annual loss not in excess of £1,000, and two years later the *New Statesman* finally produced an interim profit – of 30 shillings![48]

The *Nation* was in an even more parlous financial state than its rival, a situation no longer acceptable to the Rowntree family, supporters of Hugh Massingham's paper since 1907. The Rowntrees were exasperated by their increasingly eccentric editor, a man prone, according to Leonard Woolf, to hair-raising outbursts of verbal violence that belied a lifetime of evangelical pacificism. More and more Massingham's *Nation* adopted, in Donald Moggridge's words, a 'rather negative querulous tone in the face of the wickedness of the post-war world'.[49] In conversation and in print Massingham exceeded even Clifford Sharp in his loathing of Lloyd George; and yet he treated the Asquitheans with scarcely less venom. For the nation's salvation he now looked to Labour. Thus the *New Statesman* and the *Nation*, thanks to their equally idiosyncratic editors, were being steered in directly opposite directions. For the Rowntrees, patrons of ostensibly the premier Liberal organ, Massingham's decision to join the Labour Party in December 1922 was the last straw. Yet by this time he had gathered together a glittering array of contributors, albeit sharing a similar disenchantment with their old party: H.W. Nevinson, Noel Brailsford, J.L. Hammond, L.T. Hobhouse, J.A. Hobson, and Noel and Charles Buxton. Together they constituted an intellectual powerhouse, individually and collectively seeking a fundamental shift in Liberal thinking, 'from belief in individual freedom and unfettered property rights towards concepts of "positive" freedom and social justice'.[50] Keynes, as his biographer points out, had never been a disciple of T.H. Green, regarding pre-war 'New Liberalism' as a 'typical example of Oxford Idealist muddle'. From 1922 he found himself involved in a concerted effort to update Liberalism and rejuvenate the Liberal Party in anticipation of eventual reunion under his old enemy Lloyd George: 'He believed that the Liberal temper was more readily attuned to his message than dynastic conservatism or class-war Labour.' Looking for a suitable platform from which to point out the twin follies of excessive reparations and an early return to the gold standard, Keynes found in 1923 the ideal platform for his ideas on monetary reform – the *Nation*.[51]

Eager to sell, Arnold Rowntree encouraged Massingham and his staff to seek a fresh sponsor. At the same time he began discreet negotiations with the organisers of the annual Liberal Summer School: the *Economist's* Walter Layton, and the history professor turned full-time thinker and activist, Ramsay Muir. With Cambridge represented on the Summer School Committee by Layton, Keynes and Hubert Henderson, Muir's fellow members of the 'Manchester Group' were C.P. Scott and his son Ted, and local businessman turned MP, E.D. Simon. Leonard Cadbury, Keynes, Simon and Rowntree established the New Nation Company to buy the *Nation*, on the correct assumption that Massingham would fail to raise sufficient money to exercise his option. The Rowntree Trust sold the paper for £12,500 in March 1923, although Massingham's resignation only came into effect two months later when the magazine was relaunched by his successor, the now former don Hubert Henderson (Keynes having effectively vetoed the original choice of Ramsay Muir, with whom he differed profoundly over salary, editorial control and, above all, economics).[52]

Keynes's biographers have assumed that, in partnership with Layton, he was the driving force behind the *Nation*'s change of ownership. However, Ernest Simon appears to have been a key figure in the early planning stages, seeking to reconcile his financial interest in the new venture and in the *New Statesman*. Over Christmas 1922 Simon persuaded Sharp that with him as editor a potential circulation of 20,000 would ensure a secure and profitable future for a merged *Nation* and *New Statesman*. On New Year's Day Sharp informed Sidney Webb that the New Nation Company were willing to buy his 37 management shares, and those of any other investors willing to divest their stock, on terms fixed by the relative valuation of the two papers. Sharp's initial enthusiasm for the merger was soon qualified by doubts as to whether the new board would guarantee his 'security of tenure and complete freedom of control and the political independence of the paper'. Such apprehension was wholly justified: when Ramsay Muir expressed similar concerns to Keynes in February 1923 he was told in no uncertain terms that the *Nation*'s editorial committee would energetically exercise its right to decide on content and policy, and this indeed proved to be the case.[53] To be fair to Sharp, who was on the whole a quite dreadful man, he was insistent that he could not support the deal unless Webb's 'formal consent becomes *real* consent':

> Certainly I [Sharp] shall do nothing of which you [Sidney Webb] finally disapprove, because although I may be unable to run the paper precisely on the lines you would choose I am nevertheless definitely not prepared to make it any more in opposition to your conception of what is [?] in the general interest.[54]

Although taken by surprise, on reflection the Webbs began to see the case for making a complete break given that, 'With Sharp's Liberal leanings, the *New Statesman* had ceased to be of use to us'. Simon, although himself a Liberal MP, told Sidney that he only suggested a merger because 'by far the greater part of the damage is already done'. If one can understand Beatrice correctly, Sidney felt 'any accession of strength to the Liberals by their adoption of a left policy was detrimental to the Labour Party', but there was little chance of this if Sharp was editing the new magazine and so he was quite happy to sanction the merger. Edward Whitley and Glynne Williams were hostile to amalgamation, for exactly the opposite reason, namely that the paper would not be sympathetic to collectivism. Keynes's syndicate confirmed that it would indeed be, in Beatrice's words, 'definitely Liberal in substance and form and expressly intended to exclude "collectivist dogma". Even Sharp was disillusioned.' Over dinner at the Berkeley, Williams and Whitley secured Arnold Bennett's casting vote by offering to underwrite the current deficit. They were then elected chairman and vice-chairman respectively.[55] Sharp too had decided that 'our *complete* independence is too valuable an asset to be sacrificed to anything short of sheer necessity'.[56]

The issue of 13 January 1923 denied newspaper rumours of a merger, reassuring *New Statesman* readers that the owners 'have not at any time contemplated any change of policy or attitude towards the political parties. They regard the complete independence of THE NEW STATESMAN as its cardinal feature, which they intend fully to maintain.'[57] Sharp's understanding of 'complete independence', namely that Tories, Liberals *and* socialists might be praised or damned without discrimination, was to clash more and more with Webb, Whitley and Williams's perception of independence as being a state of mind predetermined by what was in the best interests of HM Opposition. Yet initially Beatrice saw grounds for hope: 'If C.S. will only keep sober he may become disillusioned with the Asquith set – indeed he is becoming disillusioned – owing to the decline of Asquith's power and the waning of Margot's faith in his helpfulness.'[58]

That same week 'Comments' expressed regret at the imminent departure of the 'brilliant and sincere' Massingham. For Sharp, news of Keynes chairing the *Nation*'s editorial committee confirmed his worst fears. On 19 May *The Times* announced that Massingham's popular 'Wayfarer's Diary' had found a new home in the pages of the *New Statesman*. Sharp's goodwill towards a fellow editor down on his luck was not reciprocated. Massingham was a sick man who resented working for a rival he had always despised. He found the atmosphere, if not the politics, of the *Spectator* far more congenial, and in June 1923 accepted St Loe Strachey's invitation to write 'The Other Side', a series of essays which proved unexpectedly popular with his new Tory audience. To be fair to Massingham, he missed only six issues of the *New Statesman* between 26 May 1923 and his death in August of the following year, establishing 'London Diary' nearly a decade before it became synonomous with Kingsley Martin.[59] Ratcliffe and Sharp drafted a lengthy obituary to a 'master of his craft under whom it was a stimulus and a joy to work'. Sharp acknowledged that 'London Diary' had never captured the magic of the 'Wayfarer': 'We could not give him [Massingham] and he never sought to take that complete independence which was a necessary condition of his very best work.'[60] No doubt many readers asked: 'Why not?' Of course Massingham's notes were always far more inquiring and iconoclastic than anything Sharp was writing by this time, albeit, in the opinion of his biographer, never recapturing his old 'sting, his intensity of conviction, his outrage, his enthusiasm'.[61]

With the benefit of hindsight we can see that 1923 was too early for a merger of the *Nation* and the *New Statesman*. Although Simon first proposed the idea, his thinking throughout the whole episode appears to have been decidedly muddled, except when viewing the venture in purely commercial terms. Sharp clearly had no idea what purpose the Liberal Summer School Committee envisaged for the *Nation*, and once it became clear that he would be either held under a tight rein or out of a job then his initial enthusiasm waned. Sidney Webb, if Beatrice is to be believed, in effect saw the sale of the *New Statesman* as a convenient means of recouping his investment and off-loading a growing cause of personal embarrassment. He was after all by now a Labour front bench spokesman, and most Saturday mornings found him wincing over Sharp's latest caustic remark regarding the performance of the parliamentary party. It was Williams and Whitley who recognized that, given the intellectually formidable team they would in future be working with, the final result would have been a *de facto* take-over rather than a genuine merger and meeting of minds. The Keynes who chaired the *New Statesman and Nation* from 1931 was in a very different position from the optimist of eight years earlier; at that time eager to restore his party's electoral fortunes and expound the case for modern Liberalism as a 'philosophy of government' firmly rooted in Cambridge economics.[62] The Liberal Party was in dire straits, but not in a terminal condition. For all the heroic endeavours of Cole, Laski, Tawney and others, the Labour Party still lacked the firm intellectual underpinning which the 'Manchester Group' and more significantly their Cambridge allies offered Lloyd George before and, more importantly, after he assumed the leadership of a reunited party. The 1924 and 1929 elections were arguably killer blows, the latter result proving especially cruel given the imagination, innovation and intellectual rigour of the action programmes spawned by the Liberal Industrial Inquiry.[63] As his biographer recognised, Keynes looked to a revitalised Liberal Party sharing office with Labour. He laboured hard to provide the intellectual underpinning for the programme such an alliance would require to be credible and fruitful. The absence of an electoral breakthrough in 1929, Labour's traumas in office, and then the disastrous showing of the Liberal Party in 1931, left Keynes 'politically homeless'.[64]

In 1923, with his hopes intact, and a determination bordering on ruthlessness to see the *Nation* succeed, Keynes would easily have seen off any attempt by *New Statesman* survivors to fly the flag of collectivism. Indeed, he would have seen off the *New Statesman* itself, in the same way that after 1931, in a stark reversal of fortunes, Martin (ironically under Keynes's chairmanship) ensured that the character of the *Nation* was subsumed into his personal vision of what an unequivocably socialist weekly should be – and in the same way that after 1988 *New Society*, from a much stronger initial position, soon surrendered its identity. Not for the first time since 1913, the fortunes of the Labour Party and of the *New Statesman* were inseparable. Whitley and Williams, unsung heroes, ensured the survival of a non-aligned review that, although clearly drifting under Sharp, nevertheless offered a manifest left-of-centre perspective on the world. It is not too outrageous to say that the Labour Party needed the *New Statesman*, even if it did not know it. Another two years were to pass before MacDonald belatedly acknowledged the need for a sympathetic weekly magazine not boasting the imprimatur of the ILP.[65] In 1923 the *New Statesman* remained the most reputable non-partisan outlet for socialist ideas, as Cole's enormous contribution to the general debate on Labour's task once in office shows. The magazine neither sold its soul to the new Liberal establishment nor compromised its independent position with regard to the Labour Party: Cole had no time for vague promises of the New Jerusalem, and the most Sharp could ever offer MacDonald and his colleagues was a support so heavily qualified that it is little wonder Sidney Webb was all ready to withdraw at the first opportunity.

DEALING WITH MACDONALD, 1923–24

In 1923 France, supported by Belgium, occupied the Ruhr. Week after week the *New Statesman* led with Europe. Sharp and Lloyd's message was simple, consistent and predictable: the French had to learn that Germany was still at the heart of the European economy, and that insistence upon full reparations was as counter-productive as it was vindictive. If this lesson could not be learnt, then the failing Bonar Law, or after May 1923 the inexperienced Baldwin, had to terminate *entente* with a militaristic nation intent on 'European hegemony'. Nor was the *New Statesman* alone in its demands. Few newspapers had a good word to say about the French. Their concern for national security, even after the 1925 Locarno agreement on the Rhineland, and their clear dissatisfaction with the Dawes Plan, fuelled hostile public opinion throughout the 1920s. Baldwin was of course always happy to leave such matters to his Foreign Secretary, being preoccupied with what he saw as more urgent matters at home. This was as true in the 1920s as in the early years of Appeasement. In 1923 few people knew anything about the Prime Minister, and all greatly underestimated him. For Sharp, the government's record abroad seemed an easy target. By November Baldwin's decision to seek a mandate for protectionism was dismissed as a crude distraction from the inseparable issues of unemployment at home and Britain's failure to impose a revised peace settlement in Europe.[66]

As David Marquand and Maurice Cowling were the first to point out, by opening to doubt the assumptions on which British foreign policy had been based since 1904, the crisis over France's entry into the Ruhr discredited not only the government but also both wings of the Liberal Party: Grey, if not the architect was certainly the builder of the *Entente Cordiale*, while by 1912 Lloyd George was already the lost leader of Radical 'Little Englanders'.[67] Such circumstances favoured a Labour Party well briefed by its new recruits from the progressive intelligentsia and led by a man whose opposition to war in 1914, if not vindicated and condoned, could now at least be comprehended. We have already seen how both Lloyd and Sharp acknowledged MacDonald's unique authority to address the House on foreign affairs. While acknowledging differences in other areas, the *New Statesman* regularly endorsed the Labour leader's view of reparations as counter-productive, and his fear that by playing down French bellicosity Baldwin and Curzon endangered an already fragile peace. The Independent Liberals, in order to reconcile similar concerns over the reparations issue with Grey's familiar empathy towards France, urged a League of Nations guarantee of French security and a German presence at Geneva – the eventual outcome of Locarno. Earlier enthusiasm notwithstanding, Sharp shared Labour's more sceptical view of the League. He accepted MacDonald's position that, before any arbitration over reparations could take place at Geneva, international agreement was needed on a restructured and more representative League that in consequence would hold greater 'moral authority'. Events from the Japanese invasion of Manchuria to the outbreak of war might suggest that an early strengthening of the League was a missed opportunity, but once in office MacDonald had to give absolute priority to improving Franco-German relations, aware that rewriting the Covenant so soon after its inception was a major undertaking few nations would greet with enthusiasm, let alone a Foreign Office over which he still had only tenuous control.

From 1919 until his return to the Commons in 1922 MacDonald was rarely mentioned in the *New Statesman*, with the exception of his narrow defeat in the East Woolwich by-election of February 1921. Yet in these years he remained on the NEC as party treasurer, was re-elected to the NAC, and as joint secretary of the second International played a key role in ensuring the ILP did not affiliate to the Comintern thereby marginalising the nascent British Communist Party.[68] For a paper so closely associated with the labour movement (whether Sharp liked it or not), it was ironic that on the whole politics meant Parliament. Considering that MacDonald was by trade a journalist, with his work appearing regularly in the ILP papers and New York's *Nation*, as well as occasionally in the national press, it is perhaps surprising that Webb did not invite him at least to approach Sharp.[69] The latter was not averse to accepting signed articles by active politicians: for example, Sir Herbert Samuel upon his return from Palestine.[70] In November 1923 the *New Statesman* rediscovered MacDonald, now chairman and leader of Labour's newly elected 142 MPs. In terms of standing and breadth of support within the Labour Party this was MacDonald's finest hour: even the ILP's 'Red Clydesiders' admired his wartime stance; middle-class former Radicals rightly judged him of like mind, particularly on foreign affairs; while most trade unionists had a grudging respect, particularly when he came to dominate the new National Joint Council (NJC) intended to bridge the industrial and political wings of the movement. Soon he found himself lionised as a potential statesman of European stature by an editor many Labour supporters now looked on as a virtual traitor, including no doubt MacDonald himself. Cole at the same time was echoing MacDonald's view of successive by-elections as a straight struggle between capitalism and democratic socialism:

> If a Centre Party is to be built on the basis of opposition to Socialism as the Labour Party interprets it, it would be inevitably to all intents and purposes a Conservative Party. Union of Liberals and Conservatives on such an issue would not create a powerful political combination but drive all reformers into the Labour fold

– perhaps not such a bad thing as Labour would certainly be broadened and deepened by new influences among its rank-and-file.[71]

Cole had a particular axe to grind about too many sinecured second-rate trade unionists, but his prediction of a marginalised Liberal Party was of course unerring. His error lay in underestimating the strength of a Conservative Party that was to dominate the whole of the interwar period. A fortnight later, with piquant irony, Cole reassured wavering Liberal voters that Labour was 'constitutionalist to the backbone . . . and at times it seems more parliamentarian than the parliamentarians themselves'. Here was a man with no illusions regarding the quality of the Opposition front bench.[72]

On the eve of the December 1923 general election a now reunited Liberal Party was forecast to win two-thirds of previously Tory constituencies, admittedly while sacrificing seats in the north of England to Labour. Sharp's gloomy acknowledgement that reunion had failed to span an ominous gulf between unreconstructed anti-socialists and coalitionists complemented the insistence of Cole and Webb that voters faced only two clear alternatives: competition, individual struggle and social division under the Conservatives, or co-operation, collective endeavour and common reward under Labour. As it was now 'a national party, based on ideas rather on an exclusive appeal to a particular class', Labour was congratulated for having widened its social composition. Needless to say, the *New Statesman* claimed credit for Labour's move away from its narrow working-class base and its equally narrow reformist preoccupations. By making such extravagant claims the paper was setting itself up as an easy target; but it could with some justification claim to have advanced the new orthodoxy well before MacDonald (let alone the electorally hapless Arthur Henderson) was back at Westminster and in a much stronger position to plan the Liberals' early demise.

If the *New Statesman* was going to rehabilitate itself in the eyes of Labour supporters and be forgiven for the fiasco of the preceding election, then this was the moment. Instead Sharp overrode the advice of colleagues and again called for partnership, albeit this time with Asquith as Foreign Secretary in a coalition headed by MacDonald. Conflicting signals were being sent out not just within the same issue, but within the same editorial notes. Cole and Webb were applauding Labour's success in marginalising Liberalism, while their editor was at the same time suggesting the party take several steps backward on its mapped-out path to power.[73] In reality there was no way a mistimed election, and a shotgun marriage of Asquith and Lloyd George, would force the Labour Party into abandoning its strategy and encouraging the Liberals' revival as a potential party of government. Yet again, thanks to its editor, the *New Statesman* was left looking directionless and a mass of contradictions. How much longer would the board, especially Williams and Whitley, tolerate such a state of affairs?

The issue of 8 December went to press before the election results were known. While Sharp drafted an article for the *Daily News* on why Labour now had to accept the case for a coalition with the Liberals, Massingham was imploring the Webbs to do all in their power to stop it. Since leaving the *Nation* Massingham had been advancing the idea of a 'genuine' Labour weekly to no avail, and like so many converts had embraced his new faith with an evangelical and fundamentalist fervour. Nevertheless, MacDonald entrusted him with finding out from Reginald McKenna, chairman of the Midland Bank, how the City would view a Labour government.[74] That same afternoon Sharp showed Sidney his article, unaware that over lunch the Webbs and Henderson had agreed that Labour must assume office, offering a moderate programme and presuming unconditional Liberal support. Confirmation came the following night from MacDonald and the rest of the NEC. Owing to apparent apathy among those Liberals with whom he was in contact, Sharp felt obliged to shelve his coalition plea. Nevertheless the *Daily News* did publish an amended version early in January 1924 which infuriated Sidney Webb, first because it appeared under Sharp's own name, and second because it suggested MacDonald would need Liberal help to complete his Cabinet.[75]

A fortnight earlier Sharp was already pointing out to readers that Sidney was no longer chairman, and had been 'for some time in disagreement with us on certain momentarily important issues'. What he really meant, of course, was that Webb had quarrelled with him, and not necessarily the paper as a whole. Nevertheless, a lengthy leader went on to deny that Labour candidates had suffered embarrassment and defeat as a result of the *New Statesman*'s coalition sympathies and belief that Labour's proposal of a capital levy was presently impractical: 'for the views expressed editorially in this journal no official member of the Labour Party is directly or indirectly responsible. We support the Labour Party upon every item of its programme that we regard as practical; but we are independent and intend so to remain.'[76]

While doubtless no candidate could attribute defeat to the *New Statesman*, it was clearly disingenuous to suggest that neither Cole nor Lloyd enjoyed editorial responsibility. Sharp had ultimate responsibility, but in practice Lloyd had a definite influence over policy decisions. It was thanks to him and his next-door neighbour that the paper had not taken the fatal step of wholeheartedly embracing the Independent Liberals. Anticipating an immediate improvement in the 'whole tone and temper of English political life', Sharp kept calling in successive issues for a coalition. When MacDonald finally did form a government on 22 January his decision to combine the premiership with being Foreign Secretary was welcomed by Lloyd and Sharp, and all talk of coalition quietly faded away. Whips were urged to liaise closely, and Labour was advised not to alienate the growing number of left wingers on the backbenches.[77]

Sharp had little option but to shut up once Asquith decided that dealing with the Tories was too risky, and a better tactic was to give Labour plenty of rope with which to hang themselves. The *New Statesman*, or rather its editor, explained that Asquith was a 'very wise man' whose intuitive knowledge of 'the temper of British Liberalism' allowed him to appreciate the average Liberal voter's preference for MacDonald rather than Baldwin. This observation, as inaccurate as it was embarrassing, was already in print when Sir Edward Grey announced that his party was not offering Labour a chance to rule but rather imposing upon the Tories a sabbatical in which to reflect upon recent mistakes.[78]

Particularly impressed by John Wheatley, the 'Red Clydesider' appointed to the Ministry of Health, Sharp at first urged Liberal collaboration with the 'ablest Government we have had for ten years'. Yet in his coverage of Labour's 259 days in office Sharp all too often ignored the wishes of directors clearly sympathetic to the struggling administration. In the spring of 1924 he angered the board by writing another highly provocative commentary for the *Daily News* and signing it as the editor of the *New Statesman*. Arguing that Labour had grown in spite of, and not because of, socialism, Sharp insisted that the 'Liberalism of the average Englishman' made nonsense of MacDonald's declared intention to destroy the one party with a hope of securing a clear majority. The Prime Minister's success at the Foreign Office was unlikely to impress voters as much as the failure to tackle unemployment or housing. Without an immediate coalition or 'definite and close co-operation', the nation was doomed to another hung Parliament, culminating eventually in 'Tory reaction'. As in so many earlier articles, Sharp simply refused to acknowledge fundamental differences between Labour and the Liberals. A startling break from his own editorial policy – greeted with approval by the *Daily News*'s editor but with horror by *New Statesman* readers – was Sharp's view that a minority Liberal administration was preferable to a government which drafted bills acceptable only to the ILP and then amended them drastically in order to secure passage through the Commons. In reality the ILP had precious little influence over policy, other than housing via Wheatley. Also, the notion that Asquith could assume office at the head of a genuinely reforming minority government, let alone expect tacit support from Labour, was absolute nonsense. No wonder the likes of Webb, Williams and Whitley were furious. From now on the editor was living on borrowed time.[79]

Arguably Sharp gave the Prime Minister an easy ride, urging the now familiar Francophobe approach to foreign policy and congratulating him on his diplomatic triumphs in the summer of 1924. Yet high praise was invariably qualified. Thus, the price of Franco-German accord under the terms of the Treaty of London was a dereliction of duties: absence from the House, failure to co-ordinate domestic policies, and approval of his minister of state's Anglo-Russian Treaty.[80] Nevertheless, MacDonald's success in securing mutual acceptance of the Dawes Plan and the French evacuation of the Ruhr marked a clear vindication of Labour's decision to accept office and seek a settlement in Europe:

> by succeeding where all his recent predecessors had failed, he [MacDonald] has earned great credit not only for himself but also

for a Government which in other directions has not been conspicuously successful. Having played for the highest stake and won he can afford to ignore his minor losses.[81]

In September, by which time Labour's honeymoon period was well and truly over, Lloyd and Robert Dell (sacked as Paris correspondent in early 1915 for alleged defeatism, but recruited again in the early 1920s) were nevertheless recording the very favourable impression MacDonald made on his first visit to Geneva.

With Henderson marginalised by yet again losing his seat, and then forced to accept the Home Office against his better judgement, MacDonald took all the credit for raising Britain's profile within the League. To be fair to Sharp, however ungracious his timing, he was right in suggesting that the Prime Minister had failed to spur on those colleagues holding economic portfolios, particularly with regard to the acid test of any Labour administration – providing real jobs. For the first but by no means the last time in its history, the *New Statesman* experienced divided loyalties. What position should a left-of-centre paper adopt when Labour was in power?[82] More immediately, could the *New Statesman* flinch from attacking 'one of its own', in this case its co-founder? Cole was increasingly scathing about Labour's fatalistic view of recovery, yet all too well aware that Sidney Webb was President of the Board of Trade and chairman of the Cabinet committee on unemployment. In May ultimate responsibility for unemployment was transferred to Philip Snowden, of all people. As Chancellor of the Exchequer, Snowden had produced an April budget which had effectively ended any chance of a major public works programme to create jobs. Recommending to the House a finance bill Gladstone would have been proud of, he saw no irony in attracting greater approval from the Opposition benches than from his own: Treasury officials cooed and the City loved it. Seeing Labour's initial performance in the context of Fabianism's 'slowly attained, incomplete and mixed communal control', Beatrice nevertheless acknowledged a policy vacuum over unemployment – for which Sidney, despite remaining part of MacDonald's 'inner circle' (although certainly not his social circle), had paid the price. Labour leaders were at fault in implying, if not asserting, that the prevention of unemployment was an easy and rapid task instead of being a difficult and slow business involving many complicated transactions and far more control of capitalist enterprise than any one has yet worked out.[83]

Meanwhile Snowden revealed himself as privately sharing Sharp's view – by the late summer of 1924 being regularly voiced in the *Evening Standard* – that socialism was dead and Labour's leaders were in reality Liberals. Arguing that the likes of MacDonald and Snowden were no longer socialists could of course be judged unusually perceptive, and plenty of ILP backbenchers would have muttered endorsement. But to claim a huge ideological vacuum on the left was another matter. What was especially prescient was Beatrice's conclusion that 'if circumstances pointed the way – if the fortunes of Liberalism rose, and those of Labour declines – the Snowdens [sic] might be found in a Liberal Cabinet'.[84] Six years later Snowden found himself among all but a handful of Liberals in a National Government. Eventually this unreconstructed (and during the August 1931 crisis unrepentant) free-trader resigned rather than accept even the most diluted form of economic nationalism.[85]

Cole and Lloyd were clearly uneasy about criticising a struggling administration, and at first deliberately played down ILP unease over MacDonald's hesitant approach to 'constructive socialism': conference recognised that abolishing capitalism was a 'slow and carefully thought-out process'. Their patience strained by Snowden's budget, the two leader-writers saw his ineffectual handling of unemployment as confirmation that here was a one-time man of the left seduced by Treasury orthodoxy: to create jobs, why not follow Wheatley's example over municipal housing and circumvent Whitehall opposition by drawing upon party not civil service ideas? Almost every issue throughout July and August called on the government to announce its plans for tackling unemployment. The Unemployment Insurance Bill and the notion of funding increased relief through rationalisation were applauded as temporary initiatives pending Labour's belated adoption of a medium-term economic strategy. Lloyd's over-riding concern was whether Snowden was now so easily swayed by his officials that he might approve the Bank of England's request for sterling to return to the gold standard at its pre-war parity. Clearly influenced by

Keynes, Lloyd rightly surmised that such a move would be highly deflationary, as events a year later confirmed.[86]

Throughout 1923 and 1924 Lloyd's articles on the economy had often echoed what Keynes was writing at the same time in the *Nation*, particularly his argument against a return to the gold standard in all but very exceptional circumstances. Keynes believed that the free flow of gold would force Britain to inflate and deflate at the same rate as elsewhere in the developed world, thus sacrificing the advantage of domestic price stability that could be secured by empowering the Bank of England to control the clearing banks' reserves – and thereby determine directly the supply of credit, and indirectly the level of economic activity. This was a period in which Keynes was writing prolifically on monetary policy, with the ideas first floated in the *Nation* and the Reconstruction Supplements of the *Manchester Guardian Commercial* developed at greater length in *A Tract on Monetary Reform*, first published in December 1923. Lloyd would have been familiar with the literature, and with the furious debate Keynes engaged in with another LSE Fabian, Edwin Cannan. An Oxford economist and a veteran socialist, Cannan rejected the notion that banks could fuel credit provision and defended the gold standard as an infallible means of controlling money supply. Keynes denied the gold standard could regulate inflation simply by limiting the issue of cash, and thereby determining the level of public expenditure: this was too narrow a view of how spending could be controlled. Answering Cannan's critique of the *Tract*, Keynes insisted, in Skidelsky's words, that 'the volume of business activity and to a large extent the quantity of money itself are jointly determined by the community's spending, or what he would later call "effective demand"'. In the summer of 1924 Cannan and Keynes presented conflicting evidence to the Committee on the Currency and Bank of England Note Issues. This high-powered committee, initially under Austen Chamberlain's chairmanship, had been established on Treasury advice by MacDonald and Snowden, both of whom anticipated a final recommendation that sterling should be again fixed to gold. Keynes's advice that such a step would be highly deflationary was repeated in the next issue of the *Nation*, as well as noted by Lloyd in the *New Statesman*.[87]

Lloyd's articles suggest an equally keen interest in Keynes's support for state intervention to shift British savings from foreign and imperial investment to capital construction at home. With unemployment firmly stuck at 10 per cent, the economy needed a kick-start. True, a prerequisite of increased domestic investment was renewed business confidence; but this should be brought about by *lowering* the rate of interest, and in particular by easing credit facilities for securing new capital equipment. The case had already been made in the *Tract* for credit control to stabilise prices, thereby providing further encouragement for potential investors. However, Keynes now considered private enterprise as no longer in a position to generate recovery by itself: it needed to forge a partnership with the public sector. Thus a further stimulus for investment would be to spend £100 million on funding major capital projects – housing, roads, electrification. Supporting Lloyd George's appeal in the *Nation* for a programme of public works, Keynes calculated that up to 100,000 jobs could be created by using the Sinking Fund and other budget surpluses to encourage public *and* private investment in Britain rather than to repay loans from overseas.[88]

Lloyd was clearly impressed by what was appearing in the *New Statesman*'s nearest rival. In consequence, he found himself endorsing the case for public intervention being made by Lloyd George and the Liberal Summer School economists, while elsewhere in the paper Sharp was still fantasising about Asquith and Grey reclaiming their lost estates. Note that the editor gave Lloyd and Cole almost complete autonomy to co-ordinate their economic thinking, and in consequence express freely the magazine's jaundiced view of Labour's monetary and employment policies in the summer and autumn of 1924. Sharp had no objection to his main leader-writers criticising MacDonald's administration, nor did he mind such criticism being expressed from an unequivocally socialist perspective: the two men were reliable, and they produced good copy. Beatrice Webb, who in her diary was on the whole surprisingly tolerant of the Coles, given that she disagreed with them over so much, saw an isolated Douglas as paying the price for 'bad comradeship in days gone by':

If there were a real revolutionary movement, I suppose the Coles would be somewhere in it, but they would be distrusted by revolutionaries and anti-revolutionaries alike. . . . He [GDH] is too much of the aristocrat and the anarchist, too childish in his likes and dislikes – he is not an artist – to succeed with an Anglo-Saxon democracy.[89]

Beatrice tempered her remarks by adding a rider to the effect that Cole was wholly lacking in ambition and showed little interest in material gain.[90] He and Margaret were going through a process of painful adjustment, belatedly embracing the realities of humdrum Labour politics in smoke-filled ward offices and conference hotels. As for the shop floor, Cole had never fully understood the reformist priorities of most organised labour, and if he had perhaps he would never have become a guild socialist. Although he was loath to break with the ideals of guild socialism and still deeply suspicious of the state, Cole's collaboration with Lloyd injected a greater sense of realism into his writing. Even when an editorial read more like a seminar paper, there was still a passion in his insistence that the priority for any Labour government must be to provide its natural supporters with work.

As Stephen Howe recognised in his anthology of *New Statesman* writing, Cole's report on the ILP's Summer School was an important insight into his thinking in the dog-days of MacDonald's first administration. Socialism had never been so popular, albeit for many 'a disembodied faith in the soul of a dead idea. . . . Guild Socialism, if it has not secured acceptance for its own schemes, has at any rate made short work of State Socialism in its traditional forms.'[91] For Cole the ILP – 'the pioneering propagandist body of Socialism' – was stuck in an ideological vacuum.[92] Viable policies were formulated, but 'in a strictly empirical and particularist spirit, as if each problem stood by itself and had to be judged by its merits'. Cole lamented the absence of 'a clear unifying principle in the light of which all problems could be seen in their true aspect. In short, in this representative gathering of Socialists, there appeared no common basis of Socialist doctrine.'[93]

The pragmatists, arguing that in present circumstances the government simply had to do the best it could, were outnumbered by those calling for 'a plain declaration of its Socialist faith'. But, asked Cole, if Parliament was challenged to reject 'really Socialist measures', what would those measures be, and *would they really be socialist?* ILP leaders might eventually succeed in finding 'for the old soul of Socialism a new bodily habitation', but any notion of a rigid ideological blueprint could be left to the Communists. The 'new [evolutionary] Socialism, more regardful of the claims of the wage-earner, will be less regardful of vested interests in property', more receptive to fresh ideas from across the political spectrum, and less hostile to 'strange new companionships'. In this respect Cole's report on the travails of the ILP was by no means all doom and gloom, but one can readily understand why Howe drew parallels with Labour's soul-searching in the aftermath of the 1987 defeat.[94]

Cole's article was clearly a lament, but it concluded on an optimistic note and, like so much of his work at this time, was written in a spirit of constructive criticism. The now ageing Young Turk's coming to terms with the constraints of parliamentary politics, but without compromising on the continued importance of idealism underpinned by rigorous intellectual debate, suggests Lloyd's growing influence. A Fabian academic equally at home licking envelopes and standing on doorsteps, Lloyd was the educated middle-class Labour activist *par excellence*. Cole's new-found tolerance reached its apogée in October 1924 when, despite all the disappointments of the preceding 10 months, he gave a guarded welcome to Labour's election manifesto.[95] Labour's achievements in office were, to say the least, modest, and its record on unemployment was lamentable. But the lesson for both Lloyd and Cole – the former especially influenced by Keynes demonstrating again and again that the state did have the capacity to facilitate economic regeneration if the political will was there – was that limited power was better than none at all. With Labour in office there was at least the possibility of action over unemployment, whereas any change of government guaranteed apathy and indifference. Either way, the New Jerusalem would still be a long time coming.

SHARP'S FIRST DISMISSAL, OCTOBER 1924

In an attempt to end Soviet isolation the government had recognised the regime, and secured a trade treaty plus compensation for British holders of bonds from before the Revolution. By early August it was public knowledge that the

Cabinet was split over sanctioning a loan to the Russians, with Snowden particularly hostile. Aware that both opposition parties had also denounced the original deal, MacDonald and Ponsonby pressed on with negotiating a more water-tight agreement. Throughout the protracted negotiations Sharp had dismissed any final treaty as a costly distraction.[96] On this basis in early September he launched a devastating attack on the Prime Minister. The *New Statesman* accused MacDonald of ignoring the advice of ministers, advisers and most MPs by pursuing a policy clearly not in the national interest:

> If his [MacDonald's] signature is dishonoured, as doubtless it will be, he has only himself to blame; but unfortunately he will not be the only sufferer. He will have wantonly destroyed a very valuable material asset, namely the reputation which Great Britain has hitherto possessed for keeping its foreign policy clear of party politics and honouring its bonds.[97]

Much of this was pompous balderdash, but it was an astonishing rebuke of a leader whose surprisingly adroit handling of foreign affairs had won plaudits on both sides of the House – and from Sharp himself. As editor he could over-ride accusations of inconsistency from Lloyd and Cole, but he could scarcely ignore the fact that a major shareholder and co-founder of the *New Statesman* was a senior minister in MacDonald's government.

Webb was no great admirer of his leader, but no-one would have accused him of betraying confidences. It was common knowledge that ministers were unhappy about credit to the Russians, and anyway Sidney had been generally impressed by MacDonald's performance in office. According to Beatrice, he had 'altogether surpassed our expectations as a brilliant politician and competent statesman'.[98] Praise indeed from someone who over the years had more often loathed than loved Lossiemouth's most famous son. Sharp clearly gave no thought to the embarrassment he was causing Sidney Webb because he kept on attacking the Russian loan until Parliament reconvened. September was a difficult month for the Prime Minister following his admittance that Sir Alexander Grant, a lifelong friend and chairman of McVitie and Price, had provided a car and chauffeur plus running costs funded by shares in his biscuit company. Grant's baronetcy was wrongly interpreted in some newspapers as the price of his generosity. The incorruptible image of Labour – and most especially of its leader – was without doubt tarnished, compounding the damage inflicted by the Campbell case.[99] Although Lloyd George was deeply hostile to any deal with Russia, ministers hoped to calm an increasingly frenetic situation by getting Asquith to accept postponement of ratification until the next Parliament. On 22 September the Liberal leader publicly rejected any compromise, fuelling speculation around Great Queen Street that Sharp, a guest at Sutton Courtney throughout September, was a party to his decision. Labour could no longer rely on the Liberals' support in the Commons, but Sharp could have had no idea that their call for a select committee to investigate the Campbell case would be linked to a Tory motion of censure and thus be treated by MacDonald as a matter of confidence. Defeated by 364 votes to 198, the Prime Minister sought a dissolution and a general election on 29 October.

The first Labour government left office, not in a blaze of glory over a matter of principle, but over a rather tawdry matter which reflected badly on everyone involved. Allied to this was a treaty for which few but Downing Street, the Foreign Office and the CPGB had a good word to say. The irony was that, despite repeatedly denouncing any deal with Bolshevik Russia, Sharp defended the Attorney General's decision to drop charges against Campbell. In his view only the Communists would gain from the publicity, and complete freedom of the press was a luxury which Britain could still afford.[100] This was small comfort to any Labour supporter who felt the *New Statesman* had in its own small way contributed to the departure from office of a party which readers had been encouraged to vote for, albeit with varying degrees of enthusiasm, since 1918 – and which was to be endorsed again on the eve of the poll in October 1924. Repeated assertions of independence could not camouflage obvious contradictions and inconsistencies in the paper's editorial line. Something had to be done, and the onus was on the board to take action speedily and even ruthlessly.

On 11 October Sharp's fierce criticism of MacDonald culminated in a 'furiously malignant attack' which Beatrice Webb attributed to his being drunk when he wrote it.[101] Blithely ignoring the fuss surrounding the Russian treaty, Sharp acknowledged MacDonald's 'immense success' at the Foreign Office before dismissing him as an 'utter failure' as prime minister – a man vain, over-sensitive, suspect in a crisis, ungenerous to the Liberals, and above all deeply jealous of H.H. Asquith. This astonishing tirade concluded by finding MacDonald's conference speech hysterical, despicable, nonsensical and clear evidence of a party leader of suspect integrity who, if he insisted on an election, should never again enjoy office. Readers were confused by reading an editorial overtaken by events – and accompanied by an enthusiastic call from Cole for all conference decisions to be incorporated into Labour's manifesto.[102]

Sidney Webb was now in an even more invidious position. He immediately resigned his directorship, as from the previous January; a decision Whitley privately regretted in the absence of an emergency board meeting. Whitley wrote to Webb explaining that he and Williams had already made clear to Sharp their deep disapproval of an article written 'in very bad taste'. However, the chairman was reluctant to change editor as he feared the *New Statesman* would become a 'Labour paper pure and simple', and as such preach only to the converted. Hedley Le Bas later convinced Williams that his fears would be groundless. Whitley meanwhile agreed on the need for the magazine to remain independent of Labour, but by means of 'kindly and fair criticism as of a father or elder brother and not stabs in the back and hitting below the belt'. In his view, such 'great possibilities' necessitated Sharp's departure if the *New Statesman* was not to become an unequivocally pro-Liberal organ once directors such as himself had retired.[103]

Lloyd, acting as spokesman for the staff, felt torn between loyalty to Sharp, who in his capacity as editor had a right freely to criticise Labour, and sympathy for Whitley's view that the *New Statesman*'s survival necessitated a general statement of support for the party. Both Lloyd and Cole at first intended to resign, Sharp having broken a promise that the first draft of his leader would be rewritten in the light of their criticism (he conceded his judgement had been 'clouded by fatigue', or what today we would describe as 'tired and emotional': drunk). Instead, they agreed to remain and 'rescue' the paper. Angry readers as well as angry writers forced Sharp to publish a more balanced editorial in the next issue, accompanied by heavily pro-Labour contributions from Cole and Sisley Huddleston.[104] Lloyd was still unhappy, but he accepted that a total *volte-face* was impossible overnight. All he could do was hope that

> the unholy alliance between the Tories and the Liberals will have its effect in weakening his [Sharp's] anti-Labour and pro-Liberal attitudes. He maintains that his attitudes are not really pro-Liberal; but . . . it *seems* so to all the world – and in effect, appearance becomes reality.[105]

Convinced that Sharp was about to be dismissed, Lloyd interrupted an emergency board meeting and, in a dramatic and really quite remarkable display of loyalty, paid tribute on behalf of all the *New Statesman* staff to an editor of 'invaluable efficiency'. Clifford Sharp had made his paper a 'great institution', and with hindsight he now saw that a political weekly could be both independent and a 'Socialist journal in the broad, reasonable, critical, common sense meaning of Socialism'. Lloyd argued that the directors were being unfair to Sharp in leaving him free for 11 years to determine editorial policy, and then suddenly dismissing him – with minimal staff consultation – because they disapproved of a particular article. There was, in Lloyd's opinion, a far greater risk of losing readers as a result of sacking Sharp than as a consequence of retaining him.[106] This intervention, reminiscent of staff discontent over the departures of Bruce Page and Stuart Weir in the 1980s and of a semi-public campaign in 1994 to ensure the renewal of Steve Platt's contract, was well-intentioned but quite clearly wrong.[107] How often over the next six years did Mostyn Lloyd regret defending a man who, for all his love of the *New Statesman – his* paper – was no longer up to the job. Sharp needed help and support, but simply pretending that his attack on MacDonald was an aberration, and that at heart all was well, was as unfair to him as it was to the magazine itself. There was at least one director who recognised this. Although Williams was sympathetic, Hedley Le Bas rightly questioned Lloyd's ability to restrain Sharp and regain Labour's confidence in the paper. As the board had already decided on a successor, Le Bas insisted that fellow directors adhere to an earlier decision to secure Sharp's resignation. This decision had been agreed over lunch by all but Bennett, and had not been affected by the present editor's spirited defence of his actions at the commencement of the meeting.[108]

The discussion in its entirety lasted three hours, and on the two occasions when Sharp was present became particularly heated. There is some evidence to suggest that Le Bas, a business associate of MacDonald, was determined from the outset to install a new regime at Great Queen Street. He disputed Sharp's claim, as the man who had successfully launched the *New Statesman*, to have some say in its future: this was the prerogative of the shareholders. Le Bas also rejected a claim for heavy financial compensation. What he was not prepared for was Sharp's unexpected offer to buy all the shares at par, and the other directors' subsequent agreement to adjourn the meeting for 14 days. Sharp immediately wrote to Sidney Webb, confident of his support in raising the cash to buy out Whitley and Williams, and then regain the confidence of the other shareholders. Although he was not explicit about his final intentions when writing to Webb, presumably Sharp hoped to isolate Le Bas and offer him no alternative other than to sell his stake in the company. This was a ridiculous scenario as Sharp had no chance of raising sufficient money, and the board should have squashed the idea at the outset. Webb was aware that claims of easy access to capital were totally spurious, and there is no evidence that he even acknowledged Sharp's letter. Instead, he chose to take Sharp at his word when he claimed to be totally indifferent to the outcome, and in actual fact sacrificing a desire to travel for the sake of old loyalties. Here was a rather pitiable figure, but if even these pathetic claims had helped stir old emotions there was nothing Sidney could do, or wished to do: he had no spare cash to invest, he had no desire to return to the board, and he had no incentive to do so if Sharp would still not guarantee Labour wholehearted support.[109]

Granted a fortnight's reprieve, Sharp and Lloyd collaborated on a pre-election issue which expressly called for the return of a Labour government with a working majority in the Commons, and equally clearly denounced those Liberals supporting the Tories' anti-socialist crusade. On 25 October 1924 *The Times* reproduced the front-page denial of an official Labour Party statement that the *New Statesman* was now controlled by 'a group of influential Liberals'. Meanwhile, even Le Bas and Whitley were impressed by a letter from staff and regular contributors affirming their support for the present editor, and their intention to resume the Tuesday lunches in order to ensure 'regular consultation about matters of political policy'. This was coded language for ensuring Sharp would not go off the rails again. A long talk with Lloyd made a deep impression on Williams, but ironically Sharp's real saviour was Shaw. Nearly 10 years later he recalled with gratitude how 'G.B.S. came to my moral rescue in a most generous fashion' by interceding on his behalf.[110] Shaw's lobbying of Williams and Webb was a major factor in the decision to reinstate Sharp, despite directors' suspicion that his farcical endeavour to launch a boardroom coup was merely a delaying tactic. Sharp noted with great magnanimity that 'they did it very charmingly. So that the question of buying them out does not arise'.[111] Glynne Williams painted a very different picture: when informed his notice of dismissal was being withdrawn Sharp was visibly relieved and embarrassingly penitent, even when Bennett insisted that he could no longer boost his income by writing for the *Evening Standard* in his capacity as *New Statesman* editor. No doubt he was also warned to keep off the bottle, and an improvement in the quality of his copy at this time suggests temperance, albeit temporary, as well as repentance.[112]

Sharp had encouraged his chances of reinstatement with an unusually astute post-election assessment of Baldwin and his potential for reviving a strong 'two nations' Tory tradition. Although ostensibly the Conservatives had won because of voter dissatisfaction with minority government (a spurious claim, but all part of 'the healing process'), the new prime minister was 'a very honest and humane and straightforward politician, and in certain respects is far ahead of his own party in his understanding of the realities of modern politics and of the necessity of dealing drastically with evil social conditions'.[113] Sharp noted sadly the Paisley voters' ungenerous treatment of 'unquestionably the greatest figure in English [*sic*] political life', but his remarks were far more muted than might have been expected: an expression of regret, no more. There was even tacit acceptance that MacDonald had the satisfaction of knowing the Liberal MPs were now little more than an 'impotent faction' too often at odds with their new leader.[114] On 6 December 1924 the *New Statesman* announced that its net sales for the previous month were 11,562, and exceeded by only one other sixpenny weekly (the *Spectator*). Was there ever a more appropriate moment at which to overtake the

Nation in the battle for the hearts and minds of the nation's progressive intelligentsia? The irony, of course, was that as both a political and literary review the *Nation* under Henderson was in the mid-1920s far superior to the *New Statesman*; and, as was to be expected, was far more innovative in promoting macro-economic policy. In urging the Labour government to take action on unemployment, Lloyd applauded the practical application of Keynes's ideas, but he rarely contributed any original thought of his own.

LABOUR'S EFFORTS TO PURCHASE A POLITICAL WEEKLY, 1925

There is a postscript to the story of Labour's first experience of power, and of the mutual suspicion between Fleet Street and Downing Street that culminated in the furore surrounding the Zinoviev letter.[115] Throughout his period in office MacDonald regularly complained about lack of support from the *Daily Herald* and the *New Leader*, let alone the *New Statesman*. Even before Sharp's tirade against him, the Prime Minister had warned Brailsford at a rare meeting that he was 'very sick of the Labour press. It has been conducted by men who seem to have misunderstood their position that they assumed they were Government & movement in one.'[116] This brief note in MacDonald's diary offers an insight into his perception of the relationship between Labour's leaders once in office and the rest of the movement which they had had almost by design to leave behind: the familiar tension of national and party interests.

Once the general election was over and Labour were again in opposition, MacDonald found time to launch a syndicate, including the veteran journalist Sir Robert Donald and the ex-minister and NUR leader Jimmy Thomas, a man handy to advise on shifting newspapers but scarcely an expert on how to secure them. The intention was to counter the irresponsible and misrepresentative reporting of the Liberal press, and 'enable the real Party point of view to be expressed'.[117] Much time was wasted on trying to buy *Reynold's News*, but for eight months in 1925 'an inordinate amount of time and energy' was taken up by a scheme of Le Bas to secure a controlling interest in the most obvious and the most vulnerable of the political weeklies.[118] MacDonald first informed Sidney Webb of his intention to acquire the *New Statesman* on 7 April, and was given every encouragement. Webb offered assistance and advice but pointed out that he studiously avoided Sharp, being 'wholly out of sympathy with his product which, besides being utterly unappreciative of the Labour Party, is now hard and wooden and sterile'.[119]

With Whitley willing to sell, Le Bas was confident of buying out Harben's much smaller interest. Meanwhile, despite Webb's confident expectation that the chairman would dispose of the 53 management shares necessary to finalise control, Williams delayed any final decision until September, when he sold only half his holding. Two months later Williams announced his retirement from the board, and Le Bas, who had resigned over Sharp's reinstatement, again became a director. Unlike Sharp's fantasies, this really was a boardroom coup. Having personally financed all transactions, except the sale of E.D. Simon's shares for which Donald drew on his own capital, Le Bas returned MacDonald's cheque for £500, a rather modest amount given that the estimated cost of gaining control of the *New Statesman* was at least £6,000.[120] This was when the Labour leader first realised that his personal involvement had been exploited to the advantage, not of the party, but of individual members of the consortium. So long as MacDonald naively anticipated a *New Statesman* trust analogous to that of the *Manchester Guardian*, the original shareholders had assumed that Le Bas was acting on his instructions and with his full approval.[121] In reality, Le Bas was working to his own agenda. Once the dust had settled the only tangible benefit for the Labour Party was the election to the board of H.B. Lees-Smith, a colleague of Lloyd at the LSE and a close friend of MacDonald, who in 1929 appointed him President of the Board of Education. Not surprisingly, Lees-Smith supported Le Bas's renewed call for a revitalised and revamped *New Statesman*, offering a more overtly pro-Labour message, and appealing to a much broader audience.[122] Given Le Bas's obvious determination to secure a major shareholding in the company, by fair means or foul, it is puzzling that he did not maintain the momentum and insist that the editor should now go. It was obvious that the kind of paper he envisaged would never emerge so long as Sharp remained at Great Queen

G. Bernard Shaw phot.   Emery Walker Ph. sc.

Beatrice Webb

1. Beatrice Webb photographed by GBS

2.   Sidney Webb as a cabinet minister, 1924

3.   George Bernard Shaw, 'the principal shareholder'

4. Nick Garland's 1973 *New Statesman* caricature of the Webbs and GBS

THE NEW
STATESMAN
A Weekly Review of Politics and Literature

VOL. I. No. I.]　　　　SATURDAY, APRIL 12, 1913　[REGISTERED AT THE G.P.O. AS A NEWSPAPER.]　[SIXPENCE

CONTENTS

All MSS. and letters relating thereto should be addressed to the Editor, at 10 Great Queen Street, Kingsway, London, W.C.

THOSE who would have it that we are a nation of sentimentalists will never find a more conclusive demonstration of their proposition than that which has been provided by the British Press during the past week in its comments on the coercion of Montenegro. We are, most of us, of course, so abysmally ignorant with regard to foreign affairs that sentiment is always apt to have more than its proper share of influence in the determination of our views about them; but usually, when we are offered a choice of views, there is one that is much more obviously sentimental than the rest. In the present controversy, however, this distinction is wanting. In point of sentiment there seems to be nothing to pick between the two opposing parties.

*　　　*　　　*

The issue is as to who shall have Scutari. The larger party, which supports the Montenegrin claim, begs us to remember that it was Montenegro which for centuries alone upheld the banner of Christianity in the Balkan peninsula, that it was Montenegro which fired the first shot in this war against the unspeakable Turk, that it is Montenegro which so far has suffered the heaviest losses and made the fewest acquisitions, and last but not least, that it was Montenegro—not Albania—which inspired some of the finest poems of the late Lord Tennyson. On the other side it is urged by individuals claiming to have made personal inspection of the nationalities of the inhabitants of Scutari that it is an Albanian town—by a substantial majority—and that consequently to hand it over to Montenegro would be to violate the most fundamental of national rights. We need not stay to inquire what, if this doctrine be accepted, will have to be done

about Quebec, Hongkong, Pretoria, Calcutta, Belfast and the rest. Nor need we anticipate the probable unwillingness of the Albanian tribesmen to be formed into anything that could be described as an autonomous nation. All these things are for the moment, at all events, beside the point. The outstanding fact in the situation, the only fact that can possibly weigh with those who are responsible for determining British action, is that Austria has put her foot down.

*　　　*　　　*

The conflict which rages round the possession of Scutari is indeed at bottom a question of race, but the races concerned are the Austrians and the Slavs, not the Montenegrins and the Albanians. Austria, who sees her Empire, her very existence, threatened by the successes of the young Slav nations, has hitherto allowed her bellicose impulses to be curbed by the Great Powers (*Les Grandes Impuissances* as they have been irreverently termed on the other side of the Balkans ever since they forbade the war last autumn). She has seen the Slavs of Bulgaria established in territory within a few dozen miles of the gates of Constantinople, she has seen the Slavs of Servia spread southwards to the Aegean Sea, she has seen the coveted road to Salonika closed to her for ever; and she has submitted. But, to see the Slavs of Montenegro in possession of Scutari and the adjacent Adriatic coast is, if we are to believe Sir Edward Grey, more than she is prepared to stand. She will rather fight. That being so, there is no more to be said. Europe is not going to war over Scutari, even though the sympathies of every nation except Austria are with " gallant little Montenegro." The claims of sentiment in this affair, as we have seen, cancel each other out, and we may therefore with an easy conscience allow ourselves to be guided by common sense.

6. Clifford Sharp, pioneer editor

7. Arnold Bennett – drawn
   for the *New Statesman*
   by his successor as
   director, David Low

Arnold Bennett

8. Lloyd George – Low's
   portrait of Sharp's
   erstwhile enemy

9. H.H. Asquith, Lord Oxford – Sharp included his post-war hero in the 1926 supplements

10. Ramsay MacDonald – in opposition again after 1924, he sought to buy the magazine

11. 'YY' – Irish patriot, man of letters and regular columnist, Robert Lynd

12. Low's 1933 caricature of John Maynard Keynes, *New Statesman and Nation* chairman

13. David Low's memory of
    Kingsley Martin

14. Kingsley Martin –
    synonymous with the
    'Staggers & Naggers'

15. Leonard Woolf and Virginia Woolf, 1940 – one lauded Martin, and one loathed him

16. Richard Crossman – a key figure in late 1930s successes and early 1970s disappointments

Street, drunk or sober. Yet nothing happened, and the *New Statesman* carried on drifting – arguably, so too did the Labour Party.

8

'Literature is news that STAYS news' (Ezra Pound): The *New Statesman* as a literary review

ESTABLISHING A CRITICAL REPUTATION – OR NOT: JACK SQUIRE AND DESMOND MACCARTHY

Leonard Woolf recalled Sharp as rivalling the Webbs in his indifference to the creative arts, but he was always keen on reviewing and he had the good sense to leave Jack Squire alone.[1] Although well aware that Beatrice Webb thoroughly disapproved of employing such a raffish character as himself, Squire relished the prospect of a permanent base from which to observe the activities of a narrowly metropolitan English literary scene. His successor, Desmond MacCarthy, was equally enthusiastic about being ensconced in Great Queen Street, and it is with the very heavily qualified achievements of these two men of letters that much of this chapter is concerned.

Although it is hard to imagine today, through his 'Books in General' column Squire quickly established a reputation as a very readable and even a faintly provocative *belle-lettriste*, eager to promote his own poetry but more especially that of his contemporaries. From the outset he published regular literary supplements as an opportunity for well established writers to float new ideas and for young talent to see their work in print. Ironically he himself was best known as a parodist, and his widely quoted 'How They Do It' series established a great *New Statesman* tradition, maintained over the years by veterans of the weekly competition such as E.O. Parrott, Martin Fagg and poacher-turned-gamekeeper Roger Woddis. Sharp considered Squire the 'best parodist since Calverley', and admiring readers often mistook his verse for the real thing. When *The Three Hills and Other Poems* appeared later in 1913 Squire ended 'How They Do It' on the grounds that critics (quite rightly) refused to treat him as a serious poet.[2]

Squire thrived on the cabalistic, incestuous world of the Georgians. As we have seen in his dealings with Bennett, he cultivated the established literary elite of the Café Royal and the Reform Club, at first drawing heavily upon contacts established at Cambridge and through working with Orage. Fiercely proud of his chosen profession as a man of letters, Squire maintained until the end of his life that academics rarely proved sound critics of contemporary literature, where the trick was to recognise at once those few works likely to stand the test of time.[3] With hindsight, of course, Squire and his regular reviewers' track record in spotting classics, especially novels, was abysmal. But it was precisely this smugness which in Cambridge in the 1920s, in a pre-*Scrutiny* era, so infuriated I.A. Richards, F.R. and Q.D. Leavis, and other Young Turks – and which a later *New Statesman* literary editor categorically rejected.[4] However, as befits someone who has held a university chair and founded the *London Review of Books*, Karl Miller has also voiced the opinion that, by encouraging difficult writers and uncovering fresh talent, a 'properly conducted weekly need yield nothing in point of authority to any academic periodical'.[5] According to Raymond Mortimer, Sharp established a largely time-honoured principle of giving the literary editor his or her head, while insisting on a final, and often rigorous, scrutiny of the whole paper before going to press. Squire, of course, relished such freedom.[6]

We should not exaggerate the Edwardians' 'cosy, impressionistic, quasi-autobiographical' approach to the demands of weekly journalism, best epitomised by Bennett, whose influential *Evening Standard* column Q.D. Leavis later dismissed so scornfully in *Fiction and the Reading Public*.[7] A clichéd image of the Georgians as intellectual cripples, hidebound by the loyalties and conventions of minor public school and Oxbridge, too easily calls to mind Cyril

Connolly's dictum that critics who regularly declared their integrity 'discover one day that in a sense their whole life is an accepted bribe, a fabric of compromise'. These were men (overwhelmingly men) not entirely seduced by the country-weekend lifestyle.[8] The young Jack Squire was never an urbane, adroit, witty but ultimately shallow character from a Saki short story – if only because he was too eccentric for that. In later life he may have over-indulged in *avant le déluge* golden-age day-dreams, but in 1913 he could still pose as the self-disciplined, rational Fabian – the professional journalist assuming the editorship in 1917 so smoothly that most readers failed to spot the change. Squire was the confidant of both publisher and author, a charming sportsman (if not *quite* a thorough gentleman) effortlessly placating literary agents while their versifying clients awaited a guinea cheque.[9] None of this of course made Squire a better critic, but it did serve to refute charges of other-worldliness. If after Sharp's call-up he ever felt an intruder in the wartime world of high politics, his feelings towards the literary establishment were clearly quite different. Any sense of awe was easily disguised.

Under the influence of first Orage and then Bennett, Squire acknowledged, however reluctantly, that his review had to be metropolitan *and* cosmopolitan. His first supplement deliberately set out to counter allegations of smug insularity. For example, following Bennett's earlier championing of Dostoevsky in the *New Age*, MacCarthy similarly lauded Blok and Chekhov. Short stories by the latter, and by D.H. Lawrence, appeared in early issues, as did work by Marinetti and his fellow Futurists (albeit accompanied by a disclaimer, stating that their views were in no way representative of those held by the *New Statesman*).[10] Similarly, 'Books in General' prefaced criticism of Post-Impressionism and of the Cubists with a clear and balanced explanation of respective techniques and intentions. Hyams suggested that this ability to acknowledge, but inability to identify with, Modernism in the raw was an inevitable consequence of a cultural milieu rooted in amateurism. That, in effect, Squire and his ilk were intellectual dilettantes incapable of developing their critical faculties beyond mere interest. Hyams depicted them as unashamedly English men-about-town or country gentlemen incapable of agreeing upon what he mysteriously labelled a 'policy', which one can only assume to be a uniformly positive response to new ideas from across the Channel.[11] This is surely too neat an explanation: it offers a caricature of Squire and his colleagues, and it assumes a wholesale receptivity to 'The Shock of the New' scarcely evident in London before the onset of war. The real irony, even paradox, is that to writers only a novel or slim volume of verse away from the Edwardian equivalent of Grub Street, and whose very livelihoods were dependent upon brisk sales and editors' whims, it was the *avant-garde* who so often appeared unbusinesslike, amateurish and perhaps even out-moded. Squire could admire the sacrifices a writer such as Joyce was prepared to make in the interest of artistic integrity, but the eventual outcome appeared to him a creative cul-de-sac. Most young writers were journeymen not geniuses. Success meant popularity and acclamation by one's peers, but that success had to be earned – and what better way to start than as a humble reviewer?

MacCarthy and Randall Davies were respectively the magazine's first drama and art critics, and their reviews were invariably devoted to a single production or exhibition, or even to defending a previous week's comments.[12] MacCarthy had joined the *Speaker* in 1903, but when it became the *Nation* four years later Massingham – to his later regret – sacked him, along with Lytton Strachey. It was while he was working freelance for Hilaire Belloc's *Eye Witness* that MacCarthy got to know Squire. In late 1912 he met Sharp for the first time when the Webbs, probably on Shaw's recommendation, invited him down to Sussex. That weekend Sidney defined for MacCarthy their respective roles as writers and commentators: 'We are interested in the drains and stopping dry rot in the house; you in its decoration'.[13] Despite openly admitting his 'remarkable ignorance' of social questions and the current state of the economy, MacCarthy met with approval from Sidney and Beatrice. They recognised that his heart was in the right place. The archetypal rational English liberal, he refused to accept the inevitability of poverty and deprivation, even if he did little to further the cause of social justice. Arguably the cornerstone of Bloomsbury, he was at one time even closer to the Fabians than Woolf, albeit never sharing the latter's commitment to genuine political struggle. MacCarthy characterised his political philosophy as a begrudging acceptance that a limited curtailment of individual liberties was necessary for the overall benefit of society. Activism was eschewed on the grounds that campaigning for social change in the body politic necessitated a sharp focus on the dissemination of the good things in life – as opposed to just their identification and praise.[14]

Four years after despatching his first copy, MacCarthy found himself describing the 'moving and august' spectacle of Labour's London conference on events in Russia. The very word 'Labour' radiated a mysterious aura, with all its

> hopes for humanity, fears for much that makes life delightful to me, the righting of enormous wrongs and the infliction of many individuals with whom my nature is in sympathy, the possibility of a dull, lustreless civilization, but the only chance of a really noble and dignified one.[15]

Not much sign here of rushing to the barricades. If this was the dilemma of the cultured bourgeois then it is scarcely surprising that MacCarthy retreated to Sussex and Gordon Square as soon as idealism looked like becoming reality. Apart from Woolf and Keynes, this air of benign resignation became increasingly common within Bloomsbury, the other notable exception being Clive Bell. The egalitarian society would be a dull world for the aesthete, and the dry detachment and austere spirit of Sharp's prose served as a salutary reminder to MacCarthy, Lynd and, indeed, Jack Squire, that even the driest wit was dispensable.[16] Woolf later observed that the tone and style of his unsigned articles invariably matched whichever editor had commissioned them, whether it be Sharp or Massingham. When writing he found himself subconsciously acknowledging that both men were wholly different in 'temperament, style and editorial methods', and tailored his articles accordingly.[17] MacCarthy shared the same experience, recalling later that:

> Both papers often advocated the same views, but while *The Nation* supplied arguments which encouraged its readers to feel that they were the salt of the earth, the tone of the *Statesman* in arguing the same point would be 'If you want to escape being a short-sighted fool, this is the line you must take'.[18]

This captures the spirit of Sharp's paper perfectly.

Both F.R. and Q.D. Leavis of course loathed anyone and anything connected with Bloomsbury. For them MacCarthy was the walking embodiment of 'an age in which there were no serious standards current'. He and his friends represented that 'small modish literary world' of 'belletristic subjectivism' which the Leavises, along with I.A. Richards, held responsible for the absence of a popular consciousness sympathetic to *modern* poetry – as opposed to the undemanding, reassuringly nostalgic, pastoral lyricism of the Georgians.[19] This was unashamedly English poetry which to the Leavisite critic was parochial, technically slack, too often banal in its choice of subject, and above all insultingly easy to understand. It mattered little that Virginia Woolf viewed the work of Edward Marsh and Squire's shrinking band of obsolete lyricists with similar disdain. Not that MacCarthy had much contact with the best-known of the Georgian poets. His relationship with Squire was almost entirely professional; they moved in totally different circles. All his life MacCarthy was the would-be novelist who never fulfilled the promise of youth – the biographer of Byron for ever in search of that final definitive source. Lacking in self-discipline and a victim of his own popularity among the 'Bloomsberries', he used his review deadlines to excuse the absence of serious writing and serious thought. Equally damning of the likes of David Garnett and Raymond Mortimer, Queenie Leavis drew no distinction between MacCarthy and the next generation of a Bloomsbury *côterie* she judged wholly unqualified, if only by virtue of their class and connections, to recognise and promote important and innovative work. She accused the weekly press of further debasing cultural standards by imposing transient literary modes on – and thereby hastening the demise of – a 'reading public' at one time capable itself of establishing the very highest standards in contemporary taste.[20]

Reflecting on MacCarthy's apparent indolence in 1919, Virginia Woolf concluded that pleasure had slowly subverted his ambition. Half a century later Leonard Woolf suggested that MacCarthy had been unduly influenced by G.E. Moore's *Principia Ethica*, setting himself impossibly high standards. According to this generous explanation, MacCarthy was too plagued by his own doubts and inadequacies to last the course, so he turned to reviews and short stories as an acceptable alternative.[21] Whatever his excuse, MacCarthy carved himself a reputation in interwar London as a powerful and influential critic. With the passage of time he became the target of increasingly bitter attacks by those pioneers of the Cambridge English School indignant over the *New Statesman's* failure to rise above its more mediocre weekly rivals. A forlorn hope that MacCarthy's arts pages could emulate the pioneering critical work of Ford Madox Ford's pre-war *English Review* or Edgell Rickword's short-lived *Calendar of Modern Letters* was precisely that – forlorn.[22] The *New Statesman* was a wholly different animal from an overtly literary review. Despite all those subscribers whose reading supposedly started with the letters and ended with the classified ads, the front half of the magazine always determined overall editorial content, and in consequence identity; it was Clifford Sharp's paper, not Desmond MacCarthy's, or even Jack Squire's. Kingsley Martin could have every confidence in a V.S. Pritchett or a Raymond Mortimer, and each of them undoubtedly left an indelible impression, but no-one would wish to argue that the 'Staggers and Naggers' should be assessed primarily in terms of its contribution to the cultural life of mid-century Britain.

Unlike his Bloomsbury contemporaries MacCarthy had seen active service during the First World War. He served briefly with the Red Cross in Flanders in late 1914, and spent a further five months on the Western Front in the spring of 1915. It was at this time that Sharp published eight articles based on MacCarthy's experience with the BEF. In his history of the *New Statesman* Hyams wrongly implied that MacCarthy was overseas for the remaining three years of the war, when in fact he served at home in the Royal Navy. Working for Naval Intelligence inside the Admiralty left him time to carry on reviewing plays. After the Armistice MacCarthy resolved to resign his commission as soon as possible, and succeed Squire once the latter had enough sponsorship to establish his planned monthly review, the *London Mercury*. He confided in Virginia Woolf: '"I [MacCarthy] know so many people who write well" he said; if that were all, he would make a perfect editor.'[23]

In January 1920, newly appointed on an annual salary of £500, a jubilant MacCarthy discussed with friends a variety of innovations, including the very minor change of adopting 'Affable Hawk' as a pseudonym for the notes that made up 'Books in

General' (Bennett wrote as 'Jacob Tonson' if ever asked to contribute, and Squire even published anthologies under his *nom de plume* of 'Solomon Eagle', originally a lunatic in seventeenth-century London; when Sean French established a similar column in May 1994 he wisely chose not to follow tradition). 'Books in General' had been a mixture of literary gossip and Squire's highly idiosyncratic but nevertheless entertaining commentary on the current state of the arts. Like Bennett and Orage, Squire had seized his opportunity to promote previously unknown talent. MacCarthy, on the other hand, chose to be a lot less gossipy, often devoting the whole page to a single subject. Sensing that editorial duties had 'drugged the remnants of ambition', Leonard Woolf lamented his friend's new-found contentment, a phenomenon a bemused Virginia found 'disillusioning to behold'.[24]

Guided by the super-efficient Mrs Vincent, secretary to the editor and no doubt a woman whose tolerance of Sharp's behaviour verged on the saintly, MacCarthy responded with a previously unsuspected respect for the discipline of a weekly deadline. One can only presume that naval discipline and waging a secret war from the bowels of Whitehall had generated a well-hidden capacity for getting things done speedily and expeditiously. MacCarthy's nine-year tenure at the *New Statesman* revealed his latent talent for man-management, sub-editing and effective reporting. Sadly, such talent was less and less evident in the last 18 months when the demands of his new monthly review, *Life and Letters*, resulted in his being seen less and less at Great Queen Street. The dog-days of Sharp's editorship, in 1927–30, were of course precisely when MacCarthy was most needed: his regular presence could have helped maintain standards in the back half of the paper at a time when the front half was well-nigh falling apart.

A great conversationalist and *bon viveur*, MacCarthy's lifestyle precluded any sustained thinking about how the *New Statesman*, buoyed up by more readers and greater advertising potential, could carve a niche for itself as a review which anyone who wanted to know anything about the arts in London and beyond simply had to have. MacCarthy should have been the ideal man for the job, but trapped in a weekly treadmill and too busy reading new books to reflect on long-term goals, his urbanity and catholic taste were insufficient in themselves to promote original and provocative critical work. To be fair, he was by no means incapable of perceiving such potential in others, particularly the young; but he failed to foster talent in any sort of systematic and conscientious fashion. Thus, despite the exaggerated antipathy felt towards him by the *Calendar of Modern Letters* and then by *Scrutiny*, it is hard to dispute the conclusion of John Gross that MacCarthy's sole contribution to mid-century English cultural life was to 'keep alive a tradition of breadth, enlightenment, rational sociability, civilized forebearance'.[25]

MacCarthy's growing indifference to the *New Statesman* after 1926 meant that all too often he was absent from Great Queen Street when the paper had to be put to bed. Sharp was often too drunk to cover, and the job was left to George Stonier and to S.K. Ratcliffe, until the latter returned to New York. The damage done, MacCarthy at last resigned, succeeding Edmund Gosse at the *Sunday Times*. Stonier, a talented if somewhat eccentric individual, was given responsibility for the review pages, ostensibly under the direct supervision of Sharp. V.S. Pritchett, by the late 1920s already a regular reviewer, and growing in fame as a short-story writer, recalled Stonier as a 'sharp and candid critic with an excellent eye for the delicate and bizarre in vulgar events'.[26]

Thus by 1927 not only was the front half of the magazine rudderless, but so too was the back. Months turned into years, and neither editor nor directors saw any need to take action – a reflection of how little direct interest Bennett took in his investment by the end of the 1920s. In early 1930 a veteran hack called Clennell Wilkinson returned to Fleet Street from South Africa looking for his old drinking companion, Sharp. Desperate for a job, Wilkinson promised a weekly article from his brother-in-law, Hilaire Belloc, in return for appointment as literary editor. Although Belloc was no longer fashionable, he had been a frequent contributor earlier in the decade, and his name was still worth a few new readers. Without bothering to consult the board, Sharp agreed. It would have been hard to have found someone less qualified for the job. Wilkinson arrived at Great Queen Street 'with the martyred look of a man whom God had heartlessly appointed to save the whisky business from bankruptcy . . . a surviving Edwardian'. In August 1930, Belloc's six-month contract was not renewed. To the relief of all, Wilkinson left the next day, with the hapless Stonier resuming his thankless task. Sharp's final act, before being despatched by his directors to New York to dry out, was to appoint Ellis Roberts. This 'soft fat cooing priest', a competent but ineffectual contributor for well over a decade, was currently on the staff of the *Church Times*. No doubt to the bemusement of his new colleagues, he labelled himself a 'high Anglican man-of-letters', and dressed accordingly.[27]

Hyams rightly pointed out that by 1930 Lloyd had neither the time nor the inclination to bother about the review pages. There appeared to be merit in Roberts' appointment. Unimaginative and uninspiring he might have been, but technically he was very competent, and thus able to work largely unsupervised. The price of reliability was an astonishing £1,000 per year. The fact that staff largely approved the board offering such a high salary shows how keen everyone was to secure a professional journalist who, limited critical faculties notwithstanding, could at least do the job.[28]

The worthy Roberts did not long survive the *New Statesman's* 1931 merger with the *Nation*. The latter's literary editor, Edmund Blunden, who himself had not long before succeeded Leonard Woolf, was passed over for the new post on the mistaken assumption that he was about to take up a fellowship at Oxford. (Blunden then failed to interest Sassoon in buying the *Athenaeum* title from the *Nation*, and relaunching it as a monthly review.) Kingsley Martin later admitted that Roberts was the only *New Statesman and Nation* writer whose style and opinions he found absolutely intolerable. The two men quarrelled repeatedly and, amidst threats of litigation and apocalyptic warnings of the new venture's rapid demise, Roberts departed. Harold Nicolson agreed to compile 'Books in General' for six months, but for financial reasons declined Martin's invitation to join the editorial staff. Nicolson shrewdly recommended Raymond Mortimer as literary editor. By this time Stonier was again holding the fort, but, much as he admired his writing, Martin found him too other-worldly. Such a character assessment makes the eventual appointment of David Garnett even more surprising, particularly as Stonier stayed on to deal with much of the office work.[29]

According to Garnett, in November 1932 he was approached by Keynes, a Bloomsbury intimate for over a decade. During that time the critical acclaim 'Bunny' had received as a stylish young novelist on a par with Huxley, Michael Arlen and William Gerhardie had done little to ease a continuous state of financial embarrassment. Whatever his misgivings, no doubt reciprocated, about working with Martin, Garnett had little option but to accept Keynes's generous offer. Although his memoirs conveyed an impression of great activity and no little success, he turned out to be a particularly indolent editor whose business ineptitude constituted a major threat to his patron's hopes of imminent profitability. From the outset Garnett loathed the job, convinced it was destroying for ever his skills as a creative writer. Martin, loath to antagonise Keynes at such an early stage, hit on the idea of a six-month sabbatical, enabling Garnett to write his next novel, *Beany-Eye*. Belatedly acting on Nicolson's recommendation, Martin asked Mortimer to become acting literary editor. Delighted with a swift improvement in his paper's fortunes, Martin made Mortimer's post permanent, placating Garnett by asking him to retain 'Books in General'. In 1939 Mortimer took this role over as well, leaving Garnett, who bore no ill will at his friend's success, as just one of a by then glittering array of reviewers.[30] Mortimer's appointment, to a post for which he was eminently well qualified and which he was to hold with distinction for over a decade, marked the end of five years of instability, inertia, drift and a growing conservatism in terms of any pretension the paper might have had to be an arbiter of taste.

GREAT QUEEN STREET AND BLOOMSBURY

Leonard Woolf's wartime association with the *New Statesman* has been documented in earlier chapters. He had met Sharp as early as June 1913, at one of the Webbs' regular Tuesday lunches. The same year brought publication of Woolf's novel based upon his experience as a civil servant in Ceylon, *The Village in the Jungle*. Before finally accepting that he would never get anywhere writing non-fiction, he sent Squire two short stories. Virginia may have considered the *New Statesman's* literary editor 'more repulsive than words can express and malignant into the bargain', but he published both stories, in September 1913 and February 1914.[31] Regular review work began the following year. With Lloyd and Sidney Webb, Woolf covered books on politics, economics, and his specialist area, international relations. With all three sharing the same politics, and publishing their own work during or soon after the war, reviews could occasionally lapse into bouts of collective self-congratulation.[32]

Although editorial consistency undoubtedly improved in 1917–19, with writers straddling both halves of the paper under a single editor, Woolf refused to endorse Squire's call for Germany's total defeat. Differences came to a head in February 1918 when Woolf objected strongly to his editor's insistence that they agree on the future conduct of the war. In a succession of increasingly emollient notes, Squire nevertheless insisted on his right to edit copy and to 'remove any conscientious desire to say a word in favour of the Prussian evil when he is being painted everywhere a shade blacker than he is'.[33] Woolf remained unhappy and, given Squire's tortuous prose, presumably bemused. Relations worsened once Sharp returned and discovered just how far the paper had swung to the left. Woolf's increasing reluctance to review on a regular basis, particularly when the atmosphere at the *Nation* was so much more congenial, prompted placatory correspondence from Squire and even Sharp. As noted in Chapter 6, Woolf should have felt much more comfortable writing for the *New Statesman*, but he viewed Sharp's personality and politics with equal distaste. Prevarication over a long piece on reform of the Diplomatic Service, and its eventual rejection in July 1920, gave Woolf the excuse to make a clean break.[34]

The arts pages had already lost Aldous Huxley and Lytton Strachey as occasional contributors. Woolf had put Huxley in contact with Squire after the two men met at Philip and Ottoline Morrell's Garsington country house in the autumn of 1916. Huxley, a pacifist and at that time a very minor poet, was working with Clive Bell and others as a registered farm labourer. The *New Statesman* provided him with pocket money and enough experience to land a job on the *Athenaeum* when John Middleton Murry became editor in April 1919. Squire took Huxley with him to the *London Mercury*, and over a decade passed before he again wrote for the *New Statesman*.[35] Before and during the war Strachey submitted around a dozen fairly lightweight pieces, on subjects ranging from Freud to Frederick the Great. He loathed Squire almost as much as he loathed his paper, but Massingham had sacked him from the *Nation* and St Loe Strachey had refused all copy for the *Spectator* unless it was censored. Michael Holroyd has suggested Strachey's pre-war essays for the *New Statesman* on liberalism and tolerance were deliberately provocative, in order that a suitably outraged Squire would unwittingly provide their author with a glorious opportunity to denounce the paper as censorial and hypocritical. In reality, before the war, Squire's views differed from Strachey's only over sex and capital punishment – the former being hostile to sodomy and sympathetic to hanging, and quite happy to make the latter the price of the former.[36]

In 1918 Edward Shanks joined the chorus of praise for *Eminent Victorians*. But Strachey, the 'precise, vivid and witty essayist' who had 'redeemed English biography', could now afford to spurn Squire's offer to publish all new work. Why write for a magazine that denounced genuine efforts at securing a negotiated peace? No matter how vehemently Squire protested, Strachey's decision was final. Not even MacCarthy's eventual appointment made him change his mind.[37]

MacCarthy was a great networker, competing vigorously with rival editors like Middleton Murry and now Squire to exploit old acquaintances and tap new talent. Much of the run-of-the-mill work went to uninspiring but reliable regulars like Roberts, Shanks, the essayist and ex-schoolmaster E.E. Kellett, and the prolific popular novelists, Maurice Baring and Gerald Bullett – all easy targets for a rebarbative Queenie Leavis. Luckily for MacCarthy he had three years (before Leonard Woolf took up the parallel job at the *Nation*) when he enjoyed first call upon his closest friends. Agreed, Strachey was cool, and E.M. Forster offered only his thoughts on Jacobean drama in Cambridge, but Virginia Woolf (joined briefly by a mollified Leonard) contributed five reviews in as many months. This regular flow ceased following a complaint to the editor over the overt chauvinism of 'Affable Hawk' in lauding Bennett's *Our Women*. For over a year she saw little of MacCarthy, to the point of regretting 'writing sharply in the NS (but I was right)', but then the occasional piece began appearing again. Virginia wrote either at MacCarthy's invitation, or more often as a relief from the emotional intensity of writing fiction. She undoubtedly felt a much deeper obligation to her original patron, Bruce Richmond at the *Times Literary Supplement*, and to Leonard once he succeeded H.M. Tomlinson at the *Nation*.[38]

Of the other older members of Bloomsbury, Clive Bell and Roger Fry were MacCarthy's most prolific contributors. Both men had written for the paper before the war, but their disgust with Sharp and Squire over censorship, pacifism and the *New Statesman*'s jingoist coverage of the fighting led to a six-year break. Busy writing *Civilization*, Bell only occasionally contributed in the early post-war years, but Fry became the regular art critic until he made way for T.W. Earp in 1926. The quality of their criticism was unmatched by any other weekly, and in art if nothing else the *New Statesman* was a beacon of Modernism. Fry's most intuitive work remains his tributes to Cezanne, inspirer of the famous pre-war Post-Impressionist exhibitions and so much of Bloomsbury's approach to painting, and to Picasso, 'the painter who has had more influence on modern art than any other single man'. Reviewing Fry's *Vision and Design* in January 1921, Bell rightly emphasised his friend's 'power of infecting others with his own enthusiasm' – an enthusiasm capable of rousing the most philistine reader, and even the most philistine editor.[39]

Like Duncan Grant and Vanessa Bell, Fry was a member of the London Group, and he helped Keynes establish the London Artists' Association in 1926. Four close companions – Grant, Fry and the Bells – all sharing a common cultural experience, inevitably succumbed to public expressions of self-congratulation. Mutual back-slapping was endemic, despite Bell's honest criticism of Fry's first post-war exhibitions. Fry himself enthusiastically reviewed pamphlets on Duncan Grant, and his *New Statesman* essays on the latter's exhibitions with Vanessa Bell and Mark Gertler justified all three painters' pretensions to be in the vanguard of early twentieth-century English art. All this may seem cosy, even incestuous, but Fry's engagement in the Modernist experiment ranged far beyond the studios at Charleston.

In art Bloomsbury's critics may have exaggerated their charges of a cultural cabal, yet in literature the suspicion lingers that loyalty too frequently triumphed over critical detachment. Few might contest Mortimer's claims to 'write enthusiastically without one twinge of conscience' about Garnett's *A Man in the Zoo*, and to feel no qualms in judging Huxley's *Antic Hay* the most entertaining novel of 1923. It was after all a very funny novel. But how many readers of Bell's *On British Freedom* shared MacCarthy's high opinion of the 'most spirited, swift, admirably written onslaught I have read . . . since one of Shaw's prefaces'? Later in the decade the same author's study of Proust and his *Landmarks in Nineteenth Century Painting* received equally enthusiastic endorsements. Similarly, although *Queen Victoria* confirmed Strachey at the height of his critical powers, how many of MacCarthy's fellow critics hailed a 'masterpiece which will influence the art of biography'?[40] A distinct impression of uniformity in taste – a new critical orthodoxy rooted firmly in Gordon Square – was reinforced in 1922 by Robert Lynd's regular essays (but not his YY column) making way for a fortnightly alternative to 'New Novels' in which Augustine Birrell, Ellis Roberts and F.L. Lucas took turns to elucidate a common understanding of what constituted civilisation. These were by no means 'Bloomsberries', but they shared Bell and Strachey's view that civilization was firmly rooted in the eighteenth century and the Enlightenment.[41]

Thus, it was probably in the *New Statesman*'s interest that its brief tenure as Bloomsbury's house magazine came to an end early in 1923 when Keynes and his fellow consortium members secured control of the *Nation and Athenaeum*. Having at last acquired an acceptable editor in Hubert Henderson, Keynes turned to the equally thorny issue of who would run the back half of the paper. Encouraged by the chairman, whoever took on the job would be in an even stronger position than MacCarthy to rely on Bloomsbury's diverse talents. T.S. Eliot was originally offered the post as a means of escaping the bank, but his terms of appointment were wholly unacceptable. Keynes then turned to Leonard Woolf, who by then had become a regular leader-writer for the *Nation*. He offered Woolf £500 per annum, a seven-year contract and complete autonomy. The latter guarantee was to prove crucial as Henderson, who disapproved of Woolf's politics as well as his privileged position on the paper, soon found Woolf's 'constellation of stars' to be 'impossibly highbrow', unduly elitist, and irritatingly irreverent. From the first glittering issue on 5 May 1923 (with much trumpeted feature articles by Virginia Woolf and Lytton

Strachey) the new literary editor annoyed Henderson intensely by relying on his closest friends for regular copy. Henderson was further irritated by Woolf's readiness to encourage obscure talent, and his reluctance to alter or cut reviews (partly out of respect for others' opinions, and partly because he found the technical side of editing intensely boring). Woolf launched the career of more than one young writer, sometimes offering the additional outlet of the Hogarth Press; and through his own column 'The World of Books' he set new standards of quality and consistency in weekly literary journalism. Yet still the rows with Henderson persisted. On more than one occasion Woolf threatened to resign, but was duly placated by Keynes, his guardian against external as well as internal complaints.[42]

Henderson's largely unfounded charge that the *Nation*'s arts pages had become little more than a mouthpiece for Woolf's friends was, not that surprisingly, supported by MacCarthy. The irony is that in any other circumstance he himself would have been a frequent contributor. Unable to match the *Nation*'s initial rates of pay, MacCarthy envisaged all his regular reviewers deserting him, and despite Woolf's attempts at a compromise a row soon ensued. R.C. Trevelyan's mediatory efforts proved as feeble as the poems he regularly despatched to Great Queen Street, and yet on 18 May 1923 Virginia felt able to assure Fry that, 'In spite of Bob's [Trevelyan's] enormous assiduity, the row with Desmond MacCarthy is now over. But I assure you the atmosphere is full of coal dust.'[43]

Over tea two months later a placatory MacCarthy found Leonard insistent that in practice it was the *Nation*'s reviewers who were being poached. By August MacCarthy was again uncompromising and his editor was ready to back him up. Sharp objected strongly to the *New Statesman*'s regular writers having bylines in the *Nation*, and made it clear to Francis Birrell that if he wanted to go on reviewing history books then he had better remember where his first loyalty lay.[44] This firm line worked in so far as Woolf henceforth proved more accommodating, but it also brought about a 'rather distressing' interview with Birrell and Mortimer in which MacCarthy tried to claim full responsibility for cracking the whip. At this point Clive Bell and Bertrand Russell threatened a public boycott of the *New Statesman* if anyone was penalised for contributing to the *Nation*. Joined by Lucas, all four reviewers formally requested clarification of Sharp's position, on the understanding that each would then decide which weekly to write for in future.[45]

In Virginia Woolf's words, MacCarthy now 'cut up crusty' and, ironically, it was Sharp who displayed common sense and good humour in sorting out the mess. Birrell was assured of work if his signature was confined to the *Nation*'s theatre column (an agreement which cost a disgruntled Woolf £150 per annum). Mortimer's status as a member of the editorial staff precluded his writing for a direct rival – an apology and offer to write unsigned reviews in an emergency did little to placate the Woolfs. Lucas accepted exclusive fortnightly work for a negotiable fee. Russell's 'resignation' was regretfully accepted, despite private acknowledgement that he and Bell were too popular to demand exclusivity. Tongue firmly in cheek, a triumphant MacCarthy sent Woolf a note of 'surrender', signed 'Walenski'.[46]

The row with MacCarthy cast an early shadow over Woolf's seven years as a literary editor. He had a stormy relationship with Henderson, and he hated the editorial treadmill of meeting a weekly deadline. His memoirs recall how a 'violent struggle for space between politics and literature . . . corrodes and erodes the editorial mind'.[47] Extremely competitive, he resented the *New Statesman*'s steady increase in circulation in inverse proportion to the declining quality of the paper. When it came to advertising, publishers were more impressed by sales than substance, and the *Nation* suffered accordingly. Although the reviews were as good if not better, Woolf warned Keynes in late 1924 that 'we are not so good a literary paper' because MacCarthy regularly covered more books in an effort to boost advertising revenue. Why was the *Nation*'s review section shrinking when the *New Statesman*'s back half now exceeded the front by five pages? One week after the 1923 general election was perhaps not the most tactful moment at which to observe: 'You [Keynes] are materially deteriorating the literary side precisely at the moment when Sharp . . . is all out, not only to do you on the political side, but at the same time to strike you as hard as he can on the literary.'[48]

Woolf argued to no avail, and by March 1925 he was predicting a continued deterioration in the face of MacCarthy's success in attracting more advertisers. Whatever his misgivings about the job, Woolf's correspondence with Keynes throughout the mid-1920s reveals an eagerness to succeed, but also a feeling of inferiority when comparing his situation with that of MacCarthy. This sense of frustration must have become that much more acute as it became clear his rival was no longer doing a particularly good job. The fact is that Keynes and Henderson could not afford to maintain an aggressive, expansionist policy for very long. Trimming production and distribution costs, and reducing the price from 9d to 6d, had not brought profits, but rather the reverse: circulation actually fell from around 8,000 in Massingham's time to between 6,000 and 7,000. During the first seven years, at the end of which the *Nation* was just about solvent, Keynes was forced to invest a further £4,000, and seek capital injections from other members of the board.[49]

Given the somewhat tempestuous relationship MacCarthy had with the Woolfs during the four years he and Leonard were rivals, it was fittingly ironic that his valedictory column should have been an indignant reply to Bennett's attack on the late Sir Leslie Stephen in the *Evening Standard.* MacCarthy's departure deepened the gulf between Bloomsbury and Great Queen Street, albeit partially bridged by younger, more peripheral figures like Mortimer and Birrell. Only after 1931 would all those who had deserted to the *Nation* resume regular review work, including Virginia Woolf, whose most famous contribution, 'All About Books', was still to come. MacCarthy always had a good word for the Hogarth Press's early collections of Virginia's essays. He found her a 'delightful critic . . . combining with a sensibility, extremely personal and modern, a traditional sense of balance'.[50] This could have applied as readily to her fiction, the embodiment of that peculiarly English breed of Modernism 'rooted in familiar, national, provincial experience, rather than in the arcane worlds of its own making'.[51] For this reason familiarity may easily breed contempt, however unintentional: MacCarthy failed to perceive the significance of Virginia Woolf's key statement from the early 1920s, 'Mr Bennett and Mrs Brown'. The essay declared unequivocally that realism – as embodied in Bennett's fiction – was outmoded. With everything to play for, English literature trembled on the verge of a great age. Here was a commitment to experimentation that, commercial pressures notwithstanding, the *New Statesman* should have been in the vanguard of. Instead, MacCarthy now found himself defending Bennett. What had previously constituted the paper's healthy scepticism of Bohemian excess was rapidly becoming a knee-jerk distrust of anything even slightly disturbing and new.[52] Such suspicion, often teetering on the brink of outright reaction, goes a long way to explain the post-war magazine's poverty of response to fresh developments in fiction, and especially in poetry.

POETRY AND PROSE – THE POVERTY OF CRITICISM

The initials on the weekly summary 'New Novels' were for the first year those of the *Sunday Chronicle*'s most popular columnist, and Sharp's father-in-law, the veteran Fabian and roué Hubert Bland. Bland was only the first in a great tradition of questionable *New Statesman* critics, most of them with a blind spot when it came to D.H. Lawrence (for Bland *Sons and Lovers* lacked structure because the author clearly made it up as he went along). Preoccupied with poetry as he was, Squire saw no harm in the editor himself succeeding Bland. Fortunately, this arrangement lasted only a fortnight before Sharp conceded he had better things to do with his time than scan numerous third-rate novels every week.

In June 1914 Gerald Gould, then little known as a critic, took over 'New Novels', and to his eternal credit shared with Ezra Pound in the *Egoist* the distinction of recognising that *Dubliners* was the work of a genius.[53] Three years later Squire was congratulated by Bennett on his review of *A Portrait of the Artist as a Young Man*. It is hard to know why, as Squire could make neither head nor tail of Joyce, concluding with wonderfully unintentional irony that 'He is a realist of the first order ... it is doubtful if he will make a novelist'.[54] Nine years after its Paris publication MacCarthy finally found time to read *Ulysses*. Clearly exhausted by the experience, he found it obscene, tedious and often unbearable, but nevertheless containing 'more artistic dynamite than any book published for years'. Joyce was a writer 'of prodigious talent without a clear sense of direction ... the net result of the great part of his work is to show what is *not* worth doing in fiction by going one better in the direction in which the modern novel is moving'.[55] Whether deliberately gnomic, or simply damning with faint praise, at least MacCarthy recognised something significant was taking place. Similarly, George Stonier's knowledge and appreciation of contemporary European novelists, including the then unknown Kafka, had ensured an intelligent and sensitive review of Joyce's *Work in Progress.*[56]

In the early days Gould, despite early promise and a determination to raise standards, had wholly failed to appreciate the significance of *The Voyage Out*, or the maturity of Lawrence's and Conrad's wartime work. In 1914 the great Edwardians still merited individual reviews, with H.G. Wells held in especially high regard, despite his well-publicised disdain for the paper. While Squire was eager to publish any essays Bennett would let him have, Gould made no attempt to disguise his poor opinion of the novels. He saw little merit in *The Prince of Love*, published in September 1914, at a time when Bennett was already insisting Sharp withdraw a sneer more probably aimed at Wells. Objecting to an attack on popular authors making money out of the war, Bennett defended serious novelists' right to study an 'affair of human nature, a triumph of instinct', thereby denying the *New Statesman*'s claim that they had rushed into print as instant pundits on all matters military. Bennett was no doubt partly motivated by patriotism, but his main reason for signing lucrative contracts with the *Daily News* and the *Daily Chronicle* was clearly financial. However, Sharp was all too well aware that Squire had himself signed up for the weekly *Land and Water*, and as 'Solomon Eagle' for *Outlook*. Bennett's enmity was not to be taken lightly. An apology was duly despatched. Later in the war he was to make life a misery for Squire by continually carping about Gould. In March 1918 the first 'New Novels' abruptly ended when, to Bennett's undisguised delight, Gould resigned to become associate editor of the resurrected *Daily Herald* .[57]

Gould's departure left Squire even more dependent on his protégé Shanks, Ellis Roberts and the historian, critic and wartime civil servant Philip Guedalla. Guedalla wrote for an assortment of Liberal newspapers and weeklies, and his popular histories were of a sub-Strachey standard (a judgement shared by Strachey himself). Bennett admired the work ethic of Shanks, Roberts and

Guedalla, but found their reviews to be lacking 'literary method, to be too d...d sociological'.[58] If Bennett meant that they stated clearly what a book was about (in the case of the shorter notices, not having read the book – with probably the same true for the longer notices), but lacked either the critical acumen or vocabulary to judge whether or not it was well written, he was right.

Much of the time, particularly when reviewing poetry, Shanks was an embarrassment for the magazine, and yet throughout his editorial career Squire held him in the very highest regard. It would be easy to quote examples of Shanks's failings, but one may suffice here. In March 1919 the second, expanded version of *The Wild Swans at Coole* was published. With disarming honesty Shanks confessed his inability to discern any meaning whatsoever from arguably the finest individual volume of W.B. Yeats's work (in addition to the poem which gives the book its title, it includes 'An Irish Airman Foresees His Death', 'In Memory of Major Robert Gregory', 'Ego Dominus Tuus', and 'Upon a Dying Lady', the latter two having previously appeared in the *New Statesman*). Probably using Joseph Hone as an intermediary, Squire was able to publish seven of Yeats's poems between 1914 and 1917. The issue of 23 October 1920 contained the most famous poem ever to appear in the *New Statesman*, 'Easter 1916'. Yeats wrote the original version in September 1916, having it privately printed and circulated. The final version included minor changes to the descriptions of Constance Markiewicz (by 1920 a Sinn Fein MP boycotting Parliament)) and of Patrick Pearse (one of the four listed at the end who have 'dreamed and are dead'). Squire may have mocked Pound and ignored Eliot, but, at a time when most editors would have found an excuse not to publish, he let Yeats warn an English audience that 'A terrible beauty is born'. Nevertheless, the next time Yeats sought a wider circulation via the weeklies, he looked to the *Nation*. As we shall see, whenever Squire and his successors were confronted with the cutting edge of English verse, their response ranged from caution to contempt.

No writer suffered more at the hands of the *New Statesman*'s most pedestrian reviewers than D.H. Lawrence, whose travails over censorship of *The Rainbow* are noted in Chapter 5. Gould proved as insensitive as Hubert Bland, finding *The Prussian Officer and Other Stories* 'drenched in melancholy and pitiful for all its pitilessness', and *The Rainbow* 'dull, monotonous, pointless'. Reviewing *New Poems* at the end of the war Shanks declared that Lawrence's 'whole talent is rapidly becoming a grimace'.[59] Five years earlier Squire had been happy to publish two stories and two poems, and in the autumn of 1913 Lawrence's agent, Edward Marsh, sent him part of the 'Look! We have come through!' sequence. Squire replied: 'May I keep D.H. Lawrence's poem one or two days more? I want to see if I can make *a*, Head, or alternatively *b*, Tail, of it.'[60] Reluctant to turn down one of Marsh's poems, Squire delayed another month before finally sending it back.[61]

At last Lawrence attracted the reviewer he deserved when Rebecca West was appointed by MacCarthy to revive 'New Novels'. Although a novelist in her own right, who before the war had sat at the feet of Henry James, West was best known on both sides of the Atlantic as a daring and iconoclastic young journalist. This was an imaginative and adventurous appointment, which only ended when Wells hinted that she was beginning to praise the very writers most in need of attack.[62] Her reviews were intelligent, abrasive, stylish and wonderfully entertaining: 'Mr S.P.B. Mais has produced another novel [*Caged Birds*]. How long, O Lord, how long?'[63]

'Affable Hawk' and his chief fiction reviewer shared similar tastes. Both suspected Huxley's surface brilliance. Perhaps predictably, both admired Katherine Mansfield and Virginia Woolf, *Jacob's Room* confirming the latter's status as a 'supremely important novelist'. For West, *Women In Love* confirmed Lawrence's genius. In a subtle dissection of the novel she identified its obvious failures before going on to defend her contention that the four central characters were 'master-pieces of pure creation'. Reviewing a selection of Lawrence's short stories she aptly described him as King Lear wandering 'on the blasted heath of his own temperament'. Yet at the same time she was quite prepared to dismiss *Aaron's Rod* as the 'plum-silly' product of genius 'without horse sense'.[64]

Rebecca West's abrupt departure in 1922 was clearly a major blow, but it occasioned Mortimer's arrival at Great Queen Street. V.S. Pritchett in his memoirs paid tribute to the breadth of the young Mortimer's reading. After a brief wartime sojourn at the

Foreign Office, a career in literary journalism had seemed an attractive if risky option, particularly as Mortimer once confided to the Woolfs that it was 'far better to write reviews than second rate novels'.[65] His output over the years was frankly staggering. In addition to his specialist areas of literature and painting, he would cover any aspect of the arts if the regular correspondent was absent or the post was vacant. A man of obvious integrity, Mortimer's enthusiasm was infectious. Above all, as a critic, later doubling up as an editor, he was a complete professional. He shared West's high regard for Lawrence, but was not afraid to suggest that the 'ridiculous and barbarous, if not entirely unreal, view of life' displayed in *Kangaroo* had stifled its author's keen sense of poetry. MacCarthy justifiably lambasted John Middleton Murry for reproducing this review in the *Adelphi* under the headline 'The Triumph of a Fool'.[66] Mortimer was increasingly – and rightly – disturbed by the 'brutish philosophy' behind Lawrence's recent work, despite – equally rightly – finding the *England, My England* stories written 'with greater vigour and intensity than any other living English novelist'. Mortimer, later Stonier, and to a lesser degree MacCarthy himself, were for the first time placing a writer like Lawrence in a genuinely European context. They built on the legacy left by Rebecca West during her short but dazzling tenure. Readers were encouraged to be adventurous, with Mortimer one of the first critics in a non-specialist review to promote the work of Mauriac, Cocteau and, above all, that 'supreme novelist' Proust. The paper was still all too often exhorting the virtues of contemporary best-sellers long since forgotten, but the influence of Stonier and Mortimer on the next generation of *New Statesman* critics, most notably Cyril Connolly and Peter Quennell, was considerable. Commissioning younger, more receptive writers, who in the interest of their own creative work were fully cognizant of trends in contemporary fiction across the Channel, meant a more sympathetic understanding of experimentation in the novel than in verse, at least until the early 1930s and the emergence of Auden, Spender and MacNeice.

However, before the recruitment in 1927 of Quennell, a poet sent down from Oxford, and Connolly, his contemporary at Balliol, MacCarthy lumbered 'New Novels' with a series of mediocrities – Ralph Wright, John Franklin, P.C. Kennedy and the novelist Naomi Royde-Smith. To be fair, Franklin was mildly amusing, Kennedy admired *Mrs Dalloway* and recognised Hemingway's talent if not Fitzgerald's, and Wright praised Forster's great 'sensitiveness to truth' in an otherwise bland review of *A Passage To India*. Usually, however, Woolf was the victim of total incomprehension (witness Royde-Smith on *To The Lighthouse*) and Lawrence the subject of unwarranted invective (witness F.L. Lucas on the poetry of *Birds, Beasts and Flowers*, the art critic J.J. Holms on *Studies in Classic American Literature*, and to a lesser degree Kennedy on *The Plumed Serpent*). The turning-point came in July 1927 when Quennell reassessed *The Plumed Serpent*, now complemented by *Mornings in Mexico*, in the *New Statesman*'s most intelligent and enlightened essay on Lawrence since West's departure. Quennell reaffirmed a 'strange, strangely developed and fine-pointed sensibility' genuinely worthy of the name genius.[67]

Quennell and Connolly, who took over the 'white man's grave of journalism' in September 1927, were seeking to raise critical standards at precisely the moment that MacCarthy's indifference was starting to have the opposite effect. Dealing with the sympathetic but unreliable Stonier, the bibulous Wilkinson and the cathedral close mentality of Roberts, it is remarkable that the two young critics stuck to their task in the way that they did. For two years, 'New Novels' under Connolly was lucid, rigorous, demanding, witty and highly readable. Undertaken at the outset of a presumed brilliant career, the column rarely hinted at the bitterness of failure that led to *Enemies of Promise*.[68]

Unlike Connolly, Quennell deliberately made time to step off the review treadmill and publish poetry, a novel and a critical study of Baudelaire. His short stories appeared occasionally in the *New Statesman*, alongside work by Pritchett, Rex Warner, H.E. Bates and Malcolm Muggeridge, at that time leader writer and later Moscow correspondent of the *Manchester Guardian*. When the paper's fortunes were at their lowest ebb, in early 1930, Quennell had the good sense to take a two-year sabbatical, accepting a chair in English at a Japanese university. Quennell's departure, and Connolly's decision to quit 'New Novels', left Roberts treading water. Under the 'Proteus' byline anyone who was available provided a monthly round-up of new fiction, including Gerald

Bullett, the novelist and poet Viola Meynell, and Roberts himself. The latter characteristically offered a harsh, uncharitable obituary of Lawrence, and on another occasion declared Huxley's mental development to have been arrested. (It is easy to see why Sharp found Roberts, for all his High Anglican pretensions to Christian charity, to be a man after his own heart.) Following Roberts' stormy departure, Kingsley Martin repeatedly asked Virginia Woolf to become chief fiction reviewer, much to her annoyance.[69]

Garnett's failure to fill the gap left by Quennell and Connolly was symptomatic of the continued crisis within the arts pages which persisted for another four years beyond 1931, and which only the appointment of Mortimer finally resolved. Needless to say, one of Mortimer's first priorities was to re-establish the pivotal role of 'New Novels' within what was still overwhelmingly a literary review. Another priority was a fuller acknowledgement of recent developments in poetry, although to be fair Stephen Spender had seen his work published as early as February 1931 (before that Auden and Day-Lewis's early work had attracted scant critical attention). The *New Statesman* had, belatedly, to recognise that the 'low, dishonest decade' had its own generation of poets. In this respect it was repeating the experience of 1913, when Squire set out to sell the Georgians to a sceptical Fabian audience.

Squire enthusiastically championed the poets anthologised by Harold Munro and Edward Marsh, the latter an agent not only for Lawrence but also for J.D. Beresford, James Elroy Flecker and Rupert Brooke. Over dinner at the National Liberal Club, Marsh and Squire would together select poems for future issues. Brooke, who was happy for Squire to publish his travel sketches should the *Westminster Gazette* not want them, nevertheless instructed Marsh from Canada to ensure that the *Nation*, which along with the *New Age* had been an early outlet for his poems, still had access to his work.[70]

Brooke's friendship with Ben Keeling and Julius West dated back to their Cambridge days, but he strengthened his ties with the *New Statesman* by getting to know Squire much better after arriving home. Before his death in 1915 Brooke had let Squire have three poems, a reflection upon wartime Samoa under New Zealand occupation, and a semi-autobiographical sketch of a traveller who learns belatedly that war has been declared – the hero, finding himself overwhelmed by powerful images of England, for the first time realises that defence of his country must override all other emotions, including love of both mother and lover.[71] Given the dour, utilitarian image of the *New Statesman* at the onset of the First World War, it somehow seems ironic that Squire and Shanks should have been prominent in cultivating the Brooke legend. Already devastated by Flecker's death in a Swiss sanatorium, Squire was equally affected by news of Brooke's death in April 1915 en route to the Dardanelles. Throughout the war years he returned again and again to the question posed in Brooke's obituary: 'what a man of his intellectual acuteness, sensitiveness, musical perception, and feeling for words might not have done had he lived'.[72]

Deemed unfit for active service in 1914, Squire saw it as his duty to preserve the memory of the dead, and to secure recognition for serving writers. The latter attracted respect, even reverence; and in praising their endeavours to expose the 'cant and hypocrisy, cruelty and crudity of taste' prevalent at home, 'Solomon Eagle' addressed his readers in the trenches directly. Squire found Kipling's early poems almost as distasteful as *The Times*'s 'torrents . . . [of] flat, uninspired, banal' patriotic verse.[73] However, as early as Christmas 1914 Lytton Strachey had identified the most effective enunciation in verse of this war's 'mortal irony'. His review of Thomas Hardy's *Satires of Circumstance* dwelt upon the curiously prophetic nature of 'Channel Firing', a poem composed in time of peace but destined to exert an especial influence over the war poets, and in particular Siegfried Sassoon. Once, that is, Sassoon's early front-line experience had crushed any Brooke-inspired efforts to evoke and express establishment aspirations of war and patriotic duty; in other words, that 'callous complacency' of civilians which he quickly came to revile, but which in truth Squire could never fully shake off.[74]

Sassoon knew this, hence his bitingly savage satire on Squire's support for conscription, 'Memorial Tablet (Great War)'.[75] With lines like 'Two bleeding years I fought in France, for Squire:/I suffered anguish that he's never guessed', is it any wonder that the target of Sassoon's scorn soon began to question the durability of verse 'cloaked with the horrors of war . . . and smug detestation of civilians'. *The Old Huntsman* had been greeted enthusiastically in June 1917. But when *Counter-Attack* appeared a year later Squire damned with faint praise, reflecting upon the quality of verse its author would write in peacetime – when contemplating the 'things he loves instead of the things he hates'. This was doubly ironic given that before the war Squire had rejected Sassoon's early work as 'mere exercises in versifying'.[76] In *Siegfried's Journey 1916–20* the latter recalled how Squire 'reviewed me with moderation' – scarcely surprising if he was expected to swallow attacks like the above – and how he was not the only editor to keep 'on the safe side' when accepting wartime verse from Marsh or Robert Ross. Ross was a celebrated critic and a leading member of the Reform Club who was instrumental in finding Sassoon a publisher, as well as introducing both him and Wilfred Owen to Bennett. Although Owen received the *New Statesman* in France, it was Massingham and Tomlinson who first recognised the quality of his work, publishing 'Miners' in January 1918.[77] With its opposition to conscription, its highly qualified support for the war, and its antipathy towards anything vaguely militaristic and jingoistic, the *Nation* was a far more attractive proposition for any enlisted writer sick of the fighting.

Like Sassoon's, Edward Thomas's early poems received little encouragement. Godwin Baynes, a Cambridge Fabian and friend of Sharp, had first suggested approaching Thomas, who by 1913 was already highly regarded as an observer of the English countryside. Five studies of rural life had appeared in the *New Statesman* before, under Robert Frost's influence, he decided to take his interest in poetry seriously. There then followed two years of silence, interrupted only by a short story in May 1915 about two entrained NCOs comparing their respective attitudes to war and death.[78] Then, on 21 April 1917, 'Solomon Eagle' recorded Thomas's death at Arras, revealing that during the previous year his verse had appeared in print for the first time under the pseudonym of 'Edward Eastaway'. In tribute, the following week's issue contained four poems (including the much anthologised 'Adlestrop') and extracts from a letter to Frost. A further eight poems appeared at intervals throughout 1918, all of which were included two years later in the first collected edition of Thomas's work.

Another writer on the Western Front whose work first appeared in the *New Statesman* towards the end of the war was Robert Graves. Again Marsh and Ross were responsible for selling his poems to a receptive Squire (like Bennett, he greatly admired Graves's first collection *Fairies and Fusiliers*). Only two more poems appeared in 1921, and then there was a 27-year break until Graves became a regular contributor in the late 1940s and 1950s.[79] In the early 1920s, under the pseudonyms of 'Sigma Sashun' and 'SS', Sassoon contributed another 13 poems, but like Edmund Blunden, whose best-known war poem 'The Ancre at Hamel: Afterwards' was published on 12 July 1924, the trauma of the trenches refused to go away. With the passage of time Squire's successors became ever less sympathetic, Ellis Roberts striking a particularly caustic note in his review of *Memoirs of a Fox-Hunting Man*.

Squire might have been the enthusiastic promoter of a poetry rooted in an English idyll that never really was, but at least he had a passion *and* a policy. He took that passion with him to the *London Mercury*, and his 1922 *Selections From Modern Poets* confirmed him as a natural successor to Marsh. After his departure the *New Statesman* became marginally more open to genuinely contemporary verse, but it no longer aggressively pursued a policy of encouraging new, young poets. It was not until 1927 that Stonier persuaded MacCarthy to adopt a more systematic selection procedure, but even then most work was randomly selected from the accumulated manuscripts of obscure optimists. In addition, MacCarthy was always happy to publish anything passed on to him by his friends. Bell, Trevelyan, Lucas, Rylands, Princess Bibesco and even Nancy Cunard all saw their feeble scribblings in print. Thus, not only were far fewer poems being published, but much of the time they were embarrassingly bad.[80]

By the end of the 1920s the only poet of quality who regularly appeared in the magazine was Roy Campbell, whose first collection *The Flaming Terrapin* 'thrilled' MacCarthy, and whose satire on fellow-South African intellectuals, *The Waygoose*, was enthusiastically received in March 1928. In 1930 a similarly warm reception was given to *Adamstor*, a selection containing several poems published in the *New Statesman* over the previous four years. Campbell's early success depended heavily upon

Bloomsbury's generosity, yet he viciously satirised his old patrons (except MacCarthy, who had brought him back from Cape Town) in his Augustan parody *The Georgiad*. Humbert Wolfe, only one of countless targets, persuaded Roberts to publish a short, sharp counter-blast, 'The Ranciad'.[81]

Very tentatively, the post-Squire *New Statesman* entered the decade of 'critical revolution'.[82] As early as November 1920 the Georgians were being charged with insincerity, and of imposing their 'insipidity of nothingness' upon an audience no longer amenable to their sentimental, spiritually bankrupt projection of nature. By 1923 even Lucas, scarcely a literary maverick, could dismiss Marsh and Munro's post-war anthology as intolerably dull and outmoded. On the other hand, Lucas was clearly a disastrous choice to review *The Waste Land*. His reference to the 'usual abortions of modern poetry' provoked Edgell Rickword's devastating (if metaphorically inaccurate) attack in the *Calendar of Modern Letters* on this 'Canute-like … pedantic don'. If only because he was writing a book on Rimbaud, Rickword when at the *New Statesman* was rarely allowed to review anything other than nineteenth-century French literature. However, he did introduce an unprecedented discussion of aesthetics into the arts pages, as well as encourage the fiction reviewers' incipient interest in Freud and Jung. I.A. Richards did not last long either, despite offering the first serious discussion of Eliot as a poet; in the course of which he castigated Middleton Murry's surrender of solid textual analysis to spurious 'self-mystification' (too much exposure to Lawrence). Instead, genuinely modern verse had to suffer the bemusement or outright disaffection of a Shanks, a Lucas or a Roberts, the latter providing a memorable obituary of Robert Bridges: this 'truly great' poet would be remembered long after the likes of Eliot and Pound had been forgotten.

Eliot's work before *The Waste Land* was largely ignored, perhaps out of politeness as he provided a regular supply of short notices and even the occasional review during the latter part of the war. In March 1917 Squire to his credit published Eliot's call for him to justify his continued sniping at *vers libre*, and in particular the Imagist poems of Ezra Pound (a favourite target of 'Solomon Eagle') and Amy Lowell. Eliot's essay was full of common sense, politely suggesting that Squire had encouraged controversy, and that in practice there was only 'good verse, bad verse, and chaos'. For Eliot, Squire was imposing on the English tradition a wholly artificial division: between the popular lyrical verse upheld by the Georgians as a model for all contemporary poets, and a more cerebral *vers libre* we would today label Modernist.[83]

CONCLUSION

Under MacCarthy, Garnett and all the other journeymen and literary lightweights who kept the back half intact between Squire's departure and Mortimer's appointment, the *New Statesman* singularly failed to establish any sort of identity for itself as a flagship for the arts. As a literary review it scarcely bothered to cultivate a consistent and clearly discernible critical viewpoint. Editorial staff worked from week to week – individually and collectively they lacked vision. The exceptions, such as Edgell Rickword, were marginalised, or had no influence in the first place. To be fair, given wider concerns over circulation and financial viability, MacCarthy proved a skilled and resourceful literary editor for at least six of the seven years he was in charge, as his success in maximising advertising revenue showed. Under his tenure the arts pages were worthy and unexceptional, albeit on occasions infuriating, *vide* reviews of Lawrence, Joyce, and so on. The real crisis came with MacCarthy's diminishing interest and eventual departure.

In the late 1920s Sharp's drinking had a disastrous impact on the paper as a whole, but nowhere was the effect more keenly felt than in the back half, and not simply because of the circumstances in which Clennell Wilkinson was appointed. In the absence of firm leadership, morale, let alone standards, sank to an all-time low. The impression was that nobody cared; and those who really did – young writers like Mortimer, Quennell and Connolly – were still standing on the sidelines. They were either too busy as freelances trying to earn a living, or spending long periods abroad, notably Mortimer in America and Quennell in Japan. Garnett was of the same generation, but his appointment was a rare example of Keynes' generosity prevailing over his sound judgement – an error he swiftly acknowledged. Mortimer's belated appointment in 1935 ended an interregnum coinciding with an especially critical moment in twentieth-century English literature. Able to draw on a remarkable fund of goodwill in the first half of the 1930s, largely as a consequence of Martin's heroic endeavours in the front half of the paper and a sharp move to the left after 1931, the arts pages should have been a showcase for the work of Auden and his contemporaries. Bloomsbury still had a contribution to make, not least through Mortimer himself, but Spender, Day-Lewis, *et al* might easily have viewed the *New Statesman* as the preserve of those with established reputations, rather than rising stars. Back in 1913 this had never been Squire's intention, witness his commitment to what seemed the new poetry of the day. Mortimer's task over two decades later was to convince another generation of writers – politicised to a degree the Georgians could scarcely have imagined – that the back half of a now unequivocally socialist weekly had as much relevance to them as the front.

It is not surprising that Eliot's involvement with the *New Statesman* was marginal, even after the appointment of MacCarthy. He had no incentive to become involved with a magazine so dismissive of his poetry, and anyway there were other priorities, most notably the launching of the *Criterion* in 1922. Nevertheless, in reviewing the collection of essays that made up *The Sacred Wood* MacCarthy pointed to Eliot – the embodiment of the 'European mind' – as a role model for all aspiring young critics. Similarly, I.A. Richards's *Science and Poetry* and *Principles of Literary Criticism* in 1924 and 1926 respectively, and four years later William Empson's *Seven Types of Ambiguity*, were all praised for their intellectual muscle. These were critics lauded by MacCarthy and Stonier for their courage in pioneering new techniques of analysis as a means of rigorous critical revaluation. Yet the unwritten assumption seemed to be 'But this has very little to do with the weekly demands of literary journalism'. The Leavises were of course right – it had *everything* to do with ensuring that a popular review did not engage in a subtle, perhaps even unintentional form of inverse snobbery.

Where the editors of *Scrutiny* were wrong was in failing to acknowledge the constraints that arose out of producing a readable – and ideally profitable – product on the same day 52 times a year. Nevertheless, a literary editor with vision and drive might easily over-ride individual idiosyncrasies and foibles. He or she could foster those qualities conducive to a consistently high standard of critical appraisal: receptivity to new ideas; a keen sense of the foolish, the fallacious and, above all, the mediocre; an adherence to high standards in contemporary literature, but not at the expense of the popular just because it is widely read and easily accessible; and a familiarity with longer-term trends in contemporary culture cutting across national boundaries. An ideal team of reviewers could not afford to be ivory-towered, but nor could they afford to ignore what was taking place on the cutting edge of literary criticism. No wonder Edgell Rickword bemoaned the absence of a 'vital' homogeneity of view in respect of 'living literature' when he left the *New Statesman* in 1925 to found and edit the *Calendar of Modern Letters*.[84]

Mortimer's admiration for MacCarthy notwithstanding, he tolerated some astonishing outbursts of philistinism, with Lawrence and Eliot as the most distinguished victims.[85] Contrast Rickwood in the *Times Literary Supplement*, genuinely perplexed but making an intelligent and inquiring attempt to understand *The Waste Land*, with F.L. Lucas lamenting Lawrence and Eliot's sacrifice of 'their artistic powers on the altar of some fantastic Mumbo-Jumbo ... modern writers of real creative power abandon themselves to the fond illusion that they have philosophic gifts and a weighty message to deliver to the world as well'.[85] This reads like a latter-day leader in the *Spectator*, but worse was to come with Roberts' patronising review of *For Lancelot Andrewes*, which provoked F.R. Leavis's first – and from the outset characteristically trenchant – published essay.[86] With the likes of Lucas and Roberts actually in control in 1931, and no fresh face from the *Nation* able to seize the opportunity of a fresh start, Leavis could in a later article rightly bemoan the absence at the time of an 'intelligent and courageous critical organ' – a popular review committed to the same mission as the late lamented *Calendar of Modern Letters*, namely,

> that re-education which was necessary before the contemporary re-orientation of English poetry could be recognized and appreciated. But where, at that time, apart from Mr Eliot's essays, were the incitements and aids to such a re-education to be found?[87]

Where, indeed. Leavis's solution was *Scrutiny*, but this was no answer for most general readers of the weekly press.

The years of crisis: The *New Statesman* in the late 1920s

MOSTYN LLOYD AND ROBERT BRUCE LOCKHART – DEALING WITH THE BOLSHEVIKS

As early as 1925 Sharp was a shadow of his former self. In the circumstances Lloyd worked miracles, holding down a full-time job at the LSE, and yet every Thursday successfully putting the paper to bed. Editing a well-established political weekly magazine without allowing the real editor to feel usurped was a weekly triumph of tact and diplomacy. Clearly, the full-time staff at Great Queen Street, particularly John Roberts, had a key role to play. Lloyd wrote prolifically, particularly on foreign affairs where he could draw on the advice of Robert Bruce Lockhart and the expertise of a growing number of foreign correspondents, usually stringers for the *Manchester Guardian*, or *The Times* in the case of Rome's Vernon Bartlett and Paris's Sisley Huddleston. Ratcliffe provided first-class coverage of American affairs, Northcliffe rating his work the 'best informed of any then appearing in any paper in Europe'.[1]

Consistently dismissing French security fears, while lauding Gustav Stresemann's efforts to advance Germany's international rehabilitation, Lloyd shared Sharp's suspicion of Austen Chamberlain's good relations with Aristide Briand. Forging real collective security, with Germany secure and stable in the heart of Europe, necessitated a change of government in Britain. Unlike Sharp, but in common with other centre-left observers of the world stage, Lloyd placed great hope in MacDonald. By 1929 there was even speculation that, once in office, a Nobel laureate would surely follow. Predictably, the *New Statesman* applauded MacDonald's Commons motion in October 1928 demanding a 'reorientation back to independence and away from servitude to France', quoting his Reichstag speech later that month as the highest endorsement of its own views on Europe, on the need to repair Anglo-American relations, and on Britain's moral obligation to bolster the authority of the League.[2] Instinctive appeasers from the outset, *New Statesman* writers could scarcely conceive of another war. They put their faith in a strong League of Nations, a worldwide disarmament programme, a revised Versailles Treaty, and above all, a stable, democratic Germany. They were not unusually naive in purporting such a scenario as attainable; although Lloyd's enthusiasm for *Anschluss*, and his initial willingness to accept Stalin at face value, all too clearly illustrate how having an opinion on everything gives real insight into nothing.[3]

The *New Statesman*'s coverage of Soviet affairs during the period of the New Economic Policy (NEP) and the attendant power struggle that followed the death of Lenin in 1924 demonstrated, even with the benefit of hindsight, a lamentable mixture of ignorance, naïvety and false optimism. Kingsley Martin's benevolent view of the Soviet Union in the 1930s and beyond has attracted much criticism over the years, but a reluctance to condemn outright the world's only socialist state had its roots in the years of NEP. Like Lloyd, Lockhart was slow to recognise Stalin for what he was. Until as late as the 1929 Party Congress he chronically underestimated the coming man in the Politburo. Lockhart had returned to the paper in November 1927, not long before he gave up being a banker and, disregarding Sharp's advice, started editing the *Evening Standard*'s famous 'Londoner's Diary'. Lockhart was no socialist, but he was a legendary socialite and as such proved a tremendous asset to the *New Statesman*. An habitual night-clubber, by day he played golf with the Prince of Wales. When not abroad he was a regular weekend guest at Chartwell or Cherkley. An habitual gossip, he mixed as freely in literary as in diplomatic circles, where Harold Nicolson and Rex Leeper regularly passed on news from the Foreign Office. As seen in Chapter 6, Lockhart knew Russia well, albeit making enemies among the Bolshevik leadership. By contrast, his visits to post-war

Prague brought about life-long friendships with Benes and the Masaryks, and he was regarded as a great champion of Czech interests in London. Elsewhere in central and eastern Europe Lockhart fostered contacts at the highest levels.[4] Like David Low, once he became Beaverbrook's confidant his already vast number of acquaintances multiplied, extending across the Atlantic.[5] Neither the *Nation* nor the *Spectator* could boast anyone enjoying comparable familiarity with high society and with the corridors of power. Lockhart was as much at home in the Embassy Club and Fort Belvedere as Carlton Gardens and Hradcany Castle. Bennett, his fellow columnist on the *Evening Standard*, agreed with Beaverbrook that here was 'one of the most brilliant men of this generation'.

Lockhart's impact upon the *New Statesman* between 1927 and 1929, at a time when energy and enthusiasm were at a premium, was as considerable as it was unexpected. Sadly, by the early 1930s ill-health brought on by mounting debts and a punishing work schedule greatly diminished his input. In June 1930 occurred one of the great 'what ifs' – Bennett offered Lockhart the editorship of the paper. He was so much in debt, especially to his employer, that he simply could not afford to take up the offer.[6] One can only speculate on what a *New Statesman* edited by Lockhart and not Martin would have been like. Almost certainly the period of his editorship would have been far shorter, and the paper would have looked very different. The onus would have been on style, with contributors sought on the basis of 'Never mind their politics, can they write well?'. Mortimer would have been literary editor much earlier, with his *Vogue* and New York experience heavily drawn upon. The magazine would have lacked the clear political identity quickly established by Martin, and there would have been little talk of its acting as the conscience of democratic socialism, but it would have been more exciting and more widely appealing, gaining sales earlier than the 'Staggers and Naggers' actually did. The question is, of course, whether in the wider context of the 1930s later historians would have been as interested in Lockhart's style guide as in Martin's flagship of the left.

Consistent with his thinking during the civil war, Lockhart saw NEP as a unique opportunity for Britain to re-establish trade and financial links with Russia, arguing that the size of the Red Army and the activities of the Comintern increased solely in proportion to the level of Western provocation. Sharp concurred, arguing from experience that MI6 should cease operating inside Russia.[7] The *New Statesman* was similarly hostile to MI5 and Special Branch over-reacting to Soviet subversion at home, in May 1927 seeing little justification for the famous 'Arcos raid' on the Russian Trade Delegation.[8] Only after the 1929 Party Congress did Lloyd and Lockhart concede that Bolshevism had acquired a dictator responsible to no-one, least of all his own party. Having repeatedly condemned Baldwin and Austen Chamberlain for appeasing backbench and Home Office prejudice by cold-shouldering Stalin, they now urged caution in dealing with him. Unlike five years earlier, Labour's 1929 trade agreement was warmly welcomed, with sympathy expressed over Moscow's continued attacks on both party and government. The rationale behind the *New Statesman*'s position at the end of the decade was simple: Stalin could now be seen to be a ruthless dictator, but in the interest of peace and prosperity, and in particular British jobs based on Anglo-Soviet trade, he was a dictator any government – but especially a Labour government committed to bringing down unemployment – had to deal with.[9] This line of argument had an internal logic, but it was predicated on the assumption that MacDonald and his ministers had the ideas, the dynamism and the political will to reduce the jobless total. Evidence from the years in opposition did not augur well.

DOUGLAS COLE – DEALING WITH THE DOLE, AND DEALING WITH THE LIBERALS

One man who refused to let the issue of unemployment go away was G.D.H. Cole. Given the poverty of official Labour thinking on economic recovery in the face of Lloyd George and his advisers' well-publicised attempts to offer a credible Liberal alternative, the *New Statesman*'s real value to the party was via Cole's insistence on maintaining the intellectual initiative of democratic socialism. As Cole more and more exerted his influence over coverage of domestic affairs, so he advocated, in the words of a later editor, 'the *New Statesman*'s most unpopular course . . . the need to attempt an economic discourse of extreme detail and precision'.[10]

In pursuit of this task he was given every encouragement by Lloyd with whom he liaised almost daily, even after moving back to Oxford in September 1925. Cole's work was invariably lucid and precise, but his style could scarcely be described as elegant; indeed Martin thought it dull and colourless. Sharp estimated Cole was contributing over four columns a week by the late 1920s, and Woolf testified to his reliability.[11]

Throughout these years, in addition to carving out an academic career in Oxford, Cole continued to teach his WEA classes in London. Having ceased contributing to the *New Leader*, he wrote briefly for *Lansbury's Labour Weekly*, before concentrating all his efforts on the *New Statesman*. In his writing he made few concessions. Cole rarely wore his learning lightly, and no doubt many skimmed or ignored a weekly test of readers' patience and intellect. Yet, nevertheless, his work continued to articulate an unceasing anger and frustration over the appalling waste and the callous inhumanity generated by chronic structural unemployment. Week by week the committed reader could trace the evolution of Cole's thinking on social equality, until finally in April 1929 there appeared the distillation of his ideas, *The Next Ten Years in British Social and Economic Policy*. The book was deliberately practical, detailing a series of proposals that an incoming Labour government might implement in order to alleviate unemployment (including a voluntary National Labour Corps to undertake capital projects beyond the scope of private enterprise).[12] Cole was advancing ideas and practical proposals over half a decade before the emergence of what Marwick has labelled 'middle opinion', and in this respect the influence of his tutee, Hugh Gaitskell, was critical.[13] By 1929, largely through Gaitskell's efforts in the view of his biographer, Cole had come to recognise the intellectual and above all the practical limitations of guild socialism. But why abandon idealism when the realist alternative was so unattractive – Labour's record in power had been abysmal. In rigorous but never rancorous discourse Gaitskell offered a persuasive intellectual defence of evolutionary parliamentary socialism. *The Next Ten Years* defended Labour's unique claim to engage in rational economic planning, and Cole paid tribute to his former student in the preface.[14]

Through endless agonising, often brought on by discussion with

Gaitskell and the other socialist students who met each week in his University College rooms, Cole gradually acceded to the art of the possible. The logic of his position – that unemployment had to be reduced by whatever practical means were most readily to hand – was that he was a reformist. A mellowing in his opinion of the Labour leaders, duly reciprocated via his increasing input to policy formulation, reflected a slow, uneasy journey in the direction of Westminster, culminating in his adoption as Labour candidate for the King's Norton constituency in Birmingham. Cole had already acquired a formidable roster of enemies, and he never convinced those sceptics at Transport House who saw him as ivory-towered, idealistic and totally ignorant of life on the shop-floor or at the coal-face. It was easy for his critics inside the Labour Party, and particularly in the trade unions, to portray him as yet another socialist intellectual from Hampstead or the Woodstock Road. Yet few could deny Cole was well-intentioned, committed and, in his endeavours to secure the left's common agreement on a coherent programme of socialist reform, unwavering in his party loyalty. In the words of one biographer, Cole's reconciliation of socialist idealism and practical politics induced genuine creativity rather than disingenuous compromise.[15]

Keynes once described Cole as a 'writer of great ability, but a prolific journalist who does not exercise much self-criticism'.[16] This may well have been true before his return to Oxford, but succeeding years suggested a battered ego and, as discourse with Gaitskell confirmed, a growing awareness of alternative interpretations and options. By 1930 Keynes and Cole's paths crossed more and more, particularly after the *New Statesman*'s merger with the *Nation* in 1931. They never shared the symbiotic relationship Keynes enjoyed with Hubert Henderson before the two friends quarrelled (in 1930–31 over the value for money of public works, and more seriously in 1936 over the *General Theory*); but in February 1930 they jointly presented the case for reflation not retrenchment in a report of the Committee on the Economic Outlook, a sub-committee of the Economic Advisory Council (EAC). After the 1931 crisis both men served on the EAC's successor, the Committee on Economic Information. While Henderson, as joint secretary of the EAC and therefore an *ad hoc* civil servant, became increasingly sympathetic to the Treasury viewpoint, Keynes found fresh allies in his two socialist colleagues Cole and Bevin, the latter the TUC's representative on both the Committee on the Economic Outlook and the Macmillan Committee.[17]

In the years preceding Labour's second election victory, the Wall Street Crash and the subsequent 'economic blizzard', Cole and Keynes experienced a gradual convergence of ideas. As early as 1925 Cole had enthusiastically supported Keynes's opposition to a return to the gold standard. Now, although starting from wholly different political perspectives, both came to share a healthy scepticism towards free trade, and both argued the case for a public works programme ('Keynes was coming to see that public spending was needed as a complement to cheap money in order to raise prices and thus restore "normal" profits. The question of "confidence" might be met by a policy of protection'[18]). Cole of course could always fall back on the convenient assumption that a future post-capitalist society would speedily eliminate unemployment. Equally predictably, Keynes refused to accept that mass unemployment was an inevitable consequence of the contradictions of capitalism. Nevertheless, Keynes advocated, on grounds of efficiency and in consequence of humanity, ameliorative measures Cole justified solely in terms of social equality. Thus Keynes argued the case for forcing prices up to the level of the 'going' wage rate simply because the current convention of forcing wages down in line with prices was impractical. Cole could follow Keynes's reasoning, but rejected a low wage economy essentially because it was unjust and punitive.[19] Less than a year after Labour left office Cole was busy identifying feasible capital projects for a second, more purposeful administration. He knew what needed doing, but not how to pay for it – a £100 million national loan 'for the enlargement of the nation's productive capacity' sounded speculative and unconvincing.[20]

Because intellectually he saw no case for it, Cole, the veteran guild socialist, viewed liberal capitalism in conventional, nineteenth-century terms; in other words, he was thinking within the same intellectual parameters as the guardians of Treasury orthodoxy. Thus, in the mid-1920s he still accepted the shibboleth that increased public expenditure decreased the total investment available for private enterprise. Although busy discarding ideological baggage in the latter part of the decade, Cole naturally still rejected capitalism. Yet when, as a member of the EAC, he found himself wrestling with the immediate problem of making the market work, he was clearly less hidebound by convention than only a few years earlier. Keynes was an obvious influence, even before collaboration. Paradoxically, by believing capitalism remained the most potentially efficient and prosperous economic system, Keynes was much less inhibited in approaching the question of how to make it work well (he was also, of course, a far more formidable intellect than Cole). Thus, unlike Cole, he was capable by 1930 of engaging in that series of intellectual quantum leaps, most notably with respect to deficit financing, which six years later found ultimate expression in *The General Theory of Employment Interest and Money*.

In 1926–28 the General Strike and its aftermath (see below) led Cole to focus primarily upon industrial relations, defending the trade unions and the ILP's efforts to take the initiative in establishing the priorities for a future Labour government. For Labour commentators and activists alike, dealing with the jobless was still crucial, but in terms of burning political issues not the absolute priority. Thus, the *Nation*, the Liberal Summer School and the Liberal Industrial Inquiry (LII) together set the agenda with regard to lowering unemployment. After 18 months of intermittent deliberations, the LII's *Britain's Industrial Future* finally appeared in February 1928. The Liberals' 'Yellow Book' received a generally poor reception in the press, if only because of the demands its turgid prose made on the reader. In the *New Statesman*, a journal rarely hostile to turgid prose if well-intentioned, Cole applauded a 'formidable and an exceedingly interesting document' which, despite criticism of Labour's plans for the coal industry, could form the basis for a joint programme lasting the lifetime of the next Parliament. A National Investment Board's capital budget would total £100 million per annum – the same figure Cole had come up with in 1925 – but how, he asked, could new capital expenditure be funded? Beyond national investment bonds and loans, the answer was taxation, Robert Skidelsky noting the omission of any mention of an extra one shilling on income tax.[21]

Cole pointed out that, in producing an equally detailed and ambitious plan of economic reconstruction, Labour was aware that it might soon be called upon to practice what it preached. The reality of course was that Snowden was not simply indifferent, but openly hostile to the notion that, in Cole's words, the restoration of prosperity demanded a 'conscious effort and deliberate planning, in which the nation as a whole is inevitably and vitally involved'.[22] MacDonald was little better, *Labour and the Nation*'s disparate job-creation schemes giving scant impression of an overall strategy. Following the draft programme's publication in July 1928, the *New Statesman* – for which read Cole – compared MacDonald and R.H. Tawney's seamlessly crafted but ultimately empty distillation of high-flying rhetoric with the Liberals' earlier densely written equivalent. With one eye on the autumn conference, and another on his socialist credentials, Cole turned 180 degrees and denigrated the 'Yellow Book' as a 'thing of shreds and patches':

> The Liberal report means, by way of salutary reform, to strengthen the capitalist order against the threat of dissolution. The Socialist programme means to bring order out of a dissolution it regards as inevitable, by a drastic, albeit gradual, change in the basis of social organisation.[23]

This rebuff of the Liberal Party was repeated the following week. Either Sharp was on holiday or on a binge. If he was present and sober, it is hard to envisage him accepting so stark a statement of the *New Statesman*'s loyalties as Cole (and Lloyd) offered in the summer of 1928. This was 1918 all over again, and if the paper had remained unequivocally pro-Labour – and anti-collaboration with the Liberals – then at least readers would have had a clear editorial line with which to agree or disagree.

Yet by the winter of 1928–29, with the party conference long over, pragmatism again prevailed. Three essays on the state's obligation to provide work previewed the contents of *The Next Ten Years*, without Cole scoring too many party points. Then, on 1 March Lloyd George effectively launched the 1929 election campaign by pledging to reduce unemployment to an acceptable level in a year at minimal extra cost to the tax payer. The LII's report became the far more punchy and pugnacious pamphlet *We Can Conquer Unemployment*, detailing schemes to create work for 600,000; and on 10 May the Hogarth Press published Keynes and Henderson's stirring and stylish pamphlet, *Can Lloyd George Do It?*. Keynes's now familiar appetite for polemic and Lloyd George's platform oratory were taken sufficiently seriously by the Treasury as to warrant a formal reply. David Marquand rightly pointed out that many of the Liberal campaign documents' ideas could be found, albeit in a cruder, more embryonic form, in *Labour and the Nation*; they constituted a very real challenge to Labour's claim to be the only genuinely radical party.[24] The Liberals' spring offensive on jobs, and the subsequent campaign debate as to just which party was the best alternative to the Tories when it came to engineering economic recovery, finally brought to the surface deep divisions within the editorial staff of the *New Statesman* present for at least a decade.

For at least a year after the 1924 election Sharp had drawn a veil over persistent squabbling between the Asquithean rump in the Commons and a recalcitrant Lloyd George.[25] Privately he came to the view that the set surrounding Margot Asquith and her increasingly feeble but now ennobled husband were more and more out of touch with the real world. For Asquith, policies were the product of government, and scant encouragement was given to those supporters eager to advance any ideas going much beyond the Gladstonian remedies of free trade and retrenchment. Sharp was often inebriated, but never wholly incapacitated. At Great Queen Street he needed alternative policies – *Liberal* policies – to counter Lloyd and Cole's insistence that the *New Statesman* had to re-nail its colours to the flagstaff of democratic socialism. Like Keynes after 1924, Sharp's path led inexorably to an old enemy. Lloyd George, whatever his faults, was still for many the most formidable and exciting personality in British politics. From 1925 he was arguing, to the chagrin of many Asquitheans, that a modern and practical Liberal programme could still offer a radical and yet non-socialist solution to economic stagnation. As early as the spring of 1924, immediately following the winding-up of the National Liberal Party, he had marked his return to the fold with an appeal in the *Nation* for the party to promote capital investment in the industrial infrastructure. The winter of 1925–26 witnessed a new land campaign focused on Lloyd George, and intended to restore much battered party morale. Admittedly the campaign fizzled out when a specially convened Land Convention adopted Asquith's diluted alternative to Lloyd George's original proposals. But by this time Sharp had long since come round to the view of C.F.G. Masterman, another one-time opponent, that 'When Lloyd George came back to the party, ideas came back to the party'.[26]

On 12 December 1925, at the height of the land campaign, and again a month later in the aftermath of Sir Alfred Mond's defection to the Tories, leading articles called on Liberal MPs to rally round Lloyd George if they wanted their party to survive. Careful to distance Asquith (by now Lord Oxford and Asquith) from quarrels over money, Sharp now targeted two personal enemies: Walter Runciman and Vivian Phillips.[27] All this gloom and doom contrasted sharply with a New Year message from the *New Statesman* that Labour had little prospect of securing an outright majority, but the Liberal Party had every chance of recovering from its present gross under-representation in Parliament. In a conclusion carefully drafted to avoid antagonising colleagues and directors, Sharp returned to an old familiar theme:

> We may be profoundly conscious of the undesirability of any Liberal–Labour alliance, but we must recognise also the probable consequences and the price that must be paid for such political 'purity'. Perhaps it is worth paying: perhaps it is not. That is for the party leaders to decide.[28]

For all the carefully crafted air of Olympian detachment, the message was crystal clear; and by-election victories suggested some Liberal success in attracting back middle-class supporters frightened into voting Tory in 1924. In public Labour remained confident of an imminent return to power. Yet despite Henderson and MacDonald cold-shouldering Lloyd George when he sounded them out as to co-operation in the Commons, there was very real concern that a Liberal revival might prevent Labour taking office after the next election.[29]

When faced with a stark choice in May 1926 Sharp, like so many of Asquith's admirers, supported Lloyd George's more conciliatory approach to the General Strike. In the aftermath of the dispute, and ironically on the day Asquith suffered a slight stroke, a *New Statesman* leader insisted he step aside to give Lloyd George full authority to promote a progressive coalition.[30] That autumn, before and after Asquith's resignation as party leader, Sharp – doubtless to the chagrin of Cole and Lloyd – reiterated the message that a narrow class-based socialist party was unelectable in Britain, particularly with Lloyd George spearheading a Liberal revival.[31] For much of the next 12 months Cole's coverage of Labour's affairs was forced to play second fiddle to Sharp's commentary upon internal wranglings within the Liberal Party. Not only did colleagues have to grit their teeth when reading that two Liberal by-election victories marked a 'definite turning point in contemporary political history', but Cole had to put up with Sharp adding a footnote to his report on the Labour leadership's tight control over the 1927 conference.[32] One can only speculate whether the editor interfering with Cole's copy provoked an argument, but by the winter of 1927–28 Sharp was writing less and less. Publication of the 'Yellow Book' inspired him to take a fresh interest in party politics, and thus yet again the *New Statesman* found itself enthusing over a Liberal revival. Editorial consistency was at a premium, with Sharp's confident predictions of a triumph for Lloyd George and his scornful references to Labour annoying Sidney Webb intensely.[33] After all, although Webb no longer had any direct interest in the *New Statesman*, he was its co-founder, and it must have been particularly galling to find the paper crazily veering from qualified support for the Opposition Front Bench, of which he was a member, to eulogising a politician who less than a decade earlier had been its bitterest foe. Sharp had no compunction in telling the MP for Seaham Harbour to his face that 'He was contemptuous of the Labour Party; its leaders had no courage, it was based on the interests of one class, its only chance was coalition with the Liberals, and that would mean an inward split'.[34]

If Sidney Webb could no longer get Sharp dismissed, pro-Labour shareholders such as Williams and Whitley surely could. In the autumn of 1928, both before and after the board cautioned him for his intemperate language, Sharp exulted in the *New Statesman*'s almost unique concern for the 'most important of all immediate political problems', namely the need for an electoral '*entente*' comparable with that of 1906.[35] Labour were all too well aware of the longer-term benefits for the junior partner in the MacDonald–Gladstone electoral pact, and had absolutely no intention of holding out the hand of kindness to Lloyd George. In the light of Sharp's one-man campaign, wholly at odds with those colleagues who were actually producing the paper, let alone the directors, the decision not to use costly litigation as an excuse to dismiss him was a remarkable demonstration of loyalty on the part of the board. But there is no need for hindsight to see that it was an expensive and foolish gesture.

The whole purpose of unsigned leading articles was to convey to readers a common direction and a sense of unity and purpose – what made the *New Statesman* different from the *Nation*, the *Spectator* or any other political weekly. Like its rivals, it needed a recognisable identity and a clear editorial line. In fact, anonymity highlighted the deepening chasm between Sharp and his most senior staff. Readers were rightly confused by sporadic demands for an alliance that Labour's NEC explicitly, and most of the time the *New Statesman* implicitly, deemed inopportune and unnecessary. Yet, when readers wrote in to protest, Sharp gave them short shrift: anyone complaining was labelled unduly partisan and indifferent to the wider interests of the nation. Could the board afford to hang on for much longer to a man prepared for the sake of personal conviction to sacrifice some of the magazine's loyalist readers? Only months away from a crucial election Labour had to keep its nerve and resist any temptation to do a deal with Lloyd George. MacDonald's strategy was two-track: to keep the Liberals isolated and increasingly out of touch with the exercise of real power, and, above all, to maintain Labour's image as a party of moderation with its roots in the working-class but with a broad-based appeal to all non-Tory voters whatever their background. Before 1914 the appeal of 'New Liberalism' to the party managers was its message that social reform rendered Labour irrelevant – why wait years for the socialists to become a credible party of government when the Liberal Party could initiate change straightaway? A quarter of a century later the tables had been turned – if most people at a general election were choosing a government and not registering a protest, then a Liberal vote had to be seen to be a wasted vote. The week Sharp was repeating his call for an electoral pact, MacDonald recorded in his diary: 'If the three party system is to remain, it is obvious that the question of coalition in some shape or form has to be faced. Our [Labour's] immediate duty is to place every obstacle we can in the way of the survival of the three party system.'[36]

When Cole cooled towards *Britain's Industrial Future*, and gave only a qualified welcome to *We Can Conquer Unemployment*, it was because, however much he welcomed the spirit of the documents, party political considerations had to prevail. In fact Cole was actually drafting Labour's reply, *How to Conquer Unemployment*. His accompanying articles in the *New Statesman* contrasted Liberal palliatives with Labour's willingness to use public ownership of coal and the banking system to facilitate structural change, 'give the greatest stimulus to production for the home market and also add to the purchasing power of the domestic consumer so as to make this re-distribution effective'.[37] Cole was sending all the right signals for the role of a mixed economy in advancing demand-side measures to reflate the economy; and if ever implemented these were measures acceptable to Lloyd George and his wing of the party, albeit anathema to Samuel, Simon and the free trade traditionalists. The real test was whether these same proposals were acceptable to MacDonald and his colleagues, most notably Snowden, once in power. In office, would the rhetoric of socialism become reality?

Cole and Lloyd didn't need Sharp to highlight Labour's fear of Lloyd George's appeal to the voters' imagination. They were pointing it out every week in the *New Statesman*. They were also explicitly rejecting the option of a progressive alliance: at the Carlton Club meeting Baldwin had stopped Lloyd George destroying a second party, and Henderson and MacDonald had to do the same. With stakes so high, a re-run of the internal differences that had racked the *New Statesman* in 1924 seemed unavoidable, but this time the editor would not have his assistant to defend him. In any future confrontation between Sharp and Lloyd, supported by Cole, it was obvious whom the board would support. And then suddenly the rogue articles demanding coalition disappeared. The contributors' file confirms Sharp's absence for six weeks before polling day. As this was before his departure for New York one can only speculate as to the reason. For the *New Statesman* it was a particularly convenient moment for him to be *hors de combat* as a consequence of the demon drink, and neither his colleagues nor his directors would have been keen to see him during the election campaign. It does seem more than merely coincidental that Sharp should have disappeared at such a convenient time for the editorial staff. One possibility is that Williams made it clear that the paper should give Labour unqualified support, in the spirit of 1918, and that Sharp then walked out in high dudgeon. Drinking heavily, he was in no fit state to come back, proclaim editorial independence, and exercise his authority over the staff.

SHARP, LLOYD, AND COLE – DEALING WITH THE GENERAL STRIKE

The *New Statesman* was the only political weekly published during the General Strike in May 1926. It was only 10 pages long and poorly printed, but it retained the usual format, with contributions from 'YY' and 'Affable Hawk', as well as all the other regular features. With Lloyd and Cole absent organising support for the strikers, no-one questioned Sharp's decision to publish. Relying on a fortnight's supply of newsprint and a small non-unionised print shop discovered in Wandsworth, Sharp and Roberts had 12,000 copies printed, almost all for sale in London. Volunteer drivers delivered regular orders to newsagents and local subscribers, and street vendors were recruited to sell the remaining copies. A long-standing criticism of the strike organisers is that, although the TUC General Council published the *British Worker* (essentially a strike sheet preaching to the converted), they failed to get their message across to the general public because they called out the printers. Thus, the *Daily Herald* would have been a valuable weapon in the battle for public opinion, and the blinkered decision not to publish was yet another example of inadequate forethought and poor leadership. Seen in this light, getting the *New Statesman* on to the streets of the capital was a gesture of solidarity rather than an insensitive exercise in strike-breaking.

Sharp no doubt enjoyed getting one over on his rivals, most notably Henderson and St Loe Strachey, but there is no reason to doubt his intentions. Although he regarded A.J. Cook as a dangerous extremist, he had never been slow to lambast the Mineowners' Association as a cabal of blinkered profiteers. The contributors' file confirms that throughout the preceding 18 months Sharp, Lloyd and Cole were as one in supporting the miners, in attacking government collusion with the colliery owners, and in demanding national agreements on wages and conditions far beyond the recommendations of the Samuel Commission.[38] The *New Statesman*'s defence of trade union rights and its insistence that reducing labour costs was harshly deflationary, with minimal effect on overseas competitiveness, were two rare examples of consistency and unanimity. Cole, Lloyd and even Sharp after he signed up for Lloyd George, all saw public ownership as the panacea for the coal industry's ills, but recognised that politically it was a non-starter. To sum up, since the start of the dispute the *New Statesman*'s stance had been clear and uncompromising, but at the same time always realistic. Ego notwithstanding, Sharp's conscience was clear – the miners, if not their leaders, would see publishing a special strike issue as the act of an ally not a scab.

It was on this basis that a front-page article defended publication, but with one important qualification: the TUC was short-sighted in muffling friendly opinion, but neither should it have silenced its Fleet Street enemies. Why were the *Daily Mail* compositors so misguided as to provide ministers with an ideal excuse to provoke a strike? Sharp never took the easy route. He could easily have justified the paper's appearance on the grounds that it was a long-standing supporter of the miners, restated the view that Baldwin was personally responsible for the strike and for its resolution, and left it at that. Instead, he made a rod for his own back by also focusing on the paramountcy of the freedom of the press.[39] It was a theme he returned to the following week, after the strike was over, while at the same time roundly condemning the government for depicting 'patriotic moderation' as selfish extremism, and attempting to suppress church leaders' pleas for conciliation (the BBC were 'advised' not to let the Archbishop of Canterbury broadcast). There was a danger that the question of press freedom, important though it was, could overshadow the real issue of whether a general strike was a legitimate means of protecting the interests of trade unionists and, in this particular case, the miners. Sharp had done himself no favours by condemning the TUC's decision to shut down the printing presses, but this would not have worried him for one moment (neither of course would any embarrassment he might have caused Cole and Lloyd). Reflecting on the previous week's events he did in fact have much to say on the pros and cons of mass industrial action. Sharp was writing during one of his more sober (literally) and lucid moments. Although refusing to recognise the general strike as a legitimate weapon, he reserved his harshest words for a government which provoked individual trade unionists – 'profoundly and passionately convinced that they are fighting in a worthy and unavoidable fight' – to withdraw their labour in such a fashion:

> The men [needless to say, no mention of female strikers] who came out on strike did so at a heavy cost to themselves, with no prospect of personal advantage. They were fighting not for themselves, but for the miners, and they fought with a spirit and a unanimity which has never before been known in the history of industrial struggles throughout the world.[40]

For once Sharp's sardonic veneer was stripped away, and he wrote with great humanity and passion. His admiration for the strikers, especially the miners, was genuine, but at the same time he refused to accept what he saw as fundamentally illiberal acts on both sides – however callous and duplicitous Baldwin and his ministers had been, the TUC had no right to put a gun to the government's head. Once such action became the norm, the fundamental tenets of liberal democracy began to corrode.

Sharp was not slow to cultivate an idea that grabbed the national psyche almost as soon as the strike was over, namely that it was conducted in a peculiarly English spirit, somehow reminiscent of the Great War. Ever happy to subscribe to popular myth, he lauded the strikers' moderation in refusing to respond to provocation, and praised the authorities for their supposedly sensitive handling of a difficult situation. The only people excluded from an heroic part in this great national drama were the more diehard members of Baldwin's Cabinet. What was really needed was a report by Cole from the picket line – a healthy infusion of stark realism to counter-balance Sharp's more platitudinous remarks. Cole's absence was most noticeable in the advice given to the leaders of the Miners' Federation, which was as naive as it was specious. After all that had taken place over the past 10 days, let alone the past 18 months, Sharp could scarcely have expected Cook and his executive to accept the guarantees of Sir Herbert Samuel. When the Samuel Memorandum referred to an eventual 'revision of existing wage rates', the miners were convinced it had only had one direction in mind, and they were right.[41]

Needless to say, Sharp could not resist relating the strike to the battle for power within his adopted party, defending Lloyd George's conciliatory line while twice questioning on what basis Sir John Simon declared the strike illegal. More importantly, Lloyd now took up what was to become a central issue for the paper over the next 18 months: punitive action by the government in the light of what was a clear defeat for the trade union movement. Labour – and the *New Statesman* – would 'fight tooth and nail' any attempt to repeal or amend the 1906 Trade Dispute Act, or any other legislation providing for statutory rather than voluntary regulation of organised labour.[42]

Heavily involved in Oxford as a member of the University Strike Committee, Cole contributed nothing to *New Statesman* commentary during or even after the strike. His contribution came retrospectively, six weeks later. All leaders were of course unsigned, so any reader unfamiliar with the internal politics of Great Queen Street would have been puzzled to find that the TUC decision to call a general strike was now deemed to be entirely right. Where the General Council was at fault was in its inadequate preparation and unclear objectives, the latter compounding an already poor working relationship with the Miners' Federation. Cole took understandable pride in having participated, and yet his *New Statesman* article suggested that the failure of the strike was somehow reassuring: it demonstrated that the outcome of mass industrial action – in Britain at least – was not consistent with syndicalist mythology. The extra-parliamentary option, lionised on the left for so long, had failed to counter the full power of the modern state, let alone the 'self-protective instincts' of an ever-larger middle class. The prospect of another general strike was now remote, except in the unlikely circumstance of a government persistently ignoring the popular will over an issue so great as to mobilise the mass of public opinion. Like Sidney Webb in 1913, Cole argued that a strike in such conditions could justifiably be labelled 'constitutional' if it led to a general election and the government being voted out of office. Of course this implied, albeit unintentionally, that mass extra-parliamentary action could only be considered 'constitutional' (did he really mean 'legitimate'?) if it was successful; the logic of such a premise being a denial of legitimacy if, no matter how just the cause, such action proved unsuccessful.[43]

For all its faults, the *New Statesman* in 1926–27 was a campaigning paper. The poverty and distress on the coalfields was never forgotten, the deficiencies and iniquities of the Trades Disputes Bill were repeatedly highlighted, and the attempt to suspend the miners' seven-hour day was denounced as tantamount to declaring class war. Cole returned from Durham appalled by conditions and aghast that miners there 'should *ever* go back'.[44] 'Spencerism' in the East Midlands and the gradual drift back to work prefaced employers' reprisals; all of which Cole dutifully recorded in reports compiled with Fabian thoroughness, yet infused with a deep personal sense of horror and injustice. Meanwhile, beyond the paramount issue of restoring wages and conditions at the pithead, ministers were regularly lambasted for everything from dismissing the West Ham Board of Guardians (Neville Chamberlain at Health) to posing as the moral guardian of a sexually depraved nation (Joynson-Hicks at the Home Office). If divided on the composition of the next government, Cole, Lloyd and Sharp could at least agree that the present one needed replacing. They consistently underestimated Baldwin, but in this they were not unusual. Sharp, for example, portrayed the Prime Minister as a well-intentioned but weak leader: a man lacking the 'moral and mental strength' to control an increasingly reactionary Cabinet, let alone unite the nation.[45] In doing so, of course, he completely misjudged Baldwin, accepting the consensual one-nation Tory image at face value, and failing to recognise that behind the avuncular image was a steely, even ruthless character quite capable of seeing off Curzon, Beaverbrook, Churchill, Edward VIII and anyone else intent on bringing him down, including even A.J. Cook.

THE *NEW STATESMAN* AND THE ILP 1924–29: WAS THERE STILL A PLACE FOR SOCIALISM?

Labour's tentative programme, defended by Cole more in hope than anticipation, was scarcely even a diluted version of the platform adopted by the ILP as the basis of its 'Socialism in Our Time' campaign, or A.J. Cook and James Maxton's subsequent manifesto. After 1924 Cole could easily have taken a leading role in the ILP, and yet his work for the *New Statesman* revealed a growing disaffection with the 'emotional intransigence of this section of the Left . . . [which] offended his Fabian practicability'.[46] Why was this?

After 1924 the Labour pendulum swung away from the gradualism of parliamentary politics back towards direct industrial action. Many trade unionists were disillusioned by a Labour Cabinet's insistence on placing national interests above the specific needs and demands of its natural supporters – for example, in using emergency legislation if a strike threatened the maintenance of essential supplies and services. Although sharing their anger over ministers' failure to tackle unemployment, Cole acknowledged the threat to the parliamentary leadership's electoral strategy if the very heart of the movement – the trade unions – now openly questioned their party's commitment to democratic socialism. Albeit writing anonymously, Cole showed how far he had travelled, and how quickly, in a state-of-the-movement assessment in April 1925:

> in so far as the party inheirits the position of Liberalism . . . it becomes more and more occupied with questions of political expediency and strategy . . . no longer satisfied with expressing Trade Union aims; it seeks to become a 'People's Party' rallying supporters from all classes and sections of Society. . . . The Trade Unions grow more and more disposed to say that, since the politicians can apparently do nothing for them . . . they prefer to pursue their own course without any regard to questions of political expediency.[47]

'Expediency' is often a dirty word, and implicit approval could be read into that final sentence. However, when seen in the context of the article as a whole, Cole's recognition that the less obeisant trade union leaders would be happy to plough their furrow rang as a warning bell for both halves of the movement: yes, Labour had to broaden its electoral base, but unity remained crucial. In the aftermath of the Russian Revolution and the establishment of the third International this was what was unique about organised labour in Britain – the principal party of the working class had remained largely intact, with much of the credit going to the endeavours of MacDonald and Henderson while out of Parliament between 1918 and 1922. By 1925 Cole as well as Lloyd were key party activists, all too well aware of the dangers of factionalism and, more crucially, of trade union disillusion with Westminster. They both enjoyed direct lines to individual TUC and PLP leaders, albeit in the case of Cole still viewed with suspicion by the likes of Bevin and Citrine, but their real concern was with dissatisfaction on the shop-floor or at the coal-face. In the latter case, the simplest means of keeping the Miners' Federation on board was to go on campaigning for nationalisation and a decent wage.

Cole rightly anticipated that the ILP would endeavour to secure trade union support for the *New Leader*'s insistence on a 'living wage'; a campaign, originally inspired by veteran 'New Liberal' thinker J.A. Hobson, which in early 1925 offered 'an under-consumptionist solution' to unemployment.[48] A week later Cole dismissed the ILP 'Left Wing' of Brockway, John Paton and the Glasgow MPs for 'still trying to mix the oil of revolutionary Communism with the water of evolutionary Social Democracy'. He sided with Clifford Allen, Noel Brailsford and the other ex-UDC intellectuals who wanted to make the ILP an essentially policy-making body, sacrificing 'its street-corner Socialism to its political aspiration'.[49] Although this was a predictable attitude for the *New Statesman* to adopt, it ignored the fact that Maxton (Allen's successor as leader after illness forced his resignation in late 1925) and his supporters, both on the back benches and out in the country, were determined to prevent their party becoming a think tank for the progressive intelligentsia. The spirit of 'Red Clydeside' was still alive and well and, in consequence, Cole distanced himself more and more from a party which even before May 1926 was becoming isolated from mainstream Labour politics. Although he criticised MacDonald for his tactical ineptness in handling the Clydesiders, he disputed their insistence on placing the interests of the ILP above those of the parliamentary Labour Party. Nevertheless, Cole still saw a role for back-bench dissent, particularly after the 1925 conference and the annual elections to the parliamentary committee demonstrated just what a grip the old guard, and MacDonald in particular, still had over the party.[50]

Well before the General Strike – arguably well before the experience of 1924 – MacDonald's credentials as a visionary committed to major structural reform of the economy, allied to a fundamental redistribution of wealth, were exhausted in the eyes of most ILP activists. By the spring of 1926 his relations with the party's executive, the National Administrative Council (NAC), were at an all-time low. Cole questioned MacDonald's insistence that the left's activities on the floor of the House were losing Labour the next election, pointing out that most ILP MPs were ultra-loyal and that Labour needed a 'ginger group' to keep it on its toes. How this squared with Cole's view of Maxton, Brockway and their allies on the NAC as the 'vanguard of a potentially revolutionary working class' was never made clear. Cole was most sympathetic to the ILP when it was operating as a policy-making body in practice if not in name, hence his heavily qualified support for the inquiry into a national minimum wage which Brailsford instigated as a proper campaign in January 1926. The *New Leader* slogan of 'Socialism in Our Day' became the more familiar 'Socialism in Our Time' following the campaign's formal adoption at that April's annual conference.[51]

Cole saw the 'puritanical Socialist demand' of a living wage as a laudable but impractical objective which no incoming socialist government could in practice deliver. *If* 'Socialism in Our Time' had any value then it was as an instrument of propaganda, a deceptive Sorelian myth, but 'if the aim is to convert the working-class to a full-blooded Socialist propaganda it would be better, and better propaganda, to tell them so straight out'. His prediction that the ILP could expect little support from trade union leaders other than A.J. Cook was right: Bevin and other TUC stalwarts saw a state-controlled wage as a clear threat to their traditional collective bargaining role.[52] Cole acknowledged the ingenuity of Hobson's analysis of and solution to underconsumption. His objections were principally political, as indeed were MacDonald's. He may have been, in Beatrice Webb's words, an 'intellectual fanatic' (a description as flattering as it is implicitly pejorative), but he saw the importance of a coherent programme of economic planning as the prerequisite of any assault upon capital's commanding heights – and as far as the *New Statesman* was concerned, the ILP had yet to draft and adopt just such a programme.[53]

Looking back on the stormy events of 1926 Cole felt obliged to point out that the NAC's presumption of a high degree of revolutionary consciousness had been found wanting, and yet working-class voters expected the next Labour government to 'change enough to make a real and noticeable difference to our ways of life'. In the aftermath of the General Strike, with a Cabinet planning further retribution, such voters were entitled to expect a Labour Party thinking ahead and not 'too content to live on its intellectual capital'.[54] At a time when the Fabian Society was desperately in need of regeneration, and the ILP was more and more teleological in its policy-making, Labour needed hard thinking, not easy slogans. Cole's undergraduate discussion group, of which Gaitskell was such a vocal member, had grown out of the 1926 University Strike Committee, and was always kept deliberately informal. In the second half of the 1920s his mind turned more and more to alternative propagandist and policy-making bodies, operating under a Labour umbrella, but it took the trauma of 1929–31 to bring about the Society for Socialist Inquiry and Propaganda (SSIP) and the New Fabian Research Bureau (NFRB).[55]

Cole would always have a soft spot for the ILP, and the 1927 Summer School convinced him that Brailsford and the more cerebral end of the party still had much to contribute, particularly when questioning free trade as a tested cure for the nation's economic ills. Like Lloyd, he found the likes of Maxton and Brockway harder to handle, his conference report predicting clashes in a pre-election year between the NEC and an NAC flirting with the Communists.[56] He was right of course, and by Easter 1928 the 'constant air of moral superiority' adopted by the executive at the ILP's annual conference was too much even for Cole. Having previously insulted the 112 members of the parliamentary group by positing a future for the ILP as a useful 'debating society for keen Socialists', the *New Statesman* now argued that the potential for damaging Labour was so great that its founding party's best course of action was to wind itself up.[57] Remember, this was Cole and Lloyd writing, not Clifford Sharp.

That could have been the end of the story, but the contradiction remained, with the ILP now an open target for Cole and Lloyd's barbs while still being cited as a potential focus for research and debate. Pleas for the ILP to adopt a radical propagandist role could hardly be squared with Lloyd's harsh reception for the Cook–Maxton manifesto launched nationwide in June 1928.[58] The manifesto's unequivocal dismissal of gradualism constituted a genuinely revolutionary approach to unemployment, and indeed to the prevailing economic system as a whole. This was a socialism that did not assume capitalism had to be made to work in order to fund and facilitate ameliorative, reformist measures, and as such it was bound to polarise the ILP, let alone the Labour Party ('much of the energy which should be expended in fighting Capitalism is now expended in crushing everybody who dares to remain true to the ideals of the movement'[59]).

The Cook–Maxton manifesto was a direct challenge to all that the mainstream Labour Party represented at the time. At the 1928 conference the most competent and the most respected of the Clydesiders, John Wheatley – the one minister who left office in 1924 with his reputation enhanced – held up *Labour and the Nation* and declared 'it would be easier to select a Liberal programme from these measures than a Socialist programme'.[60] In his conference report Cole found himself not only projecting the party's tawdry manifesto as a more imaginative and constructive document than the 'Yellow Book', but also having to ignore telling criticism from one-time natural allies on the left (admittedly natural allies coming from an overtly statist – as opposed to Cole's guild socialist – background). Nor could the fact that this was the *New Statesman* opining, and not G.D.H. Cole by name, provide much comfort, or much cover. The impression given in a characteristically sombre and humourless leader, full of hackneyed evangelical imagery, was clearly unintentional: Cole made the Labour Party appear dull, complacent and self-righteous, and thus curiously akin to the *New Statesman* at the time. Wheatley had talked 'arrant nonsense' in his conference address, and the behaviour of the platform had been impeccable. The last conference report before the general election was as informative and as exciting as the NEC's minutes, with everyone, most of all Cole, on his best behaviour.[61] When launched at the start of the 1929 campaign, *Labour and the Nation* was warmly, and predictably, received; scarcely surprising given Cole's authorship of the accompanying pamphlet *Labour's Reply to Lloyd George*. All this would have been perfectly acceptable had Lloyd and Cole been in a position to state outright at the beginning of the campaign that the *New Statesman* would be enthusiastically supporting the Labour Party – which in effect Squire did in 1918. However, in order that harmony might prevail at Great Queen Street, and Sharp not rock the boat, no such statement was made. In theory, the *New Statesman* was not a recognised pro-Labour paper in the spring of 1929, even if in practice it was. This would not have mattered had the magazine not continued to insist that it was an independent journal with no obvious political alignment. As it was, this unsatisfactory state of affairs highlighted the confusion and crisis management that had plagued the paper throughout the second half of the 1920s.

SHARP'S FINAL YEARS

Encountering Sharp's 'fierce eye and ... brazen voice' for the first time in 1927, the young Peter Quennell was easily impressed. Here was a master of the English language, and a 'giant in his trade' who continued to command the respect of his colleagues. Well yes, free from the bottle Sharp could still rule Great Queen Street with a rod of iron, but few of his peers would have accepted Quennell's generous judgement. By the late 1920s Sharp was scarcely ever sober, and when he was he had a massive hangover that was best remedied by a stiff whisky. V.S. Pritchett provided a memorable portrait of a 'massive man . . . a glaring editorial chunk', with his 'nobly handsome face, swollen and ravaged by his dissipations'.[62]

In the summer of 1928 Sharp spent a weekend with the Webbs for the first time in six years. Beatrice found him 'physically shattered by drink' but 'sane, cynically able, and frank'. Still scornful of Labour, its leaders and its narrow class-base, Sharp remained insistent that coalition with the Liberals was the party's only credible option. A lonely and embittered figure, he found politics 'deadly dull', the world 'sombre and unlovely', and public life plagued by a 'dearth of talent'. How could anyone so world-weary inject enthusiasm and dynamism into a weekly magazine? Of course, he could not, as those who worked with him would readily confirm:

> He [Sharp] told us [Sidney and Beatrice Webb] a good deal about Beaverbrook, who had made him various offers of highly paid employment. He was tired of the *New Statesman* but hated the idea of anyone else controlling it. . . . I should not be surprised if Clifford Sharp ended by deliberately drinking himself past recovery; he seems to have lost hope either for himself or for the world . . . .[63]

By this time Sharp rarely contributed editorial notes, the major exception being the Empire which became a subject close to his heart in the dog-days of his career. He developed the habit of drinking heavily in the late afternoon; and on Thursdays of then 'invading the printer'.[64] Exercising his right as the ultimate arbiter to rewrite copy, Sharp would seriously delay the paper going to bed. This must have exasperated Mostyn Lloyd who, despite able assistance from Cole, Stonier and Ratcliffe, when he was not in New York, was by this time the *de facto* editor. One can imagine an exhausted Lloyd at home or in the LSE senior common room being called to the telephone in order to appease an irate chief compositor. No wonder standards slipped and sales stagnated. Not only that, Sharp's negligence was beginning to cost the board serious money.

In addition to bemoaning the state of the Empire, by 1928 Sharp's only regular leaders concerned a subject close to his Nonconformist heart: the constitutional crisis created by the Lords accepting and the Commons rejecting the Established Church's revision of the Prayer Book to appease its Anglo-Catholic clergy. However, his increasingly maverick behaviour heightened the risk of a last-minute editorial, long on prejudice but short on accuracy. Substituting copy at the last minute meant ignoring words of wisdom from more cautious colleagues *and* the paper's legal adviser. Every editor can expect the occasional allegation of libel or even contempt of court, but Sharp had in the past been particularly adroit at avoiding litigation. In 1928 he ran out of luck, largely through his own fault.

First, the *New Statesman* lost a costly libel suit brought by the Metropolitan Police concerning the role of the Commissioner and Assistant Commissioner in the so-called 'Savidge case'. At a time when the Home Secretary, Sir William Joynson-Hicks, was fuelling popular concern over alleged illicit sexual practices in Hyde Park, Sharp rose to defend Sir Leo Chiozza Money when he and a Miss Savidge were charged with indecent behaviour in public (and later acquitted, after complaints in the House about police behaviour and a subsequent tribunal of inquiry). Chiozza Money was not only an ex-minister, an authority in the Labour Party on the City, and the financial correspondent for the *New Statesman*, but also one of Sharp's oldest friends. Writing in the paper after the trial, Sharp was unrepentant. Neither, earlier in 1928, did he regret accusing Mr Justice Avory of a 'substantial miscarriage of justice' during his conduct of the *Morning Post*'s successful libel action against Marie Stopes. Having demonstrated an obvious contempt of court, and then libelled the most senior officers in the Metropolitan Police, it is scarcely surprising that the minutes of 30 October 1928 record the board informing Sharp that 'these comments and articles were sometimes characterized by violence of phrasing and desired that such violence be avoided in future'. The total cost of both cases helped turn a potential profit for 1928–29 into a loss of £3,618. Whitley, Williams and Bennett covered the loss with loans to the company, while effectively giving Sharp one last chance to pull himself together.[65]

Just over a year later, in December 1929 the board, with genuine reluctance, finally accepted the need to dismiss Sharp. By this time, despite Labour being again in power, his contribution to the paper comprised little more than occasional trivia for 'Comments' and the odd leader drafted late on the evening before press-day in the company of his mistress and his hip-flask. At least, to Lloyd's relief, he had stopped going to see the printers. Instead, Sharp indulged in his new passion of accompanying stunt pilots – an eccentricity which a bemused Beatrice Webb sniffily described as a 'passively reckless pursuit – significant of certain distaste for life'.[66] In a further Wodehousian twist, the board told Sharp that his employment would cease only after a 12-month paid sabbatical in New York, during which time he could dry out. Over the years *New Statesman* directors have been party to some bizarre decisions, and until the 1980s were reluctant to sack an editor outright (in 1972 Crossman was asked to continue until a successor was appointed). However, assuming that Sharp would be incapable of acquiring a drink in New York as a result of Prohibition suggests a stunning naivety. Given Bennett's knowledge of America one is tempted to conclude Sharp was sent there for reason of pure malice. However, evidence suggests the board genuinely believed that a fresh career across the Atlantic beckoned, if only he could break with old haunts and habits. A year under Ratcliffe's eagle eye was intended as a gesture of appreciation for Sharp's 16 years of service. In tandem with Orage, another editor – of more genuinely heroic proportions – exiled in the New World, Ratcliffe toured the speak-easies rescuing Sharp from alcoholic poisoning and arrest, but in a very short time he had lost everything. John Roberts, Great Queen Street's long-serving – and long-suffering – business manager, sold Sharp's 1,000 (shilling) shares in the company to pay for a ticket home. He met his erstwhile editor at the docks, and placed him in the first of several clinics. Old friends, notably Jack Squire and Robert Lynd, rallied round in a last desperate effort to save Sharp's career. He was an alcoholic, and the only cure was total abstinence. Sharp could stop drinking, but he lacked the strength of character, will-power and motivation to stay off the bottle. What was the point? All he wanted to do was edit the *New Statesman*. By 1930 he was no longer capable of doing this, even if the board had not dismissed him, and he knew it.[66] In his diary Bennett recorded Sharp's final meeting with the board following his return from New York: 'He [Sharp] never argued or protested. It really was a very sad scene. The best thing for me is not to let my imagination work on it all.'[67]

10

The rise and fall of the Labour government, and the fall and rise of the *New Statesman and Nation,* 1930–31

LLOYD, COLE, AND THE FIRST 18 MONTHS OF LABOUR IN POWER

Espying Kingsley Martin among the exultant Labour MPs and supporters gathered at Westminster on 6 August 1945, Ernie Bevin is said to have called out across a packed Central Hall, "Ullo, gloomy, I give you about three weeks before you stab us all in the back'.[1] However fair or unfair to Martin personally – and it was well known that there was no love lost between the two men – Bevin's remark ignored the fact that, contrary to popular assumption, the *New Statesman* had been surprisingly sympathetic to both previous Labour governments. In 1924 Cole especially could have been far harsher in his criticism of economic policy, while Sharp was endeavouring to bring the Liberals into the administration rather than consciously seeking to drive Labour out. Similarly, MacDonald's second administration was given a surprisingly easy ride until the latter part of 1930. Sharp had been effectively silenced, except for a valedictory leader on 25 January 1930 which urged *rapprochement* with Lloyd George.[2] Mostyn Lloyd's paper was dull, uninspiring, introspective and even at times self-indulgent, but for the first time since 1918 it did have a clear political stance.[3] Regular readers no longer had the jarring

238

experience of digesting a clarion call for undiluted socialism one week and the next a plea to accommodate Liberal faith in the free market. Although Lloyd's final issue insisted the *New Statesman* had never been the 'property of any party', by 1930 only the most insensitive subscriber would fail to recognise that here was an unequivocably pro-Labour paper.[4]

Both Lloyd and Cole emphasised to readers the difference between independence and disloyalty, and in so doing came out strongly in Labour's favour. This 'loyal grousing' paralleled that of the New Fabian Research Bureau (NFRB) and the Society for Socialist Inquiry and Propaganda (SSIP), both of which the two men began planning in the winter of 1930–31. With each organisation minimising the risk of clashes with the party hierarchy by securing formal affiliation, the accent was on breadth of discussion rather than open dissent.[5] Scepticism verging on outright hostility towards Maxton and the ILP, and waning enthusiasm for Sir Oswald Mosley as he became an ever-more maverick figure within the party, reflected a clear reluctance to challenge what, in the aftermath of the August 1931 crisis, Cole described as the labour movement's 'sentiment of collective solidarity'. In highlighting trade union antipathy towards individuals who sacrificed party unity for the pursuit of their ideas and ambitions, Cole might by then have had MacDonald in mind, but the example he in fact quoted was Mosley. The latter's experience in 1930 was a lot closer to that of Cole himself, the difference being the latter's respect for, to use Robert Skidelsky's phrase, the 'ideological cement of class solidarity'.[6] The irony is obvious, but nevertheless intellectuals like Cole and Lloyd had to accept, particularly after the trauma of 1931, that trade unionism remained at the very heart of the labour movement. Closer acquaintance with Bevin, deeply suspicious but by no means automatically hostile towards the denizens of Hampstead and Oxford, no doubt influenced Cole's previously poor opinion of general secretaries.

One general secretary whose mediocrity Cole had never doubted was J.H. Thomas, appointed Lord Privy Seal and given overall responsibility for relieving unemployment. After a disappointing King's Speech, Cole made clear what he saw as Labour's domestic agenda, with more jobs and better working conditions right at the top. Nevertheless, he urged patience, pointing out that it had been the Liberals and not Labour who had rashly promised early results.[7] Thus, throughout the second half of 1929 the *New Statesman* gave the new government an easy ride, rejecting ILP charges of ministerial inertia, and highlighting diplomatic triumphs for Henderson at Geneva and MacDonald in New York. Even the Chancellor attracted praise, albeit from a ridiculously Francophobe Sharp, predictably ecstatic over Snowden's wrecking tactics at The Hague conference on the Young Plan.[8] By December, and after the publication of a wholly inadequate White Paper on job creation, Cole switched from coded criticism of Jimmy Thomas to a *de facto* call for his replacement by one of his two junior ministers, Mosley or Tom Johnston.[9] Cole voiced what others had been saying in private since Thomas's appointment: that he was not up to the job and easily swayed by his civil servants.[10] Like Mosley, Cole's argument for an executive body to initiate a major public works programme constituted an implicit rejection of the Treasury view that state aid should only be given to export industries poised to exploit an imminent trade revival. Getting skilled workers off the dole and back into jobs, targeting overseas *and* domestic markets, was not only a cost-effective use of public money, but a direct means of enhancing purchasing and thus demand. Cole was articulating a familiar reflationary argument, then as now, albeit without the intellectual grist of a Richard Kahn.[11]

Cole's belief that Thomas was a lame duck was no longer based on hearsay, but on direct experience. When MacDonald first floated the idea of the Economic Advisory Council (EAC) in December 1929, Thomas joined Snowden and the FBI in frustrating any attempt to give it limited executive functions. The EAC, together with the Macmillan Committee, nevertheless took the heat off Thomas, helped placate an increasingly frustrated Mosley, and, it was hoped, sent positive signals to back-benchers and to constituency or shop-floor activists.[12] Chapter 9 showed that Keynes worked closely with Cole on the EAC, and with Bevin on the Macmillan Committee. Bevin's grudging respect for Cole served to complete the triangle. Arthur Henderson, who appears to have engineered Cole's membership of the EAC, agreed that Mosley should succeed the increasingly bibulous Thomas at once:

MacDonald had to spend less time monitoring Foreign Office business, and focus instead on efforts to breathe life into the economy.[13] Since writing his 1925 pamphlet *Revolution by Reason*, Mosley had regularly acknowledged his debt to Keynes. In September he sought Keynes's support for his abortive attempt to increase the road-building programme, and in January 1930 he sent him his draft memorandum on tackling unemployment. Having sought advice from Keynes and from Hubert Henderson, Mosley sent the final draft direct to Downing Street. Although Cole was not party to these preliminary discussions, John Strachey, Mosley's closest ally and a friend of both, would certainly have briefed him on the call for borrowing proportionate to the size of the jobless in order to support a centrally directed public works programme. On 15 February 1930 the *New Statesman* fully endorsed Mosley's proposals for economic regeneration and for reform in the machinery of government: in the face of global evidence, not least the shock waves generated by the Wall Street Crash, the Lord Privy Seal's faith in the trade cycle was a bewildering manifestation of fatalism and inertia.[14] Cole confidently predicted that the world slump would get 'a lot, lot worse'. Over succeeding weeks Cassandra-like predictions prefaced calls for Thomas's resignation in the interest of government and party, as much as for the sake of the unemployed. Again and again in that dreadful spring of 1930 Cole's dire warnings were overtaken by events: unemployment appeared to be rising inexorably towards two million, and Labour performed poorly at by-elections in Central Nottingham and West Fulham. Yet still the Lord Privy Seal soldiered on. In May 1930 he and Snowden orchestrated his deputy's resignation following Cabinet rejection of Mosley's memorandum. Not until the following month was Thomas very belatedly moved to the Dominions Office.

In the light of these events one would have assumed continued support for Mosley, and yet by the time he sought re-election to the NEC at the October conference the *New Statesman*'s enthusiasm had quite clearly waned. Perhaps one should not be so surprised. As 'loyal grousers', Cole and Lloyd took every opportunity to play down the very obvious divisions within the parliamentary Labour Party. Thus, in April 1930 a characteristically Gladstonian budget attracted only muted criticism, with Cole, doubtless appreciating his anonymity, making the ridiculous claim that differences between the Clydesiders and Snowden were 'only a question of degree – the former intent on an immediate redistribution of wealth, and the latter only after a revival of trade'.[15] This was only days before those very same Glasgow MPs accepted an ILP policy to follow only conference decisions as interpreted by the NAC. Party discipline in the House appeared to be breaking down, even though the Labour Whip was not immediately withdrawn. With Wheatley dead, and Maxton too regularly pilloried for his passion and his appearance, the left had no-one who could challenge the first generation Labour leadership on their own terms. Mosley was different, as Beatrice Webb noted in a particularly astute assessment of his character and his chances of one day seizing the crown. Allies such as Strachey and Fenner Brockway were, like Mosley himself, 'intruders into the world of manual workers' (and anyway he had little in common with the ILP rank and file). Success meant support from the 'natural leaders of the great organised communities of the proletariat' – power-brokers like Henderson, Bevin, Citrine and Herbert Morrison who clearly had little use for Mosley.[16] Cole's reluctance to continue championing Mosley suggests a frank realisation of his character flaws, his very real potential for destroying an already fragile government, and above all, the emptiness of his pretensions to be a credible alternative to MacDonald. The new-found hero of the conference floor and unholy ally of Red Clydeside already matched vision and imagination with an unattractive and all too obvious ambition. It did not require the creation of the New Party and then of the British Union of Fascists to recognise that, however worthy his intentions towards the unemployed, here was a man best avoided.

Thomas's departure meant that MacDonald assumed direct responsibility for unemployment, chairing the relevant Cabinet committee. Cole's acquaintance with the Whitehall machine confirmed, as if he did not know already, that Treasury orthodoxies had to be challenged. Snowden and his officials' refusal to countenance any compromise over free trade and the gold standard would always thwart interventionist policies such as those advocated by Mosley. In such circumstances, it was up to the

Prime Minister to demonstrate the strength of his convictions. How much longer could the pretext be maintained that to pay two million to do nothing was cheaper than giving them useful work? 'As well expect a man to swim with a millstone round his neck, as expect industry to flourish when both production and consumption are artificially kept down. Are we all mad, that we allow this unutterable folly to go on?'[17] Echoing sentiments voiced at the EAC, Cole outlined the case for an early restructuring of manufacturing industry through a massive input of state capital, and for a limited redistribution of wealth via direct taxation in order to improve living standards for the poorest and enhance purchasing power: 'so far from having reached the limits of "insular socialism", this country is really at a point where a substantial dose of constructive Socialism is its greatest economic need.'[18] In reality, there was nothing distinctively socialist about Cole's 'constructive Socialism', and any Liberal of Lloyd George's (and indeed of Keynes's) persuasion could happily have endorsed his plea for action. Indeed, Lloyd urged MacDonald to take seriously the Liberal leader's willingness to support any government initiatives to create jobs.

Yet if by the autumn of 1930 the honeymoon period was well and truly over, the emphasis on positive criticism remained: the post-Sharp *New Statesman* continued to manifest a remarkable degree of goodwill towards MacDonald and the majority of his colleagues, including of course its founder.[19] In consequence, Maxton, John Paton and the other ILP 'rebels' defying the Labour Whip could derive little comfort from Cole and Lloyd's leader columns. They were regularly accused of disloyalty and naivety, and their parliamentary tactics were condemned as disruptive and counter-productive. The paper's position was simple: ILP demands were unreasonable and impractical, and a Labour government was entitled to expect the loyalty of the whole parliamentary party. As late as July 1931 Cole was dismissing the ILP amendment to the Unemployment Insurance Bill as a 'Utopian demand' which would serve merely to embarrass the government.[20] Eight months earlier, in the aftermath of an unhappy conference, disappointing municipal election results and yet another uninspiring King's Speech, the real concern was not the condition of Labour in the Commons but in the constituencies.

How could ministers counter the spread of disillusion and distrust without 'a plan, bold, feasible and more attractive than tariffs for rescuing the country'?[21]

The paper was already displaying a less sceptical view of protection; but Cole's plea for an alternative was a clear acknowledgement that recovery was in no way guaranteed, and that anyway it would split the Cabinet. By this time both Cole and Lloyd were key figures in the discussions out of which emerged the SSIP and the NFRB. How far both men had moved away from Mosley since his resignation six months earlier is illustrated by the hostile reception given to John Strachey when he presented an early meeting with a draft of the policy document intended to turn rumblings of discontent into open revolt. Unlike the 17 backbenchers and A.J. Cook who did eventually sign Mosley's manifesto, Cole denounced it as a 'conspiracy against the government'. Lloyd likewise blanched at Mosley's attack on parliamentary government, highlighting the potential for abusing executive power if the nation's fate was placed in the hands of a small emergency Cabinet. In January 1931, before becoming editor, Kingsley Martin raged over so many MPs' complacency in the face of economic dislocation and social deprivation, emphasising in common with Cole and Lloyd the need for parliamentary reform. For all three men pluralism was synonymous with 'democratic socialism'; Cole after all had his roots in a guild socialism deeply suspicious of a state apparatus indifferent to grassroots opinion. It is scarcely surprising that by early 1931 the *New Statesman* was already warning of Mosley's excessive enthusiasm for concentrating the power of the state at the centre.[22]

Keynes, who according to Hugh Dalton met Mosley quite frequently in the autumn of 1930, clearly did not share these fears. In the *Nation* on 13 December he gave the manifesto a warm welcome. Not for the first time had Keynes publicly endorsed Mosley's ideas, witness his letter in *The Times* of 6 June 1930 supporting the case for a major public works programme. The difference now was that the EAC's economists' sub-committee, on which Keynes was clearly the driving force, had submitted a majority report calling for a temporary 10 per cent tariff on imports, plus a protective tariff on iron and steel to generate revenue. Keynes himself had argued for an all-round tariff, but had modified his position in order to secure the support of every member except Lionel Robbins, whose minority report Snowden predictably endorsed. The more astute *Nation* reader could have read the signs. He or she might even have speculated on the implications for a magazine synonymous with the intellectual case for free trade if its chairman and most distinguished columnist was to come out publicly in support of protection. Keynes himself must surely have reflected on the irony of the situation, and on possible damage to the *Nation* should any quarrel over editorial policy became common knowledge.[23]

THE MERGER OF THE *NEW STATESMAN* AND THE *NATION*, AND THE ARRIVAL OF KINGSLEY MARTIN, 1930–31

The first issue of the *New Statesman and Nation* appeared on 28 February 1931, and was greeted with a deafening silence. The absence of publicity reflected the lack of controversy: Bennett and Keynes had masterminded the merger with a characteristic degree of guile, calculation, compromise and prescience.[24] Rescuing Kingsley Martin from the *Manchester Guardian* was, in retrospect, a genuinely historic appointment. No apprentice editor ever chose a less auspicious moment to relaunch his or her paper as a crusading flagship of the left. Yet today Martin holds a unique position in the history of the British press. Few editors have written so much about themselves, or had so much written about them.[25] Simply to say that he took a failing Fabian weekly and increased its circulation from 14,000 to 100,000 is to belittle his achievement. Commercial success might more easily have been achieved through a deliberate decision to move down-market, all too common an occurrence in more recent times. Martin avoided this easy option, preferring to build on Sharp's early achievements. He acknowledged the scale of his task, but he also recognised the potential. With no other independent weekly left of centre, a merged *New Statesman* and *Nation* was the most obvious platform for those willing to take on the herculean task of reviving democratic socialism in Britain. If Attlee's party of government ultimately emerged from the ashes of August 1931, so also did the

New Statesman and Nation, carving out a unique role for itself in Labour's lengthy process of rehabilitation.

For this particular paper Martin was the ideal man at just the right time: from the 1930s through to the 1950s his weekly voiced first the concerns and then the aspirations of progressive middle-class opinion in Britain. But not for this reason alone did Martin become a pivotal figure on the left throughout Labour's three successive decades of trial, triumph and turmoil. Standing four-square within the English radical tradition, sometimes pig-headed, sometimes courageous, and sometimes spectacularly wrong, Martin made the 'Staggers and Naggers' the socialist conscience of the British labour movement. In doing so, of course, he made many enemies – many of them in the Labour Party. He also made many friends, particularly among a generation of African and Asian nationalists inspired and encouraged by Martin's early championing of post-war decolonisation. On occasion he could be guilty of appalling misjudgements, most evidently over the 1938 Munich agreement and, more contentiously, over his refusal to publish George Orwell's despatches from Spain; similarly, his coverage of Soviet affairs will always provoke furious debate. Yet only Martin's harshest critic would deny that the generosity, the idealism and the sheer brilliance of his journalism outweighed a naivety and inconsistency that might have destroyed any lesser editor.

Martin's radicalism was the legacy of his Nonconformist upbringing, and in particular the family values of tolerance, non-violence and co-operation. A pacifist like his father, he registered as a conscientious objector on leaving school. Experience as an orderly on the Western Front in the Friends' Ambulance Unit served only to strengthen his pacifism. In the early 1920s Martin enjoyed academic success at both Cambridge and Princeton, culminating in tenure at the LSE. In the senior common room Harold Laski quickly became a close friend and influence, introducing his young *protégé* into that close-knit yet incessantly squabbling network of union *apparatchiks*, parliamentary captains and backroom policy-makers who together were forging Labour into a credible, if deeply flawed, party of government. In 1927, following a series of disputes with the LSE's Director, William Beveridge, Martin left to carve out a fresh career in journalism. He became a leader-writer at the *Manchester Guardian*, where he clashed on more than one occasion with its legendary editor and proprietor, C.P. Scott. Although on a day-to-day basis Martin dealt with Ted Scott, any crypto-socialist editorial overlooked by the son rarely escaped the eye of the father. By the summer of 1930 Martin was lobbying hard to secure a new post, although Woolf was wrong in maintaining that he was 'dropped'. Whatever their differences over policy, Ted Scott 'could not wish for a more loyal colleague', telling Bennett that his by now chief leader-writer was 'ideally suited' for appointment to the *New Statesman*.[26] Martin told Lloyd 'in strictest confidence . . . I'd rather work with you on the N.S. than anything else', but informed Keynes only that he was seeking fresh employment in London.[27] In his reply Keynes said simply that he would ask Harold Wright, Hubert Henderson's successor at the *Nation*, to provide Martin with occasional freelance work.[28]

Before leaving Cambridge Martin had applied for a fellowship at King's. Although unsuccessful, the required thesis had impressed Keynes sufficiently for him to suggest Martin might review for the *Nation*. During the second half of the 1920s Keynes followed Martin's chequered career, doubtless impressed by his crusading zeal but wary of his impetuosity. Skidelsky has suggested that it was the knowledge that Martin was available which prompted Keynes to revive the idea of uniting his paper with its closest rival. He had first put forward the idea a year earlier at a meeting with Bennett, who, as the largest outstanding creditor on the *New Statesman* board, had assumed the chairmanship in an attempt to sort out the paper's financial and editorial problems. Keynes was in a weak bargaining position, despite the *Nation*'s success in reducing its annual losses to a manageable £250. In spite of his party's disappointing performance in the 1929 general election, he still assumed the new weekly would be pro-Liberal. Bennett, having despatched to the speak-easies of New York the only member of the *New Statesman*'s editorial staff not a paid-up member of the Labour Party, made it abundantly clear that in no way would his paper subsume its identity for the ultimate benefit of Lloyd George. According to Bennett, Keynes then dropped the matter, 'and we talked at large. He stayed till 6 p.m. and was very agreeable and most acutely intelligent.'[29] By the spring of 1930, with Lloyd clearly flagging and Cole judged inappropriate as a permanent successor, Bennett was eager to find the right editor to inject life into the paper. It was at this point that, as mentioned in Chapter 9, he failed to seduce Robert Bruce Lockhart away from Beaverbrook. Common sense must then have given way to desperation as Bennett next invited an application from J.L. Hammond, who would have been even less suitable for the job than Cole.[30]

With both Henderson and Woolf gone, Keynes's interest in the *Nation* began to flag. He received little solid support from the other directors, his health was poor and, in addition to his normal heavy workload, the Macmillan Committee proved exceptionally time-consuming. The *Nation* had served the Liberal cause well, but had failed to reap its due reward in May 1929. As if to add insult to injury, a majority of the 59 Liberals in the 1929–31 Parliament had long memories and despised Lloyd George. The likes of Sir John Simon and Walter Runciman had little interest in the electorally discredited ideas of Manchester businessmen and Cambridge dons. They scarcely scanned the *Nation*, and scorned the Summer School. For Keynes it was time either to give up entirely, or to move on. Bennett needed an editor, and he had one. Martin naturally enthused over Keynes's 'splendid plan', but urged speed as the possibility had arisen of a Cambridge lectureship in economics.[31] Keynes could easily have engineered a delay in the latter appointment, but he was as eager as Martin to resolve the issue. Bennett saw the merit of Keynes's proposal, but John Roberts, Great Queen Street's business manager, proved a tough negotiator. As far as Roberts was concerned this was a take-over in all but name. During two months of hard negotiating in late 1930 he extracted concession after concession from Keynes, the latter invariably distracted by pressing college and committee business. The shares of the new publishing company went to the two predecessor companies, and, although the *Nation* directors put up £4,500 of working capital, they found themselves in a minority on the board. Aware that the *New Statesman* group were clearly in the ascendant, Keynes reassured Liberal interests by becoming chairman of the new board. Although Martin was the popular choice for editor, and his appointment was largely a formality, final approval lay with the largest investor in the venture, Arnold

Rowntree. At a formal interview on 15 January 1931 the two men got on famously, as a result of which Rowntree insisted that Martin should also become a director.[32]

The merger was an unusually well-kept secret. The Woolfs, for example, were only put in the picture after Martin had been appointed, and were then sworn to secrecy until both papers made a joint announcement on 31 January 1931.[33] Two days before Martin's meeting with Rowntree, Keynes wrote to Lloyd George explaining why the *Nation* and the *New Statesman* could no longer go on competing for largely the same audience, but that 'an independent organ of the Left without special attachment to a political party . . . should be capable of establishing itself securely and becoming an important organ of opinion'. Lloyd George responded enthusiastically, but neither he nor Keynes could have had any illusions as to where the new paper's first loyalties would lie.[34] A weekly with Martin, Lloyd, Cole and soon Woolf in the editorial driving seat was unlikely to qualify its Labour allegiance, even in a year as turbulent as 1931. Like so many other institutions and policies in mid-century Britain, the *New Statesman and Nation* was rooted in the Liberal tradition: its very existence reflected the demise of Liberalism as a party political force, but not the disappearance of the Liberal mind, witness the role of Keynes, Beveridge and others in setting the post-war agenda. The spirit of the *Nation* was by no means dead, and indeed many contributors now filed their copy at Great Queen Street; but few would deny that the Liberal Party was now bereft of a weekly annexe to its loyal dailies, themselves gently drifting into extinction. Furthermore, although 'the *Nation* bore the stamp of Keynes, the *New Statesman* [*and Nation*] was unmistakably Kingsley Martin's'.[35]

The new paper's first issue suggested little had changed. Design changes were largely cosmetic and all the old familiar names were still there. The more astute reader might have sensed that since Christmas there had been a change of tone, Martin's presence at Great Queen Street encouraging a more acerbic treatment of ministers, most notably Snowden.[36] The *New Statesman and Nation*'s first leader was a powerful plea for the government to embrace state investment and genuine economic planning before its supporters became totally disillusioned. Highlighting the spread of autocracy abroad, Martin warned that 'the danger to democracy of not doing anything is far greater than the danger of making a mistake': the general public was enduring an 'irrelevant' hospital pantomime at Westminster 'conscious of ailments which are not assuaged by laughter'.[37] The new editor was conveying precisely the same message as Cole but with force and conviction. Cole was capable of writing with passion, but very rarely. Martin provided the drama Keynes was looking for: 'I [Keynes] think that the first number looked very well indeed. I liked your first leader and the whole paper had a solid substantial air such as the Week-end Review is 100 Miles away from.'[38] Attlee's characteristically terse note informed Martin that 'The N.S. is v.g.' – praise indeed![39]

DEALING WITH THE ECONOMY – THE DEBATE OVER TARIFFS, SPRING 1931

In March 1930 Lloyd and Cole had placed all their hopes on Mosley as the one man in the government who might get something done. Twelve months later his departure to form the New Party was dismissed as significant only in so far as ministers might be more sensitive to pressure from within the party and take Lloyd George at his word. Why should the Liberals commit political suicide by opposing policies akin to those fleshed out by Cole in a four-point emergency programme: a diplomatic initiative to stabilise world prices; a co-ordinated housing programme; an attempt to encourage work for the long-term jobless as a *quid pro quo* for not reducing benefits; and 'courageous handling of the problem of rationalisation in the depressed industries, and especially in steel and cotton'?[40] Why indeed? This was scarcely a programme to rally traditional Labour support, particularly in the north, the last two points being designed almost solely to assuage the Liberals. The first point was consistent with Cole's message throughout the winter of 1930–31 that global monetary stabilisation was crucial to recovery. This entailed cross-Channel co-operation in the money markets to control the distribution of gold, and trans-Atlantic agreement on confidence-building initiatives coming out of Washington.[41]

By 1931 Cole was beginning to acquire a healthy scepticism towards free trade. Nevertheless, a belief that alternative strategies could still be pursued prevented him following Keynes down the path of protection. He was no doubt privy to the pro-tariffs arguments Keynes had put before the Macmillan Committee as far back as 28 February 1930, and as an EAC member he would have read the majority report from the economists' committee. He was equally *au fait* with MacDonald's refusal in the spring and summer of 1930 to challenge Snowden and the other free traders in the Cabinet over vetoing a quota on wheat imports, and ratifying the League of Nations' 'tariff truce'.[42] All the evidence suggested that the Prime Minister was sympathetic to protection, but refused to make the issue a test of his authority for fear of a Cabinet split. Although the Treasury had received in October 1930 the economists' committee's report in favour of tariffs, along with Robbins's dissenting minority report, the full EAC did not get round to discussing their contents until 12 March 1931. With Snowden ill in hospital and the budget still seven weeks away, MacDonald had the opportunity – if he had the will, let alone the courage – to rally the protectionist lobby in a full-scale assault upon the Treasury. Keynes saw the importance of bringing the debate over tariffs into the public domain, if only to strengthen the Premier's backbone. He also appreciated how much free publicity the *New Statesman and Nation* would enjoy if its readers were the first to learn that the Liberal Party's most distinguished economist no longer espoused the cause of free trade.

On the same day that he congratulated Martin on the first issue he sent him a copy of 'Proposals for a Revenue Tariff', a forceful and persuasive piece summarising the economists' committee's case for protection as a counter-balance to the negative effects of any expansionist policy based on public works. By imposing flat rates of 15 per cent on manufactured and semi-manufactured goods and five per cent on foodstuffs: the balance of trade would tolerate the import of vital raw materials required for growth; with as much as £75 million worth of revenue the budget would still balance, thus reassuring overseas investors; employment opportunities would be created by relying on domestic production; and, above all, business confidence would not be undermined. Claiming to speak for '90 per cent of my countrymen', Keynes warned all free traders that, should they reject his 'counsels of expediency', an all too imminent crisis would leave power in the hands of an unreconstructed protectionist Cabinet.[43]

The article appeared on 7 March 1931, five days before the EAC was due to meet. Two days before publication Keynes sent proof copies to Lloyd George and to Snowden, with predictably contrasting responses. A third copy went to the Prime Minister, urging him to consider protection as an expansionist remedy.[44] Keynes's ploy seemed at first to have worked, but following the EAC's discussion of the full report MacDonald seized on an unexpected slowing down in the rate of job losses as an excuse to delay facing up to Snowden, by this time in hospital.[45]

If he failed to persuade MacDonald to take on his Chancellor, at least Keynes succeeded in his two other objectives: fuelling a debate that raged for weeks in the quality press, and ensuring a high profile for the relaunched *New Statesman and Nation*. Thirty years later Martin recalled, with understandable exaggeration, 'one of the greatest economic controversies which ever appeared in any newspaper'. For two months the correspondence columns were devoted almost entirely to Keynes's original article and the three-part 'Economic Notes on Free Trade' in which he sought to answer his critics, most notably Lionel Robbins whose no-holds-barred intellectual assault on his old sparring partner was written in the first week of the furore.[46] For free-traders such as Robbins and Beveridge, letters to the editor were not enough. The LSE's economists rushed into print with a heresy-denouncing pamphlet entitled *Tariffs: The Case Examined*. The Webbs must surely have appreciated the irony of their two great creations locked in horns.[47] In retrospect the whole episode was a purgative process for Keynes and Martin's new venture. The 2,000 readers lost were, one suspects, almost overwhelmingly veteran *Nation* readers whose worst fears had now been confirmed. Technically this reduced the average circulation to around 12,700, but in the medium term there was a net gain. The paper quickly began to attract interest among younger, more left-leaning readers. Sales increased: for the first few years in a fairly unspectacular fashion, but later growing in pace. At the same time, the average age of the readership began to decline. This new generation of subscribers carried plenty of ideological baggage, but not when it came to free trade.[48]

Martin was of course delighted with the results. Keynes's article had not only launched the *New Statesman and Nation* in style (albeit the second issue not the first), but the circumstances surrounding its publication had allowed chairman and editor to agree on the ground rules with regard to their working relationship. In *Editor* Martin paid tribute to Keynes for letting him get on with the paper.[49] The truth was that after nearly eight years of persistent interference in the editorial affairs of the *Nation*, Keynes found it extremely difficult not to assume a similar role once he was established at Great Queen Street. Throughout the 1930s the two men profoundly disagreed over a succession of issues, not least Martin's largely benevolent view of the Soviet Union following his 1932 visit with David Low. Boothby recalled Keynes as having '*worried*' Martin because he 'never understood economics and yet he was always *trying* to understand' (Boothby's italics).[50]

'Proposals for a Revenue Tariff' provided Martin with an early opportunity to assert full editorial independence. Endorsing Cole's view that Keynes's proposals were out of the question so long as a majority of Labour MPs and the party as a whole remained committed to free trade, Martin argued at the height of the storm that introducing flat-rate tariffs would encourage opponents to paint a distorted picture of where the government stood on protection. This was feeble stuff, and in the same leader Cole advanced an equally unconvincing economic argument. He looked to suspension of the Sinking Fund – in other words not maintaining a reduction in the net volume of the National Debt – as a short-term means of funding expansion and yet balancing the budget. The government would thus gain time to formulate plans for an economic revival based on a redistributionist fiscal policy. Here both men were surely whistling in the dark. They knew by now that there was no way this particular Labour administration would act on the premise that a 'much nearer approach to economic equality is both desirable and inevitable in the near future'.[51] A stop-gap budget when at last it came merely confirmed the obvious. Snowden anticipated a second, more severe budget later in the year, following recommendations from the May Committee on how to restore confidence in the economy. Needless to say, when Sir George May and his fellow financiers published their report on 31 July, the only item of government expenditure judged sacrosanct was the £50 million Sinking Fund.

Another joint leader, on 11 April, restated the objections and alternatives to protection. Keynes took time off from drafting the Macmillan Committee's final report to send Martin a generous letter emphasising how much they had in common with regard to overall objectives, confirming yet again the temporary nature of the tariffs, and conceding that there were many flaws in his argument: 'Don't feel that I [Keynes] in the least dissent from your decision to treat it as you [Martin] have. I think you have very likely been right from the point of view of the paper.'[52] Martin and Cole took the chairman at his word, the next week recruiting J.A. Hobson, an old adversary of Keynes, to back up their call for international co-operation not global trade barriers. This time Keynes, under enormous pressure at the time and not in the best of health, dashed off a prickly letter disparaging their hopes of a swift response:

> This applies overwhelmingly to Hobson, with his suggestion of 'international government with powers to over-ride obstructive elements of national sovereignty'. If, however, you do not expect anything to come of these hopes at present, what do you propose to do in the meantime?[53]

After the Macmillan Committee's report was made public on 13 July, just as the City was waking up to an imminent sterling crisis, Cole tried – and conspicuously failed – to answer Keynes's question. He merely repeated his earlier rejection of protection, urging a concerted effort to revive international prices and an 'attempt by measures of investment and development at home so to stimulate the efficiency of our industries as to hold our own without artificial aid to our exporting trades'.[54] Was this naivety or casuistry? The government had had nearly two years to introduce 'measures of investment and development'. One could scarcely imagine a less propitious moment for ministers to experience a Pauline conversion, and Cole knew it. So of course did Keynes – and Bevin, who signed the addendum to the Macmillan Report calling for capital development under the cover of a tariff. Bevin was alone, however, in calling for devaluation, an option which as it transpired ministers like Tom Johnston were scarcely aware of, let alone seriously considering ('No one ever told us we could do that').

DEALING WITH THE ECONOMY – THE STERLING CRISIS AND THE FALL OF THE SECOND LABOUR GOVERNMENT, SUMMER 1931

Bevin was not to be alone for long. By early August Keynes was adopting a 'realistic' view over parity in order to stem the run on sterling. Asked by MacDonald for advice, he urged a 25 per cent devaluation: suspension of gold convertibility could be followed by the establishment of a currency union based on the Empire. Keynes insisted that acting on the May Committee's recommendation of a £97 million cut in public expenditure, including a 20 per cent cut in unemployment benefit would constitute a 'most gross perversion of social justice', a view he expressed publicly in the *New Statesman and Nation* on 15 August. Keynes made no mention of devaluation in his article, a damning and deeply sarcastic indictment of Sir George May and his colleagues. Instead, he called for suspension of the Sinking Fund, further borrowing for the Unemployment Fund, and a revenue tariff to help balance the budget.[55] By this time Cole had at last accepted the case for protection. At Great Queen Street, he and Lloyd were again in charge, Martin being absent in Berlin. Cole had already demonstrated how out of touch he was with decision-making at the highest levels when leaking the May Committee's recommendations: 'one thing certain is that no Government, of any party, will carry them out.'[56] In reality, the May Report set the agenda throughout the final painful three weeks of the 1929–31 Labour government. The relevant issues of the *New Statesman and Nation* reveal an editorial staff poorly briefed and with no real idea of what was going on; insistent only that cuts in benefit and public sector wages were unacceptable within the Labour movement as a whole. Although echoing the chairman's call for action rather than retrenchment, leader-writers questioned neither the fundamental premise of a balanced budget nor the commitment to defending sterling (perhaps some future government would have 'the will and power to take still bolder steps and rid us of the incubus of the gold standard').[57] The paper put on a brave face. Now, ironically, clinging to the revenue tariff like a lifeline, it upheld the position Henderson and Willie Graham were advocating in Cabinet, and Bevin and Walter Citrine were insisting on within the TUC

255

General Council. Like most other Labour supporters then and for a long time afterwards it assumed that Snowden's opponents on the economic committee and in the Cabinet as a whole were far less compromising – and compromised – than in fact they were. Cole was well briefed on the TUC's hostility to cuts and calls for protection, but he had no knowledge of the immense pressure being put on MacDonald by opposition leaders, the Bank of England and the American money markets. In the end all reporting was overtaken by events, and Lloyd's cautious optimism was succeeded by Martin's astonishment following MacDonald's formation of a National government on 24 August.

Martin had returned home at once. In his diary he reflected upon British capitalism's success in utilising the nation's 'tradition of compromise and common sense' to cope with crisis. He had anticipated either compromise or resignation, but not 'mild dictatorship supported by the bulk of middle-class opinion and existing to obey the demands of bankers and creditors at home and abroad'. Martin lashed out at the press, with particular venom reserved for the *Manchester Guardian*. What spurred him on in the weeks leading up to the general election was the conviction that Labour had in Henderson a man of integrity and would learn from experience: the party 'should have a policy to offer, one which it can defend and implement when its turn again arrives'. Most important of all, a future Labour government must challenge the power of the City.[58] Keynes's first biographer implied that he deliberately distanced himself from the *New Statesman and Nation* because it subscribed to the 'bankers ramp' explanation of the crisis. As Martin himself pointed out, nothing was further from the truth, and the issue of 29 August went to great pains to piece together an accurate account of the previous week's bewildering sequence of events. Subsequent issues insisted that only a clear understanding of what had taken place could prevent a recurrence next time Labour took office.[59] Fury fuelled output, and each week the editor's presence could be felt throughout the front half of the magazine – righteous indignation competing with considered reflection, and often complementing each other. This was the moment at which the apprentice editor made the paper his own, no longer depending on Cole or Lloyd, or deferring to Keynes.

Nevertheless, in early September Keynes used the *New Statesman and Nation* as the principal platform on which he pursued his case for: loans not cuts; currency regulations; import controls; and, above all, devaluation.[60]

The 'impeccable authority' on which the issue of 29 August relied so heavily when reporting the past week's events was probably Ernie Bevin. Webb had retreated to Passfield Corner as soon as he could, and Henderson was doubtless far too busy holding his party together to provide Cole or Lloyd with an insider's account. The Transport Workers' Secretary was deemed the one man who had confronted Snowden and MacDonald with a credible alternative strategy. As we have seen, Cole had previously been impressed by Bevin's input to the proceedings of the Macmillan Committee and the EAC, and the two men had in recent months collaborated in launching the SSIP. In early September they co-drafted a *New Statesman* sixpenny pamphlet entitled *The Crisis: What is it, how it arose, what to do.* Not only was Bevin making one of the more tempered contributions to what was in fact a very messy and fractious election campaign, but he was also flexing his muscles with regard to the trade unions' involvement in future policy-making.[61] Cole and Martin complemented the pamphlet with a series of articles in late September and early October outlining what Labour should do upon returning to office.

What spurred Martin into looking to the future, rather than repeatedly raging over the past, was a disturbing letter from Graham Hutton. Hutton was an economist, assistant editor of *The Economist*, and a close friend of Keynes. In his letter he recalled a meeting of the Romney Street Group, a group of like-minded liberal thinkers and journalists who met regularly for lunch. They had taken advantage of Martin's absence to discuss his first six months at the *New Statesman and Nation*, and in particular his treatment of recent events. Hutton made special mention of the fact that Woolf and Cole were among those present who:

> thought it dangerous to substitute opposition, criticism, and [an] appeal to the reader's vague feelings about the thing [the August crisis] for reasoned argument and considered counter proposals. I [Hutton] understood [them] to mean that the NS has a unique chance of coming out with, first of all, a criticism and then a

programme which should rise above the present Government's and also the vague TUC ad hoc temporisations.[62]

Hutton went on to explain how the 'more advanced thinkers' expected a better-informed, more clearly defined attitude to economic affairs from the *New Statesman and Nation* than from any other weekly. Among its rivals not even *The Economist* could match a pool of financial staff comparable in knowledge and experience with those of Keynes, Cole, Nicholas Davenport and Hutton himself.[63]

Martin's scribbled comments on the back of Hutton's letter indicate a mixture of hurt, irritation and penitence. He could legitimately deny that the *New Statesman and Nation* had ever resorted to any glib and narrowly ideological explanation of what had happened – the issue of 29 August, for example, explicitly refuted any notion of a 'bankers' ramp'. Furthermore, his in-tray was stacked with letters praising the magazine's coverage and interpretation of the crisis. On the other hand, two of his closest colleagues clearly believed the tone of the paper was wrong, and that a more constructive note had to be set – in other words, it was time to move forward. To Martin's credit, he took the criticism to heart, swallowed his pride, and set to work with Cole on forging Labour's next agenda.

In retrospect, the reluctance of so many pro-Labour advisers and commentators before the summer of 1931 to accept the case for a revenue tariff was a precursor of Keynes's later experience, following the October general election. He failed to convince William Stevenson and Francis Williams at the *Daily Herald*, or even Martin at the *New Statesman and Nation*, that their papers could act as vehicles for a reconstructed Labour Party to flesh out expansionist and redistributionist policies designed to enhance purchasing power without at the same time shackling the private sector. In the winter of 1931–32 Keynes made clear his view that achieving office had exposed Labour's lack of a coherent and viable political philosophy. As if being unable to deliver the New Jerusalem was not bad enough, ministers had proved even less adept at reviving capitalism, thus seriously debilitating business confidence. Slavishly pursuing inherently deflationary policies, the Cabinet had never seriously explored the alternative options advanced by sympathetic advisers beyond Whitehall and Threadneedle Street. Labour activists knew that what Keynes was saying was right, but it did not follow that they liked it, or that they had to pursue his recommended policies: look where his advice had got Lloyd George's Liberals, reduced at the 1931 general election to a family group of four MPs. As Ben Pimlott noted, Keynes's 'firmly held view that capitalism could be made to work was far from palatable to those for whom the events of 1931 had been a welcome confirmation that it could not'.[64] He supported nationalisation of the Bank of England, but saw no evidence that a major extension of the public sector, when combined with the physical planning of production, would foster economic reconstruction and boost living standards. Thus, he rejected the assumption that slump was an inevitable phenomenon of capitalism, and that Labour had no alternative but to adopt – to use Cole's favourite phrase – a strategy of 'constructive socialism'. The 'collapse of his networks of persuasion' had left Keynes politically 'homeless', hence his return to Cambridge to regroup.[65]

It would be wrong to say Kingsley Martin was henceforth left alone, but his relationship with Keynes had entered a new, more mature phase. He began recruiting like-minded contributors, even when he knew Keynes thoroughly disapproved.[66] Familiar names from the golden years of the 'Staggers and Naggers' began to appear, all very earnest and well-intentioned, and all too often misguided in their understanding of many of the crucial issues of the new decade. Evidence of the paper's continuing shift to the left was the presence of Harold Laski and Noel Brailsford, ably supported by Cyril Joad and J.L. Hammond (effectively replacing R.H. Tawney, an occasional contributor in the late 1920s). At this stage, for coverage of foreign affairs Martin still relied heavily on Lloyd and, of course, on Leonard Woolf, whose early return to Great Queen Street was an inevitable consequence of the merger.[67]

After six months *in situ* Martin identified a need to speak directly to his readers, establishing a rapport scarcely attainable via unsigned editorials: the editor's personal perspective, as opposed to the collective opinion of the *New Statesman and Nation*.[68] On 12 September 1931 'London Diary' appeared for the first time:

> I [Martin] was responsible for didactic leading articles and editorial comments, weighed down with matured judgement and serious appraisal of many-sided questions . . . Such features disciplined exuberance and left no space for bubbles. I wanted also to speculate about the world: sometimes to go off at half cock, without pretending that I was making an *ex cathedra* pronouncement.[69]

All regular readers knew that 'Critic' was Martin, and 'London Diary' became the best-known – and often the most contentious – feature of his paper. In Anthony Howard's words, 'no journalist ever wore his heart more publicly on his sleeve'. *If* Martin's success did lie in 'turning the *New Statesman* into a paper of emotional protest, even sometimes of political sentimentality', then 'London Diary' was a major factor in that success.[70]

11

Conclusion: Eighty years of new statesmanship

Towards the end of Martin's second year as editor he came to the conclusion that someone else was using his office. He quite often found his wastepaper basket full of half-written leaders and empty whisky bottles. The mystery was solved one night in December 1932 when David Garnett made an uncharacteristic decision to work late. To his surprise, he gradually became aware that he was not alone. In Martin's chair sat a ghostly but familiar figure drafting copy while downing copious quantities of Scotch. It later transpired that by the time last orders was called Sharp had forgotten he was no longer editor. He would duly stagger from the pub to Great Queen Street, eager to put his paper, if not himself, to bed.[1]

The *New Statesman* had always been the sole focus of Sharp's affection. His marriage had been doomed from the start, and in the winter of 1932–33 he and Rosamund separated. Broke and broken, he went back to her a few months later, living off Rosamund's small private income and the odd scraps she earned from advertising agencies. Victor Gollancz had given him an advance on a biography of Cecil Rhodes, but it all went on drink. Robert Bruce Lockhart, still insistent that Sharp had been the 'best editor of a weekly paper in England' now found him 'in [a] bad way: no money and nerves gone'.[2] In April 1933 Sharp received £100 from the German press attaché, via Graham Seton Hutchinson. The latter was a writer, war hero and one-time Liberal candidate, once active in the British Legion but now prominent in smaller and less reputable veterans' groups. His growing admiration for Hitler had culminated in the recent establishment of the violently anti-Semitic National Workers'

261

Movement. The new government was keen to welcome British journalists, who would write enthusiastic paeans to the Führer upon their return home. Hutchison was a useful front-man, and in May 1933 he dutifully despatched Sharp to Germany. Having no doubt reinforced all his hosts' worst prejudices about the British, Sharp then carried out his side of the bargain, only to produce copy so dreadful that no reputable paper would touch it.[3] Fourteen years earlier, of course, he had proved equally useless as a propagandist for the Foreign Office. It would be nice to think that Sharp deliberately took the Nazis for a ride in the same way that he made clear to the PID he was nobody's poodle; the difference being that the second time around he did actually get to Berlin. However, there is no evidence to support this, and in fact he was too far gone to sabotage the best-laid plans of Dr Goebbels.

A year later, in April 1934, Sharp was still capable of contributing to the *New Statesman and Nation*'s twenty-first anniversary issue. In what proved to be a valedictory tribute to the founders' vision and industry, he made particular mention of Shaw's generosity, tolerance and support.[4] Ten months after he submitted his last copy, Sharp's liver finally gave out and he died in Farnborough Hospital. In the last year of his life he had tried desperately to stop drinking, but it was too late. His death prompted no major obituaries, and he was soon forgotten by all but the most assiduous student of Fabianism.

Thus, in any study of the left in twentieth-century Britain the *New Statesman* has always been synonymous with Kingsley Martin – and rightly so. However, Sharp does not deserve to be written out of history, or at best portrayed as a bit player in the Webbs' struggle to seize the socialist high ground. Nor does he warrant the treatment meted out in Edward Hyams' official history, where the failings of the man too often became the failings of the editor. True, after 1918 they were all too often one and the same, but we should be wary of character assassination, however unintentional. Any balanced assessment of Sharp's career must acknowledge the critical role he played in the early years, and indeed the value of his contribution to the paper even when in decline. Beatrice Webb was quite right when she wrote to Martin insisting that 'Clifford Sharp made the *Statesman* and ought to have the credit for it'.[5]

Sharp was always a loner, reluctant to cultivate friends unless they satisfied an increasingly pathetic desire to feel part of an inner circle, as in his championing of Asquith and then Lloyd George. Healthy scepticism had degenerated into all-embracing cynicism by 1920, and in this respect Sharp's embrace of the Liberals was doubly ironic: not only had he signed up to a party in manifest decline, but he would have viewed with scorn and astonishment anyone else fawning upon someone as pathetic as 'Squiffy' in his cups.[6] Such behaviour would be wholly inconsequential if not for the fact that in the mid-1920s it had such a damaging impact upon the paper as a whole. Siegfried Sassoon painted a revealing portrait of Sharp at this time, describing a man as bombastic as he was boorish ('a rather shoddy imitation of a rather bounderish Roman Emperor'). Denied the decanter throughout dinner, Sassoon was silenced by his guest's 'orotund survey of the landscape of literature', observing that 'Sharp is one of those men whose mental monarchy exists mainly when he is writing his weekly article'.[7] This sums him up perfectly. As does Leonard Woolf's recollection, in old age, of a 'curiously chilly and saturnine man', sustained by an 'atmosphere of intellectual Jeyes's fluid, moral carbolic soap, [and] spiritual detergents'.[8]

In writing about Sharp, Woolf had no particular axe to grind. Apparently the two men, despite their differences after the war, got on well together. Woolf developed 'the kind of affection which one sometimes gets for an old mangy, bad tempered, slightly dangerous dog'.[9] Time is of course a great healer, and all the evidence suggests that there was no love lost when Woolf was at the *Nation* in the 1920s. Nevertheless, here we have a rare – and reasonably fair – assessment of Sharp's contribution to the *New Statesman*, by someone who was intimately involved in the paper's affairs for over half a century. Woolf dismissed Sharp's claim to a place in the pantheon of great weekly editors, alongside Orage, Massingham and Martin. Certainly he lacked the ebullience and exuberance which Woolf found so inspiring in his successor.[10] Yet even the most cursory study of the magazine would conclude that Sharp 'performed the first duty of an editor' in that 'he impressed upon his paper an indelible character, a journalistic aroma which ultimately was the personal aroma of Sharp. It pervaded every corner of the paper, every article whether signed or unsigned.'[11] Of course, that 'personal aroma' was by no means always attractive, and too often it thwarted creativity, individuality and excitement (let alone entertainment).

Although the phrase 'bleak and acrid' has been applied to Sharp's style of journalism, a fairer description must be the by now all too familiar, 'dull and worthy'. Admittedly, he could be blunt and brutal when he wanted to. Yet, ironically, editorial invective was often tempered by Sharp's own success in giving the early *New Statesman* a '"personality" representing a multiplication rather than a mere addition of our several and separate personalities' – what he went on to describe as the 'quickening' of the paper.[12] In other words, when he did strike a rebarbative note it was lost in a collective appeal to reason and common sense. The whole purpose of anonymity was to encourage a consistent and familiar viewpoint throughout the paper, and yet it was Sharp who did most to subvert such a strategy in the post-war years. The person who most faithfully adhered to the rules, albeit using the absence of a by-line to his advantage when it suited him, was the Fabians' prodigal son, Douglas Cole.

Cole's mind-numbing prose was by no means unique, reflecting editorial indifference to style and panache. In the front half of the paper content and clarity of expression were the sole criteria, but Sharp was by no means hostile to a purposeful and attractive prose style. He gave Squire and MacCarthy every encouragement in fostering fresh talent, and in commissioning work from well-established writers such as Rebecca West and Roger Fry. Unfortunately, he also tolerated a great deal of dross, such as reviews by the likes of F.L. Lucas and Edward Shanks. Overall, Sharp's failure to match the excitement and zest of the *New Age* and even the *Nation* in quality of writing further undermines any pretension to be a great editor. What he did have was a natural talent for assimilating disparate and often very dry material. More significantly, he proved capable of creating a weekly with a distinct identity and, until 1919, an obvious and unambiguous editorial line. In business affairs, his evasion of expensive litigation until 1928, and indeed his general financial prudence (despite Arnold Bennett's sensible advice that good money meant good copy), helped keep down the paper's running costs. Martin, of course, maintained the *New Statesman*'s notorious interwar reputation for parsimony. Before alcohol began to exaggerate his worst character traits, Sharp was surprisingly good at man-management, happy to delegate if he respected colleagues and their expertise. For this reason alone, the individual contributions of Squire, Lloyd and MacCarthy are vital. On the technical side, even Sharp's fiercest critics conceded that he had a masterly knowledge of layout and typography, and when it came to 'subbing' he was as swift and shrewd as anyone in Fleet Street. He put into practice all that he learnt from Orage, and his background in engineering and the law no doubt served him equally well. It is not surprising that in the early 1920s he was thought of as a future broadsheet editor. An unattractive, even an unpleasant man, Sharp was nevertheless a professional in his chosen field. In Desmond MacCarthy's words, he displayed that rare power of 'blending a whole paper into a publication with a homogeneous character'.[13]

Sharp offered the progressive intelligentsia of Edwardian England a new political and literary review, an obvious rival to the *Nation* and potentially of much wider appeal than the guild socialist *New Age*. In other words, he did exactly what the Webbs appointed him to do, more than fulfilling their initial modest expectations – of him, as well as of the paper. From the outset the *New Statesman* was taken as seriously by the LCC as by the LSE. In a Liberal administration it addressed ministers as well as mandarins. The no-frills, no-nonsense approach clearly appealed to policy-makers, academics and social investigators, but it scarcely endeared the paper to the general reader. An excess of sense at the expense of sensibility was never conducive to a large circulation, but when it came to subscribers, Sidney and Beatrice were more concerned with quality than quantity: as long as the magazine's debts were containable, the failure to generate a mass readership was of secondary importance. It took the failure to contain those debts, the appointment of Bennett to the board, the impact of war, and the far more competitive atmosphere of the 1920s, to force a review of the *New Statesman*'s potential as a profitable enterprise. Sales slowly rose in the 1920s, but it became ever more difficult to market a magazine that was increasingly dull, predictable and conservative. Sharp's fall from grace was matched by that of his creation.

Although there were notable exceptions, Sharp rejected any

'romantic notion' of the *New Statesman* as a paper campaigning relentlessly against every injustice and the political forces sustaining them. Chapter 5 noted his insistence to Beatrice Webb that their concern should be for principles not persons, protesting only when there was '*a reasonable chance of producing results*'.[14] Shaw was equally insistent that sales would never improve unless the magazine became a more dynamic and risk-taking critic of the government's conduct of the war. He quit when it became clear that the Webbs supported Sharp's more cautious approach. Ultimately, of course, healthy pragmatism gave way to calculated compromise, while indifference to personality survived at the expense of political acumen. In the 1920s Sharp alienated the Webbs, antagonised the rest of the board, and without doubt damaged the paper through his intemperate criticism of Ramsay MacDonald and other Labour leaders. Mostyn Lloyd spent most of the decade engaged in damage limitation exercises. He and Cole, with the tacit approval of several directors, kept the channels of communication open with the ILP, the trade unions, and the Labour Party itself. All too well aware that the editor's return in 1919 had thwarted hopes of the *New Statesman* remaining an independent yet unequivocal supporter of Labour, Lloyd reluctantly deferred to Sharp's insistence on acknowledging the Liberals' potential for recovery. As the paper went downhill in the 1920s, Sharp's pro-Liberal leaders clashed all too visibly with the reformist yet nevertheless uncompromisingly socialist sentiments expressed in accompanying articles. After 1927 Lloyd by default assumed responsibility for editorial policy, and in the 1929 general election Liberal hopes of a power-broking role were dashed. Sharp was already on the way out when Labour's electoral success finally killed off his vision of a fresh progressive alliance in which the experience of Asquith, and later the ideas of Lloyd George, would be vital.

The fact that he supported Asquith for so long suggests that, unlike GBS or Sidney Webb, Sharp never really understood to what extent the Great War had changed everything. Perhaps this is explained by his absence abroad throughout much of 1917–18, which we can now see was a key period for his paper, as well as for the Labour Party and for the country at large. When Sharp got back to Great Queen Street in the spring of 1919 he failed to perceive that something of a seismic shift had taken place within the labour movement, and that the *New Statesman* was carving out a new role for itself as an opinion-moulder targeting a larger but more partisan audience. Four years of coalition government had seen the transmutation of a Fabian weekly, born out of permeation and still hesitant to embrace Labour as the engine of collectivist reform, into a trenchant critic of both the Coalition and the Asquitheans. Although still selling far too few copies to thrive, for the first time the *New Statesman* could speak with a voice of authority. During the First World War it had come of age. Beatrice Webb could boast with some justification that 'Fleet Street and Whitehall count it as a great success'.[15] Bennett could clearly take much of the credit for this, but Sidney Webb remained a major influence on editorial policy throughout 1917–18. Architect with Henderson of a reconstituted Labour Party, he combined chairmanship of the *New Statesman* with burgeoning political ambitions. With Woolf, Ensor and Squire all firmly committed to Labour, in some cases even contesting parliamentary seats, the paper addressed disaffected Liberals as well as long-standing Fabians.

Opposition to the war had brought many former Radicals within Labour's fold, and few would have been attracted to a magazine so firmly committed to total victory. Yet reconciliation of pro- and anti-war elements within the labour movement proved far easier than *rapprochement* between Independent and Lloyd George Liberals. The Labour Party benefited from this, and so, in its own small way, did the *New Statesman*. Many Liberal intellectuals emulated George Trevelyan and stayed faithful to the party; but many others followed Charles Trevelyan's example and found new bedfellows in a new, more broadly based Labour Party. With Massingham similarly disaffected, these former Liberals could remain loyal to the *Nation*. Only in 1923, when Keynes and his consortium needed a journal to reassert the case for Liberalism, did Labour's newest recruits look to the *New Statesman* for more congenial reading. Of course, many of them were already familiar with the paper.

Yet the purpose and commitment of December 1918 were gone. Confusion and contradiction dogged editorial policy so long as Sharp retained both his authority and his faculties. The *New*

Statesman had emerged from the First World War an independent Labour weekly, with a readership profile sharply different from those of the *Labour Leader* and the ILP's regional papers. Given the changes in Labour's fortunes after the war, and the demise of the *New Age*, this was a unique opportunity for the *New Statesman* to establish itself as *the* forum for debate on the left. That opportunity was lost, and not seized again until Martin began to assert his independence from Keynes in the aftermath of the 1931 crisis. But if in the 1920s it was not *the* voice of the left, it was *a* voice of the left. As shown in Chapters 7 and 9, Lloyd and Cole argued strenuously the case for democratic socialism as the motor of economic renewal and social justice. Despite Sharp's hand-wringing and caveats, readers were recommended to vote Labour in 1922, 1923 and in 1924. For all the editor's embarrassing tributes to Asquith, and readiness to bury the hatchet with Lloyd George, his was increasingly a voice crying in the wilderness. Clearly this was no consolation to Sidney Webb, whom Sharp twice placed in an impossible position: during the 1922 campaign, and following the December 1923 election. Nor was it to those directors exasperated by Sharp's astonishing attack on MacDonald in the autumn of 1924. Though the latter could live with personal invective, however ill-timed, sustained criticism of the party's monetary and employment policies was a different matter. The abortive take-over in 1925 suggests that the perceived importance of the paper to the Labour leadership should not be underestimated. Yet MacDonald would have made what was already a bland, rudderless paper even more boring: relaunching the *New Statesman* as a semi-official party organ would have been the kiss of death.

In 1924 neither Cole nor Lloyd had directly attacked ministers for failing to grasp the nettle of unemployment. What they did do was to advance viable options for a minority government. Compared with 1929–31, when tolerance of Thomas and Snowden lasted little more than a year, Cole was passionate but patient. Indeed, throughout that whole six-year period when Labour was in, out, and then again in office, it is remarkable how the *New Statesman* managed to reconcile a continuing critique of economic strategy (or rather, the lack of it) with qualified loyalty to the parliamentary leadership. In the second half of the 1920s

Sharp's new-found predilection for Lloyd George, however embarrassing, became more and more irrelevant. A much greater influence upon a struggling paper was Cole's advisory role within the party, and from 1930 within the EAC. He never entirely abandoned the idealism of guild socialism, particularly its intrinsic suspicion of the centralist state, but his reluctance to wave the ILP flag after 1926 reflected a growing awareness of the constraints of power and an acknowledgement of the 'art of the possible'. Cole's complaint in 1929–31, as in 1924, was that, even when shown what clearly was possible, MacDonald continued to tolerate inertia and drift.

Appointment to the EAC brought Cole into regular contact with Ernest Bevin, a connection maintained through mutual involvement in the SSIP and NFRB. Collaboration led Bevin to soften his deep-rooted suspicion of intellectuals, and Cole to temper his criticism of the TUC. Even before the General Strike the poverty of leadership within the trade union movement had been a familiar editorial theme. Sharp, who like Beatrice Webb never had much time for trade unionists, was always happy to let Cole vent his spleen. Closer acquaintance with Bevin, plus the arrival of Martin, ensured a shift in the paper's perception of a new, rising generation of trade union leaders. Even more important was a shift after 1931 in those same trade unionists' perception of the *New Statesman*, reflecting a growing awareness that here was a magazine belatedly acknowledging that Labour remained first and foremost the party of the working class. Nearly two decades of editorially sidelining the trade union establishment, either on grounds of mediocrity (Webb/Sharp) or of permanent officials' isolation from the shop-floor (Cole), finally came to an end.

Lloyd of course had laboured long and hard to bring the paper back to where it was in the winter of 1918–19, and his contribution should never be underestimated. By the late 1920s his was a thankless task, albeit rendered easier by Sharp absenting himself for long periods from Great Queen Street. Losing his maverick editor in 1929 may have reduced the stress levels, but Lloyd still had to hold down what were in effect two full-time jobs. So long as MacCarthy retained his enthusiasm and commitment, the arts pages helped preserve the overall standard of the paper. After 1927 this was no longer the case, and Lloyd had to deal with people like Clennell Wilkinson and Ellis Roberts. The irony is that, under Hubert Henderson and Leonard Woolf, the *Nation* was still enjoying qualified success as a vibrant and revitalised journal – only to be swallowed up by its rival in 1931.

The reversal of fortunes between the *Nation* and the *New Statesman* after the abortive merger of 1923 was a microcosm of the political struggle taking place at national level. After Keynes and his consortium usurped Massingham in 1923 the *Nation* was once again the flagship of Liberalism, albeit of a very different order from that espoused by embittered ex-ministers gathered at Sutton Courtney. In the opinion of just about everybody other than Clifford Sharp, the *New Statesman* was pro-Labour. On all but a few critical occasions, Cole and Lloyd's partisanship cancelled out the confusion caused by Sharp's embrace of coalition, and his refusal to accept that Labour now constituted the principal progressive, anti-Conservative force in British politics. Yet even the editor applauded the strategy associated so closely with MacDonald after 1922: of projecting Labour as a national and no longer a class-based party. Where Cole and Lloyd took issue with the parliamentary leadership was in making the New Jerusalem dependent on an upturn in the trade cycle. By placing their faith in a restoration of international trade to pre-war levels, Labour's leaders merely looked to a revival of capitalism as a means of improving living standards and the quality of life. With no coherent socialist philosophy, let alone any clear programme of action, many not on the left of the parliamentary party were easily convinced that revision of the Versailles peace treaty would ease Europe's economic malaise. Here was a persuasive argument, and one especially convenient given Labour's need to look beyond former Radicals when targeting the full spectrum of disaffected Liberal opinion.

The 1924 general election marked a reversal in Labour fortunes. Yet, despite the loss of 40 seats, the party gained a million votes. The Liberals fared far worse. In losing well over a million votes, by no means all of them to Labour, the hollowness of their pretensions as a party of government were ruthlessly exposed. The same week that only 40 Liberal MPs returned to Westminster, the *New Statesman* announced net autumn sales of 11,562. As Chapter 7 suggested, it could not have chosen a more appropriate, or a crueller, moment at which to overtake the *Nation*.

Throughout the second half of the 1920s Keynes found himself in a paradoxical position *vis à vis* the relative positions of the two weeklies. The *Nation* was the better paper, particularly after MacCarthy's departure left Woolf free to draw on all his Bloomsbury contacts. Keynes and Henderson set the agenda regarding an interventionist approach to unemployment, however much Cole and Lloyd sought to distance themselves from a public works programme so closely associated in the public mind with Lloyd George. By 1929 Cole found himself arguing that official Labour policy, however uninspiring by comparison with that of the Liberals, reflected the reality and responsibility of imminent power. This line of argument was singularly unconvincing, but at the same time demonstrated how committed a Sharp-free *New Statesman* was to the return of a Labour government. When the election came, Labour consolidated its vote, holding on to a sizeable proportion of the Liberals' 1924 defectors. Even in defeat the Conservatives retained the support of a large number of one-time Liberal voters. Like its party, the *Nation* staked everything on a distinctive and dynamic reflationary programme generating electoral recovery. Instead, 1929 brought defeat, disillusion and, in the case of Keynes and Hubert Henderson, division. Both men soon found themselves heavily committed to the EAC and the Macmillan Committee. By the summer of 1930 Keynes was immersed in the 'economists' committee' debate over protection, as well as quarrelling with Henderson over the value of public works. At Westminster many Liberal MPs barely tolerated Lloyd George's leadership, let alone his ideas. No wonder Keynes's enthusiasm for the *Nation* as a motor of Liberal revival waned. In the autumn of 1929 Keynes had adopted a very bullish attitude when suggesting a merger to Bennett, but when serious negotiations began nearly a year later he was in a much weaker bargaining position. Although editorially the superior paper, the *Nation* was played out.

The *New Statesman*, on the other hand, had survived several years of mediocrity with its circulation still rising, and had everything to play for. Even before Martin's arrival, it was reasserting its identity, insisting on the intellectual initiative of democratic socialism, and pursuing a clear policy of guarded support for MacDonald's government. Lloyd's 'loyal grousers' offered positive criticism, even in the winter of 1930–31 when it was increasingly evident that, post-Mosley, too many ministers were simply out of their depth. Only with Martin's arrival in early 1931 was a more aggressive line adopted, but even then the tone was never confrontational. Following Labour's departure from office, the new editor and his colleagues reassured them-selves as to the validity of a socialist alternative still unadopted, and thus still unproven. This reversion to a more fundamentalist position reinforced Keynes's growing belief that he shared little common ground with Labour's demoralised survivors. By the spring of 1932 the focus of his work was again Cambridge. The role Keynes now adopted towards Martin and his paper was to differ markedly from his experience with Henderson at the *Nation*. Right from the outset, when Keynes had made public his support for protection, Martin was sensitive to editorial freedom. By rejecting the case for tariffs, and then by shifting his paper significantly to the left after August 1931, he sent a clear message to Keynes over who was in charge. In the course of the 1930s the two men had some almighty rows, usually with reference to the Soviet Union, but Martin's early assertion of autonomy meant that the potential for such clashes was visibly reduced.[16]

Keynes's reluctance to intervene once the new paper had bedded down was consistent with the role of most *New Statesman* directors since its inception. The boardroom battles of more recent years have perhaps encouraged the assumption that creative tension between directors and editorial staff is the norm. The early history of the magazine shows that this was by no means always true. Except at moments of crisis, directors were loath to tangle with their prickly editor. Indeed, a major criticism of the board in the second half of the 1920s was its reluctance to tell Sharp that he should go. Thirty years later, with Cole and Woolf having followed the editor on to the board, it was well-nigh impossible to suggest that Martin should contemplate retirement. Well before Keynes there were of course individual directors who exercised a disproportionate influence upon editorial policy and/or produc-tion. Bennett and Sidney Webb are the most obvious names that come to mind, both men helping fill the vacuum caused by Sharp's absence in 1917–19, albeit for the most part disguising a mutual antipathy. Throughout much of the 1920s Bennett's involvement in the paper's affairs was minimal. At the end of the decade he intervened to ensure Sharp's removal, but died before he could see the final result of his negotiations with Keynes.

Looking back on every occasion when the *New Statesman* absorbed a rival publication, Stephen Howe has suggested that each time there took place 'a meeting of minds . . . a continuity of commitment both to a liberal culture and to a radical socialist politics'.[17] Howe was writing in 1988, not long after the merger with *New Society* had been announced (and several years before *Marxism Today* was swallowed up), but clearly he had in mind the magazine born in 1931. The legacy of the *Nation*'s 'moral reformers' is too often overlooked, attention focusing not unnaturally on the *New Statesman*'s Fabian 'mechanics'. Similarly, although Raymond Mortimer always regarded MacCarthy as a role model, his success in forging a provocative and highly readable literary review owed much more to Woolf's independence of mind throughout his seven years at the *Nation*. Christopher Hitchens, introducing Howe's anthology, offered a generally flattering assessment of the early paper's performance as a literary review, quoting publication of 'Easter 1916' as evidence of an understated but nevertheless visible cultural engagement in the major issues of the day. Yet, as Chapter 8 demonstrated, publishing Yeats's poem was unusual, in so far as Squire and his successors tended to eschew politics on the arts pages – unlike Woolf, often to the irritation of both his editor and his chairman. Similarly, Hitchens' suggestion that the *New Statesman* in the 1920s was a 'natural bridge to modernism' seems more appropriate to the *Nation*, notwithstanding MacCarthy's early success in mobilising Bloomsbury.[18] Too often Q.D. Leavis displayed an other-worldly disregard for the commercial realities of literary journalism, but she was right to suggest MacCarthy's reputation was exaggerated: at a key moment in early twentieth-century English literature he failed to establish a firm critical standpoint by which the *New Statesman* might readily be recognised, and measured.

To be fair to MacCarthy, he shared Jack Squire's determination not to make coverage of literature and the arts unduly highbrow. The front half of the paper made more than enough demands upon its readers' patience and powers of concentration, as of course did Beatrice's awesomely dense supplements. Many no doubt tackled each new issue out of a sense of duty, aware that with GBS's early departure went wit, verve and panache. Radicalism did not – does not – mean having to be be serious and well-intentioned all the time. Yet Sharp and Lloyd's *New Statesman* was a singularly humourless product. As 'YY', Robert Lynd could be mildly amusing, but Squire's jokes were as contrived as they were unfunny. Admittedly, his parodies were clever, but wit was a phenomenon largely unknown to the denizens of Great Queen Street. Freelances like Rebecca West and Cyril Connolly lightened the mood, but Martin's paper had to get into its stride before it gained a little sparkle. Hyams in his official history of the *New Statesman* unintentionally caught this mix of worthiness and priggishness, scarcely leavened by a smile. This book has deliberately not devoted space to smugly lauding the virtues of 'New Statesmanship', which seems little more than a euphemism for middle-class paternalism. Hitchens quoted with approval Anthony Howard's description of the *New Statesman* as 'a missionary outpost to the middle classes', noting, *pace* Hyams, that 'A missionary operation to the middle classes is not the same as a missionary operation from the middle classes'.[19]

Any discussion of 'New Statesmanship' has invariably focused on Kingsley Martin's 30 years at Great Queen Street and then Great Turnstile. This is that rarity, a book about the *New Statesman* in which Martin is not centre-stage. Nevertheless, Chapter 10 paid tribute to his achievement in carving out an international reputation for the *New Statesman* as a flagship of the Labour left. Only *Tribune* in its Bevanite heyday ever offered any serious challenge to the title. The same chapter repeated a familiar cliché that Martin made his paper the conscience of the left.[20] All subsequent editors have had to live in his shadow, upholding a tradition of English radicalism that for much (if by no means all) of the past 30 years has seen the paper instinctively lining up with the awkward squad – and quite right too.[21] A further legacy of the Martin legend is the common assumption that before 1931 the *New Statesman* was of peripheral importance to a nascent labour movement. In most shorthand accounts of the paper's history its first 18 years are reduced to a prologue, even a caricature: a glorified organ of Fabian propaganda is seen as useful to the Webbs when carving out a new role for themselves within the Labour

Party, but then it becomes a dullish magazine limping along under a drunken editor and waiting to be reborn.

This book is a rehabilitation of the first *New Statesman, and* a rehabilitation of its editor, however unattractive he was as an individual. Clifford Sharp's creation had not only a distinct life-span – from the demise of the Poor Law campaign to the collapse of the second Labour government – but also a distinct identity. True, the *New Statesman* never came close to achieving that 'standard of compulsive readability' which Dick Crossman saw as the true measure of Martin's success.[22] By the very nature of its initial task, and the personality of its editor, it was always at heart a conservative paper. Yet, when measured against the Webbs' meagre ambitions rather than its later glories, here was an unexpected and invaluable success: invaluable in that, contrary to popular assumption, the *New Statesman*'s influence within the Labour Party, and more widely within what today we label 'the chattering classes', was wholly out of proportion to its circulation. Even in the heyday of Sharp's editorship, the paper articulated the views of a progressive intelligentsia forced by the First World War to abandon old loyalties, and to reassess its role and status in the light of Labour's *de facto* destruction of the old political certainties.

With the first *New Statesman* ignored for so long, the danger here is to exaggerate its importance, particularly in the context of the rise of Labour. Few aspects of modern British history have attracted greater attention, and yet no reputable study has deemed the *New Statesman* worthy even of a footnote. It would have been surprising, to put it mildly, if any had. We need to keep a sense of proportion. On the other hand, the primary purpose of this book has been to demonstrate that here was a purportedly socialist journal which, during and after the First World War, played a small yet significant role in the conduct of British politics, and in the formulation of domestic policy, most notably with reference to the economy. A secondary intention was to recall an era of newspaper production long since extinct. What were the trials and tribulations experienced by Sharp, Squire and their colleagues, week in, week out, when striving to put together a magazine that was topical, opinionated, and, as an added bonus, readable? Written from a distance of well over half a century, this portrait of a political weekly is inevitably incomplete. Not even the most imaginative of empathists can capture the frenetic atmosphere of Great Queen Street on a Thursday, and sadly no-one is still alive who can recall life before Kingsley Martin. Many questions remain unanswered, and much remains undiscovered, but then that is the nature of history. Yet Sharp's weekly has not totally disappeared. It survives in bound volumes, on library shelves up and down the country. Perhaps the time has come to blow off the dust, dip into the back issues, and explore the roots of an astonishingly resilient magazine. God forbid that the original *New Statesman* should be a role model for today's embattled yet buoyant successor. It might, however, be an inspiration.

Notes

Preface and acknowledgements, pp. xi–xiv.

1. J. Connell, 'Crossman for Quitting', *Time and Tide*, 2 Jan. 1954.
2. G. Orwell, *The Lion and the Unicorn Socialism and the English Genius* (London: Secker & Warburg, 1941; Penguin paperback edn, 1982), pp. 63 and 115–16.
3. See Ch. 5. Admittedly the paper's influence diminished once Sharp returned from spying in Scandinavia, only to be restored in the aftermath of 1931 when Ernest Bevin and G.D.H. Cole formed the unholiest of unholy alliances. See also Chs. 7 and 10.
4. *New Statesman & Society* and *Tribune* organised a joint conference on 21 Nov. 1994 to discuss a replacement for Clause Four of the Labour Party constitution. Both weeklies' editors helped MPs on the left of the party draft a new statement of aims and objectives. S.Platt, 'Rewriting Socialism', *New Statesman & Society*, 11 Nov. 1994.
5. E. Hyams, *The New Statesman: The History of the First Fifty Years 1913–1963* (London: Longman, 1963). S. Howe (ed.), *Lines of Dissent Writing from the New Statesman 1913 to 1988* (London: Verso, 1988).
6. See Ch. 9, note 4.

Chapter 1, Introduction, pp.1–9.

1. A. Howard, 'The rise and peaceful fall of the weeklies', *The Times*, 22 July 1978, Howard argued – unconvincingly – that, in a more affluent and more consensual era, the *New Statesman* and the *Spectator* each lost its 'traditional partisan cutting edge'. With no great battles to fight, there was no 'perpetual clash of ideas, a continuing confrontation of ideologies'. A. Howard, 'Decline and fall of the political weekly', *Journalism Studies Review*, June 1978, p. 13.
2. Martin once described the *New Statesman and Nation* as 'the one and only solvent socialist organisation in the world'. Howard, 'Decline and Fall', p. 12.
3. For a profile of the *Spectator* under Charles Moore and then Dominic Lawson, see P. Wright, 'Spectator sports', *Guardian*, 4 July 1994.
4. For the 1993 litigation, see Ch. 9, note 4.
5. 'In search of a new politics', *New Statesman & Society*, 30 Sept. 1994.
6. For the importance of the *New Age*, its editor A.R. Orage, and its pre-war promotion of guild socialism, see Ch. 2.
7. Beatrice Webb, diary, 18 April 1896, Passfield Papers.
8. The circulation of the *Spectator*, edited by John St Loe Strachey, a Free Trade Unionist, was around 4,000 copies a week in the mid-1890s.
9. For Fabianism and 'New Liberalism', see Ch. 2. In 1890 the *Speaker* was founded by J.L. Hammond to counterbalance the *Spectator*. Never viable, it was relaunched as the *Nation* in 1907, soon seeing off a short-lived challenger, the *Tribune*. H.W. Massingham edited the Liberals' premier weekly until 1923, when it was sold to a consortium led by John Maynard Keynes. For the *Nation* in the 1920s, see Chs. 7–10.
10. R. Blackburn, 'Was this the birth of Anglo-Marxism?', *The Times Higher Educational Supplement*, 7 Dec. 1979.
11. Richard Crossman suggested that August 1931 marked a new attitude to parliamentary politics. In his dog-days Sharp had become over-fascinated with Westminster machinations. Martin, on the other hand, visibly shared his middle-class readers' effortless sense of superiority to Party politicians':

> Inevitably in our two-party system, loyalty – especially when you are wrong – is the quality most appreciated. To the editor of the NEW STATESMAN this was further evidence of their moral corruption.

R.H.S. Crossman, 'Martin's weekly medicine', *New Statesman*, 3 May 1968.

12. The *Westminster Gazette*'s editor, J.A. Spender, enjoyed unique access to Sir Edward Grey at the Foreign Office and was an intimate of Asquith, after his death writing the latter's official biography. Spender's paper, like A.G. Gardiner's 'New Liberal' *Daily News* and Robert Donald's *Daily Chronicle*, was part of the 'Cocoa Press', so-called because the Rowntree and Cadbury families held major stakes in a number of Liberal newspapers, as well as the *Nation*. Ramsay MacDonald made several abortive attempts between 1906 and 1909 to purchase the loss-making *Daily News* on behalf of a pro-Labour consortium. Despite the *Manchester Guardian*'s C.P. Scott having vacated his seat, in the 1906 Parliament 22 of the 30 newspaper proprietors were Liberals, several of them Radical backbenchers. Suggesting that editors and owners' direct contact with ministers was more likely to secure action than pleas from their leader columns, Alan Lee memorably described the Liberal press as dependent upon 'the generosity of a few rich men in order to bring pressure upon a few politically powerful ones'. D. Hopkin, 'The Labour Party Press', in K.D. Brown (ed.), *The First Labour Party 1906–14* (London: Croom Helm, 1985), pp. 115–17. A.J. Lee, 'The Radical Press', in A.J.A. Morris (ed.), *Edwardian Radicalism 1900–14* (London: Routledge & Kegan Paul, 1974), p. 58. For an overview of the London-based Liberal press in Edwardian Britain, see S. Koss, *The Rise and Fall of the Political Press in Britain Vol. 2 The Twentieth Century* (London: Hamish Hamilton, 1984), pp. 75–81 and 172–4.

13. For the mixed fortunes of the *Labour Leader* and the *Clarion*, see Koss, *The Rise and Fall of the Political Press in Britain 2*, pp. 62–5 and 154–6. For a survey of the pre-war Labour press, including the origins of the *Daily Herald* and of the costly but shortlived *Daily Citizen* (£500,000 losses, 1912–15!), see Hopkin, 'The Labour Party Press', in Brown (ed.), *The First Labour Party 1906–14*, pp. 105–28. See also D. Hopkin, 'The Socialist Press in Britain, 1890–1910', in G. Boyce *et al.* (eds), *Newspaper History from the Seventeenth Century to the Present Day* (London: Constable, 1978), pp. 294–306.

14. G. Phillips, 'A National Press Archive', ibid., p. 341.

15. The left is print-based. Socialism was a typographical invention. Printers were always in the vanguard of the left. The three feet on which the left has stood are the education system, journals of opinion, and books. But the new 'videosphere' results in the domination of the present, novelty as value, the cult of the instant, the fetish of the short term. It is terrible for us, we are culturally marginalised.

Regis Debray quoted in K. Davey, 'In the dock of Debray', *New Statesman & Society*, 17 June 1994.

Chapter 2, Perplexed Fabians: Sidney and Beatrice Webb by 1912, pp. 10–33.

1. M.Cole, *The Story of Fabian Socialism* (London: Heinemann, 1961), pp. 121–2 and 155.

2. *Fabian News*, May 1907, quoted in Cole, op. cit., p. 150.

3. Edward Pease was technically the founder of the Fabian Society, in October 1883, but all of the 'Old Gang' other than Beatrice Webb – Sidney Webb, Shaw, Graham Wallas, Hubert Bland and Sidney Olivier – had joined within a year. The first generation of Fabians, particularly the Webbs, argued the benefits of the large-scale organised state (with central control of the financial and industrial infrastructure). Complementing and counterbalancing this concentration of power would be a decentralised 'Municipal Socialism', based on autonomous local authorities which could compete for national recognition as efficient providers of public utilities and effective monitors of factory conditions conducive to high productivity: Joseph Chamberlain's achievements as Mayor of Birmingham were seen as an early step on the path of 'gradualism'. In G.B. Shaw (ed.), *Fabian Essays* (London, 1889), Wallas stressed the importance of retaining entrepreneurialism, albeit kept in check by a highly progressive fiscal policy. However, Olivier envisaged a new class of salaried managers taking as much pride in working for the community as for the joint-stock companies at that time replacing more traditional

forms of business organisation. Beatrice Webb later anticipated the 'professional expert' extending 'the sphere of government by adding to its enormous advantages of wholesale and compulsory management, the advantage of the most skilled entrepreneur'. Although unimpressed by their leaders, the Webbs defended the trade unions, persuading fellow Fabians to pursue the case for a national minimum wage (the 'National Minimum') while at the same time recognising the need for financial incentives to encourage individual effort and initiative. M. Cole and B. Drake (eds), *Beatrice Webb, Our Partnership* (London, 1948), p. 120. B. and S. Webb, *Industrial Democracy* (London, 1898).

On the first generation of Fabians and their ideas, see A.M. McBriar, *Fabian Socialism and English Politics 1884–1918* (Cambridge: CUP, 1962), N. and J. MacKenzie, *The First Fabians* (London: Weidenfeld & Nicolson, 1977), P. Clarke, *Liberals and Social Democrats* (Cambridge: CUP, 1978), Lisanne Radice, *Beatrice and Sidney Webb, Fabian Socialists* (London: Macmillan, 1984), and M. Holroyd, *Bernard Shaw 1: 1856–98 The Search For Love* (London: Chatto & Windus, 1988).

4. N. and J. MacKenzie (eds), *The Diary of Beatrice Webb: Vol. 3 1905–24 The Power To Alter Things* (Cambridge, MA., 1984), 1 March 1910 and 12 March 1911, pp. 135–6 and 156.

5. For the kind of ill-will borne towards Webb by many Progressive and ILP councillors, see MacKenzie (eds), *Diary of Beatrice Webb 1905–24*, 23 July 1903, pp. 289–90.

    Differences over education legislation led to a serious breach between the Webbs and Wallas. See P. Clarke, *Liberals and Social Democrats*, pp. 87–90.

    The Fabian executive's refusal in July 1900 either to condemn or condone British action against the Transvaal and the Orange Free State, and Sidney Webb's insistence that even if wrong Liberal supporters of the war had a reasonable case, had split the Society, leaving a deep fissure between its older and younger members. After an inconsequential postal ballot, Ramsay MacDonald and 14 other anti-war members resigned.

6. Conversation between Robert Ensor and Beatrice and Sidney Webb, 8 June 1904, quoted in R. Ensor, 'Permeation' in M. Cole (ed.), *The Webbs and their Work* (London: Muller, 1949), p. 67. N. and J. MacKenzie (eds), *The Diary of Beatrice Webb: Vol. 2 1892–1905, All The Good Things of Life* (Cambridge, MA, 1983), 28 Feb. 1902, pp. 235–40.

7. The Relugas Compact of September 1905 was an agreement by Grey, Haldane, and Asquith that they would accept office only if the latter led the party in the Commons and Campbell-Bannerman held the premiership in the Lords. The agreement's collapse in December 1905 effectively aborted the Webbs' short-term ambitions for government influence, despite Beatrice's initial excitement on hearing of the Liberal Imperialists' senior Cabinet posts. Grey consulted only Foreign Office officials, and Haldane was unlikely to ask for advice on running the War Office. Asquith, at the Treasury, had always been a distant figure. According to Robert Ensor, only Churchill and Herbert Samuel, when still junior ministers, ever discussed specific departmental matters. MacKenzie (eds), *Diary of Beatrice Webb 1892–1905*, 15 Dec. 1905, p. 325. Ensor, 'Permeation', p. 70.

8. S. Webb, 'Lord Rosebery's Escape from Houndsditch', *Nineteenth Century*, Sept. 1901. For the article's origins, and its 'brilliant success', see MacKenzie (eds), *Diary of Beatrice Webb 1892–1905*, 26 July and 1 Oct. 1901, pp. 214–15 and 21. For Shaw's involvement in permeation, and his fascination with Rosebery, see Holroyd, *Bernard Shaw 2*, pp. 36–45 and 117–26.

9. All that he [Rosebery] said about the clean slate and efficiency was an affront to Liberalism and was pure claptrap. Efficiency as a watchword! This is all a mere *rechauffé* of Mr Sidney Webb who is evidently the chief instructor of the whole faction.

Sir Henry Campbell-Bannerman to Herbert Gladstone, 18 Dec. 1901, quoted in J.A. Spender, *The Life of the Right Hon. Sir Henry Campbell-Bannerman, Vol. II* (London, 1923), p. 14.

The growing distance between the Webbs and one–time Radical allies, most notably among the Progressives on the LCC, was further highlighted by the publication in 1902 of J.A. Hobson's *Imperialism*. A persuasive dismissal of many arguments advanced by the Liberal League, it convinced many young Liberal Party members that imperial expenditure was so great that, rather than stimulate domestic reform, the empire in fact hindered it. There is some suggestion from Beatrice's diary that the ill-health she experienced throughout 1901 had its origins in the relentless conspiring and lobbying that permeation entailed, but little evidence to indicate a nervous breakdown, as recently suggested. MacKenzie (eds), *Diary of Beatrice Webb 1892–1905*, 9 Dec. 1901, pp. 224–5. C. Seymour-Jones, 'Webbs of Intrigue', *New Statesman & Society*, 17/31 Dec. 1993.

10. For Helen Bosanquet's work for the Charity Organisation Society, and a discussion of her ideas, see R. McKibbin, 'Class and Poverty in Edwardian England', in *The Ideologies of Class Social Relations in Britain 1880–1950* (Oxford: OUP, 1990, paperback edn 1991), pp. 170–96, and for a comparison with Beatrice Webb's approach to social policy, see A.M. McBriar, *An Edwardian Mixed Doubles: Bosanquets versus the Webbs – a Study in British Social Policy 1890–1929* (Oxford: OUP, 1987).

11. For the 1905–9 Poor Law Commission in the wider context of the Edwardian debate on poverty, see D. Vincent, *Poor Citizens: The State and the Poor in Twentieth Century Britain* (London: Longman, 1991, paperback edn), pp. 22–39, and J. Harris, *Private Lives, Public Spirit: Britain 1870–1914* (OUP, Oxford, 1993; Penguin paperback edn 1994), pp. 240–3. *New Age* quoted in W. Martin, *The New Age Under Orage* (Manchester: MUP, 1967), p. 2.

The Webbs' concern for the building blocks of society and not for its individual members is a familiar criticism of Fabian collectivism, from both right and left. Beatrice readily acknowledged that the 'scientific' investigation of 'social institutions, from trade unions to Cabinets, from family relationships to churches, from economics to literature', owed as much to Positivism and Darwinism as to Utilitarianism. Seeing their later embrace of Stalin as consistent with a lifelong leaning towards the authoritarian 'solution' to all social evils, Woolf attacked an unduly rigid sociological method, singularly counterproductive in its response to 'problems of imperialism, international relations, and war and peace'. Cole and Drake (eds), *Our Partnership*, p. 116. L. Woolf, 'Political Thought and the Webbs', in Cole (ed.), *The Webbs and Their Work*, p. 261. See also Ch. 5, note 71.

12.   . . . those who cut themselves off from the powerful and deeply-rooted liberal traditions were likely to fail . . . even the theories and policies most at variance with the Cobdenite orthodoxies of the past, succeeded only insofar as they were allied with or operated in the framework of historic Liberalism.

E.J. Hobsbawm, 'The Fabians Reconsidered', in *Labouring Men* (London: Weidenfeld & Nicolson, 1964), p. 263.

McKibbin has argued that the Liberal government recognised the 'centrality of free trade finance to the political economy of the British working classes', and that tariff reform 'threatened the enforcement of a new social discipline . . . that would have subordinated the working class under a new fiscal-industrial order'. R. McKibbin, 'Why was there no Marxism in Britain?', in *The Ideologies of Class*, pp. 31–2.

13. The President of the Board of Trade was Winston Churchill; the constitutional crisis began with the Lords rejecting the 1909 'People's Budget' and ended when they lost their legislative veto under the 1911 Parliament Act (or alternatively, when war in August 1914 delayed the introduction of Home Rule in Ireland); and the WSPU was the suffragette Women's Social and Political Union.

14. Attlee, who was always happier in the ILP than with the Fabians ('Have we got to grow a beard to join this show?'), was hired to organise a series of lectures, mainly in London. His connection with the Webbs continued after 1919 with his appointment as a lecturer at the London School of Economics (LSE), the great Fabian creation of

the mid-1890s which, under William Pember Reeves's directorship (1908–19), became the premier centre for studying economics outside Cambridge. At the LSE Attlee worked alongside C.M. Lloyd, see Ch. 7. K. Harris, *Attlee* (London: Weidenfeld & Nicolson, 1982), pp. 25 and 29. For a profile of the young Clifford Sharp, see Ch. 3.

15. MacKenzie (eds), *Diary of Beatrice Webb 1905–24*, 1 Dec. 1912, p. 182 .
16. Hobsbawm, *Labouring Men*, p. 253.

Throughout the 1890s Marxists and 'New Liberals' alike had scorned permeation as opportunistic and fruitless, see respectively, F. Engels correspondence with K. Kautsky, and F.A. Sorge, in K. Marx and F. Engels, *Karl Marx and Frederick Engels on Britain* (Moscow, 1962), pp. 572, 574–5, and 577–580, and L.T. Hobhouse in *Manchester Guardian*, 7 July 1899.

The cost-conscious Cabinet minister was the Chancellor of the Exchequer; see report of Asquith's speech at East Fife, *The Times*, 21 Oct. 1907.

17. Among a wealth of literature on 'New Liberalism', see M. Bentley, *The Climax of Liberal Politics: British Liberalism in Theory and Practice 1868–1918* (London: Edward Arnold, 1987) and M. Freeden, *The New Liberalism: An Ideology of Social Reform* (Oxford: OUP, 1978). Peter Clarke saw no clear ideological gulf between a rising generation of Liberal thinkers and activists and their pro-Labour contemporaries, only the predictable consequences of party division and the prevailing electoral system. Thus the Liberals had become a credible social democratic force by 1914, a view challenged in, for example, R. McKibbin, *The Evolution of the Labour Party 1910–24* (Oxford: OUP, 1974). For conflicting views on the potential of 'New Liberalism' as a foundation for a new progressive alliance or movement, unfulfilled as a consequence of the First World War, see Clarke, *Liberals and Social Democrats*, and A. Howkins, 'Edwardian Liberalism and Industrial Unrest: A Class View of the Decline of Liberalism', *History Workshop Journal*, 4 (Autumn 1977), pp. 143–61. For a summary of the argument that the process of change was more fragmented than, from their respective positions, Clarke and Ross McKibbin have assessed the position of Labour and Liberals on the eve of the First World War, see D. Tanner, *Political Change and the Labour Party 1900–18* (Cambridge: CUP, 1990), pp. 419–20. For discussion of the reality of a progressive alliance at either end of the twentieth century, see D. Marquand, *The Progressive Dilemma* (London: Heinemann, 1991, paperback edn 1992), especially pp. 5–25. For the extent to which imperialism divided Fabians from Hobhouse, Hobson and C.F.G. Masterman, see P.F. Clarke, 'The Progressive Movement in England', *Transactions of the Royal Historical Society*, Vol. 24 (1974), pp. 165–6. For discussion of Clarke's and Marquand's ideas on the difference between the Fabians as 'mechanical reformers' and the 'New Liberals' as 'moral reformers', see Ch. 5.

18. Shaw attended the ILP's inaugural Bradford Convention on 13–14 Jan. 1893 to defend the Society's use of permeation. Fabians who served on the ILP's National Administrative Council did so in an individual capacity. Only one Fabian out of 129 delegates attended the London conference on 27 February 1900 which established the LRC, and yet the Society secured a member on the 12-man executive. It would not be unfair to the Fabian executive to describe its general attitude towards the trade union dominated LRC as apathetic, sceptical, and distrustful.

For the uniqueness of MacDonald and Snowden, and why there were so few similar figures in the early ILP, see McKibbin, 'Why was there no Marxism in Britain?', pp. 33–4.

19. By 1911 there were around 1,300 Fabians in London, one-third of the total membership. By 1915 there were 15 active groups. On their involvement in metropolitan Labour politics, see P. Thompson, *Socialists, Liberals and Labour The Struggle for London 1885–1914* (London: Routledge & Kegan Paul, 1967), pp. 214, 296–7 and 221. Pre-empting the argument that 'New Liberalism' could have reinvigorated the party, Thompson concluded that the depth of class divisions in Edwardian London was such as to place the local Liberal Party in terminal condition.

For the view that the consolidation of a fundamentally apolitical popular culture had by 1900 muted working-class radicalism in the capital, see G. Stedman Jones, 'Working-Class Culture and Working-Class Politics in London, 1870–1900: Notes on the Remaking of a Working Class', in *Languages of Class: Studies in English Working Class History 1832–1982* (Cambridge: CUP, 1984). See also Tanner, *Political Change and the Labour Party 1900–18.*

20.   . . . [do not] hope for a moment that the Labour Party is going to be a Socialist Party, or that the middle class proletariat can ever be persuaded to join it under existing conditions.

    G.B. Shaw to Clifford Sharp, 5 March 1907, British Library.
    Similarly, Liberal editor H.W. Massingham's view that 'sharp limits are set to the progress of a body so largely divorced from middle-class brains and middle-class sympathy as is the Independent Labour Party', *Nation*, 6 July 1907.

21. Ensor, 'Permeation', pp. 67–8.
    For examples of Beatrice denigrating ILP MPs, even after starting to work closely with them, see MacKenzie (eds), *Diary of Beatrice Webb 1905–24*, 11 Oct. 1912, 1 Dec. 1912 and 18 Feb. 1914, pp. 180, 182, and 196.

22. For Shaw, Ensor's alternative ploy of the executive adopting a simple resolution favouring close liaison with the ILP was 'inopportune', for:

    whilst we [Fabian Society executive] fully intend that the Socialism of the Independent Labour Party shall be Fabian Socialism, we don't propose that the Party shall be identical with the Fabian Society or that the Society should depart from its old policy of not running candidates.

    G.B. Shaw to Clifford Sharp, 5 March 1907, British Library. For Shaw's relationship with Wells at this time, see Holroyd, *Bernard Shaw 2*, pp. 126–47.

23. Sidney Webb to H.G. Wells, 15 June 1907, Wells Archive. For a succinct account of Wells's 1906 challenge, see M. Cole, 'H.G. Wells and the Fabian Society', in Morris (ed.), *Edwardian Radicalism 1900–14*, pp. 110–11.

24. For an example of Beatrice's belief that the NCPD 'agitation' was having a great impact, despite Asquith and Grey deliberately ignoring her when they met for the first time in three years, see MacKenzie (eds), *Diary of Beatrice Webb 1905–24*, 13 March 1910.

25. Margaret Cole to the Editor, *New Statesman and Nation*, 26 Dec. 1959.

26. The *Spectator*, edited for nearly 30 years by John St Loe Strachey, was the only Edwardian weekly in profit, despite sales declining from 22,000 in 1903 to 13,500 in 1922. For its rivals (mostly priced at 6d) a circulation above 5,000 signified success. The high cost of newsprint during the First World War forced many small circulation magazines to shrink dramatically in size (e.g. the *New Age*), go monthly (e.g. the *Athenaeum*), merge, or cease publishing (e.g. *TP's Weekly*, edited 1911–16 by Holbrook Jackson). Sales figures quoted in Martin, *The New Age Under Orage*, p. 10.

27. A. Bennett, 'The Literary Periodical', *New Age*, 8 Sept. 1910. For the popularity and influence of 'Jacob Tonson' and his column 'Books and Persons', see M. Drabble, *Arnold Bennett* (London: Weidenfeld & Nicolson, 1974), p. 165, and Arnold Bennett to Edward Garnett, 29 Nov. 1908, J. Hepburn (ed.), *Letters of Arnold Bennett: Vol. II, 1889–1915* (Oxford, 1968), p. 235. Unable to secure an acceptable regular replacement until he met Herbert Read in 1921, from 1913 Orage himself wrote the 'Readers and Writers' column hiding behind the initials 'R.H.C.'. W. Martin (ed.), 'Introduction', *Orage As Critic* (Manchester: MUP, 1974), pp. 1–2.

28. A.J. Penty, *The Restoration of the Guild System* (London, 1906).

29. Martin, *The New Age Under Orage*, p. 26. A.R. Orage to H.G. Wells, 9 June 1907, quoted in MacKenzie, *The First Fabians*, p. 344. A.J. Penty, *Old Worlds For New: A Study of the Post-Industrial State* (London, 1917), pp. 28–9.

30. For why the *New Age* was a 'devilish good paper', see Arnold Bennett to Charles Young, 4 May 1908, Hepburn (ed.), *Bennett Letters, Vol. II*, p. 223. G.B. Shaw, 'How Free is the Press', *Pen Portraits and Review* (London, 1918), pp. 41–2.

31. Hobsbawm, *Labouring Men*, pp. 255–6. Beatrice Webb, diary, Christmas 1895, Passfield Papers.

32. For pre-war Cambridge Fabianism, see B. Pimlott, *Hugh Dalton* (London: Jonathan Cape, 1985), pp. 38–57.
    Beatrice found Keeling a 'fervent rebel', he and his Cambridge contemporaries at the 1908 summer school constituting, 'a remarkable set, quite the most remarkable the Fabian Society has hitherto attracted – fervent and brilliant'. MacKenzie (eds), *Diary of Beatrice Webb 1905–24*, 13 Sept. 1908, p. 98.

33. R. Skidelsky, *John Maynard Keynes: Vol. 1, Hopes Betrayed 1883–1920* (London: Macmillan, 1983), pp. 166, 195, and 239–41. Clarke argued, albeit a long time ago, that there was nothing contradictory about Keynes speaking in support of Webb's motion given the identity of interests between 'New Liberalism' and the revisionism of R.H. Tawney or MacDonald. Clarke, 'The Progressive Movement in England', pp. 171–2. M. Holroyd, *Lytton Strachey A Critical Biography Vol. II The Years of Achievement (1910–1932)* (London: Heinemann, 1968), p. 17.
    The Apostles was the semi-secret, highly selective Cambridge society to which at the turn of the century many male members of the original Bloomsbury group belonged. The three Apostles most prominent in the history of the *New Statesman* have been Keynes, Desmond MacCarthy and Leonard Woolf.

34. 'J.C. Squire came on Saturday. Long hair, Jaegerishly dressed. But sound, competent, honest in argument.' N. Flower (ed.), *The Journals of Arnold Bennett: Vol. II, 1911–21* (London, 1932), 8 Dec. 1913, p. 75. For a full profile of J.C. Squire, see Chs. 5 and 8.

35. F.H. Keeling, *Child Labour in the United Kingdom* (London, 1910) and *The Labour Exchange in Relation to Boy and Girl Labour* (London, 1910).
    In addition, during 1910–13 Keeling wrote for the *School Child* (as 'Accelerans'), the *Economic Journal*, and for Clifford Sharp's *Crusade*. In addition to his pre-war work for the *New Statesman*, during 1914–15 he contributed three unsigned articles on life as an NCO on the Western Front. For a selection of his work, plus tributes by H.G. Wells and Arthur Greenwood, see E. Townshend (ed.), *Keeling: Letters and Recollections* (London, 1918), and reviewed in 'A Socialist Soldier', *New Statesman*, 2 Sept. 1918. Sharp's obituary appeared in 'Comments', *New Statesman*, 2 Sept. 1916. Keeling's ideas, personality, career and relationship with Dalton are fully and sensitively explored in Pimlott, *Hugh Dalton*, pp. 40–53, and 83–4.

36. See the 1930–31 merger of the *New Statesman* and the *Nation*, Ch. 10.

37. E.g. Cole and Mellor's behaviour at a Fabian conference in the Lake District on the eve of the First World War, where they drank copiously, sang revolutionary songs and raised the Red Flag, in the process horrifying not just Beatrice, but the local constabulary, *and* the delegates at the Keswick Evangelical Convention on Religious Experiences. MacKenzie (eds), *Diary of Beatrice Webb 1905–24*, 31 July 1914, p. 204.
    The Fabians' second great intellectual partnership was forged when Cole married Margaret Postgate, Cambridge graduate and wartime secretary of the Fabian Research Department (see note 49), in August 1918.

38. For a perceptive and prescient assessment of the young Cole by Beatrice Webb, see MacKenzie (eds), *Diary of Beatrice Webb 1905–24*, 3 Jan. 1915.

39. Cole, *A History of Fabian Socialism*, p. 116.

40. For the appeal of Wells to young Fabians, particularly his views on sexual freedom, see J. Lewis, 'Intimate Relations Between Men and Women: the Case of H.G. Wells and Amber Pember Reeves', *History Workshop Journal*, 37 (Spring 1994), pp. 76–98, and M. Cowling, 'A Planetary Perspective', *The Times Higher Education Supplement*, 1 Nov. 1985.

41. Cole, *A History of Fabian Socialism*, pp. 116–17.

42. A.R. Orage, 'An Editor's Progress', *New Age*, 18 March 1926, p. 235. Orage and Penty's views on workers' rights were graphically illustrated each week by the brilliant Australian cartoonist Will Dyson. Having served his apprenticeship at home on the legendary *Bulletin*, Dyson also drew for the *Daily Herald*, scarcely disguising his

syndicalist sympathies. In 1915 he left England to become an official war artist for the Australian government, but today his work is perhaps what the *New Age* is best remembered for.

43. Martin, *The New Age Under Orage*, pp. 202 and 204. Hilaire Belloc compiled 'Notes of the Week' for the first year, and a series of articles attacking Fabian collectivism that appeared in 1910 were later published in book form, a best-seller, *The Servile State* (London, 1911).

44. For GBS's annoyance with Orage, see G.B. Shaw to C.H. Norman, 24 Sept. 1908, in D.H. Lawrence (ed.), *Bernard Shaw Collected Letters 1898–1910* (London, 1972), p. 810.

45. For a full exposition of early thinking on guild socialism, see Penty, *The Restoration of the Guild System* and S.G. Hobson, *National Guilds* (London, 1914).

46. M. Cole, *The Life of G.D.H. Cole* (London: Macmillan, 1971), pp. 26–7, 70, and 75. P. Mairet, *A.R. Orage: A Memoir* (London, 1936). For a succinct explanation of social credit, and explanation of how Douglas's ideas could be reconciled with those of the guild socialists, see D. Edgell, *The Order of Woodcraft Chivalry 1916–1949 as a New Age Alternative to the Boy Scouts, Vol. II* (Lewiston, NY: Edwin Mellon, 1992), pp. 325–41. For a relatively minor writer Orage has attracted considerable biographical and critical attention, as well as appearing thinly disguised in at least two novels, see Martin (ed.), *Orage As Critic*, Bibliography, p. 211.

47. MacKenzie (eds), *Diary of Beatrice Webb 1905–24*, 11 Oct. 1912, p. 179.

48. Henry Devenish Harben was the largest shareholder of the Prudential Insurance Company, and thus extremely wealthy. He helped support the WSPU, and kept the *Daily Herald* running between its launch in Dec. 1912 and its wartime switch to a weekly in Sept. 1914.

49. MacKenzie, *The First Fabians*, p. 383. M. Cole, 'Labour Research', in Cole (ed.), *The Webbs and Their Work*, pp. 152–3.

50. B. Webb, 'Memorandum on the Committee on the Control of Industry', Oct. 1912, Passfield Papers. R. Page Arnot, *History of the Labour Research Department* (London, 1926), pp. 5–6. Page Arnot was a co-founder of the British Communist Party (CPGB) in 1920, and a lifelong member.

51. MacKenzie (eds), *Diary of Beatrice Webb 1905–24*, 3 April, 25 May and 8 Dec. 1913, pp. 187, 188–9, and 192–3.

52. Ibid., 8 March 1914, p. 198.

53. Ibid., 15 May 1915, pp. 229–30. Cole, 'Labour Research', p. 157.

54. MacKenzie (eds), *Diary of Beatrice Webb 1905–24*, 1 June 1916, p. 257.

55. Ibid., 17 July and 7 Oct. 1921, pp. 382 and 388. Although for much of its history linked to the CPGB, the LRD has proved a long-serving and valuable research agency for British trade unions.

56. 'The *New Statesman* was part of a grand design, a weekly paper born of disappointment. . . . In 1912, Beatrice Webb got real.' Seymour-Jones, 'Webbs of Intrigue', *New Statesman and Nation*.

Chapter 3, Pre-war paper-making: Founding a new radical weekly, pp. 34–48.

1. A. Smith, 'SHARP, Clifford Dyce (1883–1935)', in J. Saville and J. Bellamy (eds), *The Dictionary of Labour Biography, Vol. VII* (Oxford: OUP, 1984), and 'Heart to the right, brain to the left', *New Statesman*, 8 Jan. 1988.
    St John Ervine's recollection of Sharp as a man 'with a fair amount of mediocre talent' barely capable of putting a paper to bed was clearly prejudiced by the latter's wartime clashes with Shaw, see Ch. 5. St John Ervine, *Bernard Shaw, His Life, Work and Friends* (London: Constable, 1956), pp. 455–6. L. Woolf, *Beginning Again: An Autobiography of the Years 1911–18* (London, 1964), pp. 129–30.

2. Beatrice Webb later recalled that she was by no means impressed on meeting Sharp for the first time. Yet she at once found him 'able and responsible in his opinions, and with the power of accurate yet literary language'. MacKenzie (eds), *Diary of Beatrice Webb 1905–24*, 22 Sept. 1917, p. 287.

3. J. Briggs, *A Woman of Passion: The Life of E. Nesbit 1858–1924* (London: Methuen, 1987), pp. 313–19.
4. There are conflicting accounts of the circumstances surrounding Rosamund's adoption, see Briggs, pp. 112–17. Bland was not a total hypocrite. As befitted a co-founder of the Anti-Puritan League, he loathed prudes and prurients.
5. Clifford Sharp to H.G. Wells, 6 Dec. 1906, Illinois.
6. Briggs, *A Woman of Passion*, pp. 300–20. N. and J. MacKenzie, *The Time Traveller: The Life of H.G. Wells* (London: Weidenfeld & Nicolson, 1973), p. 226. MacKenzie, *The First Fabians*, pp. 362–3.
7. In 1930, deeply in debt and desperate for work following Sharp's departure from the *New Statesman*, Rosamund wrote on behalf of an advertising agency asking Wells to recommend a brand of cigarettes:

    Strangely enough, I [Rosamund Sharp] remember I gave you [H.G. Wells] a promise on the seashore at Dymchurch *twenty-two* years ago that I would tell you if ever I was stranded. You told me then that Clifford Sharp would be no good to me. How terribly, terribly, right you were.

    Rosamund Sharp to H.G. Wells, 26 Jan. (?1930), Illinois.
    A later letter indicated the depth of Rosamund's unrequited love, the emptiness of her married life, and how much Wells had contributed to moulding her personality:

    By degrees I [Rosamund Sharp] got used to the idea that I didn't exist except simply as a thread on which all sorts of odds and ends are stuck together . . . Yet I am glad so many of your bits stuck.

    Rosamund Sharp to H.G. Wells, 3 Sept. (?1933), ibid., and reproduced in full in Briggs, *A Woman of Passion*, p. 320.
8. H.G. Wells, *Experiment in Autobiography* (London, 1934, 1984 edn), pp. 606–7.
9. Clifford Sharp to H.G. Wells, 6 March 1908, Illinois.
10. H.G. Wells, 'On Reading the First Number of the *New Statesman*', *New Witness*, 24 April 1913.
11. Ibid.
12. Clifford Sharp to Beatrice Webb, 11 March 1912, Passfield Papers.
13. 'To the experienced journalist it must seem a mad adventure, and we [Webbs] hardly expect more than a run for other people's money and our own hard work.' MacKenzie (eds), *Diary of Beatrice Webb 1905–24*, 11 Oct. 1912, p. 179.
14. G.B. Shaw to Beatrice Webb, 10 July 1912, Passfield Papers. While Shaw was right to imply that Sidney's copy rarely dazzled, he ignored his vast output over the years, dating back to the early 1880s when, eager to leave the Colonial Office, Webb struggled to forge a fresh career as a freelance journalist.
15. MacKenzie (eds), *Diary of Beatrice Webb 1905–24*, 11 Oct. 1912, p. 179. S.K. Ratcliffe, 'The *New Statesman*', in Cole (ed.), *The Webbs and Their Work*, p. 134. For almost the whole of the period covered by this book the *New Statesman* was based at Great Queen Street, not moving to its more famous Great Turnstile offices off Lincoln's Inn Fields until 1934. On their merger in 1988 the *New Statesman & Society* established itself in more functional and less costly premises on Kingsland Road in Shoreditch, just north of the City.
    Among other Tory leaders, a young Harold Macmillan and an even younger Edward Heath may have read the 'Staggers and Naggers', as the *New Statesman and Nation* came to be known in the 1930s.
16. Hyams, *New Statesman*, p. 14.
17. A. Smith, 'LLOYD, Charles Mostyn (1878–1946)', in Saville and Bellamy (eds), *The Dictionary of Labour Biography, Vol. VII*. Mrs. T. Lloyd, 'Charles Mostyn Lloyd', 17 Nov. 1968, British Library of Political and Economic Science.
18. Sidney Webb to Beatrice Webb, 7 Dec. 1912, Passfield Papers. MacKenzie (eds), *Diary of Beatrice Webb 1905–24*, (?) Jan. 1913, p. 186. C. Sharp, 'Early Days', *New Statesman and Nation*, 14 April 1934.

19. Sidney Webb to Elie Halévy, 18 Dec. 1912, in N. MacKenzie (ed.), *The Letters of Sidney and Beatrice Webb: Vol. III, 1912–47, Pilgrimage* (Cambridge, 1978), p. 12. Clifford Sharp to Beatrice Webb, 14 Jan. 1913, Passfield Papers. Sharp acquired the services of the *Manchester Guardian*'s stringer in Berlin, Dudley Ward, and one Pierre Chavannes in Paris. The latter soon made way for another *Manchester Guardian* correspondent, Robert Dell, a man according to Nevinson 'of great knowledge, and possessing an extraordinary flair for information, upon which he based forecasts seldom fulfilled'. H. W. Nevinson, *Last Changes and Last Chances* (London, 1928), p. 59.

20. 'The Statesman will prefer to be judged by its success in maintaining, throughout its pages, a high general level of critical and constructive thought, alike in economics, politics, and literature.' 'The Statesman' subscription form, Passfield Papers. Shaw quoted in Holroyd, *Bernard Shaw 2*, p. 320.

21. MacKenzie (eds), *Diary of Beatrice Webb 1905–24*, (?) Jan. 1913, pp. 185–6. Sidney Webb to G.B. Shaw, *Webb Letters 1912–47*, pp. 13–14.

22. G.B. Shaw to 'Fellow-Fabians', 15 Feb. 1913, Passfield Papers. *Preliminary Memorandum Descriptive of Proposed Weekly Journal*, Jan. 1913, ibid.

23. The supplements and reviews of government Blue Books were seen as vital to the FRD's survival. It was assumed that there was a well-educated lay audience who would voraciously devour what was after all incredibly heavy reading. Fortunately, Beatrice was totally wrong when she anticipated the *New Statesman* becoming 'primarily an organ of research and secondarily a general weekly paper'. Beatrice Webb to Sidney Webb, [?] Dec. 1913, Passfield Papers. MacKenzie (eds), *Diary of Beatrice Webb 1905–24*, 8 March 1914, p. 198

24. Ibid., pp. 185–6. Hyams, *New Statesman*, pp. 17–18. Lytton Strachey to James Strachey, (?) May 1914, quoted in Holroyd, *Lytton Strachey: A Critical Biography, Vol. II*, p. 108.

25. MacKenzie (eds), *Diary of Beatrice Webb 1905–24*, 25 May 1912, p. 187.

26. Sharp certainly lacked 'personal magnetism', but one wonders how on earth Beatrice could conclude that 'in some ways he is too doggedly sincere'. Ibid.

27. Mairet, *A.R. Orage*, pp. 71–2.

28. H.G. Wells, *New Witness*, 24 April 1913. Eighteen months later, Sharp adopted an uncharacteristically obsequious tone in suggesting to Wells that they settle their differences; probably because Wells was one of the few people who might succeed in circumventing Lord Kitchener's ban on correspondents at the front – and despatch to Great Queen Street an exclusive report on the fighting. For Sharp and Wells during 1915–17, see Ch. 5. Clifford Sharp to H.G. Wells, 25 Oct. 1914, Wells Archive.

29. H.W. Massingham, 'The Claims of Liberalism', *Daily News and Leader*, 14 April 1913, quoted in A.F. Havinghurst, *Radical Journalist: H.W. Massingham* (Cambridge: CUP, 1974), p. 224.

30. MacKenzie (eds), *Diary of Beatrice Webb 1905–24*, 25 May 1912, p. 187.

31. Arnold Bennett to J.C. Squire, 14 Feb. and 12 Nov. 1913, New York. For Bennett's wartime collaboration with Squire, see Chs. 5 and 8.

32. Sidney Webb to Ernest Simon, 19 May 1913, MacKenzie (ed.), *Webb Letters 1912–47*, p. 20

33. Ernest Simon to Sidney Webb, 9 June 1913, ibid..

34. G.B. Shaw to St John Ervine, (?) 1913, Texas. Apologies to Michael Holroyd for copying his idea.

35. Sharp's layout and typography were so advanced that the design remained virtually unchanged until July 1957.

36. 'Comments', *New Statesman*, 12 April 1913.
    'The *New Statesman* looks as if it would devour me. I have had to provide three articles for the first number. I'm not going to sign anything in it.' G.B. Shaw to H. Granville Barker, 10 April 1913, in C.B. Purdom (ed.), *Bernard Shaw's Letters to Granville Barker* (New York, 1957), p. 190.

37. 'Wireless Indignation', *New Statesman*, 12 April 1913. Clifford Sharp, 'Early Days',

New Statesman and Nation, 14 April 1934. The contributors' file confirms Sharp's account.

38. 'The General Strike: An Imaginary Correspondence', *New Statesman*, 26 April 1913. Shaw's article appeared as an edited, unsigned letter, alongside an unsigned reply from Webb. Sending a private version of the same letter to GBS, Sidney backed Sharp's action, pointing out that when writing anonymously Shaw had to adhere to the agreed editorial line on industrial action. Sidney Webb to G.B. Shaw, 22 April 1913, MacKenzie (ed.),*Webb Letters 1912–47*, p. 19.

39. G.B. Shaw quoted in Wickham Steed, *The Press* (London, paperback edn., 1938), p. 42.

40. Holroyd, *Bernard Shaw 2*, p. 320.

41. Ibid., pp. 320–1.

42. Sharp, 'Early Days', *New Statesman and Nation*, 14 April 1934.

43. Clifford Sharp to Beatrice Webb (?), quoted in Holroyd, *Bernard Shaw 2*, p. 321.

44. 'He [GBS] is estranged from the *New Statesman* and Sharp, but he is not at all hostile. "It is not my organ, but it may be none the worse for that".' MacKenzie (eds), *Diary of Beatrice Webb 1905–24*, 25 May 1914, p. 187.

45. G.B. Shaw to John Basil Barnhill, 18 May 1918, Dartmouth College Library.

Chapter 4, The *New Statesman* in Liberal England, pp. 49–68.

1. See Ch. 10. If the printers discovered a gap when putting the two halves of the paper together then Squire scribbled a note from 'H. de B. Winton', eccentric observer of national foibles and keeper of the *New Statesman's* socialist conscience. In the early 1980s 'Edward Pygge' performed a similar function, but in the 1990s Keith Flett has rendered the role wholly unnecessary.

2. Ironically, the whole of the front page 'Comments' in the inaugural (32-page) issue were devoted not to a domestic issue but to the Montenegrin occupation of Scutari. However, the first four articles covered the Marconi scandal, social deprivation, the suffragettes and Irish land reform. Equally ironic was that the accompanying supplement dealt with literature for pleasure not solely for moral improvement, albeit including a passion-killing essay by sexologist Havelock Ellis.

3. Sidney Webb to Sir Horace Plunkett, 28 Feb. 1913, in MacKenzie (ed.), *Webb Letters 1912–47*, pp. 15–16.

4. The article on land reform is unattributed in the contributors' file.

5. Beatrice Webb to Sir Horace Plunkett, 5 March 1913, Passfield Papers.

6. 'Conditions of a Settlement', *New Statesman*, 14 Feb. 1914. Plunkett had written to *The Times* three days earlier, proposing that Ulster vote after six years of Home Rule.

7. Joseph Maunsell Hone (1882–1959) became a prominent man-of-letters in the Irish Free State. He wrote the first biography of W.B. Yeats in 1943, and was elected President of the Irish Academy of Letters in 1957. For a portrait of Hone, the 'true Irish patriot', see H.W. Nevinson, *More Changes, More Chances* (London, 1925), p. 373. 'Comments', *New Statesman*, 26 April and 24 May 1913.

8. Sharp was embarrassed when Erskine Childers scorned GBS's suggestion that Ulster become a fully detached *English* region with guarantees for the Catholic minority. 'Ulster', *New Statesman*, 14 June 1913. Erskine Childers to the Editor, *The Times*, 10 June 1913. 'Comments', *New Statesman*, 14 June 1913.

9. 'The Drums of Ulster', *New Statesman*, 19 July 1913.

10. Nevinson found 'middles' much harder to write than leaders, as 'Being an essay, it must express personality and the expression of personality (which is style) implies a drain and drag upon the heart, the brain, or other vital organ of the writer'. H.W. Nevinson, *More Changes, More Chances* (London, 1925), p. 214.

11. YY, 'A Thousand and One "Middles"', *New Statesman and Nation*, 14 April 1934. Hyams, *New Statesman*, pp. 98 and 114. Lynd had an assigned compositor at the printers to read his hastily scribbled and thus barely legible manuscript.

12. 'The Human Nature of Riots', *New Statesman*, 23 Aug. 1913. YY, 'A Thousand and One "Middles"', op. cit.

13. 'Comments' and 'Anarchists in Dublin', *New Statesman*, 6 Sept. 1913. 'Comments' and 'Larkinism: The New Force in Ireland', *New Statesman*, 13 Sept. 1913.
14. 'The Prospect of a Settlement', *New Statesman*, 13 Dec. 1913.
15. G.D.H. Cole and William Mellor to the Editor, *New Statesman*, 20 Dec. 1913.
16. 'Civil War: Why Not?', *New Statesman*, 31 Jan. 1914. 'The Alternative to Exclusion', *New Statesman*, 14 March 1914.
17. 'Wake Up Ulster!', ibid.
18. 'After the Storm', *New Statesman*, 11 April 1914. 'Comments', *New Statesman*, 2 and 16 May 1914.
19. 'Comments', *New Statesman*, 30 May, 6 June and 4 July 1914.
20. 'Comments' and 'The Political Crisis', *New Statesman*, 25 July 1914.
21. 'Comments', *New Statesman*, 8 Aug. 1914.
22. See Ch. 5.
23. For background information, see B. Caine, 'Beatrice Webb and the "Woman Question"', *History Workshop Journal*, 14 (Autumn 1982), pp. 23–43.
24. S. Benton, '1913 – high point for New Stateswomen', *New Statesman*, 15 April 1988.
25. 'The Awakening of Women', *New Statesman* supplement, 1 Nov. 1913.
26. 'Comments', *New Statesman*, 21 Feb. 1913.
27. S. Pankhurst, 'Poverty's Prisoners', *New Statesman*, 28 Feb. 1914. The article was rejected because of the ELF's expulsion from the WSPU, allegedly for ill-discipline but in reality for its overt commitment to the class struggle. The ELF worked closely with the labour movement, had a mainly working-class membership drawn from both sexes, was not aggressively anti-male, and did not encourage arson despite justifying violence against police oppression. A. Rosen, *Rise Up Women! The Militant Campaign of the Women's Social and Political Union 1903–14* (London: Routledge & Kegan Paul, 1974), pp. 217–19 and 223.
28. 'Forcible Feeding', *New Statesman*, 12 April 1913. 'Comments', *New Statesman*, 17 Jan. 1914. Brailsford and Nevinson were WSPU activists who had resigned from the *Daily News* in 1909 in protest against editorial support of forcible feeding.
29. 'The Dickinson Bill and the Militants', *New Statesman*, 3 May 1913.
30. Ibid.
31. 'Women in Industry', *New Statesman* supplement, 21 Feb. 1914. On the 'Control of Industry' report, see Ch. 2.
32. On the Fabians and eugenics, particularly Saleeby and 'maternalism', see A. Davin, 'Imperialism and Motherhood', *History Workshop Journal*, 5, (Spring 1978), pp. 22–9.
33. 'The New Statesman', *New Statesman*, 12 April 1913. 'The Blue Book Monthly', *New Statesman*, 3 May 1913. The supplements summarising the government's Blue Books were edited for the first six months by S.K. Ratcliffe and then by Ben Keeling. Civil servants and local government officials found them especially useful, Sharp later insisting that their value in terms of enhancing the *New Statesman*'s credibility far outstripped the high cost of publication. Sharp, 'Early Days', *New Statesman and Nation*, 14 April 1934.
34. C.W. Saleeby, 'The Nurture of the Race', in 'Motherhood and the State', *New Statesman* supplement, 16 May 1914. Davin, 'Imperialism and Motherhood', pp. 19 and 84.
35. D. Forsyth, 'The Health of Children Under School Age' and E. Bentham, 'The Need for the Baby Clinics', in 'Motherhood and the State', *New Statesman* supplement, 16 May 1914.
36. For a short history of the Women's Co-operative Guild, and its demands, see Davin, 'Imperialism and Motherhood', pp. 44–6.
37. M. Bondfield, 'The National Care of Maternity', in 'Motherhood and the State', *New Statesman* supplement, 16 May 1914.
38. B. Webb, 'Motherhood and Citizenship', in 'Motherhood and the State', *New Statesman* supplement, 16 May 1914.
39. Benton, '1913 – high point for New Stateswomen'.

40. 'The Future of Parties', *New Statesman*, 12 April 1913. 'Comments', *New Statesman*, 28 June 1913. MacKenzie (eds), *Diary of Beatrice Webb 1905–24*, 5 July 1913, pp. 188–9.
41. 'Comments', *New Statesman*, 7 June 1913.
42. 'The Perilous Situation of the Labour Party', *New Statesman*, 23 Aug. 1913.
43. 'The Future of the Labour Party', *New Statesman*, 24 Jan. 1914.
44. MacKenzie (eds), *Diary of Beatrice Webb 1905–24*, 6 Feb. 1914, p. 195.
45. See Chs. 7 and 9.
46. F. Keeling to Mrs E. Townshend, 14 June 1914, in Townshend (ed.), *Keeling: Letters and Recollections*, p. 175.
47. 'Comments' and 'Labour in Parliament', *New Statesman*, 31 Jan. 1914. MacKenzie (eds), *Diary of Beatrice Webb 1905–24*, 18 Feb. 1914, p. 196.
48. D. Marquand, *Ramsay MacDonald* (London: Jonathan Cape, 1977), pp. 159–61. 'The ILP', *New Statesman*, 18 April 1914.
49. M.I. Cole (ed.), *Beatrice Webb's Diaries 1912–24* (London, 1956), 22 April 1914, p. 23. The *New Statesman* was beginning to be quoted in the Commons, particularly by MacDonald. 'Comments', *New Statesman*, 28 Feb. and 28 March 1914.
50. In 1913 there were 1,459 individual strikes, compared with an annual average of 600 in the preceding six years. 'Comments', *New Statesman*, 31 Jan. 1914. 'The Latest Utopia', *New Statesman*, 20 June 1914. The fullest denunciation of workers' control was the concluding part of the Webbs' inaugural series 'What Is Socialism?'. 'XX – In Itself a Demonstration of the Impossibility of Syndicalism and Anarchism', *New Statesman*, 23 Aug. 1913. For an analysis of the Webbs' views as developed at length in this series, see Radice, *Beatrice and Sidney Webb*, pp. 200–3.

    In 1913, in *The Social Unrest: Its Cause and Solution*, MacDonald had similarly denounced syndicalism, while at the same time defending the parliamentary party's working relationship with the government. He could at least provide some sort of theoretical case for Labour's strategy. His more mediocre colleagues, for too long 'enmeshed in the intellectual and ideological universe of Liberal-Radicalism', found tacit support for the government an excuse for not having to adopt an ideological and tactical position more in tune with the ILP rank-and-file. D. Coates, *The Labour Party and the Struggle for Socialism* (Cambridge: CUP, 1975), p. 11.
51. 'Comments', *New Statesman*, 1 and 8 August 1914.
52. As well as his involvement in the Fabian Society and the ILP (parliamentary candidate for Finsbury in 1910), R.C.K. Ensor was a leader writer for the *Daily News*, and then for the *Daily Chronicle* from 1911 to 1930. To support a large family he wrote regularly for the *Manchester Guardian*, and after April 1913 became the *New Statesman's* principal commentator on foreign affairs. Ensor's claim to expertise in this field rested upon his secretaryship of the Foreign Policy Committee, chaired by the veteran Radical Leonard Courtney and set up after the Agadir crisis to agitate for greater government accountability in the conduct of international relations. In a series written under his own name Ensor articulated many of the Committee's demands, most notably a standing committee to exert parliamentary control over an almost 'despotic' foreign secretary. (Some of his views gained support from an unlikely source, the shadowy 'fixer' and one-time *protégé* of Edward VII, Lord Esher (formerly Reginald Brett). Boycotting the bipartisan Committee of Imperial Defence because of government policy on Ulster, presumably Esher was for once sympathetic to the suggestion that he 'go public'.) For Ensor's subsequent role as ultra-patriotic *de facto* military correspondent, see Ch. 5. A.J.P. Taylor, *The Troublemakers Dissent Over Foreign Policy 1792–1939* (London: Hamish Hamilton, 1957), p. 96. R.C.K. Ensor, 'Democracy and Foreign Affairs III', *New Statesman*, 17 Jan. 1914. Esher, 'The Change in Diplomacy', *New Statesman*, 29 Nov. 1913.
53. 'Comments', *New Statesman*, 8 Aug. 1914. Ignoring the fact that Sharp took the first two weeks in August off every year, Hyams speculated on his deliberate absence in order to avoid explaining why the paper no longer opposed the war. For all his faults, Sharp never avoided the tough decisions. Hyams, *New Statesman*, p. 48.

Chapter 5, Common sense about the war: The *New Statesman*, 1914–18, pp. 69–115.

1. The coverage of censorship during the First World War draws upon A. Smith, 'Censorship and the Great War: the first test of new statesmanship' in P. Hyland and N. Sammels (eds), *Writing and Censorship in Britain* (London: Routledge & Kegan Paul, 1992). For a fuller account, see A. Smith, 'The *New Statesman* 1913–31: A study of intellectual attitudes', PhD Kent, 1980, pp. 145–52.

2. Viscount Haldane remained a close friend of the Webbs and, as Lord Chancellor in 1924, a Cabinet colleague of Sidney. In 1917 he invited Beatrice to serve on his inquiry into the machinery of government, established as a spin-off from Lloyd George's Reconstruction Committee. She proved characteristically indifferent to tedium, happy to delve into minutiae of procedure and practice long after her colleagues had surrendered to somnolence. Peter Hennessy, *Whitehall* (London: Secker & Warburg, 1989), pp. 292–9.

3. 'Solomon Eagle' (Squire's *nom de plume* as a columnist), 'Books in General', *New Statesman*, 20 Nov. 1915. Lytton Strachey reported that 'That little worm Jack Squire' only agreed to mention *The Rainbow* in his 'blasted paper' on the condition that its suppression was not for mentioning '"sapphism"'. It would be '"quite impossible for the *New Statesman* to defend perversity"'. Strachey sent the magazine a wickedly ironic letter in favour of suppression, which Sharp promptly took at its word. Strachey's letter to David Garnett, 10 Nov. 1915, recounting his meeting with Squire is quoted at length in Holroyd, *Lytton Strachey: A Critical Biography, Vol. II* .

   Censorship of *The Rainbow* is further examined in D. Grant, 'D.H. Lawrence: a suitable case for censorship', in Hyland and Sammels (eds), *Writing and Censorship in Britain*, pp. 204–6. Lawrence never forgot Squire's indifference, witness his posthumous poetic assault in the 'More Pansies' section of his final volume of poetry, published in 1932. Regarding wider relations between Lawrence and the *New Statesman*, see Ch. 8.

4. C. Bell to the Editor plus editorial reply, *New Statesman*, 4 Sept. 1915.

5. To be fair, in criticising the Dardanelles and Salonika expeditions, and also the 1917 transfer of guns to Italy after Caporetto, Ensor advanced convincing logistical arguments as to the folly of deserting Flanders. Where he was clearly mistaken was in failing to foresee victory for Allenby in the Near East.

6. Although Field Marshal Sir Douglas Haig (C-in-C British Expeditionary Force (BEF) Dec.1915–19) and Field Marshal Sir William 'Wullie' Robertson (Chief of the Imperial General Staff (CIGS) Dec.1915–Feb.1918) both largely escaped criticism, army and corps commanders were judged fair game, particularly if their Unionist sympathies had been scarcely disguised before the war. When Hubert Gough (Commander 5th Army 1916–18) became Haig's scapegoat for the débâcle of March 1918, Ensor and Squire were quick to quote his involvement in the 'Curragh mutiny' as evidence of unsuitability for high command.

7. Ensor, Squire and Bennett all attacked Lloyd George for his speech of 12 Nov. 1917 in Paris implying criticism of the status quo and accepting the case for an Allied Supreme War Council, on which Robertson's rival, Sir Henry Wilson, would represent the British Army. In the spring of 1918 Ensor took even longer than Haig himself to acknowledge Foch as Allied supreme commander, while the appointment of Wilson as CIGS confirmed Milner, Bonar Law and Carson's power behind the throne. 'The "Supreme"' War Council, *New Statesman*, 17 Nov. 1917. D. Winter, *Haig's Command A Reassessment* (London: Viking, 1991; Penguin paperback edn, 1992), pp. 298–9.

   The *New Statesman* was not the only paper with Asquithian sympathies to interpret the new chain of command as an extension of Unionist influence and a further consolidation of prime ministerial power, see the *Westminster Gazette*'s editorial of 15 Nov. 1917.

8. Arnold Bennett to J.C. Squire, 29 July and 4 Aug. 1915, New York.

9. Clifford Sharp to H.G. Wells, 19 Jan. 1917, Wells Archive.

10. 'The Progress of the War', *New Statesman*, 8 Aug. 1914.
11. 'Yarned at the Reform Club with Harold Massingham (who asked why Squire had become such a Jingo!)', Flower (ed.), *The Journals of Arnold Bennett 1911–21*, 19 Dec. 1917, p. 210. On the 'Problems of Factual Testimony', see P. Fussell, *The Great War and Modern Memory* (Oxford: OUP, 1975; paperback edn, 1977), pp. 169–74.
12. 'Comments', *New Statesman*, 8 May 1915.
13. In rationalising the obvious lack of progress a fortnight after the Somme offensive was launched (the sole object was not in fact to advance, but to drain German reserves), Sharp relied heavily upon Belloc's despatches. 'Comments', *New Statesman*, 15 July 1916. Three months later, Ensor returned from the British sector characteristically 'pleased with all he saw, and confident'. Sidney to Beatrice Webb, 10 Oct. 1916, Passfield Papers. The same letter described how Ben Keeling had died revealing himself to the enemy when checking that it was Germans under fire, there having been a suggestion that the Army was shelling its own men. Presumably Webb saw no irony in the juxtaposition of his two items of news.
14. 'Comments', *New Statesman*, 3 Feb. 1917.
15. This account of official censorship during the First World War draws upon: Sir Edward Cook, *The Press in War-Time With some account of the Official Press Bureau* (London, 1920); D. Hopkin, 'Domestic censorship in the First World War', *Journal of Contemporary History*, 5 (1970), pp. 151–69; S. Inwood, 'The role of the press in English politics during the First World War, with special reference to the period 1914–16', DPhil Oxford, 1971; G. Lovelace, 'British press censorship during the First World War', in G. Boyce, J. Curran and P. Wingate (eds), *Newspaper History from the Seventeenth Century to the Present Day* (London: Sage/Constable, 1978), pp. 307–19.
16. Sharp clearly had no knowledge of the CID's existence before the spring of 1915, witness his call for just such a co-ordinating committee after the fall of Antwerp early in the war. 'Comments', *New Statesman*, 24 Oct. 1914.
17. Lord Northcliffe to H.H. Asquith, (?) Nov. 1914, quoted in Earl of Oxford and Asquith, *Memories and Reflections 1852–1927: Volume 2* (London, 1928), p. 234.
18. *Daily Mail*, 10 Feb. 1915.
19. John St Loe Strachey to (?) Hutton, 18 Feb. 1915, quoted in Inwood, 'The role of the press in English politics during the First World War', p. 90. Ironically the *Spectator* regularly called for suppression of the pacifist press.
20. 'The censorship of the news', *New Statesman*, 22 Aug. 1914. 'The Press Bureau', *New Statesman*, 21 Nov. 1914. In fact the Home Secretary, Reginald McKenna, had already repudiated any suggestion that the government intended to suppress hostile comment, and any ambiguity regarding censorship was in theory removed when Parliament passed an amendment to DORA on 25 November 1914.
21. 'Our wonderful censorship again', *New Statesman*, 13 March 1915. The Press Bureau kept a list of 50 editors to whom confidential information could be relayed. The list is unobtainable, but given his views it is unlikely that Sharp's name was on it. HO 45-297549 fo. 52, Home Office Papers, PRO.
22. Clifford Sharp to H.G. Wells, 19 Jan. 1917, Illinois.
23. Ibid.
24. Ibid. 'He [Sharp] said the journalists laughed at [H.W.] Massingham's resentment of the Government's quite polite instruction of the press on delicate questions; that this was generally approved of.' Sidney to Beatrice Webb, 7 Nov. 1916, Passfield Papers.
25. The *Nation* had remained loyal to Asquith after the formation of the second Coalition, and news of its overseas ban confirmed his followers' worst fears. Precisely who had followed the former prime minister into *de facto* opposition and who had sided with Lloyd George only became clear on 9 May 1917 when MPs voted at the conclusion of the 'Maurice debate'. 'Comments', *New Statesman*, 14 April 1917.
26. Having discussed the prohibition order with Massingham, Bennett was the initiator of the *New Statesman*'s protest, although 'In our place "The Nation" would probably not do as much.' Arnold Bennett to J.C. Squire, 11 April 1917, New York .

27. 'Sardonyx' (Bennett), 'Observations', *New Statesman*, 20 Oct. 1917.
28. FO 281 81-5050, Foreign Office Papers, PRO. For Bennett's appointment to the MOI, see Ch. 6, note 17.
29. Lovelace, 'British press censorship during the First World War', pp. 313–14. Hopkin, 'Domestic censorship in the First World War', p. 162. 'The new press law', *New Statesman*, 29 April 1916. 'Comments', *New Statesman*, 24 Nov. 1917.
30. 'Comments', *New Statesman*, 21 Aug. 1915.
31. 'Comments' and 'The seizure of Forward', *New Statesman*, 8 Jan. 1916.
32. 'A Glasgow Labour man' to the Editor, *New Statesman*, 1 Jan. 1916. 'The case of Forward', *New Statesman*, 15 Jan. 1916.
33. Ibid.
34. T. Johnston to the Editor, and 'Comments', *New Statesman*, 22 Jan. 1916.
35. 'Comments', *New Statesman*, 29 Jan. 1916.
36. The unholy alliance between Sharp and the Glasgow ILP was confirmed by the late Lord Fenner Brockway in conversation with the author, 7 Feb. 1979.
37. 'Comments', *New Statesman*, 3 April 1915.
38. G.B. Shaw to Beatrice Webb, 12 Aug. 1914, quoted in S. Weintraub, *Bernard Shaw 1914–18: Journey to Heartbreak* (London: Routledge & Kegan Paul, 1973), pp. 30 and 32–3. For Shaw's activities in the early months of the war, see Holroyd, *Bernard Shaw 2*, pp. 341–51.
39. Lord Fenner Brockway pointed out that Clement Bundock, the fiercely anti-war deputy editor of the *Labour Leader*, to whom MacDonald forwarded his copy, had little time for Sharp's pro-war paper, 7 Feb. 1979. J.R. MacDonald to the Editor, *Nation*, 29 August 1914. MacKenzie (eds), *Diary of Beatrice Webb 1905–1924*, 28 Aug. 1914, p. 218. Cole (ed.), *Beatrice Webb's Diaries 1912–1924*, 5 May 1914, p. 28. 'Comments', *New Statesman*, 10 April 1915.
40. Weintraub, *Bernard Shaw 1914–18*, pp. 44–5 and 50. G.B. Shaw to Clifford Sharp, 21 Oct. 1914, Texas. Shaw later claimed that he had wished to delay 'Common Sense' for a month, 'but I had no more control over that than the date of Christmas day'. G.B. Shaw to James Muirhead, 16 Jan. 1915, British Library. Bernard Shaw, 'Common Sense About the War' *New Statesman* special war supplement, 14 Nov. 1914. Weintraub, *Bernard Shaw 1914–18*, pp. 50–1.

   For the first four weeks following publication, sales rose above average by 600, 1,400, 700 and 900 copies. The supplement sold out in April 1915 and a pamphlet, with a new preface by GBS, appeared six months later. Neither Sharp nor the Webbs wanted this, but the *New Statesman* owned the plates and needed the money. 2,500 further copies were then sold at 6d each. Hyams, *New Statesman*, p. 75.

   Shaw's official biographer suggests he loathed Asquith because of a personal slight, and Grey because of his endorsement of harsh punitive action in Egypt during an incident in 1906. Churchill, however, was 'someone who might emerge in Europe as a Shavian-permeated superman'. Holroyd, *Bernard Shaw 2*, p. 350.
41. In fact Squire agreed with much of 'Common Sense', especially Shaw's exposure of religious hypocrisy in time of war. As 'Solomon Eagle' he denounced excessively jingoistic sermons. For a suitably irreverent quatrain, see Weintraub, *Bernard Shaw 1914–18*, p. 61. 'The Moral Outcast Theory', *New Statesman*, 14 Nov. 1914. 'Comments', *New Statesman*, 19 December 1914. The content of 'Common Sense' is analysed in detail in Holroyd, *Bernard Shaw 2*, pp. 351–4.
42. For domestic and international reaction to 'Common Sense', see ibid., pp. 354–8. A. Marwick, *The Deluge: British Society and the First World War* (London: Macmillan, 1965; paperback second edn, 1991), pp. 19–22. For the terms of the 'Treasury Agreement', 20 March 1915, see ibid., pp. 96–102, and J. Grigg, *Lloyd George: From Peace to War 1912–1916* (London: Methuen, 1985), pp. 217–22.
43. R. Miliband, *Parliamentary Socialism A Study in the Politics of Labour* (London: Allen & Unwin, 1972; paperback edn), p. 28.
44. A.J.P. Taylor, 'Politics in the First World War', *Essays in English History* (London: Hamish Hamilton, 1976), p. 229.

45. Ibid. Sidney Webb was equally hostile to any unwarranted extension of DORA, such as the direction of labour or court-martialling civilians.
46. 'About two-thirds of Shaw's statement is strictly first-class and indeed quite unequalled. Most of the rest is absurd and may do some harm.' Arnold Bennett to J.B. Pinker, 15 Nov. 1914, J. Hepburn (ed.), *Letters of Arnold Bennett, Vol. 1, Letters to J.B. Pinker* (London, 1966), p. 215. Bennett and GBS proceeded to debate the causes of the war in the columns of the *Daily News* and the *New York Times*.
47. 'The Last Spring of the Old Lion', *New Statesman*, 12 Dec. 1914.
48. MacKenzie (eds), *Diary of Beatrice Webb 1905–24*, 3 Jan. 1915, p. 221.
49. G.B. Shaw to James Muirhead, 16 Jan. 1915, British Library.
50. Weintraub, *Bernard Shaw 1914–18*, pp. 102–4. G. Bernard Shaw, 'Wanted – A Coalition of the Intelligentsia', *New Statesman*, 12 Feb. 1916.
51. Flower (ed.), *The Journals of Arnold Bennett 1911–21*, 2 March 1915, p. 126.
52. Hyams, *New Statesman*, pp. 61–2.
53. Arnold Bennett to J.C. Squire, 10 April 1915, New York.
54. Sidney Webb to Graham Wallas, 12 March 1915, MacKenzie (ed.), *Webb Letters 1912–47*, p. 52.
55. Sidney to Beatrice Webb, 14 Nov. 1916, Passfield Papers.
56. D. Lloyd George to the Editor, *New Statesman*, 18 Dec. 1915.
57. 'Comments', ibid.
58. MacKenzie (eds), *Diary of Beatrice Webb 1905–24*, 8 Oct. 1915, p. 241. Sharp had, however, tolerated GBS's brutal attack on Grey in the *New Statesman*, 17 July 1915.
59. Flower (ed.), *The Journals of Arnold Bennett 1911–21*, 7 Nov. 1915, p. 148. Arnold Bennett, journal, 7 Nov. 1915, New York.

    The *New Statesman's* loss was in fact £1,000 less than that predicted at an emergency meeting on 22 January 1915. After agreeing to press on for a further 12 months, Shaw put up another £500, Simon £600, and the Webbs £200. Sharp then wrote to Edward Whitley and the 14 smaller shareholders to appeal for a further £600. Following the November meeting A.K. Bulley, a Liverpool merchant and the organiser of the Northern Fabian Summer School, further eased the financial pressure by buying out Harben, and sending a further £500. This was, he made clear to Sidney, despite his preference for the 'international' *Labour Leader* to the 'patriotic' *New Statesman*. Hyams, *New Statesman*, p. 75. A.K. Bulley to Sidney Webb, 9 Nov. 1915, Passfield Papers.
60. Arnold Bennett, journal, 16 March 1916. Did '"slack"' refer to GBS's notorious disregard for factual accuracy?
61. In his paper, the *Irish Citizen*, 12 Sept. 1914, F. Sheehy-Skeffington wrote:

    War is necessarily bound up with the destruction of feminism. . . . Feminism is necessarily bound up with the abolition of war. . . . If we want to stop war we must begin by stopping this war. . . . The woman who does not . . . discourage recruiting has an imperfect understanding of the basis of the feminist movement.

    Quoted in R. Cullen Owens, *Smashing Times* (Dublin: Attic, 1984), pp. 98 and 120. By 1915 the Sheehy-Skeffingtons were engaged in a public dialogue with Thomas MacDonagh, one of the signatories to the 1916 proclamation of an Irish republic, defending their position of absolute pacifism, i.e. support for a nationalist armed struggle was not the logical concomitant of opposition to England's continental war. See ibid., pp. 98–101.
62. Francis Sheehy-Skeffington to G.B. Shaw, 7 April 1916, British Library.
63. R.F. Foster, *Modern Ireland 1600–1972* (London: Allen Lane, 1988), p. 484, and F.S.L. Lyons, *Ireland Since the Famine* (London: Collins, 1971, Fontana paperback edn 1973), p. 373, both provide short accounts of Sheehy-Skeffington's capture as a hostage (he was arrested while trying to stop looting), and his subsequent death at the hands of Capt. J.C. Bowen-Colthurst. For a fuller account of his murder, and the consequences of it, see R.M. Fox, 'Hannah Sheehy-Skeffington', *Rebel Irishwomen* (Dublin: Talbot Press, 1935), pp. 135–50.

Fox claimed the Sheehy-Skeffingtons learned from James Connolly that rebellion was imminent as late as Easter Saturday. Ibid., p. 140. I am grateful to my former colleague Oonagh Walsh for this reference. 'A Piece of Evidence', *New Statesman*, 6 May 1916.

64. 'Comments', 'The Tragedy in Dublin' and 'Irish Responsibilities', ibid.

65. G. Bernard Shaw, 'Some Neglected Morals of the Irish Rising', ibid. The *New Statesman*, although professing shock at his outrageous treachery in securing German weapons for the rebels, argued against the death sentence for Sir Roger Casement. This plea was almost certainly at the request of Shaw, whose fruitless efforts to draft a defence for Casement turned into a prolonged black comedy, contrasting sharply with his succinct and sagacious public appeal to Asquith for clemency. MacKenzie (eds), *Diary of Beatrice Webb 1905–24*, 21 May 1916, pp. 255–7.

66. Pre-war Territorials could no longer refuse overseas service, or seek discharge at the end of their term of enlistment (the latter restriction also applied to regulars). Many men in the course of 1914–15 had exercised their rights to discharge. I. Beckett, 'The British Army, 1914–18: The Illusion of Change', in J. Turner (ed.), *Britain and the First World War* (London: Allen & Unwin, 1988), p. 112.

Clifford Allen urged Woolf to work for the NCF, and Adrian Stephen secured his brief appointment as secretary of the original National Council for Civil Liberties. Clifford Allen to Leonard Woolf, 25 July 1916, and Adrian Stephen to Leonard Woolf, 10 Aug. 1916, Woolf Papers, University of Sussex. 'The Conscientious Objectors', *New Statesman*, 22 April 1916.

67. 'National versus Sectional Government', ibid. 'Comments', *New Statesman*, 6 May 1916. 'Socialism and Democracy', *New Statesman*, 29 April 1916. Lord Fenner Brockway (founder of the NCF) in conversation with the author, 7 Feb. 1979.

For Beatrice's highly critical eye-witness account of the NCF's first National Convention, see MacKenzie (eds), *Diary of Beatrice Webb 1905–24*, 8 April 1916, pp. 252–4. The platform speakers embraced a broad anti-war alliance of progressive campaigners, 'New Liberals' and ILP founding fathers: 'Bertrand Russell, Robert Trevelyan, George Lansbury, Olive Schreiner, [Arnold] Lupton, Stephen and Rosa Hobhouse, Dr [John] Clifford, C.H. Norman, Miss [Margaret] Llewellyn Davies and the Snowdens [Philip and Ethel]: the pacifist predominating over the rebel element'.

68. J.A. Hobson never actually joined the Labour Party, but after 1918 he became a major influence upon the thinking of the ILP, and MacDonald in particular, although of course, when the opportunity came none of his ideas ever saw the light of day. D. Cannadine, *G.M. Trevelyan: A Life in History* (London: Harper Collins, 1992; paperback edn, 1993), p. 79. Clarke, *Liberals and Social Democrats*, pp. 166–8.

Michael Bentley has argued that intellectual support for the Liberal Party in fact proved remarkably resilient. Drawing upon Martin Ceadel's distinction in *Pacifism in Britain 1914–45* (Oxford: OUP, 1980) between an absolute 'pacifism' and 'pacifisim', the latter more in accord with the traditional Radical agenda of open diplomacy, Bentley also argues persuasively that few Liberals were opposed to war on any grounds whatsoever. The same was true of the ILP, so that Ramsay MacDonald's admittedly rather tortuous position was in fact more representative than the deep-rooted convictions of, say, George Lansbury. Bentley, *The Climax of Liberal Politics British Liberalism in Theory and Practice 1868–1918*, pp. 121–3.

69. '. . . it was because the liberal conscience seemed safer in its new home than in its old home that Labour replaced the Liberals in the role of political executor to the progressive intelligentsia.' Marquand, *The Progressive Dilemma*, p. 35.

70. Ibid.

71. . . . mechanical reformists . . . believe that recalcitrant human nature can be prodded into the right path only by coercion, and that the primary aim of those who seek social change must be to get their hands on the instruments of coercion. For the moral reformist, on the other hand, social change is above all the product of persuasion and leadership, and state imposed progress is inherently suspect.

Ibid., pp. 49–51. Clarke, *Liberals and Social Democrats*, pp. 1–8. The inherently authoritarian nature of Fabian managerialism was argued by E.J. Hobsbawm in 'The Fabians Reconsidered', *Labouring Men*; and more surprisingly by Norman MacKenzie in his 1978 lecture given at and published by the LSE, *Socialism and Society: A New View of the Webb Partnership* (London: LSE, 1978).

72. Cole (ed.), *Beatrice Webb's Diaries 1912–24*, 13 Sept. 1916, pp. 69–70. Weintraub, *Bernard Shaw 1914–18*, p. 186.
73. G.B. Shaw to the Secretary, The Statesman Publishing Company, 5 Oct. 1916, Texas.
74. G.B. Shaw to Sidney and Beatrice Webb, 5 Oct. 1916, Passfield Papers.
75. Sidney to Beatrice Webb, 10 Oct. 1916, ibid.
76. Clifford Sharp to Beatrice Webb, (13?) Oct. 1916, ibid.
77. Cole (ed.), *Beatrice Webb's Diaries 1912–24*, 3 Nov. 1916, pp. 70–1.
78. Clifford Sharp to Beatrice Webb, (13?) Oct. 1916, Passfield Papers.
79. Ibid. MacKenzie (eds.), *Diary of Beatrice Webb 1905–24*, 3 Nov. 1916, pp. 266–7.
80. G.B. Shaw to Beatrice Webb, 13 Oct. 1916, Passfield Papers.
81. Beatrice Webb, diary, (?) Aug. 1918, ibid.
82. G.B. Shaw to Arnold Bennett, 9 Nov. 1916, and Arnold Bennett to G.B. Shaw, 13 Nov. 1916, Texas. Weintraub, *Bernard Shaw 1914–18*, p. 188. G.B. Shaw to St John Ervine, 16 Nov. 1916, Texas. St John Ervine, *Bernard Shaw: His Life, Work and Friends*, pp. 455–7. D. MacCarthy, *Shaw* (London, 1951), p. 216. The 'youthful' Sharp was in fact 33 in 1916.
    Holroyd placed GBS's resignation in the context of his generally stormy relations with the British press at a time when, 'Below the surface of his forbearance, layers of disillusion were forming'. Holroyd, *Bernard Shaw 2*, pp. 358–9.
83. Sidney Webb to E.D. Simon, 17 Oct. 1916, Passfield Papers.
84. Ibid. Sidney to Beatrice Webb, 13, 17 and 23 Oct. 1916, and R.B. Byles (*New Statesman* publisher) to Sidney Webb, 15 Feb. 1917, ibid. Hyams, *New Statesman*, pp. 74–5.
    For further details on management and business affairs during the paper's first decade, see ibid., pp. 71–90, and A. Smith, 'The *New Statesman* 1913–31', pp. 122–3 and 130–1.
85. Sidney to Beatrice Webb, 17 Oct. 1916, Passfield Papers. MacKenzie (eds), *Diary of Beatrice Webb 1905–24*, 3 Nov. 1916, pp. 266–7.
86. Flower (ed.), *The Journals of Arnold Bennett 1911–21*, 21 Dec. 1916, pp. 180–1. Arnold Bennett to Oswald H. Davis, 2 March 1918, J. Hepburn (ed.), *The Letters of Arnold Bennett: Vol. III, 1916–31* (London, 1970), p. 52.
87. Sidney to Beatrice Webb, 7 Nov. 1916, Passfield Papers. 'Comments', *New Statesman*, 2 and 9 Dec. 1916.
88. 'Had Zimri Peace?', *New Statesman*, 9 Dec. 1916. The title referred to the line in 2 Kings 9:31, 'Had Zimri peace, who slew his master?', with Lloyd George compared with Israel's warrior regicide.
    Riddell and Dalziel were respectively owners of the *News of the World* and *Reynold's News*; and Scott was the editor of the *Manchester Guardian* and keeper of Lloyd George's Radical conscience. Liberal ministers' relations with the press are neatly summarised in Michael Bentley's *Politics Without Democracy 1815–1914: Perception and Preoccupation in British Government* (London: Fontana, paperback edn, 1984), pp. 342–4. For much more detailed coverage, see S. Koss, *The Rise and Fall of the Political Press in Britain, Vol.1, The Nineteenth Century* (London: Hamish Hamilton, 1981), pp. 409–35, and *The Rise and Fall of the Political Press in Britain 2*, Chs. 2–8.
89. Aitken, at that time a Unionist MP, was, of course, the future Lord Beaverbrook, ennobled on 11 December 1916 for his recent endeavours in smoke-filled rooms on Bonar Law and Lloyd George's behalf. Drawing on Lord Beaverbrook's own *Politicians and the War* Vol. 2 (London, 1932), A.J.P. Taylor described his 'Kingmaker' role in *Beaverbrook* (London: Hamish Hamilton, 1972), Ch.6.
    For a detailed account of the role of the press in the crisis of December 1916, see

Koss, *Rise and Fall of the Political Press in Britain 2*, pp. 296–306. On balance Koss rejects the view, originally fostered by Asquith's circle, that his demise was the responsibility of the Unionist press, a view encouraged by Roy Jenkins in *Asquith* (London: Collins, 1964), Chs. 26–7.

90. 'Had Zimri Peace?', *New Statesman*, 9 Dec. 1916.
91. Ibid.
92. S.K. Ratcliffe, 'The New Statesman', in Cole (ed.), *The Webbs and the Their Work*, p. 137. MacKenzie (ed.), *Diary of Beatrice Webb 1905–24*, 9 Dec. 1916, p. 272. K. Martin, *Father Figures* (London, 1966), p. 192.
93. Proofs of omitted paragraphs of 'Had Zimri Peace?', Passfield Papers.
94. Ibid. For the 'second Marconi scandal', see F. Donaldson, *The Marconi Scandal* (London: Hart-Davis, 1962), pp. 245–6, and E. David (ed.), *Inside Asquith's Cabinet: From the Diaries of Charles Hobhouse* (London, 1977), pp. 216–17 and 218–19.
95. MacKenzie (eds), *Diary of Beatrice Webb 1905–24*, 9 Dec. 1916, p. 272.
96. Ibid., 7 Dec. 1916, p. 270.
97. 'The Conduct of the War', *New Statesman*, 9 Dec. 1916.
98. MacKenzie (eds), *Diary of Beatrice Webb 1905–24*, 8 Dec. 1916, pp. 270–1. 'The Passing of the Parliamentary Labour Party', *New Statesman*, 16 Dec. 1916. 'Labour and its Voice', *New Statesman*, 27 Jan. 1917. Perhaps G.R. Elton had the Webbs in mind when he lambasted 'the *New Statesman* complex, the assurance that all things human are absolutely at their worst in this country' in *Return to Essentials: Some Reflections on the Present State of Historical Study* (Cambridge: CUP, 1991), p. 111.
99. G.B. Shaw to Sidney and Beatrice Webb, 11 Dec. 1916, Passfield Papers.
100. Cole (ed.), *BeatriceWebb's Diaries 1912–24*, 3 Jan. 1917, p. 80.
101. Ibid. Samuel at least contributed a short series of articles on 'War Liberty' in May–June 1917.
102. For Sharp's conscription and Army service, see Ch. 6. MacKenzie (eds), *Diary of Beatrice Webb 1905–24*, 22 Sept. 1917, and note to original entry (?) May 1918, pp. 286–8.
103. Arnold Bennett to Elsie Herzog, 4 March 1917, Hepburn (ed.), *Letters of Arnold Bennett, Vol. III 1916–31*, p. 27.
104. J.C. Squire to Mrs James Elroy Flecker, (?) April 1917, quoted in P. Howarth, *Squire: 'Most Generous of Men'* (London: Hutchinson, 1968), p. 116.
105. Correspondence of Arnold Bennett and J.C. Squire, April 1917–Nov. 1919, New York.
106. Ibid., 17 Dec. 1917.
107. Arnold Bennett to Hugh Walpole, 1 May 1917, Hepburn (ed.), *Letters of Arnold Bennett: Vol. III 1916–31*, p. 30.
108. A.G. Macdonnel, *England, Their England* (London: Macmillan, 1933), dedicated to 'J.C. Squire The English Poet'. MacKenzie (eds), *Diary of Beatrice Webb 1905–24*, (?) May 1918, p. 288. For a fuller profile of Squire, see Ch. 8.
109. Howarth, *Squire: 'Most Generous of Men'*, p. 116. Although at the time differing with the Webbs over his lobbying for talks with Germany (understandable given the initial success of the Hindenburg offensive), Haldane actively encouraged the *New Statesman*'s calls in early 1918 for H.A.L. Fisher's Education Bill to be reintroduced into the Commons. Cole (ed.), *Beatrice Webb's Diaries 1912–24*, 3 March 1918, p. 113.
110. J.C. Squire to Edward Marsh, 2 Sept. 1918 and 14 Jan. 1919, New York. Description of Squire based on that in MacKenzie (eds), *Diary of Beatrice Webb 1905–24*, May 1918, p. 288, and of William Hodge in Macdonnel, *England, Their England*, Ch.4.
112. MacKenzie (eds), *Diary of Beatrice Webb 1905–24*, 22 Sept. 1917, p. 287. Sidney Webb to E.D. Simon, 22 Sept. 1917, Passfield Papers.
113. Sidney Webb to E.D. Simon, 30 Nov. 1917, ibid.
114. MacKenzie (eds), *Diary of Beatrice Webb 1905–24*, (?) May 1918, p. 288.
115. 'Comments', *New Statesman*, 10 Nov. 1917. Flower (ed.), *Bennett Journals*, 19 Dec. 1917, p. 210. Squire's recollection of his editorship in a 1935 interview given to the *Western Morning News*, quoted in Howarth, *Squire: 'Most Generous of Men'*, p. 114.

116. 'Comments', *New Statesman*, 23 Feb. 1918.
117. MacKenzie (eds), *Diary of Beatrice Webb 1905–24*, 25 April 1918, pp. 306–7. Only two months earlier, at Haldane's behest, the Webbs had dined with the Prime Minister (for Beatrice still 'a blatant intriguer . . . all his ways are crooked and he is obsessed by the craving for power'), on which occasion Lloyd George had sought to convince Sidney that Labour's future lay firmly within the Coalition. ('It was, in fact, a counter-thrust to the Asquith touting for coalition with the Labour Party'). According to his wife, Webb rather than Henderson was seen by Downing Street as the inspiration for Labour's 'recent success'. Beatrice took enormous pride in Sidney's newly acquired prominence within the Labour Party, even to the point of describing him in her diary as a 'man of destiny'. Ibid., 1 March and 1 April 1918, pp. 299–300 and 305.
118. 'Comments', *New Statesman*, 5 Jan. 1918.
119. Cole (ed.), *BeatriceWebb's Diaries 1912–24*, 14 and 19 Feb., and 25 April 1918, pp. 108–9 and 120. MacKenzie (eds), *Diary of Beatrice Webb 1905–24*, 1 and 7 March 1918, pp. 299–302.
120. Flower (ed.), *Bennett Journals*, 15 Jan., 11 Feb. and 13 March 1918, pp. 216, 220–1 and 222–3. Other regular members of the Writers Group included: George Parish, Graham Wallas, J.A. Hobson, G. Lowes Dickinson, Gilbert Murray, Hartley Withers, and Leonard Hobhouse. Squire was conspicuous by his absence, and the following oblique reference suggests he knew nothing of the group's existence:

> A small group of great and good men were discussing the other day the quite remarkable excellence of the number of the N.S. for February 1st. J.A. Spender remarked that the numbers varied greatly in quality & A.G. Gardiner concurred.

Arnold Bennett to J.C. Squire, 9 Feb. 1919, New York.
121. MacKenzie (eds), *Diary of Beatrice Webb 1905–24*, 4, 7 and 17 Nov. 1920, pp. 316–17 and 324. In the 'Maurice debate' of 8–9 May 1918 Asquith led a bungled attack on the competence of Lloyd George, based upon an allegation in *The Times* by the War Office's former Director of Military Operations, Sir Frederick Maurice, that the Prime Minister had lied to the Commons over the strength of the Army in France. The House was divided against the government for the only time in the war, and Liberal MPs were forced to make a public choice between loyalty to Asquith or to Lloyd George. A hundred Liberals voted for the motion, effectively killing off any hope of reconciliation before the next election, or even beyond.
    For military intrigue against Lloyd George in the spring of 1918, see Winter, *Haig's Command: A Reassessment*, pp. 328–30.
122. 'The Labour Party Conference', *New Statesman*, 29 June 1918. 'Comments', *New Statesman*, 7 and 14 Sept. and 16 Nov. 1918.
123. MacKenzie (eds) *Diary of Beatrice Webb 1905–24*, (?) Aug. 1918, p. 186.
124. At the 1918 general election both acting editor and chairman sought entry into Parliament by the back door: Squire contested his old university, Cambridge, and not surprisingly lost his deposit, but Webb put up a creditable performance in seeking one of the two London University seats.
126. For evidence of the *New Statesman's* wartime influence on international thinking on a future League of Nations, see Ch. 7.

Chapter 6, Editor or spy? Clifford Sharp and Bolshevik Russia, pp. 116–134.

1. Sidney to Beatrice Webb, 24 Jan. 1917, MacKenzie (ed.), *Letters of Sidney and Beatrice Webb, Vol. III*, p. 80.
2. Arnold Bennett to Elsie Herzog, 4 Feb. 1917, Hepburn (ed.), *Bennett Letters, Vol. III 1916–31*, p. 25.
3. Cole (ed.), *Beatrice Webb's Diaries 1912–24*, 15 May 1917, p. 90. Arnold Bennett to J.C. Squire, 28 May 1917, New York.
4. H. Brogan, *The Life of Arthur Ransome* (London: Jonathan Cape, 1984), p. 140.

5. Beatrice Webb, diary, 22 Sept. 1917, Passfield Papers.

6. Sir P. Dukes, *The Story of 'ST25': Adventure and Romance in the Secret Intelligence Service in Red Russia* (London, 1938), p. 40. Beatrice Webb, diary, 26 Sept. 1918, Passfield Papers. MI1c or the Secret Service Bureau was from the early 1920s generally known by the more familiar name of Secret Intelligence Service.

7. C. Andrew, *Secret Service: The Making of the British Intelligence Community* (London: Heinemann, 1986), pp. 309–19.

8. R. Hart-Davis (ed.), *The Autobiography of Arthur Ransome* (London, 1976), pp. 259–62. Brogan, *Life of Arthur Ransome*, pp. 160–205.

   As Brogan demonstrates, Ransome's reports were widely read and discussed, even within the War Cabinet; but his influence over opinion and policy-making in London was seriously undermined by a widespread if erroneous conviction that his regular contact with leading Bolsheviks such as Trotsky and Radek meant his advice was biased and unreliable.

9. Hart-Davis (ed.), *Autobiography of Arthur Ransome*, pp. 259–62. K. Young (ed.), *The Diaries of Robert Bruce Lockhart 1915–38* (London, 1973), 11 Oct. 1918, p. 46. Lockhart was in Stockholm for five days and, given his presence at the British Embassy, must have met – and perhaps briefed – Sharp. Access to Lockhart's unpublished diaries remain restricted, so any meetings cannot be confirmed.

10. Hart-Davis (ed.), *Autobiography of Arthur Ransome*, pp. 263–9. Brogan, *Life of Arthur Ransome*, pp. 218, 220, 229–30 and 236. AR, 'From a Moscow Diary', 11 Feb. 1919, *New Statesman*, 17 May 1919 – confirmed Ransome's close personal relationship with Lenin, as well as other prominent members of the All-Russian Executive Committee. AR, 'From a Moscow Diary: the Centro-Textile', 22 Feb. 1919, *New Statesman*, 24 May 1919.

11. Folio FO 371/4369 (656), Foreign Office Papers, PRO.

12. Sir J. Tilley and S. Gaselee, *The Foreign Office* (London, 1933), p. 285.

13. Within the PID's east European section Paton and Namier concentrated on Polish affairs, and in particular a detailed ethnic study which formed the basis of the Curzon Line. Namier's elevation from the ranks to the Foreign Office made him £400 a year better off, and proved a watershed in his academic career. L. Colley, *Namier* (London: Weidenfeld & Nicolson, 1989), pp. 10–11.

    On Seton-Watson's involvement with the PID and the Department of Enemy Propaganda, see H. and C. Seton-Watson, *R. W. Seton-Watson and the Last Years of Austria-Hungary* (London: Hutchinson, 1980), pp. 207–8, 252–2, and 276–7.

14. Allen Leeper's early death, in January 1935, prematurely ended a career as potentially glittering as his brother, who ultimately attained ambassadorial rank (in Athens).

15. 'Balfour was my enemy'. Lord Beaverbrook, *Men and Power 1917–18* (London, 1956), p. 276.

16. Ibid., pp. 289–91. Lord Beaverbrook to Lord Balfour, 20 Feb. 1918, and Lord Balfour to Lord Beaverbrook, 28 Feb. 1919, quoted in Taylor, *Beaverbrook*, pp. 145–6.

17. Bennett had agreed to join the MOI in April 1918, commencing full-time work the following month. When offered further responsibility, Bennett, perhaps wisely, 'temporised'. Flower (ed.), *The Journals of Arnold Bennett 1911–21*, 16 April, 14 May and 16 July 1918, pp. 227, 230, 231 and 234.

18. Ibid., 15 Nov. 1918, p. 242. Arnold Bennett to Lord Beaverbrook, minute paper, 4 Nov. 1918, TS/78, Beaverbrook Papers, House of Lords Records Office. Also quoted in Hepburn (ed.), *Letters of Arnold Bennett: Vol. III 1916–31*, pp. 76–7.

19. Bennett had briefly ceased writing his *New Statesman* column in the autumn of 1918. Excessive paperwork, and his position of 'supreme authority' for day-to-day decisions, proved too much even for this notorious workaholic. Arnold Bennett to J.C. Squire, 29 Sept. and 3 Oct. 1918, New York.

20. Flower (ed.), *The Journals of Arnold Bennett 1911–21*, 27 March 1918, pp. 224–5.

21. Hardinge quoted in Taylor, *Beaverbrook*, p. 146. Hardinge's interpretation flew in the face of accepted Whitehall practice: temporary appointments were, for all intents and purposes, civil servants for the duration. Taylor makes the point that these

'independent experts' could scarcely be described as 'voluntary' when most of them had been released from the armed forces. Beaverbrook himself was later to imply that the Foreign Office took the initiative in poaching the PID from the MOI. Beaverbrook, *Men and Power 1917–18*, p. 289.

22. After three years as permanent secretary, in 1928 Tyrell requested a posting abroad, and was rewarded with the Paris embassy.

23. A. Cecil, 'The Foreign Office', in Sir A.W. Ward and G.P. Gooch (eds), *The Cambridge History of British Foreign Policy 1783–1919* (Cambridge: CUP, 1923), p. 682. The principal reason for running the PID down appears to have been a 1920 search for economies within the Foreign Office, see, N. Hillmer, 'The Foreign Office, the Dominions and the diplomatic unity of the Empire', in D. Dilks (ed.), *Retreat From Power: Studies in Britain's Foreign Policy of the Twentieth Century, Vol. 1 1906–1939* (London: Macmillan, 1981), pp. 59–60.

24. Tilley and Gaselee, *The Foreign Office*, p. 285.

25. The PRO holds comprehensive records of the Foreign Office's propaganda activities in Europe after the First World War, including a memorandum on the use of the British press in an extension of anti-Bolshevik propaganda, 1919. FO 001678/009, Foreign Office Papers, PRO.

   For an examination of these activities within a wider context, see S. White, *Britain and the Bolshevik Revolution* (London: Macmillan, 1979), Chs 1 and 4.

26. Lord Strang *et al.*, *The Foreign Office* (London: Allen & Unwin, 1955), p. 43.

27. See Andrew, *Secret Service*, Chs. 6 and 7.

28. Sir William Tyrell, 'Proposed visit of Mr Sharp to Finland', 3 Dec. 1918, Folio FO 371/4369 (656), Foreign Office Papers, PRO.

29. Ibid.

30. Capt. William Stephen Saunders to Sir Esmé Howard, 19 Dec. 1918, ibid.

31. Young (ed.), *Lockhart Diaries*, 20 Nov. 1918, pp. 48–9.

32. 'Comments', *New Statesman*, 12 May 1917.

33. J. West, *1917 The Russian Revolution and British Democracy*, Fabian Tract No. 184 (London, 1917). The Leeds Convention of 3 June 1917, organised jointly by the ILP and the British Socialist Party, and with 1,150 delegates, set up the short-lived Council of Workers' and Soldiers' Delegates to promote international fraternity with the Provisional government. The October Revolution soon brought to an end this unholy alliance of revolutionaries and constitutionalists.

34. J.C. Squire, 'Introductory Memoir', in Julius West, *A History of the Chartist Movement* (London, 1920), pp. i–xii. Marquand, *Ramsay MacDonald*, pp. 213–15.

   In compiling his seventy-fifth anniversary anthology Stephen Howe recognised the quality of West's reporting when 'in the Smolny Institute as the revolution hangs in the balance': 'Smolny Nights – Petrograd, 10 November', *New Statesman*, 8 Dec. 1917, reproduced in Howe (ed.), *Lines of Dissent* , pp. 42–7.

35. 'Russia and the Bolsheviks', *New Statesman*, 17 Nov. 1917. See also Howe (ed.), *Lines of Dissent*, pp. 37–42. 'Comments', *New Statesman*, 24 Nov. and 15 Dec. 1917. 'Brest-Litovsk and After', *New Statesman*, 23 Feb. 1918. 'Comments', *New Statesman*, 16 March 1918.

36. 'Comments', *New Statesman*, 24 Nov. and 15 Dec. 1917, and 26 Jan. and 16 Feb. 1918. 'The German Strikers', *New Statesman*, 2 Feb. 1918.

37. 'The Peril of Bolshevism', *New Statesman*, 7 Dec. 1918.

38. Cole (ed.), *Beatrice Webb's Diaries 1912–24*, 20 April 1918, p. 90. MacKenzie (eds), *Diary of Beatrice Webb 1905–24*, 26 Sept. 1918, p. 313. Another of the Webbs' sources of information was their research assistant, Felix Warren Crosse, who was attached to the Foreign Office from 1919 to 1923.

39. Memorandum to Sir William Tyrell, Jan. 1918, Folio FO 371/4369 (656), Foreign Office Papers, PRO.

40. MacKenzie (eds), *Diary of Beatrice Webb 1905–24*, 12 Dec. 1918, p. 327. 'Comments' and 'Drifting Into Another War', *New Statesman*, 21 Dec. 1918.

41. Young (ed.), *Lockhart Diaries*, 3 Jan. 1919, pp. 51–2.

42. Ibid., 'Memorandum on Allied intervention in Russia (7 Nov. 1918) and 22 Nov. 1918, pp. 49–51 and 51. R.H. Bruce Lockhart, *Retreat From Glory* (London, 1934), pp. 4–5 and 16. G.D.H. Cole told Lockhart that Tyrell had once tried to recruit him for the PID. Not very surprisingly, another influence at this time was Arthur Ransome: 'Had a long talk with Ransome re Russia. There is a good deal in what he says and I [Lockhart] am inclined to agree that but for our interference and blundering events in Russia would have shaped themselves differently.' Young (eds), *Lockhart Diaries*, 10 and 24 Jan. and 2 May 1919, pp. 52–3.

    Initially Beatrice was singularly unimpressed by Lockhart, whom she clearly felt was a mass of contradictions, see MacKenzie (eds), *Diary of Beatrice Webb 1905–24*, 12 Dec. 1918, p. 328.

43. 'White Terror versus Red Terror', *New Statesman*, 19 April 1919.

44. 'Comments', *New Statesman*, 17 Jan. 1920.

45. 'Comments', *New Statesman*, 29 March 1919. 'A Policy of Ignorance and Panic', *New Statesman*, 12 April 1919.

46. 'The Triumph of Bolshevism', *New Statesman*, 24 Jan. 1920. By September 1920 Sharp thought so highly of Kamenev, whom he almost certainly first met at that year's Fabian Summer School, that he vainly tried to accompany him back to Russia for a visit. MacKenzie (eds), *Diary of Beatrice Webb 1905–24*, 4 Sept. 1920, pp. 365–7. Clifford Sharp to H.G. Wells, 15 September 1920, Illinois.

47. MacKenzie (eds), *Diary of Beatrice Webb 1905–24*, (?) Aug. 1918, p. 186.

48. The publication of Sharp's 'An Allied Peace' as a pamphlet seems to have been the final straw for Shaw. GBS drafted an introduction to *International Government*, but Woolf wisely turned it down. Mackenzie (eds), *Diary of Beatrice Webb 1905–24*, 14 Feb. 1915, p. 222. D. Wilson, *Leonard Woolf: A Political Biography* (London: Hogarth Press, 1978), pp. 62–3. Woolf, *Beginning Again*, pp. 183–4. Holroyd, *Bernard Shaw 2*, pp. 366–7. 'Suggestions for the Prevention of War', special supplements I and II, *New Statesman*, 10 and 17 July 1915. 'The Prevention of War', *New Statesman*, 10 July 1915.

49. Woolf was on the editorial committee of *War and Peace*, which became a supplement of the *Nation* in May 1917. From December 1918 he concentrated his energies on editing the successor to *War and Peace* and *International Review* – the international section of the *Contemporary Review*. Throughout the second half of the war he had also found time to act as parliamentary correspondent for the *Labour Leader!* Woolf, *Beginning Again*, pp. 189 and 191. Wilson, *Leonard Woolf*, pp. 84 and 93.

    Sharp had already attracted criticism from Ramsay Muir and A.C. Pigou in the *Nation* for suggesting international stability could best be achieved by, 'the consolidation and expansion of the largest existing units of Government on lines which whilst satisfying their aspirations, will give them that inherent stability which the British Empire has so strikingly shown itself to possess'. 'Some Considerations on the Future Settlement', *New Statesman*, 2 Jan. 1915.

50. The 'Bryce Committee' was nominally chaired by Lord Bryce, but had in fact been convened at the start of the war by Goldsworthy Lowes Dickinson, the Cambridge historian, in order to explore problems of international organisation. MacKenzie (eds), *Diary of Beatrice Webb 1905–24*, 5 June 1915, p. 232.

51. Wilson, *Leonard Woolf*, pp. 98–9. 'The League of Nations', *New Statesman*, 16 Nov. 1918.

52. Alfred Zimmern, as an active Fabian (and ultimately Oxford's Professor of International Relations, who in his 1934 *Quo Vadimus?* first used the term 'welfare state' in English), was personally acquainted with Woolf. The other principal outlet for Woolf's ideas was *War and Peace*, a monthly founded by Norman Angell in 1916 which Leonard edited and after the Armistice relaunched as the short-lived but highly esteemed *International Review*. During 1920–22 he edited a new international section of the *Contemporary Review*. All these journals were financed by the Rowntree Trust. Both Woolf's memoirs and Sir Duncan Wilson's biography provide very full accounts of his ceaseless efforts to secure a lasting peace. See Wilson, *Leonard Woolf*, pp. 60–102.

Chapter 7, Labour or Liberal? The *New Statesman* and the struggle for power, 1918–24, pp. 135–177.

1. Captain Charles Mostyn Lloyd, late of the Manchester Regiment, was 41 when he first began writing regularly for the *New Statesman*. In 1919 he replaced J.L. Hammond as the *Manchester Guardian*'s correspondent covering the Versailles peace conference, after which he secured a permanent post at the LSE. Lloyd benefited from the major expansion of the School following William Beveridge's appointment in 1919 (from 17 to 79 full-time lecturers during his 18 years as Director). In August 1922, by which time he had become Sharp's assistant editor, Lloyd was promoted to head of the Ratan Tata Department of Social Science and Administration, a post he held until retirement during the Second World War. Mostyn Lloyd was warmly regarded by all who knew him, widely respected as a self-effacing and highly principled man of great integrity and firm socialist convictions. A. Smith, 'LLOYD, Charles Mostyn (1878–1946)', in Saville and Bellamy (eds), *The Dictionary of Labour Biography*, Vol. VII. Pimlott, *Hugh Dalton*, p. 135.

2. 'Mr Lloyd George's Future', *New Statesman*, 19 April 1919. Either Desmond MacCarthy or J.R. Spender first introduced Sharp to Asquith, but exactly when is not known. Sharp was adamant that Asquith's very real chance of again becoming prime minister ruled out an ambassadorship in Washington. Neither of Asquith's biographers – Roy Jenkins and Stephen Koss – mention his being considered for any appointment in 1919 other than heading the Royal Commission on the Universities of Oxford and Cambridge. 'Mr Asquith', *New Statesman*, 7 June 1919.

3. M. Cowling, *The Impact of Labour 1920–24: The Beginning of Modern British Politics* (Cambridge: CUP, 1971), pp. 100–1. Growing criticism of Sir Donald Maclean's leadership of the 23 Free Liberal Party MPs (nicknamed the 'Wee Frees' after the Scottish sect, and also commonly referred to as the Independent Liberals, as in this book) had helped Asquith's supporters foster a sense of urgency surrounding his anticipated return to the Commons.

4. 'A Good Thing for Parliament', *New Statesman*, 28 Feb. 1920. The Paisley campaign of early 1920, where the Labour candidate J.M. Biggar was Asquith's biggest threat, killed off any faint hope of close collaboration between the two opposition parties. Over the succeeding 18 months Labour leaders, quietly encouraged by Haldane, repeatedly rebuffed approaches by Maclean and others on Asquith's behalf. On 21 May 1921 Harold Laski wrote to the *Nation* explaining at length to a principally Liberal readership why the labour movement, particularly the trade unions, repudiated almost all that the former premier now stood for. Sharp would have read Laski's letter, and clearly learned nothing from it. S. Koss, *Asquith* (London: Allen Lane, 1976, Hamish Hamilton paperback edn 1985), pp. 347 and 251. 'The Party with a Past', *New Statesman*, 13 Nov. 1920.

    In the issue following Tory MPs' famous rejection of continued coalition at the Carlton Club on 19 October 1922, and Lloyd George's immediate resignation, Sharp coolly refuted any allegation of personal malice against 'one of the ablest men who ever held high office'. Yet, rarely able to resist a smear when the opportunity arose, in the same paragraph Sharp predictably resurrected the Marconi scandal as a portent of the 'moral slackness' which had nullified his old adversary's natural talent for leadership. 'The Main Issue', *New Statesman*, 21 Oct. 1922.

5. J.W. Good, a 43-year-old Ulsterman of 'Voltairean moderation', was the author of two recent books on the Irish question, as well as the assistant editor of the *Irish Statesman* and a leader writer for the *Irish Independent*. D. Ayerst, *Guardian: Biography of a Newspaper* (Collins, London, 1971), p. 420. 'Peace in Ireland', *New Statesman*, 10 Dec. 1921.

    For detailed coverage of the *New Statesman*'s reporting and commentary upon post-war Irish affairs see D.G. Boyce, *Englishmen and Irish Troubles: The British Public and the Making of Irish Policy 1918–22* (London: Jonathan Cape, 1972), and A. Smith, 'The *New Statesman* 1913–31', pp. 155–8.

The most famous contribution to the War of Independence was the publication of W.B. Yeats's 'Easter 1916', *New Statesman*, 23 Oct. 1920. Tom Paulin has argued that the poem helped to 'mould opinion [and] consolidate links between British socialists and Irish nationalists', by ensuring *New Statesman* endorsement of an NEC inquiry condemning British reprisals. This exaggerates the importance and influence of the paper at the time, which anyway was already deeply critical of government policy. See also Ch. 8. T. Paulin (ed.), *Introduction to The Faber Book of Political Verse* (London: Faber, 1986), p. 20.

6. 'The Inevitable Settlement', *New Statesman*, 9 July 1921. 'What Could a Labour Government Offer to Sinn Fein?', *New Statesman*, 16 July 1921. Convinced in his own mind that republicanism was anathema to the majority of Irish men and women, Protestant *and* Catholic, Sharp consistently underestimated de Valera. Similarly, Lloyd in his editorial comments on the IRA (at a time when Good's coverage of the civil war was excellent), and after 1926 on Fianna Fáil, displayed scant understanding of the republican movement.

7. 'The Spokesman of Civilization', *New Statesman*, 16 Oct. 1920. 'A Great Essay in Liberalism', *New Statesman*, 9 Oct. 1920. Jenkins, *Asquith*, p. 491.

8. Hyams is clearly not a reliable source, witness his assertion, at the same time as reporting his conversation with Cole, that support for the Labour Party only became apparent in the early 1920s – precisely the moment at which Sharp brought that support into question. Hyams, *New Statesman*, p. 93.

Cole, since 1912 a Fellow of Magdalen College, escaped conscription in 1916 by persuading the Amalgamated Society of Engineers to give the FRD 'work of national importance' collating wage-agreements in the munitions industry. Leaned on by Henderson, the tribunal in Oxford accepted his plea for exemption.

9. There is a surprisingly affectionate portrait of the recently married Douglas and Margaret Cole (née Postgate) in MacKenzie (eds), *Diary of Beatrice Webb 1905–24*, 7 Nov. 1918, pp. 317–18. Beatrice Webb, diary, 10 Oct. 1918, Passfield Papers.

Cole saw far more of Lloyd than Sharp as they were next-door neighbours between 1923 and 1925. The late Dame Margaret Cole in conversation with the author, 15 Dec. 1977.

The estimate of Cole's annual contribution to the *New Statesman* is taken from L.P. Carpenter, *G.D.H. Cole: An Intellectual Biography* (Cambridge: CUP, 1973), p. 113. The Coles' private and public life in the 1920s and 1930s is well covered in B.D. Vernon, *Margaret Cole 1893–1980: A Political Biography* (London: Croom Helm, 1986), pp. 51–94.

10. Circulation figures quoted in R.E. Dowse, *Left in the Centre: The Independent Labour Party 1893–1940* (London: Longman, 1966), pp. 71 and 89.

11. B. Crick, 'A second look at half-forgotten radicals', *Guardian*, 2 Aug. 1979. Dowse, *Left in the Centre*, pp. 82–3.

12. For example, in '"Communism" and Labour Policy', *New Statesman*, 7 Aug. 1920, the anonymous Cole urged Labour leaders to look beyond immediate concerns and evolve a fresh 'evolutionary policy' of socialism in the light of what was occurring on the shop-floor. He conveyed the same message in the *Labour Leader*, 9 Dec. 1920, but this time under his by-line, as quoted in Dowse, *Left in the Centre*, p. 68.

13. Ibid., pp. 82–3.

14. The attempt of Cole, Allen, William Mellor and their fellow 'Oxford Fabians' to gain control of the Fabian Society's executive and redraft the 'Basis' (the statement of principles governing Fabian policy) is graphically described in an unintentionally hilarious account in Beatrice Webb's diary. MacKenzie (eds), *Diary of Beatrice Webb 1905–24*, 15 May 1915, pp. 229–30.

15. When the ILP leadership orchestrated the 1921 conference's rejection of a draft programme based on guild socialism, Cole gave no hint of bitterness in his *New Statesman* report. In contrast, according to Beatrice Webb, MacDonald remained 'bitterly malicious' towards the young intellectuals, particularly after the NEC's 1921 decision to disengage from the unduly heretical Labour Research Department (Cole of

course did the same once the LRD became closely associated with the Communist Party). However, MacDonald's biographer gives a different impression, suggesting that he always kept in contact with Allen and Cole, even drawing upon the latter's ideas in *Socialism After the War* (1917) and *Socialism: Critical and Constructive* (1921). In the 1920s Cole frequently contributed to *Socialist Review*, the theoretical quarterly and later monthly of the ILP which MacDonald edited. Despite their deepening policy differences across the decade, in 1929 MacDonald encouraged Cole to enter Parliament, entertaining him and Margaret at Chequers. Overall, Cole appears to have had more success in introducing MacDonald to new ideas (if not necessarily to adopting them) than he did with Henderson who, according to Beatrice, was simply left bemused. 'Comments', *New Statesman*, 2 April 1920. MacKenzie (eds), *Diary of Beatrice Webb 1905–24*, 12 July 1921 and 24 Sept. 1919, pp. 382 and 348. Cole (ed.), *Beatrice Webb's Diaries 1912–24*, 16 July 1921, p. 214. Marquand, *Ramsay MacDonald*, pp. 270 and 829 note 9, and 410–11.

16. Beatrice Webb, diary, 10 Oct. 1921, Passfield Papers. Cole was expressing his poor opinion of Labour candidates well before the end of the war: not enough 'brain workers', and too many full-time trade union officials instead of shop stewards. T. Wilson (ed.), *The Political Diaries of C.P. Scott 1911–1928* (London: Collins, 1970), 3–5 Feb. 1918, p. 333.

17. For example, in 1920, while Cole was predicting the imminent demise of the Second International, Sidney was reporting on the success of its Geneva congress. Five years earlier, praising Cole's arduous efforts as vice-president of the FRD, Beatrice had noted that:

> He and Sidney irritate each other. Cole indulges in a long list of personal hatreds. The weak point of his outlook is that there is no one that he does like except as a temporary tool; he resents anyone who is not a follower and has a contempt for all leaders other than himself. With his keen intelligence and aristocratic temperament it is hard to believe that he will remain enamoured with the crude forms of democracy embodied in the Guild Socialist idealization of the manual working class.

MacKenzie (eds), *Diary of Beatrice Webb 1905–24*, 14 Feb. 1915, pp. 222–3.

18. 'The Object of the Direct Actionists', *New Statesman*, 13 Sept. 1919. 'A Parliament Pour Rire', *New Statesman*, 2 Aug. 1919. 'The Anarchist Conspiracy', *New Statesman*, 4 Oct. 1919. Cole (ed.), *Beatrice Webb's Diaries 1912–24*, 2 and 6 Oct., pp. 168–9.

19. The Miners' Federation went on strike on 1 April 1921, the day wartime control of the coal industry and a national agreement on wages ended. J.H. Thomas's railwaymen and Ernest Bevin's dockers threatened strike action within a fortnight under the umbrella of the Triple Alliance. On 15 April, following Lloyd George's offer of a temporary settlement on wages and the miners' refusal to re-enter negotiations, the NUR cancelled its plans for sympathetic action. 'Black Friday' was seen throughout the labour movement as a major reversal, and marked the effective end of the Triple Alliance.

20. . . . we [the British] have a habit of preferring compromises and adjustments to the decision of clear-cut issues . . . the innate conservatism of the British working-class and the sense of reality which has hitherto normally characterised the British upper class appear to make the class-war a very remote and improbable contingency . . .

'Classes *versus* Masses', *New Statesman*, 2 April 1921. In a scornful Commons reply, Lloyd George assumed the writer to have been Webb, thus provoking a blistering retort from Sharp in the next issue. Here was a weekly with a tiny circulation, but it could nevertheless provoke parliamentary debate.

21. 'Comments', 'Force: the Only Remedy?' and 'The Gun That Did Not Go Off', *New Statesman*, 23 April 1921. Cole (ed.), *Beatrice Webb's Diaries 1912–24*, 24 April 1921, p. 209.

22. Dowse, *Left in the Centre*, pp. 49–50. Miliband, *Parliamentary Socialism*, p. 61.

Cowling, *The Impact of Labour 1920–25*, p. 42. Naturally the *New Statesman* exhorted 'that increasing breadth of view which has distinguished its [Labour's] outlook since the war . . . in its personnel and policy it is effectively a national party, based on ideas rather than on an exclusive appeal to a particular class'. 'Comments', *New Statesman*, 24 Nov. 1923.

23. Marquand, *Ramsay MacDonald*, p. 330.

24. The overwhelming majority of Independent Liberals had been and still were prepared to defend Grey and Asquith's handling of foreign affairs up to the spring of 1915. Unlike his brother Charles, G.M. Trevelyan after 1918 keenly defended the Liberal Party's pre-war record, culminating in his 1937 biography, *Grey of Fallodon*. Cannadine, *G.M. Trevelyan*, pp. 164–6.

25. J.M. Keynes, *The Economic Consequences of the Peace* (London: Macmillan, 1919). For Keynes's observation of the Peace Conference, and the circumstances surrounding the publication and popular reception of *The Economic Consequences of the Peace*, see Skidelsky, *John Maynard Keynes: Hopes Betrayed 1883–1920*, pp. 353–402, and for a summary of the historiographical debate, see R. Skidelsky, *John Maynard Keynes: The Economist as Saviour 1920–1937* (London: Macmillan, 1992), pp. 31–4.

26. 'The Depression', *New Statesman*, 1 Jan. 1921.

27. 'Comments', *New Statesman*, 8 Oct. 1921. 'The Labour Party and the Government', *New Statesman*, 15 Oct. 1921. Sir Eric Geddes and his fellow businessmen's Committee on National Expenditure's report was published in February 1922, setting the agenda for a *de facto* end to post-war social reform, particularly in education.

28. 'The Plight of the Coalition', *New Statesman* , 22 Jan. 1921. R.F. Harrod, *The Life of John Maynard Keynes* (London: Macmillan, 1951; Penguin paperback edn, 1972), p. 412. For Keynes's thinking on the British economy 1920–23, see Skidelsky, *John Maynard Keynes: The Economist as Saviour 1920–1937*, pp. 130–70.

29. 'The One Thing Needful', *New Statesman*, 24 Nov. 1923. Cole preferred not to mention that Labour's 1923 manifesto scarcely mentioned public ownership, focusing on free trade and the scandal of the jobless. On 3 May 1924 he conceded that state control of coal was in the present conditions 'politically infeasible'. What he failed to argue sufficiently strongly was that the mechanics of British government are such that, with sufficient political will, many of his proposals could have been introduced using the royal prerogative, thereby circumventing a House of Commons where Labour was dependent on Liberal goodwill.

30. H.H. Asquith, address to the National Liberal Club, as reported in the *Morning Post*, 25 March 1920, and quoted in Cowling, *The Impact of Labour 1920–4*, p. 99.

31. Beatrice Webb, diary, 10 Oct. 1921, Passfield Papers.

32. Ibid., 10 Dec. 1922.

33. Ibid., 10 Oct. 1921 and 20 Feb. 1922.

34. 'Comments', *New Statesman*, 28 Oct. 1922.

35. Beatrice Webb, diary, 10 Dec. 1922, Passfield Papers.

36. Ibid.

37. Clifford Sharp to David Lloyd George, 23 Jan. 1930, Lloyd George Papers. Venetia Montagu was formerly Venetia Stanley, youngest daughter of Lord Sheffield, with whom Asquith shared an extraordinarily intimate correspondence between 1910 and 1915, when she married Edwin Montagu. Asquith's sense of loss was compounded when Montagu, a faithful ally, served under Lloyd George as Secretary of State for India. Mutual grief over Montagu's early death, in November 1924, brought a renewed exchange of letters. See H.H. Asquith, *Letters to Venetia Stanley*, M. and E. Brock (eds) (Oxford: OUP, 1982). Maurice Bonham Carter was Asquith's private secretary from 1910 to 1916, and his son-in-law from December 1915. Vivian Phillips was Liberal Chief Whip, and J.A. Spender, editor of the *Westminster Gazette* and Asquith's official biographer. All these people had, of course, been close friends and confidants of Asquith for years before Sharp spent his first weekend in the country at Sutton Courtney.

38. Ibid.

39. Frances Stevenson was Lloyd George's partner in politics and love for over 40 years. Sharp clearly kept pestering him. Recovering from the prostate gland operation that had rendered him a helpless observer throughout the financial and political crisis of August 1931, Lloyd George politely – but no doubt permanently – postponed a visit from an unemployed journalist with no friends in high places who was insistent that only one man could rescue the nation from disaster. Frances Stevenson to Clifford Sharp, undated but apparently Sept. 1931, ibid.

40. David Lloyd George to Clifford Sharp, 19 Jan. 1926, ibid. Lloyd George trusted Sharp sufficiently to reveal that C.P. Scott had been consulted before drafting a rather clever reply to the complaint by Lord Oxford (Asquith) regarding his sympathetic view of the General Strike. The unfavourable publicity attracted by this difference of opinion, followed by Asquith's stroke a month later, led to his resignation as party leader on 15 October 1926. Wilson (ed.), *The Political Diaries of C.P. Scott 1911–1928*, 22–23 July 1927, pp. 487–8. Jenkins, *Asquith*, pp. 514–17.

41. Beatrice Webb, diary, 10 Dec. 1922, Passfield Papers.

42. S. Koss, *Fleet Street Radical: A.G. Gardiner and the Daily News* (London: Allen Lane, 1973), pp. 264–5 and 291, and *The Rise and Fall of the Political Press in Britain 2*, pp. 361–2.

43. Beatrice Webb, diary, 10 Oct. 1921, Passfield Papers. Sharp intended to employ Cole as the *Westminster Gazette*'s labour correspondent. C. Seymour-Ure, 'The Press and the Party System Between the Wars' in G. Peele and C. Cook (eds), *The Politics of Reappraisal 1918–1929* (London: Macmillan, 1975), pp. 232–57. For the full story of the *Westminster Gazette*, see Koss, *The Rise and Fall of the Political Press in Britain 2*, pp. 372–5.

44. Clifford Sharp to J.A. Spender, (?) November 1921, quoted in W. Harris, *J.A. Spender* (London: Cassell, 1946), p. 220. In the early 1920s Harris, already a senior foreign correspondent for the 'Cocoa Press', occasionally filed overseas reports to the *New Statesman*.

45. J.A. Spender to Sir Donald Maclean, quoted in Koss, *The Rise and Fall of the Political Press in Britain 2*, p. 374.

46. Cowling, *The Impact of Labour 1920–24*, pp. 98–9. Remarkably, the *Westminster Gazette* had a circulation of over 250,000 when it merged with the *Daily News* in 1928.

47. Beatrice Webb, diary, 10 Dec. 1922, Passfield Papers.

48. C. Sharp, 'Early Days', *New Statesman and Nation*, 14 April 1934. For details of Le Bas's report, see Hyams, *New Statesman*, pp. 81–2. Sidney Webb to Beatrice Webb, 7 Jan. 1921, MacKenzie (ed.), *Letters of Sidney and Beatrice Webb, Vol. III*, p. 145.

49. Woolf, *Downhill All The Way*, pp. 96–7. D. Moggridge, *Maynard Keynes: An Economist's Biography* (London: Routledge & Kegan Paul, 1992) p. 390. Beatrice Webb, diary, 11 Jan. 1922, Passfield Papers.

50. Skidelsky, *John Maynard Keynes: The Economist As Saviour 1920–1937*, p. 134.

51. Ibid., pp. 134–6.

52. Ibid. Moggridge, *Maynard Keynes: An Economist's Biography*, pp. 391–2. Koss, *The Rise and Fall of the Political Press in Britain 2*, p. 376.

53. Beatrice Webb, diary, 11 Jan. 1923, Passfield Papers. Skidelsky, *John Maynard Keynes: The Economist As Saviour 1920–1937*, p. 136. Moggridge, *Maynard Keynes: An Economist's Biography*, p. 391. Clifford Sharp to Sidney Webb, (?) Jan. 1923, Passfield Papers.

54. Ibid.

55. Beatrice Webb, diary, 11 Jan. 1923, ibid. Edward Whitley to Sidney Webb, 4 and 8 Jan. 1923, ibid. Glynne Williams to Sidney Webb, 5 Jan. 1923, ibid. Sidney Webb to E.D. Simon, 5 Jan. 1923, ibid. Sidney Webb to Ramsay MacDonald, 28 April 1925, MacKenzie (ed.), *Letters of Sidney and Beatrice Webb, Vol. III*, p. 235. Simon and Bennett remained directors, but were no longer expected to contribute to the losses.

56. Clifford Sharp to Sidney Webb, 9 January 1923, Passfield Papers.

57. 'Comments', *New Statesman*, 13 Jan. 1923.

58. Beatrice Webb, diary, 11 Jan. 1923, Passfield Papers.
59. Havinghurst, *Radical Journalist: H.W. Massingham*, p. 303.
60. 'Comments', *New Statesman*, 30 Aug. 1924.
61. Havinghurst, *Radical Journalist: H.W. Massingham*, p. 303.
62. Glynne Williams to Sidney Webb, 5 Jan. 1923, Passfield Papers. Skidelsky, *John Maynard Keynes: The Economist As Saviour 1920–1937*, p. 136.
63. The 1926–27 Liberal Industrial Inquiry, financed by Lloyd George to the tune of £10,000 and set up by E.D. Simon and Ramsay Muir, investigated all aspects of the economy and involved all key Liberal thinkers. Keynes was a major contributor to the final report, *Britain's Industrial Future*. The diverse and imaginative recommendations of the 'Yellow Book' provided in 1929 the basis for the Liberal manifesto, *We Can Conquer Unemployment*, and Keynes and Henderson's combative pamphlet, *Can Lloyd George Do It?*. Moggridge, *Maynard Keynes: An Economist's Biography*, pp. 457–66. For a detailed study of Keynes's involvement in Liberal politics throughout the 1920s, see Skidelsky, *John Maynard Keynes: The Economist As Saviour 1920–1937*, pp. 21–2, 134–9, 242–71 and 301–6.
64. Ibid., p. 21.
65. MacDonald's abortive attempt in 1925 to purchase the *New Statesman*, see Ch. 9.
66. 'Mr Baldwin?', *New Statesman*, 26 May 1923.
67. Marquand, *Ramsay MacDonald*, pp. 292–3, and Cowling, *The Impact of Labour 1920–24*, pp. 284–5 and 292–3. Also, for the importance of Henderson's contribution to Labour's stance in foreign affairs and related recruitment of Radicals, see K. Morgan, 'Arthur Henderson', *Labour People: Hardie to Kinnock* (Oxford: OUP, 1987; paperback edn, 1992), pp. 84–5, R. McKibbin, 'Arthur Henderson as Labour Leader', *The Ideologies of Class: Social Relations in Britain 1880–1950*, pp. 50–1 and 63–4.

   Ironically, Maurice Cowling has suggested that ten years later the National Government regarded Henderson, by now Chairman of the World Disarmament Conference, as 'too much in France's pocket'. M. Cowling, *The Impact of Hitler: British Politics and British Policy* (Cambridge: CUP, 1975), p. 27.
68. A. Morgan, *J. Ramsay MacDonald* (Manchester: MUP, 1987, paperback edn), pp. 76–86.
69. Even when Prime Minister MacDonald was always welcomed at the Press Club as a fellow professional. Morgan discovered that he did not get round to joining the National Union of Journalists (NUJ) until as late as 1927. Ibid., p. 54.
70. In June 1920 Sir Herbert Samuel had been sent to Palestine as the first High Commissioner of the British Mandate. He resigned just under five years later. See B. Wasserstein, *The British in Palestine: The Mandatory Government and the Arab–Jewish Conflict 1917–1929* (Oxford: OUP, 1991).
71. 'The Morpeth Election', *New Statesman*, 23 June 1923.
72. 'Labour Confers', *New Statesman*, 7 July 1923.
73. 'Comments', *New Statesman*, 1 Dec. 1923.
74. Harold Laski to Sidney Webb, 9 Jan. 1923, Passfield Papers. Ramsay MacDonald, diary, 10 Dec. 1923, Ramsay MacDonald Papers, PRO. MacKenzie (eds), *Diary of Beatrice Webb 1905–24*, pp. 430–1.
75. Ibid. S. Webb, 'The First Labour Government', 1924, *Political Quarterly*, 22 (1960), p. 21.
76. 'The "New Statesman", the Labour Party and the Capital Levy', *New Statesman*, 15 Dec. 1923.
77. 'The Deadlock', ibid. 'Labour and its Allies, *New Statesman*, 12 Jan. 1924.
78. 'A Revolutionary Government', *New Statesman*, 26 Jan. 1924.
79. C. Sharp, 'The Liberal and Labour Parties – An English Bloc des Gauches?', *Daily News*, 24 May 1924.
80. 'The Reparations Settlement', *New Statesman*, 23 Aug. 1924. With MacDonald combining the premiership with being Foreign Secretary, Arthur Ponsonby as minister of state at the Foreign Office enjoyed an unusual degree of responsibility.
81. Ibid.

82. Note the description of the *New Statesman* as, in 1924, a 'left of centre paper' and not a 'voice of the left' or, as Martin would have seen it, 'conscience of the left'. Given Sharp's still formidable presence in the mid-1920s, the latter labels had become singularly inappropriate.

83. N. and J. MacKenzie (eds), *The Diary of Beatrice Webb, Vol. 4 1924–1943, The Wheel of Life* (Cambridge, MA, 1985), 25 May 1924, p. 28. 'I [Sidney Webb] certainly failed to do any lasting good in this field [unemployment].' Webb, 'The First Labour Government', *Political Quarterly*, p. 21.

84. MacKenzie (eds), *The Diary of Beatrice Webb 1924–1943*, 30 Aug. 1924, p. 36.

85. When the free-trade Liberals led by Sir Herbert Samuel withdrew support for the National government in November 1932 (over the Ottawa conference's adoption of imperial preference), Snowden resigned as Lord Privy Seal.

86. 'Mr MacDonald and the I.L.P.', *New Statesman*, 26 April 1924.

> Shaw [Tom Shaw, Minister of Labour] fully admitted our common failure, which he attributed, with some justice, to the failure of all the officials to rise to the necessary audacity of imagining schemes which they felt would certainly be frowned on by the Treasury. I [Webb] take blame to myself, as he does to himself, for not making good this imagination.

Webb, 'The First Labour Government', *Political Quarterly*, p. 22. 'The Debates on Unemployment', *New Statesman*, 31 May 1924.

> If a Labour Government is not strong enough to insist on the control of credit being used to remedy unemployment, it is surely enough caution and political sagacity to veto any attempt to have it used for the deliberate purpose of depressing prices and thus inevitably increasing unemployment.

'Gold and Unemployment', *New Statesman*, 21 June 1924. 'Comments', *New Statesman*, 12 July 1924. 'One Step Forward', *New Statesman*, 23 Aug. 1924.

87. Moggridge, *Maynard Keynes: An Economist's Biography*, pp. 414–19. Skidelsky, *John Maynard Keynes: The Economist As Saviour 1920–1937*, pp. 103, 105, 147 and 153–64. 'Gold and Unemployment', *New Statesman*, 21 June 1924. 'Comments', *New Statesman*, 12 July 1924. 'One Step Forward', *New Statesman*, 23 Aug. 1924.

88. Moggridge, *Maynard Keynes: An Economist's Biography*, pp. 420–1. Skidelsky, *John Maynard Keynes: The Economist As Saviour 1920–1937*, pp. 183–6.

89. MacKenzie (eds), *The Diary of Beatrice Webb 1924–1943*, 13 Sept. 1924, 17 May 1924, p. 2. The Coles had just been to lunch, confirming the good relations they always enjoyed with the Webbs whatever their differences.

90. Ibid., p. 28.

91. 'English Socialism in 1924', *New Statesman*, 6 Sept. 1924.

92. Ibid.

93. Ibid.

94. Ibid. Howe (ed.), *Lines of Dissent*, p. 51.

95. Sidney Webb again drafted the manifesto – with minimum consultation. MacKenzie (eds), *The Diary of Beatrice Webb 1924–1943*, 1 Oct. 1924, p. 41.

96. 'Comments', *New Statesman*, 9 Aug. 1924. 'The Russian Treaty', *New Statesman*, 16 Aug. 1924.

97. 'Comments', *New Statesman*, 6 Sept. 1924.

98. MacKenzie (eds), *The Diary of Beatrice Webb 1924–1943*, 13 Sept. 1924, p. 38.

99. On 5 August 1924 police arrested J.R. Campbell on a charge under the Incitement to Mutiny Act. Eleven days earlier, in the CPGB's (Communist Party of Great Britain) *Workers' Weekly*, he had urged soldiers not to shoot fellow-workers in a class or international war. After hostile questions from backbenchers, and information from James Maxton that Campbell was a disabled war veteran deputising as editor, the Attorney General, Sir Patrick Hastings, secured Cabinet approval to drop the case. This fuelled Tory and Liberal accusations that MacDonald had allowed a government law officer to make a political rather than a purely legal decision. Hastings had in fact

made the latter, but ministers' ignorance of constitutional proprieties fuelled accusations that he had been unduly influenced by party political considerations. For a detailed study of the Campbell case, see Marquand, *Ramsay MacDonald*, pp. 364–74.

100. 'Comments', *New Statesman*, 16 Aug. 1924.

101. Beatrice Webb, diary, 10 Oct. 1924, Passfield Papers.

102. 'This Absurd Crisis', *New Statesman*, 11 Oct. 1924. On the eve of being forced out of power Labour rallied round the government at the annual conference, 'and as for the P.M., in spite of Court dress and the motor car, he has again become the idol of the left and the respected leader of the right of the labour movement respectively'. Damage limitation extended to conference firmly rejecting the CPGB's request for affiliation; in addition, Communists could not seek endorsement as Labour candidates. The concession regarding composition of the select committee (Labour for Liberal MPs), which Asquith offered in his contribution to the debate on 8 October, indicates how keen he was to avoid a general election, despite the fact that the Liberals were primarily responsible for making this the likeliest outcome. Conversely, Lloyd George, via personal intervention and the columns of the *Daily Chronicle*, had helped engineer a sense of crisis, on the assumption that in the wake of a Liberal electoral débâcle he could secure control of the party. Sharp would have been well aware how much the Asquitheans feared a substantial loss of seats in the event of an election (they lost 118), hence the ferocity of his attack on MacDonald for being prepared to go to the country. MacKenzie (eds), *The Diary of Beatrice Webb 1924–1943*, 10 Oct. 1924, p. 42. For an account of the debate, see Marquand, *Ramsay MacDonald*, pp. 375–7, and Jenkins, *Asquith*, pp. 502–3.

103. Sidney Webb to Beatrice Webb, 12 Oct. 1924, MacKenzie (ed.), *Letters of Sidney and Beatrice Webb, Vol. III*, p. 218. Edward Whitley to Sidney Webb, 15 Oct. 1924, and Glynne Williams to Sidney Webb, 21 Oct. 1924, Passfield Papers.

104. C.M. Lloyd to Beatrice Webb, 20 Oct. 1924, Passfield Papers.

105. Ibid.

106. C.M. Lloyd to Sidney Webb, 26 Oct. 1924, Passfield Papers.

107. The dismissal of Bruce Page was warranted in that the paper had suffered a dramatic slump in sales and had become, the odd security revelation by Duncan Campbell notwithstanding, extremely boring. Stuart Weir's departure was much more contentious, but at least it facilitated the arrival of Steve Platt who played a major role in reviving the *New Statesman*'s fortunes in the early 1990s and stabilising circulation, albeit only at around 20,000.

108. Glynne Williams to Sidney Webb, 26 Oct. 1924, Passfield Papers. The board intended to invite the journalist H.M. Tomlinson to become editor.

109. Clifford Sharp to Sidney Webb, 24 Oct. 1924, Passfield Papers.

110. C. Sharp, 'Early Days', *New Statesman*, 14 April 1934.

111. Clifford Sharp to Sidney Webb, 3 Nov. 1924, Passfield Papers.

112. Glynne Williams to Sidney Webb, 3 Nov. 1924, Passfield Papers. At Bennett's suggestion, Beaverbrook bought the *Evening Standard* from Rothermere in 1923, although until 1933 the latter's Daily Mail Trust retained 49 per cent of the shares with an option on the rest. With the arrival of new editorial staff, Bennett's influential literary column and David Low's cartoons, the *Evening Standard* gradually lost its image as being a very dull and stuffy paper, its readership firmly rooted in middle-class suburbia and West End clubland. When Beatrice Webb recorded her first meeting with Sharp for six years she added that 'He told us a great deal about Beaverbrook, who has made him various offers of highly paid unemployment'. This was probably flannel, but in 1924 Bennett had presumably thought Sharp would be a useful recruit for the revamped *Evening Standard*. A. Smith, 'Low and Beaverbrook, Cartoonist and Proprietor', *Encounter*, Vol. LXV, No. 5 (Dec. 1985), p. 8. MacKenzie (eds), *The Diary of Beatrice Webb 1924–1943*, 12 Aug. 1928, pp. 149–50.

113. 'Comments', *New Statesman*, 1 Nov. 1924.

114. Ibid. 'Comments', *New Statesman*, 15 Nov. 1924.

115. When the *Daily Mail* on 25 October 1924 published Grigori Zinoviev's letter inciting the CPGB to engage in various seditious activities, MacDonald at first assumed it was

genuine. He handled the ensuing controversy poorly, and Labour were even more sensitive over the affair when subsequent evidence suggested the document was a forgery. Andrew, *Secret Service*, pp. 425–45.

116. Ramsay MacDonald, diary, 25 Sept. 1924, Ramsay MacDonald Papers. MacDonald had disapproved of Brailsford's appointment as editor when the *Labour Leader* transferred from Manchester to London in 1922, before its relaunch as the *New Leader*. Not only did the paper take on the trappings of a *New Statesman* or *Nation*, but it vigorously upheld the independence of the ILP from the parliamentary leadership. For MacDonald, the whole point of bringing the weekly south was to ensure its acquiescence, not open dissent. Koss, *The Rise and Fall of the Political Press in Britain 2*, pp. 409–11.

117. Ibid., 11 April and 15 May 1925.

118. Marquand, *Ramsay MacDonald*, pp. 419–20. This was the second attempt by MacDonald to buy *Reynold's News*. He had tried in 1906, having previously failed to persuade George Cadbury to sell the *Daily News* to a syndicate similar to that formed in 1925. Hopkin,'The Labour Party Press', in Brown (ed.), *The First Labour Party 1906–14*, pp. 115–17.

119. Sidney Webb to Ramsay MacDonald, 25 April 1925, MacKenzie (ed.), *Letters of Sidney and Beatrice Webb, Vol. III*, pp. 234–5.

120. Ibid. Hedley Le Bas to Ramsay MacDonald, 4 June and 18 Nov. 1925, Ramsay MacDonald Papers. Hedley Le Bas to Glynne Williams, 26 Nov. 1925, ibid. Sir Robert Donald to Ramsay MacDonald, 31 Oct. 1925, ibid. Williams had contemplated making way for Le Bas after the initial request for Sharp's resignation. Glynne Williams to Sidney Webb, 26 Oct. 1924, Passfield Papers.

121. Sidney Webb to Ramsay MacDonald, 19 Sept. 1925, MacKenzie (ed.), *Letters of Sidney and Beatrice Webb, Vol. III*, p. 237.

122. Sidney Webb to Beatrice Webb, 25 Nov. 1925, ibid., p. 254.

Chapter 8, 'Literature is news that STAYS news' (Ezra Pound): The *New Statesman* as a literary review, pp. 178–209.

1. Leonard Woolf to Edward Hyams, quoted in Hyams, *New Statesman*, p. 57. Including the signed 'New Novels', the major reviews and two columns of short notices took up approximately four full pages of the first issue. The remainder of the eight pages between the literary editor's full-page 'Books in General' and Emil Davies's 'City Page' was taken up with publishers' advertisements. The whole paper comprised a total of 32 pages, and this remained the average size until the wartime paper shortage reduced the total number of review pages to between three and five. The format remained essentially the same until February 1931 when 'Plays and Pictures' was established as an autonomous section broken down into individual reviews, both signed and unsigned, and concluding with a list of the week's forthcoming cultural and sporting events. Until the mid-1920s when Raymond Mortimer persuaded Sharp that longer essays should be signed or initialled, all book reviews were anonymous. A decade later Mortimer, by now literary editor, persuaded Martin that all reviews should be signed, and paid for even if accepted and not published.

2. C. Sharp, 'Early Days', *New Statesman and Nation*, 14 April 1934. Bennett, Siegfried Sassoon, and Edmund Gosse all rated Squire highly as a poet. Towards the end of the First World War selections from 'Books in General', and serious verse as well as parodies, appeared in book form. The vague, uninformative communiqués of the War Office, and some of the more pompous official statements, inspired him to produce the odd satire *à la* Woddis, albeit by no means as scathing.

3. J.C. Squire, 'VI. Criticism', *Flowers of Speech* (London, 1935), p. 148.

4. *Scrutiny* was launched in 1932 by the Leavises, L.C. Knights and their allies in the revolution in studying English that had taken place in post-war Cambridge. Scornful of the standard of reviewing in the popular (non-academic) press, including the weeklies, *Scrutiny*'s editors produced a critical journal 'which has yet to be surpassed in its

tenacious devotion to the moral centrality of English studies, their crucial relevance to the quality of social life as a whole. . . . it represented nothing less than the last-ditch stand of liberal humanism, concerned . . . with the unique value of the individual and the creative realm of the interpersonal'. T. Eagleton, *Literary Theory: An Introduction* (Oxford: OUP, 1983), pp. 31 and 42. See also F. Mulhern, *The Moment of 'Scrutiny'* (London: Verso, 1979).

5. K. Miller, 'Empson Agonistes', in R. Gill (ed.), *William Empson: The Man and His Work* (London: Routledge & Kegan Paul, 1974), p. 41. Karl Miller was a literary editor particularly hostile towards what he labelled 'consensus reviewing', and this led to his resignation in 1966 soon after the future 'man of the people', Paul Johnson, became editor. Having sat at Leavis's feet, Miller believed that the *New Statesman* was wrongly cultivating a more 'popular' style instead of continuing to acknowledge the existence of specialist interests. He would surely find little to quarrel with the record of recent successors, most notably the current books, arts and media editor, Boyd Tonkin. Squire would be equally delighted with the missionary endeavour of poetry editor, Adrian Mitchell.

6. During his own period as literary editor, in the 1930s and 1940s, Mortimer only consulted Kingsley Martin over suitable reviewers for books on politics, although the latter would sometimes exercise his right to select a volume for himself. Mortimer looked on MacCarthy, who gave him his first review work, as his mentor. V.S. Pritchett and himself notwithstanding, he judged MacCarthy to have been the *New Statesman's* finest literary editor.

Despite the occasional appointment of high-profile, opinionated literary editors, such as Martin Amis and David Caute in the late 1970s and early 1980s, past practice has been for the editor simply to read the proofs on Tuesday night and approve and amend the following morning. Today, information technology renders copy accessible at any time. Individual editor's idiosyncrasies and prejudices notwithstanding, *New Statesman & Society* has since 1972 come to rely on an ever-changing but nevertheless regular team of reliable critics, whether freelance or campus-based. In the view of Anthony Howard, who introduced this practice, standards slipped alarmingly during the two-year tenure of his predecessor, Richard Crossman. The ailing ex-minister might on the spur of the moment invite anyone, if he found them interesting, to write a review. In Howard's view, this random selection undermined the principle of consistency and a common identity across both halves of the paper, thus providing further evidence of Crossman's over-riding concern for the *New Statesman* to be seen as above all a *political* (read a loyal Labour) weekly. Raymond Mortimer in conversation with the author, 6 Dec. 1977. Anthony Howard in conversation with the author, 9 Dec. 1977.

For an insider's account of Crossman's unhappy editorship of the *New Statesman* from Labour losing power in June 1970 until March 1972 when the board requested his resignation, ostensibly on grounds of ill health, see A. Howard, *Crossman: The Pursuit of Power* (London: Jonathan Cape, 1990), pp. 300–12. Howard was assistant editor, the post Crossman himself had held for 18 years under Martin.

7. D. Daiches, *The Times Higher Educational Supplement*, 19 Sept. 1977. Q.D. Leavis, *Fiction and the Reading Public* (London, 1932).

8. C. Connolly, *Enemies of Promise* (London, 1938), pp. 166–7.

9. D.H. Lawrence to Edward Garnett, 30 Sept. and 6 Oct. 1913, A. Huxley (ed.), *The Letters of D.H. Lawrence* (London, 1932), pp. 141 and 144. Squire's letters to Edward Marsh suggest that he would genuinely have liked to pay more than a guinea a poem.

10. Squire judged the Futurists' views on sex and violence 'as old as they are unattractive', while Marinetti's poetry read like 'slightly more disjointed Whitman or Henley'. 'Solomon Eagle', 'Books in General', *New Statesman*, 10 Jan. 1914.

11. Hyams, *New Statesman*, p. 158.

12. Bennett suggested Walter Sickert as a more suitable, and more eminent, successor to Davies, but Lawrence Binyon was appointed. Arnold Bennett to J.C. Squire, 8 April 1917, New York.

MacCarthy reviewed *St Joan* over successive weeks, and he never flinched from public debate, whether via his column or on the correspondence pages. The very first review enthusiastically praised Bennett's pre-war play, *The Great Adventure*. Bennett's early memoranda to Squire contained flattering references to the theatre page, but by the end of 1917 his opinion had altered: MacCarthy was now referred to as 'poor, amateurish', 'very disappointing', and irresponsible in his indifference to deadlines. Ibid., 2 April and 5 May 1917, 20 Jan. and 8 April 1918, and 9 Feb. and 12 May 1919.

Today's *New Statesman & Society* has come full circle with, for example, Jonathan Romney rarely reviewing more than one cinema release, and Boyd Tonkin happy to address readers' complaints. However, throughout most of the intervening eight decades columnists have preferred to provide an overview of all the week's new productions, films and exhibitions.

13. D. MacCarthy, 'The Webbs as I saw them', in Cole (ed.), *The Webbs and their Work*, p. 120.
14. Ibid. D. MacCarthy, 'Apprenticeship', *Humanities* (London, 1935), pp. 17–18.
15. D. MacCarthy, 'A Glimpse of the Labour Party', ibid., p. 22.
16. Ibid., p. 20.
17. Woolf, *Beginning Again*, p. 131.
18. MacCarthy, 'A Glimpse of the Labour Party', *Humanities*, p. 20.
19. On the 'patriotic ruralism' of the Georgians, and the appeal of the rural myth to early twentieth-century socialists such as Squire and Ensor, see M.J. Weiner, *English Culture and the Decline of the Industrial Spirit 1850–1980* (Cambridge: CUP, 1981, Penguin paperback edn, 1985), pp. 58–61 and 62–4. Francis Mulhern drew attention to Q.D. Leavis's early essay insisting that 'The Discipline of Letters is seen to be simply the rules of the academic English club', and her later attack on the 'class affiliations of Bloomsbury culture' in 'Caterpillars of the Commonwealth Unite', *Scrutiny*, VII (1938), in Mulhern, *The Moment of 'Scrutiny'*, pp. 24–5, 32 note 81, and 122–4.
20. Q.D. Leavis, 'The Background of Twentieth Century Letters', *Scrutiny*, VIII (1939), pp. 74–5. F.R. Leavis, *New Bearings in English Poetry* (London, 1950), p. 14.
    Mulhern explores Q.D. Leavis's assertion in *Fiction and the Reading Public* that 'the people with power no longer represent intellectual authority and culture', leaving most critics either 'civilised' amateurs like MacCarthy or affectedly 'common' like Squire, or alternatively 'literary entrepreneurs' (Mulhern's term) like Bennett; he also makes the point that in Cambridge and beyond: 'The changes wrought by Richards and his contemporaries in the internal constitution of literary criticism implied a major revision of its comparative intellectual status. The 'revolution' in the discipline was also a revolution of literary criticism against the palsied cultural regime of post-war England.' Mulhern, *The Moment of 'Scrutiny'*, pp. 39–40 and 28.
    Ironically, Terry Eagleton's insistence that Leavis's belief in an 'essential Englishness' was essentially petit bourgeois ('English as a subject was in part the offshoot of a gradual shift in class tone within English culture: "Englishness" was less a matter of imperialist flag-waving than of country dancing; rural, populist and provincial rather than metropolitan and aristocratic') suggests that such 'chauvinism modulated by a new social class' would have suited Jack Squire and his ilk down to the ground. Eagleton, *Literary Theory: An Introduction*, p. 37.
21. A.O. Bell (ed.), *The Diary of Virginia Woolf, Vol. 1: 1915–19* (London, 1977), (?) Jan. 1919, pp. 241–2. Woolf, *Beginning Again*, pp. 134–5. In May 1914, for no apparent reason, MacCarthy had applied for an assistant librarianship at the House of Lords, but despite references from Sharp and Edward Marsh (then Churchill's private secretary) he failed to secure the post. Desmond MacCarthy to Edward Marsh, 30 May (1914), New York.
22. For a brief history of the *Calendar of Modern Letters* (March 1925–July 1927), and its claim that 'in the absence of an authoritative value-system, the properly "classical" discipline of criticism had lapsed into a subjectivism that was especially flagrant in the writings of its irresponsible and aesthetically reactionary academic exponents' (notably

Squire at the *London Mercury*), see Mulhern, *The Moment of 'Scrutiny'*, pp. 16–19.

23. Bell (ed.), *Woolf Diary, Vol. 1: 1915–19*, 15 Nov. 1918, p. 218.
24. A.O. Bell and A. McNeillie (eds), *The Diary of Virginia Woolf, Vol. 2: 1920–24* (London, 1978), 17 and 20 Jan. and 5 May 1920, pp. 9, 10 and 34.
25. J. Gross, *The Rise and Fall of the Man of Letters* (London: Weidenfeld & Nicolson, 1969), p. 267.
26. Hyams, *New Statesman*, p. 160. V.S. Pritchett, *Midnight Oil* (London, 1974, paperback edn), p. 169. MacCarthy edited *Life and Letters* from June 1928 to 1934, when another Great Queen Street regular, Hamish Miles, took over. The *New Statesman* initially gave the new monthly plenty of free publicity, and both magazines boasted many of the same contributors.
27. Pritchett, *Midnight Oil*, pp. 168–9. V.S. Pritchett to Edward Hyams, quoted in Hyams, *New Statesman*, pp. 156 and 161.
28. Ibid., pp. 161–2. MacCarthy had never sought a pay rise because of the paper's poor finances, but he was extremely annoyed to learn that Roberts was receiving double his salary. Desmond MacCarthy to Kingsley Martin, 1 July 1931, Kingsley Martin Papers.
29. Hyams, *New Statesman*, p. 163. K. Martin, *Father Figures*, p. 199. N. Nicolson (ed.), *Harold Nicolson Diaries and Letters 1930–39* (London, 1966), 19 Oct. 1932, p. 122.
30. Hyams, *New Statesman*, p. 164. Raymond Mortimer in conversation with the author, 6 Dec. 1977. D. Garnett, *The Familiar Faces: Vol. 3, The Golden Echo* (London, 1962), pp. 145 and 151.
    Keynes's papers at the Marshall Library, Cambridge University, reveal that it was Garnett who approached Keynes, in early September 1932. According to Skidelsky, Garnett received an annual annuity from Keynes after 1935, in which year he advised Martin on how to install Mortimer without a residue of ill will (as confirmed in *The Familiar Faces*). Skidelsky, *John Maynard Keynes: The Economist As Saviour 1920–1937*, pp. 528 and 536.
31. Woolf, *Beginning Again*, pp. 99–100, 114 and 130. Virginia Woolf, diary, 26 May 1919, New York, also quoted in Holroyd, *Lytton Strachey: A Critical Biography, Vol. II*, p. 351.
32. For a more detailed consideration of Woolf's review work, see Wilson, *Leonard Woolf*, pp. 119–20.
33. J.C. Squire to Leonard Woolf, 4, 6 and 8 Feb. 1918, Leonard Woolf Papers.
34. Correspondence of J.C. Squire and Clifford Sharp with Leonard Woolf, 1918–19, ibid.
35. S. Bedford, *Aldous Huxley: A Biography, Vol. 1, 1894–1939* (London: Chatto & Windus/Collins, 1973), pp. 82 and 107.
36. GLS, 'Avons-nous changé tout cela?', *New Statesman*, 2 Dec. 1913. GLS, 'Bonga-Bonga in Whitehall', *New Statesman*, 17 Jan. 1914. Holroyd, *Lytton Strachey: A Critical Biography, Vol. II*, p. 101. Squire clearly had a high opinion of Strachey as a writer, having previously sought to set him up as a ghost-writer for Augustus John.
37. 'The Art of Biography', *New Statesman*, 1 June 1918. Edward 'Dick' Shanks was a former editor of *Granta* at Cambridge. His wounds in France led to a posting in the War Office, where he began reviewing for Squire and writing verse. In 1919, with Squire one of the judges, Shanks became the first winner of the Hawthornden Prize. He was then appointed assistant editor of the *London Mercury* where he consolidated his reputation as a mediocre and deeply conservative critic. Lytton Strachey to J.C. Squire, (August?) 1918, quoted in Holroyd, *Lytton Strachey: A Critical Biography, Vol. II*, p. 349.
    Strachey and Virginia Woolf took every opportunity to vent their spleen over Squire; for example, see Virginia Woolf to Lytton Strachey, 29 Aug. 1921, N. Nicolson and J. Trautmann (eds), *The Question of Things Happening: The Letters of Virginia Woolf, Vol. II 1912–22* (London, 1976), p. 478.
38. Virginia Woolf to the Editor, *New Statesman*, 9 and 16 October 1920. After her second letter expressed dissatisfaction with the original reply of 'Affable Hawk', MacCarthy withdrew his remarks on the grounds that, 'If the freedom of women is impeded by the expression of my views, I shall argue no more'. Bell and McNeillie

(eds), *Woolf Diary, Vol. 2: 1920–24*, 22 Jan. 1922, p. 157. Woolf, *Downhill All The Way*, pp. 61–3.

Vita Sackville-West shared her friend's distaste for regular reviewing, but her review work for the *New Statesman* increased in the late 1920s as her husband, Harold Nicolson, became more involved with the paper.

39. R. Fry, 'Picasso', *New Statesman*, 29 Jan. 1921. Mortimer, a Francophile who judged Picasso 'much the greatest genius alive', and Osbert and Sacheverell Sitwell, helped deputise for Fry when he toured France and Spain in 1923 and 1924–25. Fry's involvement with the paper ceased following his return to the *Burlington Magazine* which he had at one time edited, and his agreement to write for Woolf at the *Nation*. Mortimer and Francis Birrell were happy to review anything – plays, exhibitions, books – as long as they got paid. By contrast, Edward Sackville-West was very selective, writing on little other than music.

40. 'Queen Victoria', *New Statesman*, 23 April 1921. In 1923 Clive Bell devoted a lengthy essay to eulogising Strachey, and five years later *Elizabeth and Essex* received the accolade of a review by the editor. Sharp, no friend of the author, judged it an unconvincing literary *tour de force*, with too little Elizabeth and too much Strachey. C.S., 'The Littleness of the Elizabethans', *New Statesman*, 1 Dec. 1928.

41. Augustine Birrell, former Liberal Cabinet minister and close associate of the Stephen family, was the father of Francis Birrell, in the early 1920s an intimate friend of Keynes. F.L. Lucas was a Classics don in post-war Cambridge who taught literature but resented bitterly the formal establishment of an honours degree in English. Long suspicious of Eliot, by the end of the 1920s he was targeting I.A. Richards and Q.D. Leavis. Lucas's ferocious attack on *Fiction and the Reading Public* spurred the Leavises and their circle to begin planning a successor to the *Calendar of Modern Letters*. Mulhern, *The Moment of 'Scrutiny'*, pp. 30–1.

42. Woolf, *Downhill All The Way*, pp. 97 and 130. Skidelsky, *John Maynard Keynes: The Economist As Saviour 1920–1937*, pp. 138–9. Moggridge, *Maynard Keynes: An Economist's Biography*, pp. 392–3. F. Spotts (ed.), *Letters of Leonard Woolf* (London, 1990), pp. 274–6. This edition contains on pp. 283–301 a selection of Woolf's correspondence during his period as literary editor of the *Nation and Athenaeum*, including, on pp. 284–5, a combative letter to Hubert Henderson, 26 September 1923, stating clearly the basis on which their working relationship must be maintained. For Virginia's unflattering assessment of Henderson, see Bell and McNeillie (eds), *Woolf Diary, Vol. II, 1920–24*, 11 Sept. 1922, p. 268.

43. Virginia Woolf to Roger Fry, 18 May 1923, N. Nicolson and J. Trautmann (eds), *A Change of Perspective: The Letters of Virginia Woolf, Vol. III, 1923–28* (London, 1977), p. 478.

44. Bell and McNeillie (eds), *Woolf Diary, Vol. II, 1920–24*, 8 July 1923, p. 352. Francis Birrell to Leonard Woolf, 30 Aug. 1923, Leonard Woolf Papers.

45. Bell and McNeillie (eds), *Woolf Diary, Vol. II, 1920–24*, 5 Sept. 1923, pp. 264–5. Francis Birrell to Leonard Woolf, undated, Leonard Woolf Papers. Clive Bell, Bertrand Russell, F.L. Lucas, Francis Birrell, and Raymond Mortimer to Clifford Sharp, (?) Sept. 1923, ibid.

46. Desmond MacCarthy to Clive Bell, Bertrand Russell, F.L. Lucas, Francis Birrell and Raymond Mortimer, 15 Sept. 1923, ibid. Raymond Mortimer to Leonard Woolf, 13 Sept. 1923, ibid.

By the time Mortimer returned from a tour of Persia and Russia in 1926 (later written up for the *New Statesman*), Virginia Woolf had changed her mind about him, persuading MacCarthy to re-employ him. In 1928, the year Mortimer unsuccessfully sought to earn a living in the USA, she pronounced him 'flowing, scintillating, brilliant'. Back in London a year later, he returned to the *New Statesman* and the *Nation* (and *Vogue*), meanwhile collaborating with Birrell on an unpublished play. After both papers merged in 1931, and Birrell became film critic, Mortimer, although no friend of Ellis Roberts, was appointed MacCarthy's assistant drama critic. Raymond Mortimer in conversation with the author, 8 Dec. 1977. Virginia Woolf to Vita

Sackville-West, 8 Dec. 1926, Nicolson and Trautmann (eds), *Letters of Virginia Woolf, Vol. III, 1923–28*, p. 307. Virginia Woolf to Edward Sackville-West, (?) Jan. 1927, ibid., p. 316. Virginia Woolf to Clive Bell, 21 April 1928, ibid., p. 487. Virginia Woolf to Clive Bell, 28 Jan. 1931, N. Nicolson and J. Trautmann (eds), *A Reflection of the Other Person: The Letters of Virginia Woolf, Vol. IV, 1929–31* (London, 1978), p. 283. Desmond MacCarthy to Leonard Woolf, (undated), Leonard Woolf Papers.

47. Bell and McNeillie (eds), *Woolf Diary, Vol. II, 1920–24*, 19 Dec. 1923, p. 278. Woolf, *Downhill All The Way*, p. 140.
48. Leonard Woolf to J.M. Keynes, 13 Dec. 1924, Leonard Woolf Papers.
49. Leonard Woolf to J.M. Keynes, 15 March 1925, ibid. Skidelsky, *John Maynard Keynes: The Economist As Saviour 1920–1937*, p. 139. One economy was for Woolf's annual salary to be reduced by one-fifth.
50. 'Affable Hawk', 'Books in General', *New Statesman*, 5 Nov. 1927.
51. M. Bradbury, *The Social Context of Modern English Literature* (Oxford: OUP, 1971), p. 20, quoted in Mulhern, *The Moment of 'Scrutiny'*, p. 17.
52. 'Affable Hawk', 'Books in General', *New Statesman*, 5 November 1927.
53. 'New Novels', *New Statesman*, 27 June 1914. Gould was a lecturer at London University as well as a contributor to the *Daily Herald*.
54. 'Solomon Eagle', 'Books in General', *New Statesman*, 14 April 1917. Arnold Bennett to J.C. Squire, 14 April 1917, New York.
55. 'Affable Hawk', 'Books in General', *New Statesman*, 31 March 1931.
56. 'Mr James Joyce in Progress' and 'New Novels', *New Statesman*, 28 June 1930.
57. Arnold Bennett to the Editor, *New Statesman*, 5 Sept. 1914.
58. Arnold Bennett to J.C. Squire, 14 April 1918, New York.
59. 'New Novels', *New Statesman*, 26 Dec. 1914 and 23 Oct. 1915. Shanks's review of Lawrence's *New Poems* appeared on 14 December 1918.
60. J.C. Squire to Edward Marsh, (?) Dec. 1913, quoted in C. Hassall, *A Biography of Edward Marsh* (New York: Harcourt Brace, 1959), p. 262. The unidentified poem was probably one of several that appeared in *Poetry* in January 1914.
61. J.C. Squire to Edward Marsh, 29 Dec. 1913 and (?) Jan. 1914, New York. Lawrence was only interested in payment. Although in Nottingham he had met the Webbs, Snowden and MacDonald at the home of the antiquarian and Labour activist William Hopkins, after he began teaching in Croydon he 'lost touch with the old "progressive" clique . . . [as] the socialist are so stupid and the Fabians so flat'. Having read the first issue, he wrote to his former colleague A.W. McLeod, 'What a measly thing Shaw's *New Statesman* is God help him!'. Two months later he asked McLeod for the magazine's address, intending to submit the 'sketches' which eventually appeared in the *English Review* in September 1913 and in *Twilight in Italy* in 1918. Fry's successor as art critic, Thomas Earp, although an old friend and admirer from Nottingham, could see little merit in the controversial paintings Lawrence briefly exhibited at the Warren Gallery in August 1929. As a result, like Squire, he was suitably berated in the posthumous 'More Pansies'. Yet more scorn is poured on 'socialist intellectuals' in a conversation between Constance Chatterley and her sister Hilda. D.H. Lawrence to William Hopkins, 24 Aug. 1910, quoted in H.T. Moore, *The Priest of Love: A Life of D.H. Lawrence* (London: Heinemann, 1974, Penguin paperback revised edn, 1976), pp. 154–5. D.H. Lawrence to A.W. Mcleod, 21 May and 22 July 1913, H.T. Moore (ed.), *The Collected Letters of D.H. Lawrence, Vol. 1* (London, 1962), pp. 205 and 215. D.H. Lawrence, *Lady Chatterley's Lover* (London: Penguin paperback edn, 1960), pp. 251–2.
62. H.G. Wells to Rebecca West, (?) Aug. 1922, quoted in G.N. Ray, *H.G. Wells and Rebecca West* (London: Macmillan, 1974), p. 123.
63. 'New Novels', *New Statesman*, 8 July 1922. In a dispute with a reader over the quality of women novelists, West concluded that 'In fact I'm right all along. But then, I generally am'. Rebecca West to the Editor, *New Statesman*, 16 Dec. 1922.
    In a BBC radio interview Dame Rebecca recalled that: 'Clifford Sharp hated me and I was proud of it. He was a *born* fascist – brutal, stupid, horrible . . . we had terrible

rows. He was just a tiresome drunk. He was very much supported by Beatrice Webb – she was the greatest *ass* there ever was.' Quoted in C.H. Rolph, *Further Particulars* (Oxford: OUP, 1987; paperback edn, 1988), pp. 142–3.

64. 'Notes on Novels', *New Statesman*, 9 July 1921, and 24 June and 8 July 1922.

65. Raymond Mortimer in conversation with the author, 6 Dec. 1977. Bell and McNeillie (eds), *Woolf Diary, Vol. II, 1920–24*, 22 July and 5 Sept. 1923, pp. 257 and 264. Pritchett, *Midnight Oil*, p. 202.

66. 'New Novels', *New Statesman*, 29 Sept. 1923. 'Affable Hawk', 'Books in General', *New Statesman*, 17 Nov. 1923.

67. 'Mr Lawrence in Mexico', *New Statesman*, 23 July 1927.

68. Connolly was probably responsible for persuading Roberts to accept an article on hop-picking by his old friend from prep. school and Eton, Eric Blair. George Orwell's diary of 17 days in the hop-fields of Kent later provided material for *A Clergyman's Daughter*, but extracts formed the basis of his first *New Statesman* article. With only four published reviews, plus 'The Spike' in the *New Adelphi*, Orwell saw his second full essay in print only nine days after first putting pen to paper in Bermondsey Public Library. Did Connolly simply notice that a manuscript from Eric Blair had arrived at Great Queen Street, or did he in fact meet up with Orwell much earlier than after his enthusiastic review of *Burmese Days* in the issue of 6 July 1935? Should Crick have accepted the reliability of Connolly's testimony in his 1973 memoirs *The Evening Colonnade*, simply dismissing Denys King-Farlow's claim that Orwell told him 'Without Connolly's help I don't think I would have got started as a writer when I came back from Burma'? Orwell's experience that autumn of sleeping in 'kips' in central London provided background for a second article, and the last before Martin rejected his exposure of the Communists' role in suppressing the Catalan anarchists and the POUM in May 1937 during the Spanish Civil War. E. Blair, 'Hop-picking', *New Statesman and Nation*, 17 Oct. 1931. E. Blair, 'Common Lodging Houses', *New Statesman*, 3 Sept. 1932. P. Stansky and W. Abrahams, *The Unknown Orwell* (London: Constable, 1972), pp. 239–40. B. Crick, *George Orwell: A Life* (London: Secker & Warburg, 1980; Penguin paperback edn, 1982), pp. 215–17 and 265–6.

On Orwell and the *New Statesman*, see B. Crick, 'Introduction', in A. George (ed.), *Unwelcome Guerrilla: George Orwell and the New Statesman, An Anthology* (London: New Statesman, 1985, paperback edn), pp. 5–10.

69. Virginia Woolf to Kingsley Martin, 5 June and 4 Nov. 1932, N. Nicolson and J. Trautmann (eds), *The Sickle Side of the Moon: The Letters of Virginia Woolf, Vol. V, 1932–35* (London, 1979), p. 283. Woolf's letters and diaries are littered with derogatory remarks concerning Martin, 'that stupid, but entirely well meaning, but muddled but incredibly bat eyed, mole snouted, dark, grouting and grovelling in the mire of Fleet Street, man . . .'. Virginia Woolf to Ethel Smythe, 1 Nov. 1933, ibid., p. 242.

70. Rupert Brooke to Edward Marsh, 6 Sept. and 1 Oct. 1913, G. Keynes (ed.), *The Letters of Rupert Brooke* (London, 1968), pp. 506 and 570. Other contributors to the Georgian anthologies whose work appeared in early issues included W.H. Davies, Hilaire Belloc, Walter de la Mare and John Freeman.

71. Rupert Brooke, 'An Unusual Young Man', *New Statesman*, 29 Aug. 1914.

72. J.C. Squire, 'Rupert Brooke', *New Statesman*, 1 May 1915.

73. Howarth, *Squire, Most Generous of Men*, pp. 93–115. 'I ['Solomon Eagle'] do not know whether people read Kipling in the trenches. Most of my correspondents at the front allege with the customary politeness of soldiers that their one solace is found in the perusal of the *New Statesman*.' 'Solomon Eagle', 'Books in General', *New Statesman*, 30 Jan. 1915. Life on the Western Front for Squire's correspondents must have been very harsh indeed!

74. Lytton Strachey, 'Mr Hardy's New Poems', *New Statesman*, 19 Dec. 1914. On the influence of *Satires of Circumstance* on Sassoon, see Fussell, *The Great War and Modern Memory*, pp. 3–7. S. Sassoon, *Siegfried's Journey 1916–1920* (London, 1945), p. 29.

75. S. Sassoon, 'Memorial Tablet (Great War)', in J. Reeves (ed.), *Georgian Poetry* (London: Penguin, 1962, paperback edn), p. 100.

76. 'Books in General', *New Statesman*, 24 Nov. 1917 and 3 Aug. 1918. Sassoon, *Siegfried's Journey 1916–1920*, p. 104. Squire's persistence in seeing Sassoon as an archetypal Georgian is reflected in the titles of four of the five poems he published: 'Thrushes', 'Idyll', 'Butterflies', and 'Vision'.

77. Bennett confided to Owen how highly he regarded Sassoon, perhaps encouraging Squire to publish his work. Though expressing sympathy for Sassoon's feelings about the war, he advised him to withdraw his 'Soldier's Declaration'. Sassoon, *Siegfried's Journey 1916–1920*, pp. 38, 50, 55–6 and 100. Wilfred Owen to Siegfried Sassoon, 27 Nov. 1917, H. Owen and J. Bell (eds), *Wilfred Owen: Collected Letters* (Oxford, 1967), p. 511, Wilfred Owen to Mrs Susan Owen, 19 Oct. 1918, ibid., p. 597. For Sharp's cavalier treatment of Sassoon after the war, see R. Hart-Davis (ed.), *Siegfried Sassoon, Diaries 1923–5* (London, 1985), 30 April 1925, pp. 238–9.

78. E. Farjeon, *Edward Thomas, The Last Four Years: Book One of the Memoirs of Eleanor Farjeon* (Oxford, 1958), p. 170. Edward Thomas to Eleanor Farjeon, 7 May 1913, ibid., p. 11. Edward Thomas, 'Soldiers Everywhere', *New Statesman*, 24 Nov. 1917.

79. 'Solomon Eagle', 'Books in General', *New Statesman*, 24 Nov. 1917. In the same column Squire expressed more muted praise for Ivor Gurney's *Severn and Somme*, and not surprisingly professed his ignorance of (Private) Isaac Rosenberg. R. Graves, *Goodbye To All That* (London, 1929; revised paperback edn, 1960), pp. 120, 205, 225 and 264. Graves's *New Statesman* poems later appeared in *Country Sentiment* (London, 1920).

80. Hyams, *New Statesman*, p. 160. Two unlikely poets, A.L. Rowse and Jacob Bronowski, made their *New Statesman* debuts in verse, as did the future drama critic and literary editor, T.C. Worsley, at that time a young teacher heavily influenced by Sassoon. Elizabeth Bibesco, Asquith's daughter and the wife of a Rumanian aristocrat, infuriated Keynes in the 1930s by insisting on being present at editorial lunches.

81. R. Campbell, *Light On A Dark Horse* (London, 1951; paperback edn, 1971), pp. 260–1. Humbert Wolfe, 'The Ranciad', *New Statesman and Nation*, 27 June 1931.
     The Georgiad was partly inspired by Wyndham Lewis's post-war satires, most notably *The Apes of God* which Sharp asked Campbell to review. Roberts rejected his original review in a long pompous letter. Campbell then contacted Wyndham Lewis and together they privately published *Satire and Fiction, also 'Have With You to Great Queen Street!' The History of a Rejected Review*, by Roy Campbell (Enemy Pamphlet, No. 1, London, 1930), a pamphlet containing a preface, the original review, correspondence including that of Roberts, and assorted reviews and letters praising *The Apes of God*. Campbell's association with the *New Statesman* was instantly terminated.

82. M. Bradbury (ed.), 'A review in retrospect', introduction to *The Calendar of Modern Letters*, Vol. 1, March–Aug. 1925, p. viii.

83. T.S. Eliot, 'Reflections on *vers libre*', *New Statesman*, 3 March 1917.

84. Bradbury (ed.), introduction to *The Calendar of Modern Letters*, Vol. 1, March–Aug. 1925, p. xi–xii.

85. F.L. Lucas, 'The Waste Land', *New Statesman*, 3 Nov. 1923. MacCarthy could scarcely demand more moderate language from Lucas when he himself had accused Eliot of steering dangerously towards pedantry, and of joining Joyce up a linguistic cul-de-sac. D. MacCarthy, 'New Poets III – T.S. Eliot', *New Statesman*, 8 Jan. 1921. 'Affable Hawk', 'Books in General', *New Statesman*, 4 Nov. 1922.

86. Leavis made the elementary point which most *New Statesman* critics from Squire onwards had wilfully ignored: 'His [Eliot's] poetry is more conscious of the past than any other that is being written in English today. This most modern of the moderns is more truly traditional than the "traditionalists".' F.R. Leavis, 'T.S. Eliot – A Reply to the Condescending', *Cambridge Review*, Feb. 1929.

87. F.R. Leavis, 'Towards Standards of Criticism', *'Anna Karenina' and Other Essays* (London, 1967), p. 232.

Chapter 9, The years of crisis: The *New Statesman* in the late 1920s, pp. 210–237.

1. Northcliffe quoted in C. Sharp, 'Early Days', *New Statesman and Nation*, 14 April

1934. Bartlett was a first-class reporter who had spent seven years in Europe for Reuters and the *Daily Herald* before Northcliffe persuaded him to join *The Times*. Huddleston wrote prolifically on France between the wars (22 books) and was Paris correspondent for at least eight British and American publications. Knowing every café intellectual from Aragon to Drieu La Rochelle, he became a naturalised citizen during the Vichy years. S. Huddleston, *In My Time: An Observer's Record of War and Peace* (London, 1938).

2. 'Comments', *New Statesman*, 6 Oct. 1928. 'British Foreign Policy', *New Statesman*, 20 Oct. 1928. R. MacDonald, *Forward*, 22 Dec. 1928, quoted in Marquand, *Ramsay MacDonald*, p. 473. For the Leader of the Opposition's high profile approach to foreign affairs on both sides of the Atlantic 1927–9, see ibid., pp. 465–74, and for speculation about him as a future Nobel Peace Prize winner, see Morgan, *J. Ramsay MacDonald*, p. 142.

3. 'The Future of Austria', *New Statesman*, 23 July 1927. To be fair to Lloyd, the Austrian Social Democrats had sought *Anschluss* in 1919, and in the 1920s its ultimate attainment remained consistent with their internationalist ideals.

4. Young (ed.), *Lockhart Diaries*, 2 March and 9 May 1928, pp. 68 and 69–70. Drawing on the voluminous diaries rather than the memoirs, which largely ignore the Fleet Street years, Kenneth Young provided a lively portrait of Lockhart as journalist and socialite in ibid., Introduction, pp. 17–19.

5. In 1926 Robert Lynd introduced Sharp to David Low, by then in his last year at the *Star* before being enticed by Beaverbrook to the *Evening Standard*. The result was a series of 20 *portraits chargés*, published as offset plate-stamped inserts. A second series appeared in 1933, three years after Low replaced Bennett on the board, and a year after his tour of Russia with Kingsley Martin produced the jointly authored *Low's Russian Sketchbook* (London: Gollancz, 1932). A. Smith, 'Low and Lord Beaverbrook: The Cartoonist and the Newspaper Proprietor', *Encounter*, Dec. 1985, pp. 7–24. C. Seymour-Ure and J. Schoff, *David Low* (London: Secker & Warburg, 1985, paperback edn), pp. 35–8 and 73–4

6. Young (ed.), *Lockhart Diaries*, 23 May 1928 and 25 June 1930, pp. 70 and 123. By the spring of 1930 Lockhart was writing so much for the *Sunday Express* and the *Evening Standard* that he no longer had time to edit 'Londoner's Diary', eventually handing the job over to Harold Nicolson. Debt obliged him to resume regular contributions to the *New Statesman*, and in addition to writing on Russia he complemented F.A. Voigt's incisive but intermittent Berlin reports until the latter was expelled in 1933. In the aftermath of a nervous breakdown and convalescence in Switzerland, and still at Beaverbrook's beck and call, Lockhart was increasingly unreliable with his copy. Yet Lloyd and then Martin continued to rely heavily upon his analysis of events in Germany. As a result, the *New Statesman and Nation* seriously underestimated the threat from National Socialism, even after Martin's visit to Berlin in August 1931, failing to appreciate the depth of Hitler's popularity and the strength of antagonism between the Communists and the Social Democrats. For coverage of the rise of National Socialism, see A. Smith, 'The *New Statesman* 1913–31', pp. 278–83.

   A scholar, a 'lewd and leftist' intimate of the German liberal intelligentsia, and a correspondent for the *Manchester Guardian* throughout the years of the Weimar Republic, in the winter of 1939–40 Frederick Voigt worked alongside Crossman in the Political Intelligence Department that Lockhart was commissioned to re-establish at the start of the war.

7. 'The Dangerous Irresponsibility of the Secret Service', *New Statesman*, 18 June 1927.

8. 'Comments' and 'These Melodramatists', *New Statesman*, 21 May 1927. 'A Stupid Business', *New Statesman*, 28 May 1927. For the Arcos raid of 12–15 May 1927, see Andrew, *Secret Service*, pp. 458–9 and 469–72, and Rolph, *Further Particulars*, pp. 62–4. In his other persona, as PC (ultimately Inspector) C.R. Hewitt of the City of London Police, Rolph participated in the Arcos raid, providing an hilarious account in the second volume of his memoirs.

9. 'Comments', *New Statesman*, 1 June 1929. Lockhart's access to intelligence on Russia

was via John Wheeler-Bennett at the Royal Institute of International Affairs (Chatham House), see Young (ed.), *Lockhart Diaries*, 27 Aug. 1929, p. 105. For more detailed treatment of coverage in the 1920s and early 1930s of Russia, and of Fascist Italy, see A. Smith, ' The *New Statesman* 1913–31', pp. 257–77, and 'The Response of British Intellectuals to Fascist Italy 1922–32', Kent MA, 1975, pp. 238–88.

10. 'The future and the Left', *New Statesman*, 4 Jan. 1980. The editor was Bruce Page.

11. . . . one could be absolutely certain of receiving by the first post on Wednesday morning an impeccable article, of exactly so many thousand words, on one of those topical, but grimly gritty, subjects, which are the despair of editors – and after of readers – for they lie in the depressing region where economics, industry, trade unionism produce the most important, insoluble, and boring problems.

L. Woolf, *The Journey Not the Arrival Matters: An Autobiography of the Years 1939–1969* (London, 1969), p. 137. C. Sharp, 'Early Days', *New Statesman and Nation*, 14 April 1934.

12. G.D.H. Cole, *The Next Ten Years in British Social and Economic Policy* (London, 1929), pp. vii–ix.

13. Influenced by Keynes, appalled by fascist or communist alternatives, and convinced that the free-market philosophy of pre-1914 was wholly inappropriate to the economic circumstances of the Depression, by the second half of the 1930s a growing body of 'middle opinion' looked to planning – the long-term management of the economy and of welfare provision, combined with more efficient organisation of parliamentary government – as the only means of resolving mass unemployment, and securing a higher level of prosperity and social justice for all. A significant number of those involved in PEP (Political and Economic Planning) and The Next Five Years Group became critics of the National government's foreign as well as its domestic policies, most notably Harold Macmillan, then a maverick Tory backbencher. A. Marwick, 'Middle Opinion in the Thirties: Planning, Progress and Political "Agreement"', *English Historical Review* (April 1964), pp. 285–298. R. Skidelsky, 'Keynes and the left', *New Statesman & Society*, 16 April 1993.

14. P. Williams, *Hugh Gaitskell: A Political Biography* (London: Jonathan Cape, 1979), pp. 20–1 and 43.

15. '. . . he [Cole] sought to infuse as much of the socialist spirit as he felt the electorate and the problems of the time could bear, and the Labour Party could be persuaded to fight an election with.' Carpenter, *G.D.H. Cole: An Intellectual Biography*, p. 133.

16. Quoted by Skidelsky, *John Maynard Keynes: The Economist As Saviour 1920–1937*, p. 691.

17. Unlike the EAC, with its remit from MacDonald to advise on short- and medium-term handling of the economy, the Macmillan Committee on Finance and Industry was an inquiry set up two months earlier, on 25 November 1929, to report on the influence of the banking system. Like Bevin (General Secretary, TGWU), Keynes sat on both bodies, and the working relationship established by the two men paralleled and complemented that established by Keynes and Cole. Indeed, in many respects it was a lot stronger, and, looking ahead to the Second World War, far more profitable. Skidelsky, *John Maynard Keynes: The Economist As Saviour 1920–1937*, pp. 343–6 and 363–7. Moggridge, *Maynard Keynes: An Economist's Biography*, pp. 495–6 and 536.

18. Skidelsky, *John Maynard Keynes: The Economist As Saviour 1920–1937*, p. 362.

19. Ibid.

20. 'The Way to Deal with Unemployment', *New Statesman*, 1 Aug. 1925.

21. An example of how over the years the 'Yellow Book' has acquired a semi-mythical status can be found in J. Campbell, 'The Renewal of Liberalism: Liberalism without Liberals', in Peele and Cook (eds), *The Politics of Reappraisal 1918–39*, pp. 88–9. Skidelsky, *John Maynard Keynes: The Economist As Saviour 1920–1937*, p. 268. 'Liberalism and the Industrial Future', *New Statesman*, 11 Feb. 1928.

22. 'British Industry and the Future', *New Statesman*, 17 Dec. 1927. The horrors of deficit spending for the Labour Front Bench was aptly illustrated by Snowden's

warning at the 1928 conference of the 'terrible price' of manipulating the credit system to create jobs, quoted in Marquand, *Ramsay MacDonald*, p. 481.

23. 'The Policy of Labour', *New Statesman*, 11 July 1928.
24. Marquand, *Ramsay MacDonald*, p. 485.
25. See Koss, *Asquith*, pp. 271–80.
26. David Lloyd George, 'The Statesman's Task', *Nation*, 12 April 1924. C. Wrigley, *Lloyd George* (Oxford: Blackwell, 1992, paperback edn), pp. 124–5. Masterman quoted in L. Masterman, *C.F.G. Masterman* (London: Nicholson & Watson, 1939), p. 346.
27. 'Liberal Quarrels', *New Statesman*, 12 Dec. 1925. 'Comments', *New Statesman*, 30 Jan. 1926.
28. 'Comments', *New Statesman*, 30 Jan. 1926.
29. Wrigley, *Lloyd George*, pp. 128–9. Thus, in *Reynold's News*, 6 June 1926, in the aftermath of the General Strike, Snowden wrote that if Lloyd George continued to reanimate the Liberal Party it could become a 'determining force in British politics for some years to come . . . So long as he is in politics he can never be ignored.'
30. 'The Incomprehensible Split', *New Statesman*, 12 June 1926. For the confrontation between Asquith and Lloyd George during and after the General Strike, see Koss, *Asquith*, pp. 276–81, Jenkins, *Asquith*, pp. 514–17, and T. Wilson, *The Downfall of the Liberal Party 1914–35* (London: Collins, 1966), pp. 329–36.

    Sharp chose this moment to offer a one-year contract to A.P. Nicholson, a veteran 'Cocoa Press' lobby correspondent (*Daily News*, *Daily Chronicle*) currently with the one Liberal paper to support Asquith's outright condemnation of the strikers, the *Westminster Gazette*.
31. '"True Liberalism"', *New Statesman*, 4 Sept. 1926.
32. 'Comments', *New Statesman*, 2 April and 8 Oct. 1927.
33. Beatrice Webb to Lord Haldane, 14 Aug. 1928, MacKenzie (ed.), *Webb Letters*, p. 301.
34. Beatrice Webb, diary, 12 Aug. 1928, Passfield Papers.
35. 'Comments', *New Statesman*, 20 Oct. 1928. Beatrice Webb to Lord Haldane, 14 Aug. 1928, MacKenzie (ed.), *Webb Letters*, p. 301. 'The Coming Liberal–Labour Alliance', *New Statesman*, 10 Nov. 1928.
36. Ramsay MacDonald, diary, 6 Nov. 1928, Ramsay MacDonald Papers.
37. 'The Two Problems of Unemployment', *New Statesman*, 30 March 1929.
38. See, for example, 'Where We Stand in the Coal Strike', *New Statesman*, 17 April 1926. Sir Herbert Samuel chaired the Royal Commission, appointed in September 1925 to examine the current state of the coal industry. In its report, published on 11 March 1926, it rejected the colliery owners' demand for longer hours, but effectively sanctioned a reduction in wages. The first half of April was taken up with fresh negotiations between the Mining Association and the Miners' Federation, and the second half witnessed abortive attempts at arbitration by the government and the TUC Industrial Committee. Failure to secure the withdrawal of lock-outs led to the TUC General Council taking responsibility for a general strike in support of the miners. The government broke off last-minute negotiations on the night of 2–3 May, following the refusal of *Daily Mail* compositors to set an editorial attacking the trade unions.
39. 'This Unnecessary Strike', *New Statesman*, 8 May 1926.
40. 'Panic and Pugnacity', *New Statesman*, 15 May 1926.
41. 'Comments', *New Statesman*, 15 May 1926.

    Sidney says the forty miners' member are obdurate about any reduction in wages or lengthening of hours and were furious with J.H. Thomas for suggesting that if the coal-owners' notices were withdrawn, the miners would consider the question of a temporary reduction of wages during the immediate re-organization of the industry.

    Beatrice Webb, diary, 7 May 1926, Passfield Papers.
42. 'Comments', *New Statesman*, 22 May 1926.
43. 'Some Lessons of the Late General Strike', *New Statesman*, 19 June 1926. Sidney

Webb was wholly opposed to the General Strike, as confirmed by Beatrice who privately reflected on when such action was justified and when not (in this case, 'in order to compel the employers of a particular industry to yield to the men's demands', definitely not). See Beatrice Webb, diary, Passfield Papers, 4 May 1926.

44. Cole (ed.), *Beatrice Webb's Diaries 1924–1932*, 24 Oct. 1926, p. 124.
45. 'Just You Wait', *New Statesman*, 30 Oct. 1926. Sharp's loathing of Baldwin was so intense that he, rather than Cole, assumed responsibility in the spring of 1927 for the *New Statesman*'s aggressive campaign against passage of the Trades Disputes Bill.
46. Carpenter, *G.D.H. Cole: An Intellectual Biography*, p. 131.
47. 'The Labour Party, the ILP, and the Trade Unions', *New Statesman*, 11 April 1925.
48. Ibid. Dowse, *Left in the Centre*, pp. 130–1. For details of the 'living wage' proposals and 1925–26 *New Leader* campaign, see F.M. Leventhal, 'H.N. Brailsford and the *New Leader*', *Journal of Contemporary History*, 9 (1974), pp. 107–8.
49. 'A Socialist Dilemma', *New Statesman*, 18 April 1925.
50. 'Comments', *New Statesman*, 19 Dec. 1925.
51. 'The ILP Conference', *New Statesman*, 10 April 1926. Marquand, *Ramsay MacDonald*, p. 450. For details of the 'Socialism in Our Time' campaign and the response of the Labour leadership, see ibid., p. 453, and Miliband, *Parliamentary Socialism*, p. 152.
52. 'The ILP Conference', *New Statesman*, 10 April 1926.
53. Cole (ed.), *Beatrice Webb's Diaries 1924–32*, 1 Sept. 1926, p. 119. Weiner has pointed out that in public MacDonald opposed the 'living wage' on the grounds that it implicitly accepted the capitalist myth that material enrichment was more important than improving the quality of life. Weiner, *English Culture and the Decline of the Industrial Spirit 1850–1980*, pp. 121–2.
54. 'The Labour Party and the Future', *New Statesman*, 1 Jan. 1927.
55. See Ch. 10.
56. 'Where is Socialism Going', *New Statesman*, 27 Aug. 1927. 'The Rivals in Conference', *New Statesman*, 15 Oct. 1927.
57. 'Mr Snowden and the ILP', *New Statesman*, 7 Jan. 1928. 'The ILP', *New Statesman*, 14 April 1928. The fullest history of the ILP suggests that MacDonald enjoyed the support of a majority of the 112 MPs, as well as the party's regional press, and branches in Scotland, Bradford and Bermondsey. Dowse, *Left in the Centre*, pp. 140–1.
58. 'Comments', *New Statesman*, 23 June 1928.
59. Cook–Maxton Manifesto, June 1928, quoted in Miliband, *Parliamentary Socialism*, p. 157.
60. John Wheatley, Labour Party Annual Conference Report, 1928, quoted in ibid., p. 158.
61.   It comes natural to them [J. Maxton and A.J. Cook] to think and speak in terms, not of a five or ten years' programme of practical reforms, but of a life to come.... So they think the Labour Party has given up its faith and surrendered its arms, though in fact it has only sat down to beleaguer the city of capitalism instead of taking it by storm.

   'The Policy of Labour', *New Statesman*, 14 July 1928. 'The Labour Party and the Nation', *New Statesman*, 13 Oct. 1928.
62. P. Quennell, *The Marble Foot: An Autobiography 1905–38* (London, 1976), p. 153. Pritchett, *Midnight Oil*, p. 168.
63. Beatrice Webb, diary, 12 August 1928, Passfield Papers.
64. Quennell, *The Marble Foot*, p. 153.
65. 'Comments', *New Statesman*, 28 Jan. 1928. For detailed accounts of both cases, see Hyams, *New Statesman*, pp. 83–5 and 102–6. Sixty-five years and one day later came the next serious threat from litigation to the paper's continued existence. For the eightieth birthday relaunch issue Steve Platt – with a rashness worthy of the late Sharp, and with a similar indifference to boardroom concerns – co-authored a cover

story linking John Major with the caterer Clare Latimer. Foolish, even scurrilous, but by no means definitely libellous, the article resulted six months later in out-of-court settlements once it became clear how poor were the chances of persuading a jury to deliver a verdict against the Prime Minister. The paper was further hit by having to cover the distributors' indemnity costs, and by W.H. Smith and Menzies refusing to distribute the cause of the controversy. The fact that Menzies continued not to stock the magazine, and that Major and Latimer refused to accept the very full expression of regret that appeared the following week, fuelled speculation that the Conservative Party saw an opportunity to achieve a long-desired goal, namely killing off the left's most famous weekly. *New Statesman & Society* spent ten months seeking to raise £250,000 with which to cover legal costs and settlements. In November 1993 the paper was saved from going under, or having a former Tory MP, Derek Coombs, become the major shareholder, by socialist millionaires Philip and Geraldine Jeffrey injecting £400,000 into a restructured company. Reprimanded for using the letters page as a means of rallying support against the Coombs bid, Steve Platt survived, and after a sticky meeting with the board, had his contract renewed in spring 1994. Platt personally was in a much stronger position than Sharp, burnt out and drink-sodden, but his paper was under far greater threat than in 1928. S. Platt and N. Mann, ' . . . the curious case of John Major's "mistress"', *New Statesman & Society*, 29 Jan. 1993. 'The Prime Minister and the New Statesman', *New Statesman & Society*, 5 Feb. 1993. J. Dugdale, 'New life for the Statesman', *Guardian*, 1 Nov. 1993. 'The future of NSS', *New Statesman & Society*, 12 Nov. 1993.
66. Beatrice Webb, diary, 12 August 1928, Passfield Papers.
67. Hyams, *New Statesman*, p. 117. Hyams quoted Leonard Woolf's failure to recognise the seriousness of Sharp's condition as conclusive evidence that he was discreet in his drinking. However, the majority of evidence suggests his alcoholism was evident to all.
68. Bennett quoted in R. Pound, *Arnold Bennett* (London: Heinemann, 1952), p. 338.

Chapter 10, The rise and fall of the Labour government and the fall and rise of the *New Statesman and Nation*, 1930–31, pp. 238–260.

1. C.H. Rolph, *Kingsley: The Life, Letters and Diaries of Kingsley Martin* (London: Victor Gollancz, 1973), p. 310.
2. The man whom only conscription could silence bowed out with an unintentionally ironic tribute to his old adversary, insisting that 'What matters is not what Mr. Lloyd George did ten or twelve years ago, but what he is going to do tomorrow.' 'Liberalism', *New Statesman*, 25 Jan. 1930.
3. Nobody at Great Queen Street seriously questioned the tone, length and style of Cole's articles, which, however worthy and prescient, were often taxing. Devotees of the front half were not expected to sit down, relax, and enjoy a good read. It was another eight years before Crossman, as assistant editor, made the heretical suggestion that Cole and Harold Laski were in fact very boring and thus 'killing the paper'. Howard, *Crossman: The Pursuit of Power*, p. 76.
4. 'Comments', *New Statesman*, 21 Feb. 1931.
5. A. Bullock, *The Life and Times of Ernest Bevin: Vol. 1, Trade Union Union Leader 1881–1940* (London: Heinemann, 1960), p. 500. As late as August 1931 Cole was reassuring a sympathetic MacDonald that the NFRB would not simply be demanding an ever-greater 'largesse to the community', but producing realistic and relevant policy documents 'inspired by Socialist ideas throughout'. See Ramsay MacDonald to Captain Bennett, 8 Aug. 1931, quoted in Marquand, *Ramsay MacDonald*, pp. 609–10. For Cole and 'Zip' (SSIP), see M. Cole, 'The Society for Socialist Inquiry and Propaganda' in A. Briggs and J. Saville (eds), *Essays in Labour History 1918–39* (London: Croom Helm, 1977), pp. 190–203.
6. 'The Policy of the Trade Unions', *New Statesman and Nation*, 5 Sept. 1931. R. Skidelsky, *Oswald Mosley* (London: Macmillan, 1975), p. 223.
7. 'Comments' and 'The Temper of Trade Unionism', *New Statesman*, 29 June 1929.

8. Cole (ed.), *Beatrice Webb's Diaries 1924–32*, 18 Aug. 1929, p. 216.
9. 'The First Six Months', *New Statesman*, 7 Dec. 1929. 'Comments', *New Statesman*, 14 Dec. 1929.
10. H.B. Lees-Smith, a future Cabinet minister (March–August 1931, President of the Board of Education) as well as a *New Statesman* director, happily passed on his inside knowledge that Thomas was 'in the hands of that arch-reactionary, Horace Wilson', deliberately avoiding Mosley and Johnston (and George Lansbury, the First Commissioner of Works), and relying on the benevolent protection of the Prime Minister. MacKenzie (eds) *The Diary of Beatrice Webb 1924–1943*, 28 July 1929, pp. 183–4.
11. 'Work or Doles?', *New Statesman*, 5 Oct. 1929.
12. Marquand, *Ramsay MacDonald*, pp. 523–4. Skidelsky, *John Maynard Keynes: The Economist As Saviour 1920–1937*, pp. 343–5.
13. MacKenzie (eds), *The Diary of Beatrice Webb 1924–1943*, 2 Dec. 1929, pp. 202–3. For a devastating portrait of Thomas, already a broken man and with still six months to serve as Lord Privy Seal, see ibid., 21 Dec. 1929, p. 205.
14. 'Mr Thomas and his Colleagues', *New Statesman*, 15 Feb. 1930.
15. 'Mr Snowden's Budget', *New Statesman*, 19 April 1930.
16. MacKenzie (eds), *The Diary of Beatrice Webb 1924–1943*, 29 May 1929, pp. 217–18.
17. 'The Two Millions', *New Statesman*, 16 Aug. 1930.
18. 'The Limits of Socialism', *New Statesman*, 17 May 1930.
19. Sidney Webb was now Lord Passfield, with ministerial responsibility for both the Colonial and Dominion Offices until the latter portfolio was transferred to Thomas on 5 June 1930.
20. 'Comments', *New Statesman*, 26 April 1930. 'Comments', *New Statesman and Nation*, 4 July 1931. Cole could speak with authority on the subject of national insurance, being chairman of an EAC sub-committee that adopted a surprisingly hard line in its recommendations on preventing expenditure from getting out of control. See Marquand, *Ramsay MacDonald*, pp. 585–6.
21. 'Comments', *New Statesman*, 11 Oct. 1930. 'Parties and Programmes', *New Statesman*, 1 Nov. 1930.
22. 'A New Reform Bill?', *New Statesman*, 31 Jan. 1931. For Cole and Lloyd's changing view of Mosley, and the 1930–31 origins of 'Zip' (SSIP), see Cole, 'The Society for Socialist Inquiry and Propaganda', pp. 193–7. For Cole's view of the role of intellectuals in rebuilding Labour after 1931, the fate of 'Zip', and the longer-term importance to Cole of the NFRB, see R. Dare, 'Instinct and Organization: Intellectuals and British Labour after 1931', *The Historical Journal*, 26, 3 (1983), pp. 687–90 and 694–5.

   Martin's indifference in the late 1930s to the day-to-day conduct of party politics – an emotional detachment which bemused Attlee – had its origins in the final painful months of Labour's second period in office. Clement Attlee to Kingsley Martin, 9 May 1937, Kingsley Martin Papers. 'Kingsley [Martin] believed, to the end of his life, that Britain would sooner or later turn to some "controlled" kind of dictatorship, and would discover too late that the "controller" had withered like an umbilical cord.' Rolph, *Kingsley: The Life, Letters and Diaries of Kingsley Martin*, pp. 209–10.
23. C.M. Lloyd to Beatrice Webb, 10 Dec. 1930, quoted in Williams, *Hugh Gaitskell*, p. 45. G.D.H. Cole to Beatrice Webb, (?) Dec. 1930, quoted in Skidelsky, *Oswald Mosley*, p. 239. 'More Plans', *New Statesman*, 13 Dec. 1930.

   An example of how insensitive Mosley was to the loyalties, traditions, and code of behaviour peculiar to the Labour Party was his rumoured attempt to persuade 'Uncle Arthur' to challenge MacDonald for the leadership. See Marquand, *Ramsay MacDonald*, p. 580.

   For Keynes's contacts with Mosley and membership of the EAC committee of economists, see Skidelsky, *John Maynard Keynes: The Economist As Saviour 1920–1937*, pp. 363–78. For Robbins' direct line to Snowden, via his former LSE tutor Hugh Dalton (in 1930 a junior minister at the Foreign Office), see Pimlott, *Hugh Dalton*, pp. 162–3.
24. The 1988 merger with *New Society*, although greeted with similar indifference by all

but the *Guardian*, was marked by recrimination and a lingering ill will over appointments; see A. Smith, 'Roots of a new hybrid', *The Times Higher Educational Supplement*, 8 July 1988.

25. For autobiography, biography and tribute, see K. Martin, *Father Figures* (London, 1966) and *Editor* (London, 1966), Rolph, *Kingsley: The Life, Letters and Diaries of Kingsley Martin*, and M. Jones (ed.), *Kingsley Martin: Portrait and Self-Portrait* (London: Barrie & Jenkins, 1969).
26. L. Woolf, 'Kingsley Martin', *Political Quarterly*, 40 (1969), p. 241. E.J. Scott to Kingsley Martin, (?) July 1930, Kingsley Martin Papers. For Martin's experience at the *Manchester Guardian*, see P. Clarke, *Liberals and Social Democrats*, pp. 253–4, and Koss, *The Rise and Fall of the Political Press in Britain 2*, p. 497. For accounts of the merger other than Martin's own memoirs, see Hyams, *New Statesman*, pp. 108–25, and Rolph, *Kingsley: The Life, Letters and Diaries of Kingsley Martin*, pp. 149–61.
27. Kingsley Martin to C.M. Lloyd, 3 July 1930, Kingsley Martin Papers. Martin wrote to Woolf, J.L. Hammond and other friends in London asking them for any help they could give him in securing a new job. He made no mention of his *New Statesman* hopes to Woolf, intimating instead that he would resume his academic career. Kingsley Martin to Leonard Woolf, 19 Aug. 1930, Berg Collection.
28. J.M. Keynes to Kingsley Martin, 20 Aug. 1930, Kingsley Martin Papers.
29. The fellowship thesis was published in 1924 under the title, *The Triumph of Lord Palmerston: A Study of Public Opinion in England before the Crimean War*. Skidelsky, *John Maynard Keynes: The Economist As Saviour 1920–1937*, p. 388. Bennett quoted in Pound, *Arnold Bennett*, p. 338.
30. Young (ed.), *Lockhart Diaries*, 25 June 1930 and 29 March 1931, pp. 123 and 159. Clarke, *Liberals and Social Democrats*, pp. 254–5. Sidney Webb made a conscious decision not to intervene at the end of the year when the board appeared to be choosing between Cole and Martin. He clearly had no inkling that Cole was interviewed solely out of courtesy. Sidney Webb to Beatrice Webb, 11 Dec. 1930, MacKenzie (ed.), *Letters of Sidney and Beatrice Webb, Vol. III, 1912–47*, p. 341.
31. Kingsley Martin to J.M. Keynes, 26 Nov. 1930, J.M. Keynes Papers.
32. J.M. Keynes to Kingsley Martin, 8 Jan. 1931, Kingsley Martin Papers. Correspondence between J.M. Keynes and Arnold Rowntree, Jan.–Feb. 1931, J.M. Keynes Papers. Hyams, *New Statesman*, pp. 115–23.
33. Virginia Woolf to Vanessa Bell, 25 Dec. 1930, Nicolson and Trautmann (eds), *Letters of Virginia Woolf, Vol. III, 1929–31*, p. 263. Virginia Woolf to Clive Bell, 28 Jan. 1931, ibid.
34. J.M. Keynes to D. Lloyd George, 13 Jan. 1931, David Lloyd George Papers. D. Lloyd George to J.M. Keynes, 14 Jan. 1931, ibid.
35. Skidelsky, *John Maynard Keynes: The Economist As Saviour 1920–1937*, p. 389.
36. 'Comments', *New Statesman*, 14 Feb. 1930.
37. 'The Alternatives', *New Statesman and Nation*, 28 Feb. 1931.
38. J.M. Keynes to Kingsley Martin, 1 March 1931, Kingsley Martin Papers.
39. Clement Attlee's note reproduced in Martin, *Father Figures*, p. 207.
40. 'The Labour Party and the Future', *New Statesman and Nation*, 14 March 1931.
41. '1931 – The Economic Outlook', *New Statesman and Nation*, 3 Jan. 1931.
42. Marquand, *Ramsay MacDonald*, pp. 554–64.
43. J.M. Keynes, 'Proposals for a Revenue Tariff', *New Statesman and Nation*, 7 March 1931. Keynes was paid £100 by Lord Rothermere to write a more popular version for the *Daily Mail*, thus gaining even more publicity for the original piece *and* for the weekly which published it.
44. On plans to despatch proof copies, see J.M. Keynes to Kingsley Martin, 1 March 1931, Kingsley Martin Papers. For Snowden's negative response and Keynes's reaction, see Skidelsky, *John Maynard Keynes: The Economist As Saviour 1920–1937*, pp. 387–8, and Moggridge, *Maynard Keynes: An Economist's Biography*, p. 509. J.M. Keynes to Ramsay MacDonald, 5 March 1931, Ramsay MacDonald Papers, quoted in Marquand, *Ramsay MacDonald*, p. 590.

45. Ibid., p. 591.
46. Martin, *Editor*, p. 57. Robbins argued that Keynes had overestimated the revenue yield by as much as £30 million, and that anyway there were much better ways of generating revenue than via tariffs. He lamented that the man who 'shattered the moral foundations of the Treaty of Versailles should now turn his magnificent gifts to the service of the mean and petty devices of economic nationalism'. Lionel Robbins to the Editor, *New Statesman and Nation*, 14 March 1931.
47. For Beatrice's contrasting impressions of Keynes and Beveridge ('who heartily dislikes Keynes and regards him as a quack in economics'), see MacKenzie (eds), *The Diary of Beatrice Webb 1924–1943*, 23 Sept. 1931, p. 260. 'Economic Notes on Free Trade' were short single column articles dealing with specific points raised by, among others, fellow director E.D. Simon, Ramsay Muir and Evan Durbin. For a summary of the arguments advanced on both sides in the two months before Keynes left for Chicago at the end of May, see Skidelsky, *John Maynard Keynes: The Economist As Saviour 1920–1937*, pp. 386–7, and Moggridge, *Maynard Keynes: An Economist's Biography*, p. 509. For a concise exposition of how Keynes's views on protection evolved during 1930–31, see ibid., pp. 511–14.
48. Circulation figures quoted in Hyams, *New Statesman*, p. 122.
49. Martin, *Editor*, p. 56.
50. Lord Boothby quoted in Rolph, *Kingsley: The Life, Letters and Diaries of Kingsley Martin*, p. 195.
51. 'Mr Snowden's problem', *New Statesman and Nation*, 28 March 1931. Martin was reluctant to embrace protection so long as he and Lloyd were regularly castigating Beaverbrook (and Rothermere) for launching the Empire Crusade (a line Keynes very much approved of). Thanks to S.K. Ratcliffe, whose reporting of the Simon Commission was published as a pamphlet in July 1930, the *New Statesman* had for some time had a keen interest in India rapidly achieving dominion status. This was anathema to Sharp, but he had effectively been silenced on the subject. Martin, who from the outset greatly admired Gandhi, Nehru and the other Congress leaders, saw the Empire Crusade as Beaverbrook's attempt to bring down Baldwin and Hoare, the Tories' leading advocates of cross-party cooperation on India. If the Conservative Party was absent from the forthcoming Round Table Conference then the prospects of delegation and devolution across the sub-continent would be greatly diminished (ironically, in March 1931 Beaverbrook chose Bruce Lockhart to mastermind the Empire Crusade candidate's campaign against Duff Cooper in the St George's by-election). 'Comments', *New Statesman and Nation*, 7 and 14 March 1931. 'Mr Baldwin and Lord Rothermere', *New Statesman and Nation*, 21 March 1931. J.M. Keynes to Kingsley Martin, 21 March 1931, Kingsley Martin Papers. For the origins of Martin's thirty-year feud with Beaverbrook, see Martin, *Editor*, p. 37, and 'Our Reply to Lord Beaverbrook', *New Statesman and Nation*, 23 May 1931.
52. J.M. Keynes to Kingsley Martin, 12 April 1931, Kingsley Martin Papers.
53. J.M. Keynes to Kingsley Martin, 19 April 1931, ibid.
54. 'Money, Wages, and Expansion', *New Statesman and Nation*, 18 July 1931.
55. J.M. Keynes to Ramsay MacDonald, 5 Aug. 1931, Ramsay MacDonald Papers. J.M. Keynes, 'Some Consequences of the Economy Report', *New Statesman and Nation*, 15 Aug. 1931.
56. 'Comments', *New Statesman and Nation*, 25 July 1931.
57. 'Comments', *New Statesman and Nation*, 15 and 22 Aug. 1931.
58. Kingsley Martin's 1931 diary quoted in Rolph, *Kingsley: The Life, Letters and Diaries of Kingsley Martin*, p. 209. Martin, *Editor*, pp. 53–4. 'Comments' and 'Was It a Bankers' Conspiracy?', *New Statesman and Nation*, 29 Aug. 1931. 'The Little Devil Doubt', *New Statesman and Nation*, 5 Sept. 1931.
59. 'Comments' and 'Politics and the Pound', *New Statesman and Nation*, 5 Sept. 1931. Harrod, *A Life of John Maynard Keynes*, pp. 517–18. Martin, *Editor*, p. 54. 'Comments', *New Statesman and Nation*, 12 Sept. 1931.
60. On 21 September 1931 Keynes chose the paper's weekly lunch to reveal that

Snowden would suspend convertibility, declaring that, 'At one stroke, Britain has resumed the financial hegemony of the world'. Rolph, *Kingsley: The Life, Letters and Diaries of Kingsley Martin*, pp. 164–5.

61. Bullock, *The Life and Times of Ernest Bevin: Vol. 1, Trade Union Union Leader 1881–1940*, pp. 501–2.

62. Graham Hutton to Kingsley Martin, 4 Sept. 1931, Kingsley Martin Papers. On the Romney Street Group, see Rolph, *Kingsley: The Life, Letters and Diaries of Kingsley Martin*, p. 169.

63. Ibid. Nicholas Davenport was a stockbroker, a company director and a writer. Keynes, a close friend and business associate, persuaded him in 1923 to write a financial column for the *Nation*. He transferred to the *New Statesman and Nation*, and as 'Toreador' was a stalwart of the paper for years. By 1932, convinced that Labour politicians and policy-makers needed regular briefings on what was happening in the City, he established the XYZ Club as a semi-clandestine discussion group to complement the more formally organised SSIP and NFRB. Francis Williams, in the 1930s City editor of the *Daily Herald* and later Attlee's first press secretary in Downing Street, believed that he and his fellow-members could 'claim to have exercised in a quiet sort of way more influence on future Government policy than any other group of the time'. This was largely because Dalton and Gaitskell were key members, the former providing a crucial link with the NEC's policy-making bodies. F. Williams, *Nothing So Strange* (London, 1970), p. 112. Pimlott, *Hugh Dalton*, pp. 222–4. See also N. Davenport, *Memoirs of a City Radical* (London, 1970), and E. Durbin, *New Jerusalems: The Labour Party and the Economics of Democratic Socialism* (London: Routledge & Kegan Paul, 1985), pp. 82–3.

64. Skidelsky, *John Maynard Keynes: The Economist As Saviour 1920–1937*, pp. 437–8. B. Pimlott, *Labour and the Left in the 1930s* (Cambridge: CUP, 1977), p. 39. For Keynes, Hobson and Evan Durbin's theoretical differences over the 1931 sterling crisis, see Clarke, *Liberals and Social Democrats*, pp. 268–70.

65. Skidelsky, *John Maynard Keynes: The Economist As Saviour 1920–1937*, pp. 437–8 and 436.

66. Rolph, *Kingsley: The Life, Letters and Diaries of Kingsley Martin*, pp. 195–6. Clearly the relationship with Keynes was crucial, as Rowntree and the other directors appear to have been happy to let their new editor get on with it, particularly as a circulation creeping up towards 30,000 by the mid-1930s meant the paper was in profit. Having contributors like Low, and ultimately Cole and Woolf, as fellow directors probably made life easier for Martin, but at the same time increased the possibility of unnecessary discussion of editorial policy taking place at boardroom level. Martin understandably liked to cultivate the idea of a generally harmonious board. Martin, *Father Figures*, p. 206.

67. 'In the early days . . . someone once said that we were all three much of a muchness, the difference between us being that "Kingsley Martin snarled, C.M. Lloyd nagged, and Leonard Woolf bit".' Woolf, *Downhill All The Way*, p. 244. First signs of disharmony – and future tension with Keynes – followed Lloyd's visit to Russia in the autumn of 1931. Until Martin went himself in 1932, returning enthusiastic but far more sceptical than Lloyd and the Webbs, the *New Statesman and Nation* repeatedly extolled proletarian achievements, glossed over abuses of human rights, and expressed a sympathy for Soviet fears of renewed 'imperialist aggression' that coloured the editor's judgement until at least 1948.

For coverage of Soviet affairs in the early 1930s, see Smith, 'The *New Statesman* 1913–31', pp. 266–9, and for Martin's early clashes with Keynes over Russia (a foretaste of what was to come later in the 1930s), see Rolph, *Kingsley: The Life, Letters and Diaries of Kingsley Martin*, pp. 172–3.

68. Martin, *Editor*, pp. 22–3.

69. K. Martin, *Critic's London Diary* (London, 1960), p. xi.

70. Howard, *Crossman: The Pursuit of Power*, p. 73. Woolf, Mortimer and Norman MacKenzie were among later contributors, but 'London Diary' was always the editor's

personal fiefdom, and as such safe from last-minute rewriting by horrifed colleagues. Crossman believed that one reason why he remained assistant editor despite so many rows was his talent for writing paragraphs in Martin's own inimitable style. Ibid., p. 76.

Chapter 11, Conclusion: Eighty years of new statesmanship, pp. 261–276.

1. Garnett, *The Familiar Faces 3*, pp. 150–1.
2. Young (ed.), *Lockhart Diaries*, 15 Dec. 1932 and 19 April 1933, pp. 237 and 252.
3. Ibid., 5 June 1933, p. 257. R. Griffiths, *Fellow Travellers of the Right: British Enthusiasts for Nazi Germany 1933–39* (London: Constable, 1980; Oxford: OUP, 1983, paperback edn), pp. 101–2 and 124.
4. C. Sharp, 'Early Days', *New Statesman and Nation*, 14 April 1934.
5. Beatrice Webb to Kingsley Martin, 4 April 1934, Kingsley Martin Papers.
6. S.K. Ratcliffe suggested that Sharp was always the same, even as a young man: '[H.W.] Massingham had a strong moralistic attitude to his work and to life itself; whereas Sharp gave the impression of being cynical and was certainly immoral.' Ratcliffe quoted in Hyams, *New Statesman*, p. 15.
7. Hart-Davis (ed.), *Siegfried Sassoon Diaries 1923–1925*, 30 April 1925, pp. 238–9. Sassoon's description echoes Woolf's less harsh observation that 'Kingsley's mind was not tuned to eternity and the music of the spheres, but to a period of exactly a week'. L. Woolf, 'Kingsley Martin', *Political Quarterly*, 40 (1969), p. 242.
8. Woolf, *Beginning Again*, pp. 129–30.
9. Leonard Woolf, quoted in G. Spater and I. Parsons, *A Marriage of True Minds: An Intimate Portrait of Leonard and Virginia Woolf* (London: Hogarth Press, 1978), p. 159.
10. Woolf, 'Kingsley Martin', p. 244. For Woolf's relationship with Martin post-1931, see F. Leventhal, 'Leonard Woolf and Kingsley Martin: Creative Tension on the Left', *Albion*, 24, 2 (Summer 1992), pp. 272–94.
11. Woolf, *Beginning Again*, p. 131.
12. C. Sharp, 'Early Days', *New Statesman and Nation*, 14 April 1934.
13. MacCarthy, 'Apprenticeship', *Humanities*, p. 20.
14. Clifford Sharp to Beatrice Webb, (13?) Oct. 1916, Passfield Papers.
15. Beatrice Webb, diary, (?) Aug. 1918, ibid.
16. He may have kept him at arm's length, but Martin's relationship with Keynes was undoubtedly stormy, see Leventhal, 'Leonard Woolf and Kingsley Martin: Creative Tension on the Left', *Albion*, p. 279, and K. Martin, 'Arguing with Keynes: A Memoir', *Encounter*, 20, 2, Feb. 1965.
17. Howe (ed.), *Lines of Dissent*, Preface, p. xi.
18. C. Hitchens, ibid., Introduction, p. 12.
19. Ibid., pp. 2 and 6.
20. At his memorial service, Martin's one–time assistant editor offered a variation on the cliché: 'I [Norman MacKenzie] would prefer to say that it [*New Statesman and Nation*] was in many ways the unconscious of the Left. The secret of its success was that Kingsley was able to articulate – and willing to publish – ideas that so many others felt but could not express.' Orwell would scarcely have concurred with this claim, nor the subsequent assertion that 'He preferred to say what he believed to be right, rather than what seemed to be expedient'. N. MacKenzie, in M. Jones (ed.), *Kingsley Martin: Portrait and Self-Portrait* (London: Barrie & Jenkins, 1969), p. 41.
21. Edward Pearce's upbeat assessment of Steve Platt's *New Statesman & Society* noted that: 'Any paper of the left is necessarily more circumspect these days. But we aren't feeble either. The old New Statesman of Clifford Sharp and Kingsley Martin no longer seems a reproachful ancestor, unlived up to and wincing in its picture frame.' Note the surprising mention of Sharp. Excluding the *New Statesman*, was this his first appearance in a newspaper since 1935? E. Pearce, 'Time to bury the hatchet', *Guardian*, 24 Feb. 1993.
22. R.H.S. Crossman, 'Martin's weekly medicine', *New Statesman*, 3 May 1968.

Bibliography – Primary Sources

Full publishing details of any secondary material (essays, books, theses) are available where they appear in the footnotes for the first time.

PAPERS AND DIARIES

Arnold Bennett:
    (1) Berg Collection, New York Public Library
    (2) The Humanities Research Centre, University of Texas at Austin
R.C.K. Ensor: Corpus Christi College, Oxford
Foreign Office and Home Office Papers: Public Records Office, Kew
John Maynard Keynes: Royal Economic Society, Cambridge
Mrs T. Lloyd, memoir of Charles Mostyn Lloyd, 17 Nov. 1968: British Library of
    Political and Economic Science
David Lloyd George: Beaverbrook Library, Record Office, House of Lords
Edward Marsh: Berg Collection, New York Public Library
Kingsley Martin:
    (1) Berg Collection, New York Public Library
    (2) University of Sussex
Desmond MacCarthy: Berg Collection, New York Public Library
James Ramsay MacDonald: Public Records Office, Kew
Lord Oxford and Asquith: Bodleian Library, University of Oxford
Rainbow Circle: British Library of Political and Economic Science
George Bernard Shaw:
    (1) Passfield Papers, British Library of Political and Economic Science
    (2) British Library
    (3) Berg Collection, New York Public Library
J.C. Squire: Berg Collection, New York Public Library
Sidney and Beatrice Webb:
    (1) Berg Collection, New York Public Library
    (2) Passfield Papers, British Library of Political and Economic Science
H.G. Wells: H.G. Wells Archive, University of Illinois, Champaign-Urbana,
    Illinois
Leonard and Virginia Woolf:
    (1) University of Sussex
    (2) Berg Collection, New York Public Library

INTERVIEWS

Lord Fenner Brockway	7 February 1979
Dame Margaret Cole	15 December 1977
Raymond Mortimer, CBE	6 December 1977
C.H. Rolph	22 November 1977

NEWSPAPERS AND PERIODICALS

Calendar of Modern Letters
Daily Chronicle

Daily Herald
Daily Mail
Daily News
Economist
Evening Standard
Fabian News
Forward
Life and Letters
Manchester Guardian
Nation
New Age
Nineteenth Century
Labour / New Leader
New Statesman / and Nation / & Society
Observer
Scrutiny
The Times
Westminster Gazette

CONTEMPORARY WORKS

Amery, L.S., *My Political Life: Volume One, England Before the Storm 1896–1914*, London, Hutchinson, 1953.

Bartlett, V., *This Is My Life*, London, Chatto & Windus, 1937.

Beaverbrook, Lord, *Men and Power 1917–1918*, London, Hutchinson, 1956.

Bennett, A., *Books and Persons: Being Comments on a Past Epoch 1908–1911*, London, Chatto & Windus, 1974.

— *The Evening Standard Years*, Mylett, A. (ed.), London, Chatto & Windus, 1974.

— *The Journals of Arnold Bennett: Volume 2, 1911–1921*, Flower, N. (ed.), London, Cassell, 1932.

— *The Journals of Arnold Bennett: Volume 3, 1921–1928*, Flower, N. (ed.), London, Cassell, 1933.

— *Letters of Arnold Bennett: Volume 1, Letters to J B Pinker*, Hepburn, J. (ed.), Oxford, OUP, 1966.

— *Letters of Arnold Bennett: Volume 2, 1989–1915*, Hepburn, J. (ed.), Oxford, OUP, 1968.

— *Letters of Arnold Bennett: Volume 3, 1916–1931*, Hepburn, J. (ed.), Oxford, OUP, 1970.

Bevin, E. and Cole, G.D.H., *The Crisis: What it is, how it arose, what to do*, London, New Statesman and Nation, 1931.

Brockway, F., *Inside the Left: Thirty Years of Platform, Press, Prison and Parliament*, London, Allen & Unwin, 1942.

Brooke, R., *The Letters of Rupert Brooke*, Keynes, G. (ed.), London, Faber, 1968.

Bruce Lockhart, R.H., *The Diaries of Sir Robert Bruce Lockhart: Volume One, 1915–1938*, Young, K. (ed.), London, Macmillan, 1973.

—*Giants Cast Long Shadows*, London, Putnam, 1960.

— *Retreat From Glory*, London, Putnam, 1934.

Campbell, R., *The Collected Poems of Roy Campbell*, London, Bodley Head, 1949.

BIBLIOGRAPHY

— *Light on a Dark Horse,* Hollis & Carter, London, 1951, Penguin, 1971.

Cole, G.D.H.,*The Next Ten Years in British Social and Economic Policy,* London, Macmillan, 1929.

Cole, M.I., *Growing Up Into Revolution,* London, Longman, 1949.

Connolly, C., *Enemies of Promise,* London, Routledge, 1938.

Cook, E., *The Press in Wartime, With Some Account of the Official Press Bureau,* London, Macmillan, 1920.

Davenport, N., *Memoirs of a City Radical,* London, Weidenfeld & Nicolson, 1974.

Dukes, P., *The Story of 'ST25': Adventure and Romance in the Secret Intelligence Service in Red Russia,* London, Cassell, 1938.

Ensor, R.C.K., *England 1870–1914,* Oxford, OUP, 1935.

Farjeon, E., *Edward Thomas, The Last Four Years: Book One of the Memoirs of Eleanor Farjeon,* Oxford, OUP, 1958.

Fry, R., *Letters of Roger Fry: Volume One, 1878–1913,* Sutton, E. (ed.), London, Chatto & Windus, 1972.

— *Letters of Roger Fry: Volume Two, 1913–1934,* Sutton, D. (ed.), London, Chatto & Windus, 1972.

Garnett, D., *The Familiar Faces: The Golden Echo, Volume Three,* London, Chatto & Windus, 1962.

Graves, R., *Goodbye To All That,* London, Jonathan Cape, 1929, Penguin revised edn, 1960.

Grey of Fallodon, Viscount, *Twenty–five Years: Volume One, 1892–1916,* London, Hodder & Stoughton, 1926.

Hewins, W.A.S., *The Apologia of an Imperialist: Forty Years of Empire Policy, Volume One,* London, Constable, 1929.

Hobhouse, C., *Inside Asquith's Cabinet: From the Diaries of Charles Hobhouse,* David, E. (ed.) London, Murray, 1977.

Huddleston, S., *In My Time: An Observer's Record of War and Peace,* London, Jonathan Cape, 1938.

Keeling, F.H., *Keeling: Letters and Recollections,* Townshend, E. (ed.), London, Allen & Unwin, 1918.

Keynes, J.M., *The Collected Writings of John Maynard Keynes: Volume XVIII, Activities 1922–1932. The End of Reparations,* Johnson, E. (ed.), Cambridge, CUP, 1978.

— *The Economic Consequences of the Peace,* London, Macmillan, 1919.

Labour Research Department, *The Press Studies in Labour and Capital: Volume II,* London, Labour Publishing Company, 1923.

Lansbury, G., *The Miracle of Fleet Street: The Story of the 'Daily Herald',* London, Labour Publishing Company, 1925.

Lawrence, D.H., *The Collected Letters of D.H. Lawrence: Volume One,* Moore, H.T. (ed.), London, Heinemann, 1962.

— *The Collected Letters of D.H. Lawrence: Volume Two,* Moore, H.T. (ed.), London, Heinemann, 1962.

— *The Complete Poems of D.H. Lawrence: Volume Two,* de Sola Pinto, V. and Roberts W. (eds), London, Heinemann, 1969.

— *The Letters of D.H. Lawrence,* Huxley, A. (ed.), London, Heinemann, 1932.

Leavis, F.R., *'Anna Karenina' and Other Essays,* London, Chatto & Windus, 1967.

— *New Bearings in English Poetry,* London, Chatto & Windus, 1932.

— (ed.), *Towards Standards of Criticism: Selections from The Calendar of Modern Letters 1925–1927,* London, Lawrence & Wishart, 1976.

Leavis, Q.D., *Fiction and the Reading Public*, London, Chatto & Windus, 1932.

Lloyd George, D., *War Memoirs: Volume I*, London, Ivor Nicholson & Watson, 1938.

Mairet, P., *A.R. Orage: A Memoir*, London, Dent, 1936.

Marsh, E., *A Number of People: A Book of Reminiscences*, London, Heinemann, 1939.

— *Rupert Brooke: A Memoir*, London, Sidgwick & Jackson, 1918.

Martin, K., *Critic's London Diary*, London, Secker & Warburg, 1960.

— *Editor*, London, Hutchinson, 1968.

— *Father Figures*, London, Hutchinson, 1966.

Marx, K. and Engels, F., *Karl Marx and Frederick Engels on Britain*, Moscow, Progress Publishers, 1962.

MacCarthy, D., *Humanities*, London, MacGibbon & Kee, 1935.

— *Shaw*, London, MacGibbon & Kee, 1951.

Nevinson, H.W., *Last Changes: Last Chances*, London, Nisbet, 1928.

— *More Changes, More Chances*, London, Nisbet, 1925.

Nicolson, H., *Harold Nicolson: Diaries and Letters: Volume One, 1930–1939*, Nicolson, N. (ed.), London, Collins, 1966.

Owen, W., *Wilfred Owen: Collected Letters*, Owen H. and Bell, J. (eds), Oxford, OUP, 1967.

Oxford and Asquith, Lord, *Memories and Reflections: Volume 2, 1852–1927*, London, Cassell, 1928.

Page Arnot, R., *History of the Labour Research Department*, London Publishing Company, 1926.

Pease, E.R., *The History of the Fabian Society*, London, Fabian Society, 1916.

P.E.P., *Political and Economic Planning Report on the British Press*, London, P.E.P., 1938.

Pritchett, V.S., *Midnight Oil*, London, Chatto & Windus, 1971, Penguin, 1974.

Quennell, P., *The Marble Foot: An Autobiography*, London, Collins, 1976.

Ransome, A., *The Autobiography of Arthur Ransome*, Hart-Davies, B. (ed.), London, Jonathan Cape, 1976.

Rickword, E., *Essays and Opinions 1921–1931*, Young, A. (ed.), Manchester, Carcanet New Press, 1974.

Rolph, C.H., *Further Particulars*, Oxford, OUP, 1987, paperback edn, 1988.

Sassoon, S., *Siegfried's Journey 1916–1920*, London, Faber & Faber, 1945.

__ *Siegfried Sassoon Diaries 1923–1925*, Hart-Davis, R. (ed.), London, Faber & Faber, 1985.

Scott, C.P., *The Political Diaries of C.P. Scott 1911–1928*, Wilson, T. (ed.), London, Collins, 1970.

Shaw, G.B., *Bernard Shaw's Letters to Granville Barker*, Purdom, C.B. (ed.), New York, Theatre Arts Books, 1957.

— *Collected Letters 1895–1910*, Lawrence, D.H. (ed.), London, Reinhardt, 1972.

— *Ten Portraits and Review*, London, Constable, 1932.

Spender, J.A. and Asquith, C., *Life of Herbert Henry Asquith, Lord Oxford and Asquith*, London, Hutchinson, 1932.

Squire, J.C., *Flowers of Speech*, London, Allen & Unwin, 1935.

— *The Honeysuckle and the Bee*, London, Heinemann, 1937.

Statesman Publishing Co. Ltd., *Preliminary Memorandum Descriptive of Proposed New Weekly Journal*, London, 1913.

Steed, W., *The Press*, London, Penguin Special, 1938.

Tilley, J. and Caselee, S., *The Foreign Office*, London, Putnam, 1933.

Toynbee, A.J., *Acquaintances*, Oxford, OUP, 1967.

Ward, A.W. and Gooch, P. (eds.), *The Cambridge History of British Foreign Policy 1783–1919*, Cambridge, CUP, 1923.

Webb, B., *Beatrice Webb's Diaries 1912–1924*, Cole, M.I. (ed.), London, Longman, 1952.

— *Beatrice Webb's Diaries 1924–1932*, Cole, M.I. (ed.), London, Longman, 1956.

— *The Diary of Beatrice Webb: Volume Two, 1892–1905, All the Good Things of Life*, MacKenzie, N. and J. (eds), Cambridge, MA, The Belknap Press of HUP, 1983.

— *The Diary of Beatrice Webb: Volume Three, 1905–1924, The Power to Alter Things*, MacKenzie, N. and J. (eds.), Cambridge, MA, The Belknap Press of HUP, 1984.

— *The Diary of Beatrice Webb: Volume Four, 1924–1943, The Wheel of Life*, MacKenzie, N. and J. (eds), Cambridge, MA, The Belknap Press of HUP, 1985.

— *Our Partnership*, Drake, B. and Cole, M.I. (eds), London, Longman, 1948.

Webb, S. and Webb, B., *The Letters of Sidney and Beatrice Webb: Volume III, Pilgrimage 1912–1947*, MacKenzie N. (ed.), Cambridge, OUP, 1978.

Wells, H.G., *Experiment in Autobiography*, London, Jonathan Cape, 1934, unexpurgated edn, 1984.

— *The New Machiavelli*, London, The Bodley Head, 1911.

West, J., *A History of the Chartist Movement*, London, Constable, 1920.

Williams, F., *Nothing So Strange*, London, Cassell, 1970.

Woolf, L., *Beginning Again: An Autobiography of the Years 1911–1918*, London, Hogarth Press, 1964.

-- *Downhill All the Way: An Autobiography of the Years 1919–1939*, London, Hogarth Press, 1967.

— *The Journey Not the Arrival Matters: An Autobiography of the Years 1939–1969*, London, Hogarth Press, 1969.

— *Letters of Leonard Woolf*, Spotts, F. (ed.), London, Bloomsbury, 1990.

Woolf, V., *The Diary of Virginia Woolf: Volume One: 1915–1919*, Olivier Bell, A.O. (ed.), London, Hogarth Press, 1977.

— *The Diary of Virginia Woolf: Volume Two: 1920–1924*, Olivier Bell, A.O. and McNeillie, A. (eds), London, Hogarth Press, 1978.

— *The Question of Things Happening: The Letters of Virginia Woolf, Volume II: 1912–1922*, Nicolson, N. and Trautmann, J. (eds), London, Hogarth Press, 1976.

— *A Change of Perspective: The Letters of Virginia Woolf, Volume III: 1923–1928*, Nicolson, N. and Trautmann, J. (eds), London, Hogarth Press, 1977.

— *A Reflection of the Other Person: The Letters of Virginia Woolf, Volume IV: 1929 and 1931*, Nicolson, N. and Trautmann, J. (eds), London, Hogarth Press, 1978.

— *The Sickle Side of the Moon: The Letters of Virginia Woolf, Volume V: 1932–1935*, Nicolson, N. and Trautmann, J. (eds), London, Hogarth Press, 1979.

Wyndham Lewis, P., *The Letters of Wyndham Lewis*, Ross, W.K. (ed.), London, Methuen, 1963.

Yeats, W.B., *The Letters of W.B. Yeats*, Wade, D. (ed.), London, Hart-Davis, 1954.

Index